E-Government Research:
Policy and Management

Donald Norris
University of Maryland, Baltimore County, USA

IGI PUBLISHING
Hershey • New York

Acquisition Editor:	Kristin Klinger
Senior Managing Editor:	Jennifer Neidig
Managing Editor:	Sara Reed
Development Editor:	Kristin Roth
Copy Editor:	Ashlee Kunkel
Typesetter:	Lindsay Bergman
Cover Design:	Lisa Tosheff
Printed at:	Yurchak Printing Inc.

Published in the United States of America by
    IGI Publishing (an imprint of IGI Global)
    701 E. Chocolate Avenue
    Hershey PA 17033
    Tel: 717-533-8845
    Fax: 717-533-8661
    E-mail: cust@igi-global.com
    Web site: http://www.igi-global.com

and in the United Kingdom by
    IGI Publishing (an imprint of IGI Global)
    3 Henrietta Street
    Covent Garden
    London WC2E 8LU
    Tel: 44 20 7240 0856
    Fax: 44 20 7379 0609
    Web site: http://www.eurospanonline.com

Library of Congress Cataloging-in-Publication Data

E-government research : policy and management / Donald Norris, editor.
    p. cm.
  Summary: "This book provides scholars and practitioners with a critical mass of research on the integration, management, implications, and application of e-government. Covering such issues as e-government adoption and diffusion; social and performance issues of e-government; and information security, privacy, and policy, this book is an essential resource to any library collection"--Provided by publisher.
  ISBN-13: 978-1-59904-913-7 (hardcover)
  ISBN-13: 978-1-59904-957-1 (e-book)
 1. Internet in public administration. 2. Electronic government information. 3. Public administration--Data processing--Management. 4. Government information--Management. I. Norris, Donald F.
  JF1525.A8E237 2008
  352.3'802854678--dc22
                              2007041953

British Cataloguing in Publication Data
A Cataloguing in Publication record for this book is available from the British Library.

E-Government Research: Policy and Management is part of the IGI Global series named *Advances in Electronic Government Series (AEGR)* (ISSN: 1935-3073).

All work contributed to this book is original material. The views expressed in this book are those of the authors, but not necessarily of the publisher.

Advances in Electronic Government Research Series (AEGR)

ISBN: 1935-3073

Editor-in-Chief: Mehdi Khosrow-Pour, D.B.A.

E-Government Research: Policy and Management

Donald Norris; University of Maryland Baltimore County, USA

IGI Publishing • copyright 2007 • 300+ pp • H/C (ISBN: 978-1-59904-913-7) • US $99.95 (our price)

Virtual technology is increasingly prevalent in all spheres of daily life, including infiltration into governmental policies, processes, infrastructures, and frameworks. E-Government Research: Policy and Management provides scholars and practitioners with a critical mass of research on the integration, management, implications, and application of e-government. Covering such issues as e-government adoption and diffusion; social and performance issues of e-government; and information security, privacy, and policy, this book is an essential resource to any library collection.

Current Issues and Trends in E-Government Research

Donald Norris; University of Maryland Baltimore County

CyberTech Publishing • copyright 2007 • 319 pp • E-Book (ISBN: 1-59904-285-1) • US $63.96 (our price) • H/C (ISBN: 1-59904-283-5) • US $85.46 (our price)

As emerging trends and research threads surface in the area of e-government, academicians, practitioners, and students face the challenge of keeping up-to-date with new and innovative practices. Current Issues and Trends in E-Government Research provides a complete synopsis of the latest technologies in information policy, security, privacy, and access, as well as the best practices in e-government applications and measurement. Current Issues and Trends in E-Government Research presents the most current issues in e-government hardware and software technology, adoption and diffusion, planning and management, and philosophy.

DISSEMINATOR of KNOWLEDGE

Hershey • New York

Order online at www.igi-global.com or call 717-533-8845 x10 –
Mon-Fri 8:30 am - 5:00 pm (est) or fax 24 hours a day 717-533-8661

E-Government Research:
Policy and Management

Table of Contents

Preface

Considerable hype surrounds e-government and e-government research. Much of the hype is promulgated by e-government advocates and by scholars and researchers, who should have known better, but who appear to have gotten caught up in the advocacy around e-government. The first chapter in this book should go a long way toward dispelling the notion that e-government is somehow special or has special properties to advance a governmental reform agenda or to produce unquestionably positive outcomes.

The first and, to my mind, most important chapter in this book, was authored by Ken Kraemer and John King, two of the most prominent names in the study of information technology (IT) and government. Through an extensive review of literature on IT and government, Kraemer and King examine whether IT has been an instrument of administrative reform in the U.S. They conclude that this has not been the case in the history of IT and government in the U.S. Indeed, instead of being an instrument of reform, IT has served the interests of those in power and has supported existing administrative and political structures and arrangements. Kraemer and King conclude by questioning whether this finding from the history of IT and government might not have application to e-government, notwithstanding claims to the contrary. As a result, they are properly skeptical that e-government adoption will produce governmental reform any more than IT adoption did previously.

In the second chapter, my colleague Ben Lloyd and I examine the empirical research on e-government published in refereed journals through the end of 2004. We cast a very wide net, using several search engines and databases to find articles in refereed journals which employed some form of empirical methodology or which examined empirical data.

We examined these articles using several criteria and concluded that, for the most part, the published research on e-government is neither particularly vast nor very good. Most articles were published in less than stellar journals, used less than rigorous methodologies, addressed or tried to advance theory, developed or formally tested hypotheses, included acceptable literature reviews, or stayed with their data when drawing conclusions. We concluded by expressing our hope that e-government research in the near future would improve in quality and sophistication.

Chapter III presents another paper based on a literature review, but its purpose is different from the review conducted by Kraemer and King. Ryad Titah and Henri Barki reviewed 75 articles related to e-government adoption and acceptance published between 1990 and

2007 in leading academic journals and conference proceedings. Contrary to earlier studies, they found work that demonstrated a wider array of research methods, conceptual perspectives, and findings, all pointing to "fairly considerable diversity in the topics, constructs and interrelationships considered by different studies." Based on their review, they proposed a research framework for the complex interdependencies and interactions between organizational, managerial, technical, political, and individual factors that were found by past research to influence e-government adoption and acceptance.

Chapter IV shifts focus to Web surveys. Here, Tony Carrizales, Marc Holzer, and Aroon Manoharan present findings from a 2005 survey of the Web sites of large municipalities worldwide. In particular, they examined the following features of these Web sites: security, usability, content, online services, and citizen participation. The top performing cities, based on this analysis, were Soeul, New York, Shanghai, Hong Kong, and Sydney. The authors found very few differences between the 2005 and 2003 surveys, but did find—not surprisingly—that the digital divide between developed and lesser developed nations continues.

In Chapter V, Lawrence Pratchett, Melvin Wingfield, and Rabia Karakaya Polat present findings from their study of local government Web sites in England and Wales with particular attention to the potential of these sites to deliver e-democracy. They found that local governments are providing many features on their Web sites that can facilitate e-democracy. However, for the most part, local governments in England and Wales have not tapped the full potential of the Internet to deliver e-democracy and that there is considerable variation among local governments in their delivery of e-democracy.

Genie N. L. Stowers' examination of user help and navigation features on Web sites is Chapter VI. Stowers' sample included a large number of federal government sites, all 50 states, and cities over 100,000. She found patterns across governments of help and navigation features, leading her to conclude that these features had diffused rather well within the public sector. However, she concluded that all was not well in Web land and that Web developers should work to install features on Web sites to assist users in finding information more easily.

In Chapter VII, Sangmi Chai, T. C. Herath, I. Park, and H. R. Rao examine data from a survey of adult Americans conducted by the PEW Research Center. They were interested in learning what motivated users of governmental Web sites to make return visits to those sites. They hypothesized that several factors including the users' satisfaction, perceived performance of the site, and whether sites ask users for confidential information would affect the intention to return. They also hypothesized that gender and race will play moderating roles on continuation intentions. They found that, indeed, a user's intention to return was affected by the user's satisfaction with the Web site, perceived performance of the site, the requirement for confidential information, and that both gender and race had moderating effects on intentions of repeated use.

Our focus now shifts away from Web site analysis to three chapters that look at the use of the Internet for political activism, citizen engagement, and civic deliberation. Chapter VIII features an analysis of political activism in Britain by Pippa Norris and John Curtice. Their chapter is also noteworthy because it nicely summarizes the current debate about the potential of the Internet for strengthening political activism. Drawing on data from the British Social Attitudes Survey from 2003, Norris and Curtice find, first, that political activism via the Internet is not as simple as it sounds. Different types of political activism are associated with different segments of the population, for example. Moreover, they found that the online population is likely to engage in forms of political activism (e.g., more cause oriented) that are quite different from more traditional forms (e.g., campaign activities).

In Chapter IX, Yu-Che Chen and Daniela V. Dimitrova provide an exploratory study of civic engagement via governmental Web sites. They used a sample of Internet users to examine both the demand and supply sides (availability of governmental Web sites) of civic engagement. Their findings highlight the importance of the supply side for promoting civic engagement. Additionally, Chen and Dimitrova found several factors associated with online civic engagement, particularly including perceived benefits and off-line political activism.

Laurence Monnoyer-Smith provides Chapter VIII. Her exploratory study examines the online participation of French citizens in a public debate in 2001 held by the French National Public Debate Commission over the issue of the location of a third international Parisian airport. Although online participation was limited, Monnoyer-Smith believes that this example shows the added value that Internet participation can provide. Here, she argues, it widened the profile of participation and expanded the nature of participants' arguments and their means of expression.

In Chapter XI, Jeremy Millard examines the attitudes and behavior of European users to e-government citizen services. The study comes from the 2005 eUSER project that surveyed 10,000 households in 10 European Union member states. Although there were variations in the findings based on nation of residence, Millard found that face-to-face contact remains the predominant mode of interacting with government in most countries. In the UK, telephone and mail have surpassed face-to-face contact. However, the evidence is also strong that e-government users also continue to make high use of all other channels. They are "flexi-channellers." Also, over 40% of e-government users act as social intermediaries using online services on behalf of an average of 2.4 members of their family or friends, and even higher numbers in the new member states of the EU where infrastructures and e-services are not so well rolled-out, so the impact of e-government is wider than first appearances. Millard's study also identified a number of reported barriers to citizen use of e-government. But, those barriers diminish somewhat after users begin accessing governmental information and services online.

Chapter XII moves from citizen use of the Internet to use by public officials. Here, Chan-Go Kim and Marc Holzer examine data from a survey of 895 public officials in Korea about their intentions to use online policy forums to inform their decision making. They examined individual and organizational factors and system characteristics. Their analysis indicates that three variables were related to public officials' intentions to use online forums. These were perceived usefulness, the officials' attitudes toward citizen participation, and information quality.

Chapter XIII constitutes another shift in focus for this volume. In this chapter, Julianne Mahler and Priscilla Regan examine what has become known as Web governance, which they argue is "concerned with the control and content for agency Web sites." In this study, they trace the history of efforts by Congress and OMB to specify Web site content rules, track the evolution of interagency groups that developed the rules, and examine agency activities to create Web governance procedures.

They found that the process of developing Web governance was decentralized and collaborative. Although there were guidelines, they were hardly demanding about either format or content. Moreover, within agencies studies, the process reflected "business as usual." However, this situation was different in interagency settings where there was more networking and collaboration. Perhaps one important reason for these findings is that OMB did not impose its will on federal agencies. This allowed agency practitioners in both organized forums and in informal interactions to develop the guidelines for Web governance. According to Mahler and Regan, this represents a paradigm shift in the way that the federal government goes about developing such guidelines.

In Chapter XIV, Mila Gasco and Jeffrey Roy compare e-government in Catalonia, Spain and Ontario, Canada. In particular, they examine the impacts of e-government both on administration and democracy in complex multilevel governmental environments. Both Cataloina and Ontario were known as having invested aggressively in e-government and in both jurisdictions and that e-government was consciously used as an agent of governmental reform. After reviewing the evolution of e-government in both subnational jurisdictions, they conclude that the evidence "tempers the view that e-government will immediately and radically transform the public sector." In both Ontario and Catalonia, e-services predominated over e-democracy.

Mack C. Shelley, Lisa E. Thrane, and Stuart W. Shulman study generational differences in IT use and political involvement in our final chapter, Chapter XV. Here they examine data from a 2003 survey of adults in three American states. They found profound generational differences with respect to IT and to use of IT in political activities. For example, younger respondents were more favorably inclined toward IT and more likely to desire public IT and e-participation. They conclude by noting that "e-citizenry will compound existing societal divisions" in which those favorably disposed to IT will be advantaged and those not favorably disposed will be disadvantaged.

As is clear from these chapters, e-government is still in its formative years. Its evolution is far from complete. As a result, researchers should continue to examine e-government from a variety of perspectives, using a variety of research methodologies. They should also engage in comparative analysis in order to understand what is occurring with respect to e-government around the globe.

Chapter I

Information Technology and Administrative Reform:
Will E-Government be Different?

Kenneth Kraemer, University of California, USA

John Leslie King, University of Michigan, USA

Abstract

This article examines the theoretical ideal of information technology as an instrument of administrative reform and examines the extent to which that ideal has been achieved in the United States. It takes a look at the findings from research about the use and impacts of information technology from the time of the mainframe computer through the PC revolution to the current era of the Internet and e-government. It then concludes that information technology has never been an instrument of administrative reform; rather, it has been used to reinforce existing administrative and political arrangements. It assesses why this is the case and draws conclusions about what should be expected with future applications of information technologies—in the time after e-government. It concludes with a discussion of the early evidence about newer applications for automated service delivery, 24/7 e-government, and e-democracy.

Introduction

The past several decades have seen many studies of the impacts of information technology (IT) in business organizations and comparatively fewer studies in government organizations. The concerns of researchers have been largely the same across both sectors—effects on efficiency and effectiveness, changes to organizational structure, and impacts on work. Studies in government, however, have been unique in their concern with whether IT is a catalyst or instrument of administrative reform.

We define administrative reform as efforts to bring about dramatic change or transformation in government, such as a more responsive administrative structure, greater rationality and efficiency, or better service delivery to citizens. Toward these ends, governments historically have undertaken structural reforms, such as city-manager government; budget reforms, such as the executive; performance and program budgets; financial reforms, such as unified accounting; personnel reforms, such as merit-based employment and pay; and many others. Computing has been viewed as an instrument of such reforms and also as a reform instrument, per se. Such instruments are illustrated by urban information systems, integrated municipal information systems, computer-based models for policymaking, geographic information systems, and, most recently, e-government. The rhetoric of these computing-based reform efforts has been that computing is a catalyst that can and should be used to bring about dramatic change and transformation in government (Fountain, 2002; Garson, 2004; Gasco, 2003; Reinermann, 1988; Weiner, 1969).

The question of whether computers will bring significant organizational change is nearly half a century old. In a classic 1958 *Harvard Business Review* article, "Management in the 1980s", Leavitt and Whisler forecast that IT would replace the traditional pyramidal hierarchy in organizations with a lean structure resembling an hourglass, and productivity would soar through the elimination of most middle managers. Laudon's (1974) path-breaking *Computers and Bureaucratic Reform* raised the question of administrative reform specifically with respect to local government. IT generally is considered to have the potential to bring about administrative reform. For example, Fountain (2002) says, "Technology is a catalyst for social, economic and political change at the levels of the individual, group, organization and institution" (p. 45). Yet others have argued that information technology does not tend to produce such reform and that it is implausible that IT could cause such changes in the first place (King & Kraemer, 1985; Kraemer & King, 1986; Laudon, 1974).

The era of e-government, which can be defined as the use of IT within government to achieve more efficient operations, better quality of service, and easy public access to government information and services is now underway. The IT world that surrounds public administration in the United States has changed markedly. Technology diffusion within the society has been pervasive, with personal computers and the Internet extending to the majority of American households. Internet-based e-business and e-government services rapidly are connecting businesses, households, and governments, thereby creating a much richer and more subtle IT environment. By 2002, 67% of adults using the Internet had visited a government Web site (57% a federal site; 54% a state site; and 42% a local site) (Dean, 2002). Nearly all federal agencies and most state governments provide some information or services on the Web (Fountain, 2001). The vast majority of city and county governments (95%) had Web sites in 2004 (Norris, 2006), many offering non-financial services (e.g., requests for services, government records, maps) and less than 10% offering financial services (e.g., paying taxes, utility bills, parking tickets, and licenses/permits) (Norris, 2006; Norris & Moon, 2005). Thus, most of these services involve one-way, easy-to-implement information services; very few permit citizens to complete transactions with government. Forrester Research (2000) estimated that by 2006, governments would receive 15% of their total financial collections over the Web.

Indeed, investment in information technology at all government levels has increased, new capabilities are more diffused throughout government agencies, technical expertise is stronger and more widely spread, and governments successfully have institutionalized modern principles for management of IT. If anything, there should be greater readiness for administrative reform from IT than ever before.

It seems likely that these changes would be sufficient in order to trigger the long expected administrative reforms, but Machiavelli's admonition about the perils of dramatic change is as relevant in the 20th century as it was in the 15th century.[1] This article argues that IT remains a useful instrument of incremental administrative change, but it is no more likely to bring about administrative reform today than it was two decades ago. This article recapitulates four key propositions of the reform hypothesis, discusses empirical evidence related to each, assesses the reform hypothesis in light of research results, raises relevant caveats, and concludes with a summary of the likely future relationship between IT and administrative reform.

Reform Through Information Technology

The main problem with the claim that information technology is an instrument of administrative reform is the lack of evidence to back it up.[2] Faced with this, proponents respond that the potential of IT to produce reform is thwarted because of top management's failures to distribute the technology efficiently, to empower lower-level staff, to re-engineer the organization along with computerization efforts, and to become hands-on knowledge executives themselves. Much of the benefit that IT could bring to organizations is lost due to poor management, but this does not explain the failure of the reform hypothesis. It merely shifts the argument onto different grounds.

The reform hypothesis is misguided fundamentally, because it assumes that organizational elites want their organizations to change and that they are willing to use IT to accomplish such change. The empirical evidence suggests that IT has been used most often to reinforce existing organizational arrangements and to power distributions rather than to change them (Attawell & Rule, 1984; Danziger et al., 1982; Dutton & Kraemer, 1985; Dutton et al., 1987; Holden, 2003; King & Kraemer, 1986; Kling, 1974, 1980; Kraemer & King, 1979, 1987; Kraemer & Perry, 1979; Laudon, 1974; Perry & Kraemer, 1979).

Based on a review of the research on e-government (Fountain, 2001, 2002; Holden, 2003; Holden et al., 2003; Kaylor et al., 2001; Layne & Lee, 2001; Moon, 2002; Norris & Moon, 2005; Norris, 2005, 2006), we believe that this fundamental trend will continue into the foreseeable future. For example, Fountain (2001) initially assumed that the Internet "would overwhelm organizational forms and individual resistance and ... would lead to rapid organizational change" (pp. x-xi). However, after researching the use of the Internet in U.S. federal agencies, Fountain (2002) concluded that "even the most innovative uses of IT typically work at the surface of operations and boundary-spanning processes and are accepted because they leave the deep structure of political relationships intact" (p. 45). Similarly, West (2004) concludes that "the e-government revolution has fallen short of its potential to transform service delivery and public trust in government" (p. 15). Norris' (2006) review of multiple e-government studies finds that "[l]ocal e-government ... remains mainly informational. ... nowhere is it achieving the potential positive impacts claimed by its most ardent advocates. ... e-government is not transformational, at least yet. ... e-government, like IT and government before it, is incremental. ... the trajectory of local e-government that has been observed to date will likely continue into the foreseeable future."

Decisions about IT use are made by top managers and their direct subordinates. They use IT in the broad interests of the organization, but those broad interests usually intersect with their own interests. They use IT to enhance the information available to them; to increase their control over resources; to rationalize decisions to superiors, subordinates, and clients; to provide visible deliverables with the aid of the technology; and to symbolize professionalism and rationality in their management practices. These aims do not necessarily work against the welfare of the organization, simply because they work for the welfare of managers. Yet, such aims usually are not associated with and are frequently antithetical to administrative reform.

The following sections examine four key components of the reform hypothesis and provide the contrasting results of research that call those components into question. These empirical results are drawn primarily from experiences in the United States, and it is possible that the experiences in other countries have been quite different. Nevertheless, given the traditions of administrative reform in the U.S. and given the fact that the U.S. arguably leads the world in the levels of governmental and private investment in IT, one would expect the reform hypothesis to be strongly corroborated in the U.S. context. The fact that it is not corroborated bears consideration.

IT and Administrative Reform: The U.S. Experience

U.S. public organizations have been applying IT unabated since digital computers were first introduced in the early 1950s. Picking only one era for closer examination—the mid to late 1980s—it is possible to see the magnitude of U.S. investment in the technology. Federal agencies had more than 20,000 mainframes and minicomputers and, even in those early days of the microcomputer, had more than 200,000 installed. Federal agencies alone employed more than 100,000 IT specialists and spent more than $15 billion annually on computerization (GSA, 1986; OTA, 1985). State and local governments had well over 3,000 mainframes and minicomputers and more than 40,000 microcomputers, employed 35,000 IT specialists, and spent more than $8 billion annually on IT (Caudle & Marchand, 1989; Kraemer et al., 1986; NASIS, 1989). That level of investment has grown substantially in the years since.[3] In short, U.S. public administration has been an enthusiastic user of IT.

U.S. public administration also has been a fertile ground for research into the extent and effects of IT use (Bretschneider, 1990; Caudle, 1990; Caudle & Marchand, 1989; Danziger & Kraemer, 1986; Danziger et al., 1982; Dutton & Kraemer, 1978; Dutton & Guthrie, 1991; Fountain, 2002; George & King, 1991; Holden, 2003; Kling, 1980; Kraemer & King, 1986). The empirical findings are somewhat fragmented and sometimes contradictory, but nevertheless, they can be brought together for how they bear on the following four reform propositions:

- Computers have the potential to reform public administrations and their relations with their environments.
- Information technology can change organizational structures and, thus, is a powerful tool for reform.
- Properly used, information technology will be beneficial for administrators, staff, citizens, and public administration as a whole.
- The potential benefits from information technology are under-realized due to a lack of managerial understanding of what the technology can do and an unwillingness of managers to pursue the potential of the technology when they do understand it.

The following four sections examine each proposition in turn.

Reform Proposition 1. Computers have the potential to reform public administrations and their relations with their environments.

A good example of this was Gibson and Hammer's (1985) claim that today's applications of information technology can dramatically change the way individuals, functional units, and whole organizations carry out their tasks. As a case in point, computer technology was seen as an instrument of administrative reform at the federal level in projects of the U.S. Department of Health, Education and Welfare and in many state and local governments, as well, in the mid- and late 1970s (Kling, 1980). These were efforts to create Information and Referral (I&R) systems in order to consolidate the many public and private local agencies that served large urban areas. I&R systems were believed to help by sharing information about clients, needs, resources, and performance among all participating agencies, improving both service delivery to clients and the allocation of social service resources. Additionally, such systems might facilitate administrative consolidation, central budgeting, and performance monitoring in ways that administrative reforms had failed to accomplish. Despite huge investments, however, this strategy for services integration failed, because the local social service agencies failed to see the benefits to them from the reforms. The I&R systems had no power to bring about services integration indirectly, and they expired along with the whole reform effort.

IT can help effect some reforms, such as centralization of budgeting and accounting systems that allow greater citizen and elected official control over government resources (Kraemer et al., 1981). Computerization often required recalcitrant finance directors and department heads to reveal long-established practices that did not meet the expectations of professional financial controls. Also, second-generation financial automation brought sophisticated capabilities for cost accounting and billing on a fee-for-service basis, which helped government managers to enact new means of enhancing revenues in the face of fiscal limitations set by citizen referenda. Administrative practices, such as centralized accounting and budgeting and services integration, might have failed in the face of organizational growth and decentralization if not for application of IT, but IT was not the cause of such reforms. They were grounded in the early 20th-century efforts to increase professionalism in government management, and, at best, IT was an enabler of these reforms.

Finding on Reform Proposition 1: *Experience with information technology and administrative reform has shown the technology to be useful in some cases of administrative reform but only in cases where expectations for reform are already well established. IT application does not cause reform and cannot encourage it where the political will to pursue the reform does not exist.*

Reform Proposition 2. Information technology can change organizational structures and, thus, is a powerful tool for reform.

This proposition is grounded in the belief that information technology can impact directly the data structures of public administration, enforcing or relaxing traditional hierarchical forms. Mainframe-based computerization was seen as reinforcing hierarchical organizational structures by consolidating data and expertise, while microcomputers were seen as facilitating organizational decentralization through distribution of data and expertise throughout government.

The empirical evidence suggests that the main impact of IT application has been to reinforce existing structures of communication, authority, and power in organizations, whether centralized or decentralized (Attewell & Rule, 1984; Danziger et al., 1982; Dutton & Kraemer, 1977, 1978; George & King, 1991; King, 1983; Kraemer, 1980; Laudon, 1974; Pinsonneault, 1990; Pinsonneault & Kraemer, 1997, 2002; Robey, 1981). This finding is consistent in research on computerization in both city and federal agencies. In the case of local governments, it is true regardless of the form of government. Computerization in city manager governments reinforces the power and control of the professional manager; in strong mayor governments, it reinforces the elected mayor; in commission governments, it reinforces the power of individual commissioners.

The reform proponents argue that these findings are based mainly on the era of centralized mainframe computing. Yet, the research shows that even in the mainframe era, decentralized government organizations had decentralized mainframe computing arrangements (King, 1983). Moreover, even when focused on microcomputers, the data do not support the proposition (Kraemer et al., 1986; Kraemer et al., 1992). Microcomputers have been used extensively for local text processing and other functions that do not support core government functions. To the extent that microcomputers do relate to core functions, it is through their use as intelligent terminals providing user access to centralized servers that support the large-scale processing tasks central to the government's operations.

Even if IT itself is indifferent to power distribution, senior organizational leaders are not. Recent research suggests that use of IT is correlated with both increases and decreases in the number of middle managers in organizations, but the changes are contingent on particular organizational conditions that influence the views of senior leadership (Klatsky, 1970; Pinsonneault, 1990; Pinsonneault & Kraemer, 1997). For example, when middle managers in government organizations control IT deployment decisions, they tend to use the technology to increase their numbers. In contrast, when top managers are in control, they tend to use the technology to reduce the number of middle managers, especially when environmental triggers such as fiscal stress stimulate the need for change (Pinsonneault & Kraemer, 2002).

IT has had little discernible effect on organization structure and seems to yield somewhat greater centralization in already centralized organizations in support of existing organizational arrangements. Other organizational structures also appear to be compatible with IT application, including matrix organizations involving dual authority arrangements. There is no good evidence to support or refute this idea in government organizations, but one would assume that IT application in the context of these newer organizational forms also would be used to reinforce those structures; it would not change them (Vitalari, 1988).

Finding on Reform Proposition 2: *IT application has brought relatively little change to organization structures and seems to reinforce existing structures.*

Reform Proposition 3. Properly used, information technology will be beneficial for administrators, staff, citizens, and public administration as a whole.

Proponents of this proposition argue that information technology has the potential to decentralize administration, reintegrate and enhance work life, open access to data within the government and with citizens outside, and rationalize decision making on complex problems through computerized modeling. Such changes, it is hoped, will further democratize government by bringing citizens more fully into planning and administration activities of the government itself, especially in areas of citizen concern.

There is little dispute that IT is beneficial to the organizations that use it, especially in the area of productivity (Jorgensen et al., 2003; Lee & Perry, 1998; Lehr & Lichtenberg, 1998). In the case of government, such benefits come mainly from long-standing applications to structured and repetitive tasks at the core of government operations: the day-to-day, transaction-oriented information processing of administrative agencies concerned with producing bills, recording payments, paying vendors and employees, recording public documents, answering citizen inquiries, and so forth (Danziger & Kraemer, 1986). These applications meet real needs of public agencies and represent substantial investments. They are not bold, innovative moves to reform public agencies; they simply are useful adaptations of the technology in order to improve administrative performance. They reinforce the conservative values of governmental efficiency and social control inherent in U.S. governments for decades. However, they do not serve the needs of special citizen groups, such as the poor, the homeless, the aged, or the handicapped (Kraemer & Kling, 1985).

There have been relatively few examples of IT applications aimed at broader, more liberal citizen service provision. An interesting example is Santa Monica, California's

PEN system, a public information utility designed to provide information, electronic mail, and conferencing among citizens and the city government through networked microcomputers located in public places and via remote links from people in their workplaces and homes. In many ways, the PEN system did achieve its goals, but it did so in the context of a city with legendary biases of political liberalism. In their case study of the PEN system, Dutton and Guthrie (1991) describe it as "reinforcing the values and interests of a liberal democratic community supportive of citizen participation" (p. 295). The technology was used to reinforce community values (in this case, liberal democratic values), not to reform them.[4] Once again, the empirical evidence suggests that those who control IT deployment and application determine whose interests are served by the technology.

Finding on Reform Proposition 3: *The benefits of information technology have not been distributed evenly within government organizational functions; the primary beneficiaries have been functions favored by the dominant political-administrative coalitions in public administrations and not those of technical elites, middle managers, clerical staff, or ordinary citizens.[5]*

Reform Proposition 4. The potential benefits from information technology are underrealized due to a lack of managerial understanding of what the technology can do and an unwillingness of managers to pursue the potential of the technology when they do understand it.

There is no question that some managers are more effective than others at applying IT successfully, but this has little to do with the reform hypothesis. The proposition states that managers lack the understanding necessary to motivate application of IT. In fact, IT is being applied widely in government with the full approval of all levels of the managerial hierarchy. Moreover, governments with professionalized administrations actually are more likely to adopt and apply IT (Danziger et al., 1982; Dutton & Kraemer, 1977). The issue is not that managers fail to understand the potential of IT; they understand that potential perfectly well when it comes to their own interests, and they exploit it aggressively in the pursuit of those interests. Those interests are in line with more traditional and conservative values of government in the U.S., as noted previously. In the occasional instances in which a government organization pursues a different political agenda, such as in Santa Monica, IT is applied toward those ends.

Findings on Reform Proposition 4: *Government managers have a good sense of the potential uses of IT in their own interests, and in cases where their interests coincide with government interests, they push IT application aggressively.*

Problem with the Reform Hypothesis

The U.S. experience with IT in government fails to support the reform hypothesis. The benefits of IT use are focused largely on administrative efficiency and not on reform of administrative organization, practices, or behavior. Two underlying assumptions govern the reform hypothesis, as it has been articulated, that reform is required in government and that IT can be used to carry out such reforms. Both of these assumptions are questionable.

The reform hypothesis suggests that reform is necessary without specifying why. Government organizations may be flawed and subject to improvement, but that does not mean that they are doing a poor job at their objectives. Most government organizations are bureaucracies with hierarchically organized distributions of authority, resources, and responsibility flowing downward to work units and information about organizational performance flowing back upward as a means of control. Most government managers want to keep organizations that way for good reasons. The bureaucratic form is highly refined from many decades of continuous study and improvement. It has evolved into a comprehensive set of conventions that work quite well at doing complicated tasks with reasonable performance on a sustained basis over many years. Government managers understand this form of organization, which makes them experts at using it to accomplish governmental objectives. None of this suggests that managers are averse to performance improvements; indeed, the U.S. research clearly shows senior government managers are strongly supportive of efforts to improve efficiency, productivity, and organizational control. What about the current system is broken? The reform hypothesis does not say.

IT application in the U.S. actually fits the agenda of improved government within the established bureaucratic model. For example, computerization in financial systems provides new information and control mechanisms simultaneously to senior executives, central financial managers, and department heads. Subordinates using such systems might find themselves under greater financial surveillance from their supervisors, but they also gain greater control over the details of their budgets, especially with respect to patterns of spending through real time, and accurate information about current balances. These systems allow managers at any level to enact immediate and across-the-board changes affecting subordinates, such as the elimination of funds for all open positions, enactment of budget cuts, assignment of overhead expenses, and so forth (Kraemer et al., 1981). This effect of IT use is not power-neutral; it reinforces the general hierarchical structure of bureaucratic organization even while giving managers at each level greater leverage over the operations below.

Even in cases where there are good reasons to reform government, the application of IT has a poor record as a lever for change. The short-run impacts of IT use have been far less pervasive and dramatic than forecast. Orientations, tasks, and interactions among managers and workers might change, but the changes in standard operating procedures tend to be modest. It is more common that IT is made to conform to existing behavior and practice than to change such a practice. Case studies covering 30 years of computing in cities (Kraemer et al., 1986) and federal agencies (Westin & Laudon, 1986) indicate that reform has been limited mainly to the information processing function within organizations and not to the broader aspects of organizations. The indirect influence of information technology to achieve genuine reform within the political administrative system is far less powerful than the direct intervention of executive, legislative, or judicial change. In theory, IT might lead to new administrative structures; in practice, it does not, and it probably should not.

Implications and Conclusion

Proponents of the reform hypothesis might respond to the foregoing analysis with the objection that much of the evidence presented in the analysis is from studies of government IT application prior to the 1990s, when the Internet became a major force. The potential of the Internet to alter the prospects of e-government dramatically can be inferred from the transformation of business organizations using IT and especially the Internet during and after the dot.com boom. This is a fair observation and deserves careful response.

It is true that much of the research cited in the previous arguments was done in the 1960s, 1970s, and 1980s, and that important changes in technology occurred between the 1990s and the present. Nevertheless, the studies cited were careful to account for the actual changes that might be associated with the application of IT to specific tasks in government organizations and not to changes that were specific to particular technologies. The reform hypothesis was an explicit focus of much of this research, and every effort was made to find evidence for the hypothesis. The most systematic of these studies refuted the hypothesis in fundamental ways that are relevant not only for the 30-year period of the studies but more generally into the 1990s and today. More important, studies done since the 1990s (Fountain, 2001, 2002; Holden, 2003; Holden et al., 2003; Kaylor et al., 2001; Moon, 2002; Norris,

2005, 2006) corroborate the basic findings of the earlier work—IT has not reformed or transformed government administration. The facts of today do not necessarily dictate the reality of tomorrow, but in the absence of evidence to the contrary, it is safe to assume that IT use will not result in the reforms that proponents of the reform hypothesis claim.

The role of the Internet bears attention, because the Internet (by which we broadly refer to computer networking) is a fundamental enabling component of e-government. Indeed, one might argue that the experience of the pre-Internet period is irrelevant to e-government, because without the Internet there would be no e-government. Again, the focus of this article is not on the broad question of whether IT affects government organizations; it is on the narrower question of whether IT use is likely to result in government reform. The Internet permits computers to communicate with each other and humans to communicate with computers and with each other via computers. It affects how tasks can be done and how work can be organized, but that does not mean that those tasks or the nature of the work itself will be altered in fundamental ways.

Use of IT has dramatically affected many business organizations and sectors in the past decade. Some business organizations and even whole sectors of business have undergone radical change since the Internet arrived. IT has brought major produc-tivity gains to business organizations (Jorgensen et al., 2003), and, in most cases, those gains are specifically tied to changes in the ways organizations do business (Brynjolfsson & Hitt, 2003). A good example is seen in the personal computer industry (Dedrick & Kraemer, 2005). Competitive market forces required firms to change the organization of their activities from vertical, supply-driven models to virtual, demand-driven models In order to better match supply and demand and to avoid the cycles of excess inventory and product shortages that had plagued PC companies. Dell Computer pioneered this change, which happened to fit well with the capabilities of the Internet, and soon was copied as it took market share from the other vendors. PC makers reorganized their activities around information processes—order management, planning and coordination, and customer relation-ship management. This allowed them to substitute information for inventory and to respond to market signals more quickly and more effectively. IT did not directly create new value in the PC industry; it allowed information processes to be redefined in ways that improved efficiency and added value to the customer.

While this dramatic example is compelling, it is important to note that the catalyst of industry change was a company—Dell Computer—that was a relative newcomer to an industry that already had been destabilized by eroding profitability and intense competition. Dell did not so much reform the PC industry as create an entirely new and superior model for the industry. Despite considerable effort and investment, no other personal computer company yet has been able to match Dell's efficiency (Dedrick & Kraemer, 2005). Other dramatic examples of business change associated with IT use, such as Wal-Mart, Amazon.com, eBay, and Google, show a similar pattern of forcing dramatic rethinking of the whole business enterprise.

One must be careful in drawing conclusions from such studies and applying them to government. The overall effects of IT on business are more complicated than they might first appear. While Amazon.com, eBay, and Google are stunning examples of the dot.com era, many companies that tried to change their industries or to create new industries failed completely and disappeared when the dot.com boom went bust. In addition, business and government organizations exhibit fundamental differences that influence the outcomes of IT use. Few business organizations have their tasks and work specified under statute or executive order; businesses, unlike governments, are free to decide what things to do and how to do them. Business organizations are driven mainly by market forces, which encourage radical innovation and can be characterized by Schumpeter's gales of creative destruction. Government organizations, in contrast, are driven by political/institutional forces that are not and cannot be subjected to destructive changes without severe consequences for their constituents.

This does not mean that governments have little to learn from the changes seen in the business world. Examples from business prove that even well-established production systems can be changed dramatically to produce results that are of benefit to consumers. At minimum, these examples provide hope that government services can be improved in ways that bring benefits to citizens through careful application of IT. In order for that to happen, however, the leadership of government organizations must establish the broader goals of the reform efforts, develop new models of electronic governance and electronic service delivery, and then bring IT carefully into consideration. Today's e-government initiatives are part of a broader government reform agenda that emphasizes customer service and greater responsiveness to citizens (Executive Office of the President, 2003; National Performance Review, 1993). If this, indeed, is the will of the existing governmental power structure, IT might play a role in the reform. But that is not a foregone conclusion, and what actually happens remains to be seen.

A more difficult challenge arising from the arguments in this article is the question of what practitioners, researchers, and others who are interested in e-government should do in response to this assessment. One might conclude that e-government is a mere passing fad that will flare and then fade, as many other management fads have in the past (e.g., management by objectives or zero-base budgeting). This would be overreaching. The argument here is a cautionary note about e-government and significant government reform. It is not a criticism of e-government, per se, nor is it a claim that e-government will fail to produce significant long-term changes in the nature and conduct of government. Returning to business organizations, there is considerable evidence to suggest that profound transformations in whole sectors have occurred over time through the use of IT. Yates' (2005) studies of IT in the rise of system approaches in American management between 1860 and 1920 and of the remaking of the U.S. insurance industry in the early 20th century provide elegant proof of the transforming power of IT enablement. King and Lyytinen's (2005) study of transformation in the automobile industry in the 20th century provides insights about the role of IT in reshaping industrial ecologies. There is good reason to believe that e-government initiatives might affect government dramatically over the coming decades.

The question of whether expectations for e-government are realized or dashed depends on what those expectations are. This article suggests that claims that e-government will fundamentally alter governmental structure, performance, citizen engagement, and so on (Executive Office of the President, 2003; National Performance Review, 1993) are likely to be dashed, given that IT in and of itself consistently has proven to have little bearing on those kinds of government reforms. IT is a general-purpose engine that can enable reform efforts, but unless the other factors required for reform are in place, the role of IT is immaterial. IT also has been used to thwart reform efforts, a fact that many who support the reform hypothesis overlook. True reform begins and ends with political will, and along the way, IT can play myriad roles.

Perhaps most important for e-government practice and research, nothing in this argument refutes the hope that IT will improve government operations and enable new government services. E-government, at least in principle, offers a great deal to government organizations facing increasing demands, shrinking resources, and, in many cases, more fractionated political climates. IT can be used to make important marginal improvements in efficiency and effectiveness and, in some cases, to create truly innovative government responses to challenges. IT has brought such benefits to many organizations and many sectors, and there is nothing to preclude government organizations from enjoying such payoffs from thoughtful IT investment. A challenging agenda for e-government practice and research remains, even if government reform is removed from the agenda.

Another point that is seldom mentioned in the reform discussion might be added to the agenda: the implications of e-government in changing the political dynamics whereby government leaders are elected and appointed. As was pointed out in a 1987 study of the use of computer models in the federal government, IT had failed conspicuously to alter fundamental dimensions of the federated governmental apparatus of the United States, but the same could not be said for the processes of political mobilization (Kraemer et al., 1987). The most recent U.S. presidential election was replete with examples of the ways in which IT can alter political balances and fortunes, including the Internet-based fundraising drives that allowed Democratic campaign financing to keep up with Republican financing and the effects of Weblogs and Internet-based news sites covering the campaign on the mobilization of public opinion, to the controversies regarding electronic voting (Nardi et al., 2004a, 2004b). It is in some ways fitting that the most significant impacts of IT on government thus far have been in the most political dimensions of government—the determination of who governs. This condition is likely to persist and is highly relevant to both practice and research in the realm of e-government.

References

Attewell, P., & Rule, J. (1984). Computing in organizations: What we know and what we don't know. *Communications of the ACM, 27*(12), 1184-1192.

Bretschneider, S. (1990). Management information systems in public and private organizations: An empirical test. *Public Administration Review, 50*(5), 536-545.

Brynjolfsson, E., & Hitt, L. M. (2003, January 27). *The catalytic computer: Information technology, enterprise transformation, and business performance.* Unpublished manuscript.

Caudle, S. L. (1990). Managing information resources in state government. *Public Administration Review, 50*(5), 515-524.

Caudle, S. L., & Marchand, D. A. (1989). *Managing information resources: New directions in state government.* Syracuse, NY: Syracuse University.

Danziger, J. N., Dutton, W. H., Kling, R., & Kraemer, K. L. (1982). *Computers and politics.* New York: Columbia University Press.

Danziger, J. N., &. Kraemer, K. L. (1986). *People and computers.* New York: Columbia University Press.

Dean, J. (2002). E-government hits the mainstream survey says. *GovExec.com.* Retrieved February 26, 2002, from http://govexec.com/dailyfed/0202/022602j1.htm

Dedrick, J., & Kraemer, K. L. (2005). The impacts of IT on firm and industry structure: The personal computer industry. *California Management Review, 47*(3), 122-142.

Dutton, W. H., Blumler, J. G., & Kraemer, K. L. (1987). *Wired cities: Shaping the future of communications.* Boston: G.K. Hall.

Dutton, W. H., & Guthrie, K. (1991). An ecology of games: The political construction of Santa Monica's public electronic network. *Informatization in the Public Sector, 1*(4), 279-301.

Dutton, W. H., & Kraemer, K. L. (1977). Technology and urban management: The power payoffs of computing. *Administration and Society, 9*(3), 304-340.

Dutton, W. H., & Kraemer, K. L. (1978). Management utilization of computers in American local governments. *Communications of the ACM, 21*(3), 206-218.

Dutton, W. H., & Kraemer, K. L. (1985). *Modeling as negotiating: The political dynamics of computer models in the policy process.* Norwood, NJ: Ablex Publishing.

Executive Office of the President. (2003, April). *E-government strategy: Implementing the president's management agenda for e-government.* Washington, DC: EOP.

Forman, M. (2003, May 12). Memorandum for the chief information officers Re: procedures for requesting funds from the e-government fund. Office of Management and Budget (OMB).

Forrester Research. (2000, August 30). *Sizing U.S. e-government*. Cambridge, MA: Forrester.

Fountain, J. E. (2001). *Building the virtual state: Information technology and institutional change*. Washington, DC: Brookings Institution Press.

Fountain, J. E. (2002). *Information, institutions and governance*. Cambridge: Harvard University.

Garson, G. D. (2004). The promise of digital government. In A. Pavlichev, & G. D. Garson (Eds.), *Digital government principles and best practices* (pp. 2-15). Hershey, PA: Idea Group Publishing.

Gasco, M. (2003). New technologies and institutional change in public administration. *Social Science Computer Review, 21*(1), 6-14.

General Services Administration (GSA). (1986). *Automatic data processing inventory*. Washington, DC: General Services Administration.

George, J. F., & King, J. L. (1991). Examining the computing and centralization debate. *Communications of the ACM, 34*(7), 63-72.

Gibson, C. F., & Hammer, M. (1985). Now that the dust has settled: A clear view of the terrain. *Indications, 2*(5), 5-12.

Gronlund, A. (2003). Emerging electronic infrastructures: Exploring democratic components. *Social Science Computer Review, 21*(1), 55-72.

Holden, S. H. (2003). The evolution of information technology management at the federal level: Implications for public administration. In G. D. Garson (Ed.), *Public information technology: Policy and management issues* (pp. 53-73). Hershey, PA: Idea Group Publishing.

Holden, S. H., Norris, D. F., & Fletcher, P. D. (2003). Electronic government at the local level: Progress to date and future issues. *Public Productivity and Management Review, 26*(3), 1-20.

Jorgensen, D. W., Ho, M. S., & Stiroh, K. J. (2003, January 27). Lessons from the US growth resurgence. In *Proceedings of the First International Conference on the Economic and Social Implications of Information Technology* (pp. 453-470), Washington, DC.

Kaylor, C. H., Deshazo, R., & Van Eck, D. (2001). Gauging e-government: A report on implementing services among American cities. *Government Information Quarterly, 18*(4), 293-307.

King, J. L. (1983). Centralized vs. decentralized computing: Organizational considerations and management options. *ACM Computing Surveys, 15*(4), 319-345.

King, J. L., & Kraemer, K. L. (1985). *The dynamics of computing*. New York: Columbia University Press.

King, J. L., & Kraemer, K. L. (1986). The dynamics of change in computing use: A theoretical framework. *Computers Environment and Urban Systems, 11*(1/2), 5-25.

King, J. L., & Lyytinen, K. (2005). Automotive informatics: Information technology and enterprise transformation in the automobile industry. In W. H. Dutton, B. Kahin, R. O'Callaghan, & A. W. Wychoff (Eds.), *Transforming enterprise* (pp. 283-312). Cambridge, MA: MIT Press.

Klatzky, S. R. (1970). Automation, size and the locus of decision making: The cascade effect. *Journal of Business, 43*(2), 141-151.

Kling, R. (1974). Automated welfare client tracking and service integration. *Communications of the ACM, 21*(6), 484-493.

Kling, R. (1980). Social analyses of computing: Theoretical perspectives in recent empirical research. *Computing Surveys, 12*(1), 61-110.

Kraemer, K. L. (1980). Computers, information and power in local governments. In A. Mowshowitz (Ed.), *Human choice and computers, 2* (pp. 213-235). New York: North-Holland Publishing.

Kraemer, K. L., Dickhoven, S., Tierney, S. F., & King, J. L. (1987). *Datawars: The politics of modeling in federal policymaking*. New York: Columbia University Press.

Kraemer, K. L., Dutton, W. H., & Northrop, A. (1981). *The management of information systems*. New York: Columbia University Press.

Kraemer, K. L., & King, J. L. (1979). A requiem for USAC. *Policy Analysis, 5*(3), 313-349.

Kraemer, K. L., & King, J. L. (1986). Computing and public organizations. *Public Administration Review, 46*(6), 488-496.

Kraemer, K. L., & King, J. L. (1987). Computers and the Constitution: A helpful, harmful, or harmless relationship? *Public Administration Review, 47*(1), 93-105.

Kraemer, K. L., King, J. L., Dunkle, D., Lane, J. P., & George, J. F. (1986). *The future of information systems in local governments*. Irvine, CA: University of California, Irvine.

Kraemer, K. L., King, J. L., Dunkle, D., & Perry, J. L. (1992). *Distributable computing and organizational democratization: A test of conventional wisdom*. Irvine, CA: University of California, Irvine.

Kraemer, K. L., & Kling, R. (1985). The political character of computerization in service organizations: Citizen interests or bureaucratic control. *Computers and the Social Sciences, 1*(2), 77-89.

Kraemer, K. L., & Perry, J. L. (1979). The federal push to bring computer applications to local governments. *Public Administration Review, 39*(3), 260-270.

Laudon, K. (1974). *Computers and bureaucratic reform*. New York: John Wiley and Sons.

Layne, K., & Lee, J. (2001). Developing fully functional e-government: A four stage model. *Government Information Quarterly, 18*(2), 122-136.

Leavitt, H. J., & Whisler, T. L. (1958). Management in the 1980s. *Harvard Business Review, 36*(6), 41-48.

Lee, G., & Perry, J. L. (1998). *Are computers boosting productivity? A test of the paradox in state governments* (Working Paper). Irvine, CA: University of California, Irvine.

Lehr, W., & Lichtenberg, F. R. (1998). Computer use and productivity growth in US federal government agencies, 1987-1992. *The Journal of Industrial Economics, 46*(2), 257-279.

Moon, M. J. (2002). The evolution of e-government among municipalities: Rhetoric or reality. *Public Administration Review, 62*(4), 424-433.

Nardi, B., Schiano, D., & Gumbrecht, M. (2004a). Blogging as social activity, or, would you let 900 million people read your diary? In *Proceedings of the Conference on Computer-Supported Cooperative Work* (pp. 222-228). New York: ACM Press.

Nardi, B., Schiano, D., Gumbrecht, M., & Swartz, L. (2004b). Why we blog. *Communications of the American Association for Computing Machinery, 47*(12), 41.

National Association for State Information Systems (NASIS). (1989). *Information systems technology in state government.* Lexington, KY: Council of State Governments.

National Performance Review. (1993). *From red tape to results: Creating a government that works better and costs less, and reengineering through information technology* (accompanying report of the NPR). Washington, DC: U.S. Government Printing Office.

Norris, D. F. (2005). Electronic democracy at the American grassroots. *International Journal of Electronic Government Research, 1*(3), 1-14.

Norris, D. F. (forthcoming). Electronic government at the American grassroots: The state of the practice. In A. V. Anttiroiko, & M. Malkia (Eds.), *Encyclopedia of digital government.* Hershey, PA: Idea Group Reference.

Norris, D. F., & Moon, M. J. (2005). Advancing e-government at the grass roots: Tortoise or hare? *Public Administration Review, 65*(1), 64-75.

Office of Technology Assessment (OTA). (1985). *Automation of America's offices.* Washington, DC: U.S. Congress.

Perry, J. L., & Kraemer, K. L. (1979). *Technological innovation in American local governments.* New York: Pergamon.

Pinsonneault, A. (1990). *The impact of information technology on the middle management workforce: An empirical investigation.* Unpublished doctoral dissertation, University of California Irvine, Irvine, CA.

Pinsonneault, A., & Kraemer, K. L. (1997). Middle management downsizing: An empirical investigation of the impact of information technology. *Management Science, 43*(5), 659-679.

Pinsonneault, A., & Kraemer, K. L. (2002). Information technology and middle management downsizing: A tale of two cities. *Organization Science, 13*(2), 191-208.

Reinermann, H. (1988). Vor einer "verwaltungsreform?" Informationstechnisch motivieerte ziele und "systemkonzepte" der verwaltungspolitik. In H. Reinermann, H. Fiedler, K. Grimmer, K. Lenk, & R. Traunmuller (Eds.), *Neue informationstechniken neue verwaltungsstruckturen?* (pp. 38-50). Heidelberg, Germany: R.V. Decker & C.F. Muller.

Robey, D. (1981). Computers, information systems and organizational structure. *Communications of the ACM, 24*(10), 679-687.

Vitalari, N. (1988). *The impact of information technology on organizational design and the emergence of the distributed organization.* Irvine, CA: University of California Irvine.

Weiner, M. E. (1969). *Service: The objective of municipal information systems.* Storrs, CT: University of Connecticut.

West, D. M. (2004). E-government and the transformation of service delivery and citizen attitudes. *Public Administration Review, 64*(1), 15-27.

Westin, A., & Laudon, K. (1986). *Information technology and the Social Security Administration: 1935-1990* (Research Monograph). Washington, DC: Office of Technology Assessment.

Yates, J. (2005). *Structuring the information age: Life insurance and information technology in the 20th century.* Baltimore: Johns Hopkins University Press.

Endnotes

[1] The exact quote from Niccolo Machiavelli's *The Prince*, which you can find at http://www.brainyquote.com/quotes/authors/n/niccolo_machiavelli. html, is as follows: "There is nothing more difficult to take in hand, more perilous to conduct, or more uncertain in its success, than to take the lead in the introduction of a new order of things".

[2] This literature spans more than 30 years and is illustrated by the National Performance Review of 1993. *From Red Tape to Results: Creating a Government that works Better and Costs Less*, and *Reengineering through Information Technology* (accompanying report of the NPR). Washington, DC: US Government Printing Office.

[3] By 2002, federal government spending for IT was $45 billion annually, with $45 million set aside for e-government projects, increasing to $150 million by 2006 (Forman, 2003).

[4] In a recent analysis of e-democracy in four municipalities in Sweden, Gronlund (2003) concluded that the various e-democracy initiatives reinforced the current procedures of formal politics by complementing them with increased direct communication with citizens rather than citizen participation and influence. Moreover, he concluded that this should be seen as a measure designed to reinforce the politicians' position rather than the citizens', as the agenda was set by the politicians.

[5] In every government, there is a coalition of political and administrative leaders who have broad power and control over the organization. In simplest terms, this might

be the city manager and city council in a council-manager form of government, the commissioners and CAO in the commission form of government, and the mayor and other top elected officials in the strong mayor form of government. These coalitions sometimes are referred to as the organization's power structure and might well include others lower down in the hierarchy. This explanation is similar to Laudon (1974) and Danziger et al. (1982).

This work was previously published in International Journal of Electronic Government Research, Vol. 2, Issue 1, edited by D. F. Norris & P. Fletcher, pp. 1-20, copyright 2006 by IGI Publishing, formerly known as Idea Group Publishing (an imprint of IGI Global).

Chapter II

The Scholarly Literature on E-Government:
Characterizing a Nascent Field

Donald Norris, University of Maryland, Baltimore County, USA

Benjamin A. Lloyd, University of Maryland, Baltimore County, USA

Abstract

The authors conducted a comprehensive review of articles on the subject of e-government that were published in refereed scholarly journals through the end of 2004 to serve as a baseline for future analysis of this emerging field. They found over 100 e-government articles, but only 57 with empirical content. The authors then examined the articles using 12 analytical categories. They conclude that the scholarship about e-government comes primarily from the United States, and from authors trained in the social sciences. Few e-government articles adequately used the literatures that were available (e.g., IT and government, e-government, or any specialized literatures), and few created or tested theory or hypotheses. Articles employed both qualitative and quantitative methodologies, but many contained conclusions that were not supported by their data or analyses. The authors conclude that e-government research is a young and growing field that has yet to achieve adequate scholarly rigor.

Introduction

Within the past dozen or so years, governments across the globe and at all levels have adopted electronic government (a.k.a., e-government) as a means of delivering of governmental information and services 24 hours per day, seven days per week. Nearly all national governments, most sub-national or state governments, and large numbers of local governments have established Web sites through which they provide e-government. In the U.S., the federal government has a strong e-government presence through its portal FirstGov.gov, and all federal departments and agencies have Web sites. All 50 states have Web sites as do most state agencies and departments. Finally, more than 95% of U.S. local governments with populations of 10,000 and larger have Web sites.

Although governments have adopted e-government rapidly, e-government remains a relatively new phenomenon. For example, about two-thirds of local government Web sites in the U.S. are 10 years old or less (Holden, Norris, & Fletcher, 2003; Norris & Moon, 2005). This means that research into e-government is even younger because research typically lags behind practice by a few years.

Nevertheless, over the past few years, a small but growing body of scholarly literature about e-government has begun to emerge. Most of this scholarship has been published in traditional journals in a few key fields, including the social sciences, information systems, computer science, and business administration.

Although research in the field of e-government is still in its early days, now would be an appropriate time to pause and take stock of the field via an examination of the scholarly literature that has been published in it to date. In this article, we examine articles about e-government that have been published in refereed scholarly journals. We chose to focus only on articles in refereed journals because, in academic circles, these are the "gold standard" that defines the scholarship in a field.[1]

Method

As active researchers in the field, we endeavor to keep in touch with the scholarship and believe that we know the published works reasonably well. Thus, we began our search for articles about e-government by developing a list of works known to us. To ensure that we did not miss any relevant articles, we next searched the bibliographies of those initially identified works to find published articles of which we were unaware.

To expand the search further, we used 13 online article databases at the UMBC library (Academic Search Premier, Business Source Premier, CAIO, EconLit, Emerald Library, ERIC, Infotrieve, JSTOR, LLBA, PAIS, PsycInfo, Social Sciences Abstracts, and Sociology Abstracts) to find yet additional articles about e-government. In these databases, we used "e-government," "electronic government," and "digital government" as our search terms. Depending on the design and capabilities of each database, we looked for articles that had at least one of these terms in either the title or abstract, or had one of the terms assigned to it as a subject term or keyword. We then examined the bibliographies of all of these articles to identify works that we had not otherwise found. Through these methods, we identified over 100 articles about e-government published in refereed journals.[2]

Next, we read the articles to determine if they involved analysis of empirical data, or merely represented authors' ruminations and speculations (no matter how well considered) about e-government. Our interest is with the empirical scholarship in the field, that is, works that undertake some form of quantitative or qualitative analysis of the empirical data or evidence about e-government. Thus, we eliminated articles that were essentially speculative in nature, and selected for further consideration only those articles that contained and analyzed empirical data. (By empirical data, we mean data derived from any research method involving "observation", whether qualitative or quantitative.[3]) This left us with 57 empirical articles published in refereed journals through the end of 2004.

We chose to limit our review to the period from the appearance of the first empirical article about e-government to the close of 2004 because by the beginning of 2005 four new refereed journals devoted to e-government had begun publication.[4] We therefore examined only articles that appeared prior to the establishment of those journals. As such, this review should provide a good overview of the type and quality of published empirical works from the earliest days of e-government research.

In order to understand these works and their contributions to the nascent field of e-government research, we established 12 categories for examining them. These categories are:

- **Year published:** Publication dates indicate both when e-government research began to appear and whether the number of works published about e-government annually has grown over time.

- **Type of journal:** Here we were interested in knowing the disciplines in which articles about e-government have appeared and whether articles have appeared in journals of a certain discipline more often than in another. We categorized the journals as being either in the social sciences or in information technology (or IT, which also includes both computer science and information systems).[4]

- **Type of issue:** Did the article appear in a general issue of the journal or in a special issue devoted to e-government? This may indicate whether e-government research is being mainstreamed or whether a few journals have "jump started" e-government research with focused issues on the subject.

- **Type of article:** What was the overall nature of the article? Did it involve data set analysis (e.g., from a survey or other data set), case study or studies, and Web site analyses?

- **Type of data:** What sort of data or evidence did the authors use in their analysis? Our categories were survey data, Web site content analysis, and "case data," which we defined as being narrative descriptions of e-government programs or projects; We considered combining these two categories (type of article and type of data) because they are similar. At the same time, however, each has distinct value. For example, some of the case study articles used survey data, while others used simple case stories.

- **Discipline of lead author:** This category allowed us to learn the disciplines from which authorship emanated. Our categories were: social sciences, IT (including computer science and information systems), business and management, and communications. In cases when an author was located in the information systems department of a business school, we considered that author's discipline to be IT. We also included a category for practitioners of e-government programs who are outside of academia. In cases of multiple authorship (of which there were 34 articles), we used the discipline of the lead author only.

- **Authors' location(s) of origin:** Here, we determined whether the author(s) were based at a university or other location in the United States, or at a location outside of the U.S., or, if there were multiple authors, were they located both inside and outside of the U.S.? This allowed us to determine whether the scholarship on e-government is dominated by authors based in the United States, or if it is truly an international field.

- **Formulate theory:** Next we wanted to learn if an article involved the development of original theory or the application of existing theory?

- **Test of theory:** Likewise, we wanted to know if an article engaged in the formal testing of original or existing theory. Arguably, articles that develop or test theory can be viewed as being more rigorous than those that do not. Those that do may also be more closely linked to prior scholarship in related fields than those that do not.

- **Formulate hypotheses or research questions:** This category enabled us to ascertain if an article developed formal hypotheses or research questions that then helped to drive or guide the research.

- **Test of hypotheses or research questions:** Likewise, did the article involve the testing of hypotheses or research questions? Here again, articles that formulate and test hypotheses or research questions arguably can be considered more rigorous than those that do not.

- **Type of analysis:** Here we asked if the authors engaged in qualitative or quantitative data analysis or some combination thereof. If quantitative, what sort of analysis (e.g., descriptive statistics, correlation analysis, regression analysis)? Readers should note, however, that we agree with Yin (2004) and do not assert a hierarchy of research or analytical methods. That is, we do not argue that some methods of analysis (i.e., quantitative) are better than others (i.e., qualitative).

Thus far, our categories have been descriptive and reasonably objective. This information allows us to tell a basic story about the types of works about e-government that have been published in scholarly journals. However, an analysis of the scholarly literature about e-government would not be very satisfying or useful if it did not go beyond describing such things as types of journals, types of articles, types of data, and the like. Hence, we developed more qualitative (and frankly more subjective) categories for examining these works. We discuss these below.

- **Adequacy of literature review:** Sir Isaac Newton was reported to have said that he had been able to achieve great scientific breakthroughs in part because he "stood on the shoulders of giants." By this he meant that he read everything that came before him that was relevant to his work. This remains excellent advice for scholars today. Hence, we were interested in learning if the articles we reviewed had stood on the shoulders of giants. To do so, we examined their literature reviews. In particular, we looked for reviews of literature from the nascent field of e-government as well as the well-developed field of IT and government. Did the authors cite appropriate works from those literatures? Several of the articles also involved issues beyond e-government alone (e.g., bureaucracy, participation, etc.). Thus, where relevant, we examined whether the authors cited and used appropriate works from those literatures as well. Regarding e-government literature reviews, our characterization became increasingly strict over time. We did not expect much of articles published in 1999 and 2000, because there was not much e-government literature to cite (including literature published in other than peer-reviewed journals). However, we expected far more of articles published in 2003 and 2004 in terms of their e-government literature reviews simply because of the greater volume of material available to inform scholarship. We characterized the literature reviews as weak, moderate, or strong based on the strength of the literature reviews in the bodies of the articles and the numbers of citations in the bibliographies.

- **Support for conclusions:** We read each article with a view toward understanding the extent to which the authors' conclusions were supported by the evidence and analysis presented in the work. We also examined the articles for whether their methodologies produced data that could reasonably be employed to produce or support the conclusions drawn. In other words, were the data "good" and did the authors stick to the data when drawing conclusions, or did they "go a bridge too far"? An example of an article where the conclusions strayed too far from its data is one that examined the contents of governmental Web sites and drew its conclusions about governmental openness and responsiveness based solely on Web site contents. Another example would be an article that used data from a survey which had a very low response rate, and whose respondents were not representative of the population being described. We ranked articles as having weak, moderate, or strong evidentiary support for their conclusions.

Clearly, these subjective categories leave some room for disagreement. However, we believe that they represent at least a beginning point for developing a better understanding of the scholarship in this emerging field. Moreover, the two authors each read all of the articles independently and coded them separately. Inter-coder reliability was greater than 95%.

Findings

We discuss our findings in the following paragraphs. We then summarize the findings and draw conclusions about the nascent field of e-government research.

Year Published

There was a slight but steady increase in the number of empirical articles about e-government published each year between when the first empirical article appeared and the end of 2004. The first two articles appeared in 1999, about four to five years after the governments began adopting e-government in earnest. This number increased to three in 2000, six in 2001, and 13 in 2002. Then, in 2003, 16 articles appeared, followed by 17 in 2004 (Table 1).

Type of Journal

There was a nearly equal distribution of articles by discipline of the journals in which the articles appeared. A slight majority (30, or 53%) were found in journals of the social sciences, while the remaining 27 (47%) were from journals in the information systems, information technology, or related fields. Of the 27 articles in IT journals, 14 were found in *Government Information Quarterly (GIQ)*. The social

Table 1. Number of articles published by year

1999	2
2000	3
2001	6
2002	13
2003	16
2004	17

Table 2. Number of articles published by journal

Social Science Journals 30	
Social Science Computer Review	7
Public Administration Review	3
Public Performance & Management Review	3
Administration & Society	2
Journal of Public Administration Research and Theory	2
Administration	1
The American Review of Public Administration	1
Governance: An International Journal of Policy, Administration, and Institutions	1
International Journal of Public Administration	2
International Journal of Public Sector Management	2
New Media & Society	1
Political Communication	1
Public Administration	1
Public Administration and Development	1
Social Science Quarterly	1
State and Local Government Review	1
Information Systems, Information Technology and related Journals 27	
Government Information Quarterly	14
Journal of Electronic Commerce in Organizations	5
Bulletin of Science, Technology and Society	1
Information & Management	1
Information and Communications Technology Law	1
International Journal of Electronic Business	1
Journal of Computer Information Systems	1
Journal of Computer Mediated Communication	1
Journal of Government Information	1
Technological Forecasting and Social Change	1

science journal with the most empirical e-government articles was *Social Science Computer Review (SSCR),* which had seven. The remaining articles were dispersed among 24 different journals (Table 2).

In addition to identifying the types of journals in which articles were published, examination of the table also reveals something about the relative prestige of the journals publishing e-government works. Arguably, only three top-ranked journals appear here: Public Administration Review, Journal of Public Administration Research and Theory, and Administration and Society. This suggests that e-government research is not yet seen as mainstream work in the top journals in either the social sciences or information sciences.

Type of Issue

Of the 57 articles, 40 (70%) were published in general issues of journals, while 17 (30%) came from one of eight special e-government issues (Table 3). Four of the eight special issues were in GIQ (issues 18:2, 18:4, 19:4, and 20:4), and two were in Social Science Computer Review (21:1 and 22:1). The others were in Public Performance and Management Review (26:4) and the Journal of Electronic Commerce in Organizations (1:4). Clearly, the publication of e-government research has

Table 3. Number of articles by type of issue

General Issue	40
Special Issue (about e-government)	17

Note: One article appeared in a journal special issue devoted to public information systems management (not e-government). Therefore we did not include it among the special issues devoted to e-government.

Table 4. Number of articles by type*

Case Study	21
Data Set Analysis	19
Web Site Analysis	16
Theoretical	2

*Adds to 58 because one article was both a data set analysis and a Web site analysis

been jump-started by these special or focused issues about e-government. Without them, the number of articles published about e-government would likely have been considerably smaller. Nevertheless, the great majority of articles appeared in regular issues of these journals.

Type of Article

Our survey yielded some variety in terms of article type. Case studies (21, or 37%) were the most common, followed closely by analyses of large data sets (19, or 33%), and Web site analyses (16, or 28%). Only two articles were primarily theoretical in nature (2, or 4%). As we noted earlier, we eliminated theoretical articles that had no empirical content from consideration here. The two theoretical articles that we included in the survey, while mainly theoretical, contained empirical content with which to test or justify the theory. One article was designed as both a data set analysis and a Web site analysis, so the percentages here add to more than 100 (Table 4).

For the most part, the case study articles were not produced from well-designed case studies in the sense that Yin (2004) means, that is, methodologically-rigorous cases that will produce highly reliable results and can be replicated. These articles, instead, were based on what Grönlund (2004) calls "case stories". Therefore, our use of the term "case study" should be considered rather generous as applied herein.

Type of Data

Survey data (24 articles, or 42%) and data obtained by content analyses of Web sites (22 articles, or 39%) were the most common types of data found in the articles. Fourteen articles (25%) used only case data. One article, which we labeled as "other,"

Table 5. Number of articles by type of data*

Survey Data	24
Web Site Content	22
Case Data	14
Other	1

*Adds to 61 because four articles used both survey data and Web content data

Table 6. Number of articles by discipline of lead author

Social Sciences	29
Information Technology	17
Communications	4
Business	5
Practitioner	2

analyzed state laws mandating Web posting of government documents. Again, the percentages add to more than 100 because four articles used both survey and Web site analysis data (Table 5). As we noted above, the case data were developed largely from case stories, not rigorously designed case studies.

Discipline of Lead Author

The majority of lead authors of the articles came from the social sciences (29, or 51%). The second-most common discipline for authorship was IT (17, or 30%), followed by communications (4, or 7%), and business (5, or 9%). E-government practitioners within the U.S. federal government wrote the two remaining articles (Table 6).

It is somewhat surprising that more than one and one-half as many articles were written by social scientists as by information and computer scientists. It is surprising because funding for e-government research is not as readily available to social scientists as to information and computer scientists. Nevertheless, it was social scientists who published most of the empirical research in the field during this period. Information and computer scientists produced less than one-third of the articles about e-government.

Authors' Location of Origin

The author(s) of 33 of the articles (58%) were based in locations in the U.S., while the author(s) of 19 of the articles (33%) were based outside of the U.S. Five additional articles (9%) were written by multiple authors originating from both inside and outside the U.S. (Table 7).

Table 7. Number of articles by author(s) location of origin

United States	33
Outside of the U.S.	19
Both	5

Table 8. Did the author(s) formulate original theory or expand existing theory?

Yes	14
No	43

Table 9. Did the author(s) engage in the testing of original or existing theory?

Yes	14
No	43

Formulate Theory

The overwhelming majority of articles (43, or 75%) did not formulate new theory nor extend existing theory; only 14 (25%) did so (Table 8).

Test of Theory

Only 14 (25%) of the articles engaged in the testing of theory, while 43 (75%) did not (Table 9). It is important to note that of the 14 articles that formulated or extended theory, 12 tested the theory using empirical evidence. Two articles that formulated theory did not test it. Conversely, of the 14 articles that tested theory, two involved the testing of theory that was neither new nor extended from its original form.

The absence of theory development and testing may suggest works that are less sophisticated or rigorous or that are less well connected to prior relevant scholarship that should inform this new field. This may also be indicative of the newness of the field itself.

Formulate Hypotheses or Research Questions

In many academic disciplines, the formulation of hypotheses and research questions in a research article is a sign of research sophistication and methodological rigor. Of the 57 articles which we examined in this survey, only 19 (33%) formulated hypotheses or research questions; 38 (67%) did not (Table 10).

Table 10. Did the author(s) formulate hypotheses or research questions?

Yes	19
No	38

Table 11. Did the author(s) test hypotheses or research questions?

Yes	19
No	38

Test of Hypotheses or Research Questions

Another test of research rigor and sophistication is whether hypotheses and research questions are formally tested in analyses. Of the articles that formulated research questions or hypotheses, all 19 tested them (Table 11).

The absence of formulating and testing hypotheses and research questions may suggest certain weaknesses in the field of e-government research as well as its recent origin.

Type of Analysis

Slightly more than three-quarters of the articles (44, or 77%) employed some form of quantitative analysis, while 33 (58%) employed qualitative analysis. Totals here are greater than 100 percent because 20 (35%) of the articles used both quantitative and qualitative methods. Of the 44 articles with quantitative analyses, 41 (93%) used descriptive statistics, 13 (30%) used correlation analysis, 13 (30%) used regression analysis, and one article employed factor analysis. Less than half of the quantitative articles (18, or 41% of the 44) employed more than one quantitative method (e.g., a combination of descriptive statistics and either correlation or regression analysis).

Table 12. Types of analyses used

Qualitative	33
Quantitative	44
Descriptive Statistics	41
Correlation Statistics	13
Regression Analyses	13
Factor Analysis	1

Nearly half (21, or 47%) of the articles that used quantitative methods presented only simple descriptive statistics (Table 12).

Adequacy of Literature Reviews

Here we examined the articles' literature reviews in three areas: e-government, IT and government, and any special topic (e.g., bureaucracy, participation, etc.) that the author(s) addressed in the article. For the most part, the literature reviews were unimpressive. Relatively few of the authors of these works "stood on the shoulders of giants". We rated only seven (12%) of the e-government literature reviews as strong, compared with six (11%) that were moderate, and 44 (77%) that were weak. The bibliographies of the latter typically contained few, if any, citations from the available e-government literature (either articles, books, book chapters, monographs, or Web postings). The weakness of the e-government literature reviews was not a function of the lack of literature in the field. It was a function of the authors' failure to cite relevant literature that was available at the time that the article was written.

For the IT and government literature, a literature that e-government scholars should examine because it provides considerable theoretical underpinning for e-government research and also provides direction for e-government research in terms of empirical findings, again the articles failed to impress. We rated only five articles (9%) as strong in terms of their reviews of the IT and government literature. We rated eight (14%) as moderate, and 44 (77%) as weak. Here again, weak bibliographies typically contained few, if any, citations from the IT and government literature, a literature which, as of this writing, is at least three decades old.

The specialized literatures fared somewhat better. Nine articles did not address issues beyond e-government that would have required such literature reviews. Of the 48 that had specialized literatures, we rated 16 (33%) as strong in their reviews of specialized literature, 12 (25%) as moderate, and 20 (42%) as weak (Table 13).

Table 13. Articles by adequacy of literature reviews

Type of Literature	Strong	Moderate	Weak
E-Government	7	6	44
IT and Government	5	8	44
Specialized*	16	12	20

* Nine articles did not require specialized literatures; therefore there are 48 articles considered in this category.

Support for Conclusions

Finally we examined these articles to ascertain if their conclusions were supported by their data or analyses. We were conservative in our determinations about whether an article's conclusion was supported. For us to give an article a "strong" support rating, its conclusions must have clearly and reasonably followed from its evidence or analysis. In other words, the author or authors "stuck to their data." Articles that received "moderate" or "weak" ratings went "a bridge too far" with their conclusions. That is, their authors exceeded reasonable inferences that could have been drawn from their data. Additionally, we gave "weak" ratings for support for conclusions to articles that suffered from serious methodological flaws that would have rendered their data questionable. One of the articles contained no explicit conclusions so the number in the table totals 56.

Of these 56 articles, the data strongly supported the conclusions in only one-third of them (18, or 32%). We found the conclusions in another 15 (27%) of them to have been supported moderately. The remaining 23 (41%) contained conclusions in which either: a) the authors went beyond their data in drawing conclusions, and/or b) the authors' methodologies and data were seriously "challenged" (Table 14).

Examples of articles whose conclusions were not supported well or at all by their data or analyses or whose methodologies were challenged included those in which conclusions were based on surveys with exceptionally small sample sizes or response rates or which used data from non-representative samples of respondents and articles which employed correlation and/or regression analyses of variables from data sets that did not make good bedfellows.[5]

Conclusion

What can be said from this examination of the published scholarship in the nascent field of e-government research? Since we do not want to be criticized for "going a bridge too far", that is, for going beyond what the data from the articles permit us to say, we will be cautious in drawing conclusions.

Perhaps the first conclusion is that, through the end of 2004 (that is, during arguably the first 12 years or so of e-government, and arguably eight years of published e-government research), relatively few (only 57) empirical articles about e-government have been published in peer-reviewed academic journals. What is more, only seven (13%) of those articles appeared in what are generally considered the leading journals (e.g., *Public Administration Review, Journal of Public Administration Research and Theory, and Administration and Society*). All of the other articles appeared in lesser-ranked journals.

Second, the empirical literature on e-government in this period was distributed almost equally between journals in the social sciences and journals in the information sciences. Within the subset of articles appearing in IT journals, however, more than half (14 out of 27) were published in a single journal, *GIQ*, which led in this category because of the number of special issues on e-government that it had published.

Third, most of the authors (as determined by lead author's discipline) of these articles were from the social sciences (51%). This is at least somewhat surprising because funding for e-government research is more available to computer and information scientists than to social scientists.

Fourth, the most common types of empirical data found in the articles were survey data (42%) and Web site content analysis data (39%), each of which were used in 40% of the articles. Case study data (which were mostly from "case stories" and not rigorously-developed case studies) was used less often, appearing in 25% of the articles, while one article used a content analysis of state legislation. Four articles used a combination of survey and Web site analysis.

Fifth, 77% of the articles used some form of quantitative analysis, most frequently descriptive statistics, and often in conjunction with some form of correlation or regression analysis. A majority (57%) employed some form of qualitative analysis. Twenty articles employed both qualitative and quantitative analyses.

Sixth, only about one-quarter of the articles (25%) formulated new theory, or extended existing theory in a new way, or engaged in explicit testing of theory. Only slightly more (33%) formulated explicit hypotheses or research questions and tested them.

Seventh, of the authors who formulated or extended theory, nearly all (12 of 14, or 86%) formally tested the theory, while all who formed hypotheses or research questions engaged in formal testing. The scant number of articles that formulated theory, hypotheses, and research questions and that tested theory, hypotheses, and research questions suggests a lack of rigor in the published works in the emerging field of e-government research and also the relatively recent origin of the field.

Eighth, for the most part the authors of these articles did not heed Sir Isaac Newton's advice to "stand on the shoulders of giants". With exceptions as noted, the reviews of the e-government and the IT and government literatures were unimpressive. Here, we considered only 13 literature reviews in each category (23%) to be adequate (rated as either strong or moderate). The remaining articles (44, or 77%) received "weak" ratings. The articles were somewhat better when it came to reviewing specialized literatures (e.g., bureaucracy or participation) that were also topics of the articles. Here, 28 (58%) were rated as adequate, while 42% received "weak" ratings. (Because of their topics, nine articles did not need or contain reviews of specialized literatures.)

Finally, a number of the articles (23, or 41%) went a "bridge too far" and presented conclusions that were not supported by their data or analyses or whose data suffered from methodological deficiencies. In only about one-third (18 or 32%) of the articles were conclusions strongly supported by the data or evidence presented, and in a quarter (27%) of them, conclusions were moderately supported.

Our review of the small but growing body of literature in the field of e-government, from its beginning through the end of 2004, strongly suggests that this is, indeed, a new field of scholarship that it is just "getting its legs." Relatively few articles on e-government had been published in peer-reviewed articles in this period, fewer still were empirical in nature, and yet fewer appeared in leading scholarly journals. Indeed, the latter finding may help to explain the number of relatively weak articles that were published; they appeared in lesser-ranked journals.

Although the published empirical articles demonstrated a range of (mainly quantitative) methodologies, few contained strong or even adequate links to previous scholarship in either the e-government or IT and government fields. Additionally, a surprising number of the articles drew conclusions that went beyond what their data or analyses would support.

As e-government itself continues to grow and evolve, what might we expect of the field of e-government research? We would both hope to see more and stronger (that is, more rigorous) articles, articles representing research from a wider range of disciplines, articles that employ a wider variety of research methodologies, and more articles that develop and test theory, hypotheses, and research questions. We would also hope that future articles would be linked more strongly to prior research (a.k.a., the relevant literatures), and that their conclusions would be more strongly supported by their data and analyses.

With the publication of four new journals devoted to e-government research beginning in 2004 and 2005, at the very least, the quantity of articles about e-government can be expected to increase. Beyond the issue of quantity, however, and, given the findings of this research, we can only wonder whether the field can sustain four journals or whether their existence will result in the continuing publication of research into e-government that lacks rigor and sophistication and is not adequately connected to prior relevant scholarship.

Whether our hopes and expectations for e-government research are fulfilled will require continuing examination of articles published in peer-reviewed journals—the gold standard of research in virtually any field.

References

Anderson, K. V., & Henriksen, H. Z. (2005). The first leg of e-government research: Domains and application areas, 1998-2003. *International Journal of Electronic Government Research, 1*(4).

Grönlund, Å. (2004). State of the art in e-gov research—A survey. In R. Traunmuller, (Ed.), *EGOV 2004, LNCS 3183* (pp. 178-185). Berlin: Springer-Verlag.

Holden, S., Norris, D. F., & Fletcher, P. D. (2003). Electronic government at the local level. *Public Performance & Management Review, 26*(4), 325-344.

Korosec, R. L., & Norris, D. F. (in press). *E-government among Florida municipalities: A comparison to national data and trends.* Baltimore: Maryland Institute for Policy Analysis and Research, University of Maryland, Baltimore County.

Norris, D. F., & Moon, M. J. (2005). Advancing e-government at the grassroots: Tortoise or hare? *Public Administration Review, 65*(1), 64-73.

Titah, R., & Barki, H. (2006). E-government adoption and acceptance: A literature review. *International Journal of Electronic Government Research, 2*(3), 23-57.

Yin, R. K. (2004). *Case study research design and method.* Thousand Oaks, CA: Sage Publications.

The 57 Empirical E-Government Articles

Barnes, S., & Vidgen, R. (2004). Interactive e-government: Evaluating the Web site of the UK inland revenue. *Journal of Electronic Commerce in Organizations, 2*(1), 42-63.

Becker, S. (2004). E-government visual accessibility for older adult users. *Social Science Computer Review, 22*, 11-23.

Beynon-Davies, P., Williams, M. D., Owens, I., & Hill, R. (2004). The electronic procurement of ideas. *International Journal of Electronic Business, 2*(1), 3-19.

Cairns, G., Wright, G., Bardfield, R., van der Heijden, K., & Burt, G. (2002). Exploring e-government futures through the application of scenario planning. *Technological Forecasting and Social Change, 71*, 217-238.

Cho, Y. H., & Choi, B. (2004). E-government to combat corruption: The case of Seoul metropolitan government. *International Journal of Public Administration, 27*, 719-735.

Cooper, C. (2002). E-mail in the state legislature: Evidence from three states. *State and Local Government Review, 34*(2), 127-132.

Cresswell, A., & Pardo, T. (2001). Implications of legal and organizational issues for urban digital government development. *Government Information Quarterly, 18*, 269-278.

Cullen, R., & Houghton, C. (2000). Democracy online: An assessment of New Zealand government Web sites. *Government Information Quarterly, 17*, 243-267.

Dawes, S., Pardo, T., & Cresswell, A. (2004). Designing electronic government information access programs: A holistic approach. *Government Information Quarterly, 21*, 3-23.

Deakins, E., & Dillon, S. M. (2002). E-government in New Zealand: The local authority perspective. *The International Journal of Public Sector Management, 15*(5), 375-398.

Doty, P., & Erdelez, S. (2002). Information micro-practices in Texas rural courts: Methods and issues for e-government. *Government Information Quarterly, 19*, 369-387.

Fagan, J. C., & Fagan, B. (2001). Citizens' access to on-line state legislative documents. *Government Information Quarterly, 18*, 105-121.

Fagan, J. C., & Fagan, B. (2004). An accessibility study of state legislative Web sites. *Government Information Quarterly, 21*, 65-85.

Ferber, P., Foltz, F., & Pugliese, R. (2003). The politics of state legislature Web sites: Making e-government more participatory. *Bulletin of Science, Technology, and Society, 23*(3), 157-167.

Gilbert, D., Balestrini, P., & Littleboy, D. (2004). Barriers and benefits in the adoption of e-government. *The International Journal of Public Sector Management, 17*(4), 286-301.

Golden, W., Hughes, M., & Scott, M. (2003). Implementing e-government in Ireland: A roadmap for success. *Journal of Electronic Commerce in Organizations, 1*(4), 17-33.

Grönlund, Å. (2003). Emerging electronic infrastructures: Exploring democratic components. *Social Science Computer Review, 21*, 55-72.

Ho, A. T. (2002). Reinventing local governments and the e-government initiative. *Public Administration Review, 62*, 434-444.

Ho, A. T., & Ni, A. Y. (2004). Explaining the adoption of e-government features: A case study of Iowa County treasurers' offices. *The American Review of Public Administration, 34*(2), 164-180.

Holden, S., Norris, D., & Fletcher, P. (2003). Electronic government at the local level. *Public Performance & Management Review, 26*(4), 325-344.

Holliday, I. (2002). Building e-government in East and Southeast Asia: Regional rhetoric and national (in)action. *Public Administration and Development, 22*, 323-335.

Joia, L. A. (2003). A heuristic model to implement government-to-government projects. *Journal of Electronic Commerce in Organizations, 1*(4), 49-67.

Kaylor, C., Deshazo, R., & Van Eck, D. (2001). Gauging e-government: A report on implementing services among American cities. *Government Information Quarterly, 18*, 293-307.

Kim, S., & Kim, D. (2003). South Korean public officials' perceptions of values, failure, and consequences of failure in e-government leadership. *Public Performance & Management Review, 26*, 360-375.

Kinder, T. (2002). Vote early, vote often? Tele-democracy in European cities. *Public Administration, 80*(3), 557-582.

Koh, C., & Prybutok, V. (2003). The three ring model and development of an instrument for measuring dimensions of e-government functions. *Journal of Computer Information Systems, 43*(3), 34-39.

Kuk, G. (2003). The digital divide and the quality of electronic government service delivery in local government in the United Kingdom. *Government Information Quarterly, 20*, 353-363.

LaPorte, T., Demchak, C., & de Jong, M. (2002). Democracy and bureaucracy in the age of the Web: Empirical findings and theoretical speculations. *Administration & Society, 34*, 411-446.

Lee-Kelley, L., & James, T. (2003). E-goverment and social exclusion: An empirical study. *Journal of Electronic Commerce in Organizations, 1*(4), 1-16.

Li, F. (2003). Implementing e-government strategy in Scotland: Current situation and emerging issues. *Journal of Electronic Commerce in Organizations, 1*(2), 44-65.

Macintosh, A., Robson, E., Smith, E., & Whyte, A. (2003). Electronic democracy and young people. *Social Science Computer Review, 21*, 43-54.

Martin, S., Chamberlin, B., & Dmitrieva, I. (2001). State laws requiring World Wide Web dissemination of information: A review of state government mandates for documents online. *Information and Communications Technology Law, 10*(2), 167-179.

McGregor, M., & Holman, J. (2004). Communication technology at the Federal Communications Commission: E-government in the public interest? *Government Information Quarterly, 21*, 268-283.

McNeal, R., Tolbert, C., & Mossberger, K. (2003). Innovating in digital government in the American states. *Social Science Quarterly, 84*(1), 52-70.

Melitski, J. (2003). Capacity and e-government performance: An analysis based on early adopters of Internet technologies in New Jersey. *Public Performance and Management Review, 26*, 376-390.

Moon, M. J. (2002). The evolution of e-government among municipalities: Rhetoric or reality?. *Public Administration Review, 62*, 424-433.

Musso, J., Weare, C., & Hale, M. (2000). Designing Web technologies for local governance reform: Good management of good democracy? *Political Communication, 17*, 1-19.

Potter, A. (2002). Accessibility of Alabama government Web sites. *Journal of Government Information, 29*, 303-317.

Reddick, C. (2004a). Public sector e-commerce and state financial management: Capacity versus wealth. *Social Science Computer Review, 22*, 293-306.

Reddick, C. (2004b). A two-stage model of e-government growth: Theories and empirical evidence for U.S. cities. *Government Information Quarterly, 21*, 51-64.

Shelley, M., Thrane, L., Shulman, S., Lang, E., Beisser, S., Larson, T., & Mutiti, J. (2004). Digital citizenship: Parameters of the digital divide. *Social Science Computer Review, 22*, 256-269.

Shi, W. (2002). The contribution of organizational factors in the success of electronic government commerce. *International Journal of Public Administration, 25*(5), 629-657.

Steyaert, J. (2000). Local governments online and the role of the resident: Government shop versus electronic community. *Social Science Computer Review, 18*, 3-16.

Steyaert, J. C. (2004). Measuring the performance of electronic government services. *Information & Management, 41*, 369-375.

Stowers, G. (1999). Becoming cyberactive: State and local governments on the World Wide Web. *Government Information Quarterly, 16*, 111-127.

Thomas, J. C., & Streib, G. (2003). The new face of government: Citizen-initiated contacts in the era of e-government. *Journal of Public Administration Research and Theory, 13*(1), 83-102.

Thompson, C. (2002). Enlisting online residents: Expanding the boundaries of e-government in a Japanese rural township. *Government Information Quarterly, 19*, 173-187.

Timonen, V., & O'Donnell, O. (2003). Development of e-government in Ireland: Remaining issues and challenges. *Administration, 51*(3), 3-20.

Waddell, P., & Borning, A. (2004). A case study in digital government: Developing and applying urbansim, a system for simulating urban land use, transportation, & environmental impacts. *Social Science Computer Review, 22*, 37-51.

Wang, Y. (2003). The adoption of electronic tax filing systems: An empirical study. *Government Information Quarterly, 20*, 333-352.

Weare, C., Musso, J., & Hale, M. (1999). Electronic democracy and the diffusion of municipal Web pages in California. *Administration and Society, 31*(1), 3-27.

Welch, E., & Wong, W. (2001). Global information technology pressure and governmental accountability: The mediating effect of domestic context on Web site operations. *Journal of Public Administration Research and Theory, 11*, 509-538.

West, D. (2004). E-government and the transformation of service delivery and citizen attitudes. *Public Administration Review, 64*(1), 15-27.

Whitson, T., & Davis, L. (2001). Best practices in electronic government: Comprehensive electronic information dissemination for science and technology. *Government Information Quarterly, 18*, 79-91.

Wong, W., & Welch, E. (2004). Does e-government promote accountability? A comparative analysis of Web site openness and government accountability. *Governance: An International Journal of Policy, Administration, and Institutions, 17*, 275-297.

Zhang, J. (2002). Will the government 'serve the people'? The development of Chinese e-government. *New Media & Society, 4*(2), 163-184.

Zhou, X. (2004). E-government in China: A content analysis of national and provincial Web sites. *Journal of Computer Mediated Communication, 9*(4).

Endnotes

[1]   See also Grönlund (2004), Andersen and Heinriksen (2005), and Titah and Barki (2006).

[2]   We would also like to thank Prof. Ronnie L. Korosec, University of Central Florida, who as part of an e-government research project on which she is working with Prof. Norris, identified four empirical articles that our search missed.

[3]   For a definition of empirical, see Merriam-Webster Online at http://www.m-w.com/cgi-bin/dictionary?book=Dictionary&va=empirical&x=17&y=15 retrieved April 26, 2005.

[4]   We categorized these journals as either from the social sciences or information systems and technology based on their titles and typical contents. Other scholars might categorize them somewhat differently.

⁵   There is a story (no doubt, apocryphal) about an introductory statistics course in which the instructor assigned students the task of correlating the incidence of traffic accidents with the occurrence of high tide. The students found that there was a high correlation; when high tide occurred, more traffic accidents occurred. The instructor's point was twofold: 1) Correlation does not equal causation (high tide occurred during rush hour!); and 2) some variables ought not to be correlated at all (it makes no sense to do so).

This work was previously published in International Journal of Electronic Government Research, Vol. 2, Issue 4, edited by D. F. Norris, pp. 40-56, copyright 2006 by IGI Publishing, formerly known as Idea Group Publishing (an imprint of IGI Global).

Chapter III

E-Government Adoption and Acceptance:
A Literature Review and Research Framework

Ryad Titah, HEC Montréal, Canada

Henri Barki, HEC Montréal, Canada

Abstract

Despite increased research interest on e-government, existing research has not adequately addressed two key issues concerning the implementation and integration of e-government systems: a better understanding of the factors influencing the adoption and acceptance of e-government systems, and a better understanding of the factors that influence the effective usage of these systems. The objective of the present chapter is to lay the groundwork for the development of a theoretical framework of e-government systems implementation. Based on an extensive review of the literature the chapter provides a synthesis of existing empirical findings and theoretical perspectives related to e-government adoption and presents the premises of a conceptual model that reflects the multidimensional nature of the acceptance and use of e-government systems.

Introduction

Electronic government refers to the use of information technologies (IT) to improve the efficiency, effectiveness, transparency, and responsibility of public governments (Kraemer & King, 2003; World Bank, 2007). Viewed as radical, yet unavoidable transformation projects (Jaeger, 2003), the implementation of e-government systems has been attracting increased research interest, and is believed to constitute one of the most important IT implementation and organizational change challenges of the future (Marche & McNiven, 2003; Warkentin, Gefen, Pavlou, & Rose, 2002). According to some estimates, e-government systems are already helping save 2% of the annual U.S. gross domestic product (GDP) (UNDP, 2001). However, the realized savings are still far less than what is potentially possible. For example, World Bank (2007) figures indicate that even the countries that are most advanced in the implementation of e-government systems are able to capture only 20% of their real savings potential. Moreover, implementation failures of e-government systems are also common and often lead to adverse financial consequences (e.g., the Gires project in Québec or the Canadian Firearms Registry which cost $400M and $1 billion, respectively) (Radio Canada, 2003).

Despite the potentially significant impacts of e-government systems on public administrations, organizations, individuals, and society, there is presently a dearth of systematic and thorough studies on the subject (Jaeger, 2003; Kraemer & King, 2003, p.12). In addition, the research themes, as well as the research approaches and perspectives employed in the study of e-government implementations also exhibit significant diversity, making it difficult to reach conceptual clarity on the subject (Grönlund, 2005a). Finally, several authors remain skeptical (Kallinikos, 2003, 2004; Kraemer & King, 2003) regarding the relevance of a radical transformation of the public bureaucratic model, with others seriously questioning the viability of the outcomes that result from IT-led transformations of institutionalized governmental processes (Ciborra, 2005; Du Gay, 2003, 2004; Kallinikos, 2004; Stokes & Clegg, 2002).

Given the importance and complexity of the topic, and the lack of published comprehensive literature reviews of e-government adoption and acceptance, the present chapter provides a synthesis of existing empirical findings and theoretical perspectives on this subject, and presents the theoretical premises of a conceptual framework that reflects the multilevel and multidimensional nature of the adoption and acceptance of e-government systems.

The chapter is organized as follows: the first section presents an analytical framework for conducting the literature review; the second section describes the main findings from this review; and the third section provides a discussion of the findings and the conclusions of the study.

Past Research on E-Government Adoption and Acceptance

Three data sources provided the input for our literature review of e-government adoption and acceptance: 1) ABI/INFORM and the ACM digital library; 2) *Government Information Quarterly, Information Systems Research, International Journal of Electronic Government Research, Journal of MIS, MIS Quarterly, Organization Studies, Organization Science, Public Administration Review,* and *Social Science Computer Review*; and 3) Americas Conference on Information Systems (AMCIS), International Conference on Information Systems (ICIS), and Hawaii International Conference on System Science (HICSS) conference proceedings. Our search targeted the identification of articles published since 1990 that presented either 1) reviews and studies of e-government adoption or acceptance in the IS domain, 2) reviews and studies of e-government adoption or acceptance in the public administration field, or 3) reviews and studies related to IT enabled organizational change in the public sector.

It should be noted that electronic government is a multifaceted concept that can involve four types of stakeholders (government, citizens, businesses, and employees) in five used contexts: government-to-citizen (G2C), government-to-business (G2B), government-to-employee (G2E), government-to-government (G2G), and internal efficiency and effectiveness of e-government systems (IEE). While past e-government implementation efforts have focused mainly on internal efficiency and effectiveness (IEE) (Kraemer & King, 2006), current e-government initiatives are more centered on networked electronic provision of services to the four types of stakeholders identified above. The present review includes all studies related to e-government adoption and acceptance in the five different used contexts listed above.

As the present review is specifically focused on e-Government adoption and acceptance, it represents a more focused and fine-grained complement to recent reviews of the more general e-government literature (e.g., Andersen & Henriksen, 2005; Grönlund, 2005b; Norris & Lloyd, 2006). In fact, the adoption and acceptance studies targeted by the present search correspond to two of the four e-government contextual research domains identified by Andersen and Henriksen (2005) of (1) diffusion management and (2) administrative e-services[1]. Further, our search specifically selected articles published in top IS, public administration and organization studies journals, as well as in top IS academic conference proceedings. Although European, Asian, or other specific regional IS conferences were not included in the search, the contributions of international research on e-government adoption were well represented in the surveyed peer-reviewed publications (see Tables 1 through 5). Note also that the present search did not take into account research published in monographs or in other specialized e-government journals (e.g., *Electronic Journal of e-Government, Journal of e-Government*) or conferences (e.g., DEXA/EGOV; d.go). While acknowledging these limitations, the variety and quality of the publications included in the present search is thought to provide an adequate and reliable sample of existing research on e-government adoption and acceptance. It is interesting to note that 52% of the papers identified in Andersen and Henriksen's (2005) review were in the two categories mentioned above, corresponding approximately to 86 out of the 167 papers they found. Our literature search identified 99 articles related to e-government adoption and acceptance that conceptually map onto Andersen and Henriksen's (2005) two categories. This suggests that the present review appears to have adequately captured past research on e-government adoption and acceptance. However, it should be acknowledged that, while our review is aimed at synthesizing a significant portion of e-government adoption and acceptance research, it inevitably left out some segments. For instance, work on e-government cultural barriers (Margetts & Dunleavy, 2002) or on complex e-government change processes and mechanisms (Dunleavy & Margetts, 2000) were not included in the present review because of their specialized publication outlet. A few other specialized journals, monographs, and conferences were also excluded.

The 99 papers were content analyzed following a three step procedure. First, based on an emergent coding method (Allard-Poesi, 2003), preliminary analysis of the articles' abstracts was conducted and led to the inference of the five main research themes. Second, the selected articles were carefully read and analyzed by the first author. Third, the face validity of the chapter classification categories and theme inferences was separately assessed by both authors. Note that while both authors agreed on the classification of the articles, an interrater reliability score was not calculated. While the absence of a formal interrater score represents a limitation to the inferences drawn, the detailed description of each article's content enables a relatively straightforward assessment of the face validity of the proposed framework.

Five topic categories were identified to broadly represent the subject matter investigated by the 99 articles: (1) the influence of managerial practices on e-government adoption and acceptance; (2) the influence of organizational and individual characteristics on e-government adoption and acceptance; (3) the influence of governmental subcultures on e-government adoption and use; (4) the influence of IT characteristics on e-government adoption and acceptance; and (5) the assessment of e-government impacts. The articles of each category are listed in Tables 1 to 5 with the content of each article presented based on the concept-centric approach suggested by Webster and Watson (2002), using the following elements: (1) theoretical framework, (2) methodology, (3) level of analysis, (4) technology, (5) variables or key concepts, and (6) main results or arguments.

Topic 1. The Influence of Managerial Practices

Research related to the influence of managerial practices on e-government adoption and acceptance aims at the identification and/or measurement of specific management strategies and behaviors that are thought to significantly affect e-government adoption and acceptance either by governmental agencies or by citizens and businesses. For example, a practice that has received significant research attention and that is posited as having an important effect on governmental agencies' adoption is process reengineering. Several authors (e.g., Cahill, 2006; Golden, Hughes, & Scott, 2003; Kawalek & Wastall, 2005; Scholl 2003, 2005; Thong, Yap, & Seah, 2000) have empirically shown that the absence of a clear and well executed process reengineering strategy significantly hinders e-government adoption and success. Related to this factor, there is also the influence of management support and leadership (Chan & Pan, 2006; Homburg & Beckers, 2002; Ke & Wei, 2004; Pardo & Scholl, 2002). For example, Thong et al. (2000) found that management support was a significant factor that influenced e-government acceptance. Chan and Pan (2006) also found that leadership was a key resource in e-government acceptance. In the same vein, Gauld (2007) identifies 14 ill-managed elements that explained the implementation failure of an e-government system. Similarly, the establishment and exercise of a formal governance structure, as well as the perception of neutrality vis-à-vis this structure (Thong et al., 2000) were also found to be major enabling factors of e-government adoption and usage. Moreover, several authors (e.g., Davison et al., 2005; Esteves & Joseph, 2006; Layne & Lee, 2001; Tan, Pan, & Lim, 2005) have proposed e-government development stage models, and suggested the presence of different adoption enabling factors, adoption inhibiting barriers, implementation challenges, and intervention strategies for different maturity stages. Finally, some authors have also argued that e-government acceptance was significantly enhanced when all stakeholders were involved in the process (Chan & Pan, 2003; Esteves & Joseph, 2006; Jain & Patnayakuni, 2003). For example, Jain and Patnayakuni (2003) posit that the most legitimate e-government stakeholder, that is, the public, was left out of the critical conceptualization, development, and implementation phases of e-government.

In sum, managerial action appears to play a key role in facilitating the critical aspects of process reengineering and integration, and in developing the main governmental capacities for adaptation and innovativeness. Little is known however about the specific actions managers need to undertake in order to foster organizational innovativeness via new knowledge acquisition, assimilation, transformation, and exploitation (Boynton, Zmud, & Jacobs, 1994; Zahra & George, 2002), or about the practices they need to undertake in order to positively influence and sustain e-government adoption and acceptance.

Topic 2. The Influence of Organizational and Individual Characteristics

Research related to the influence of organizational or individual characteristics attempts to identify the attributes that explain how or why dissimilarities among individuals or governmental agencies influence their adoption and acceptance of e-government systems. For example, one organizational characteristic that is thought to significantly influence the adoption of e-government is red tape (excessive bureaucratic regulation). While some authors have found red tape to be negatively related to organizational adoption (e.g., Bretschneider & Wittmer, 1993; Moon & Bretschneider, 2002), others observed no significant relationship between red tape and e-government adoption (e.g., Welch & Pandey, 2005), although red tape was found to be significantly and negatively associated with information quality. Size is another organizational factor that has been shown to affect e-government adoption. For example, Norris and Moon (2005) found that adoption of Web sites was strongly related to local government size. Similarly, Caudle et al. (1991) found that small government agencies were more interested in technology transfer than large agencies. Further, Ho (2002) argues that extended adoption and usage of e-government systems was hindered because of the e-government "paradigm," which emphasizes coordinated network building and one stop customer service, thus contradicting the bureaucratic paradigm, which emphasizes standardization and division of labor.

A significant research stream within this topic group has investigated the influence of individual characteristics on e-government adoption by following the tradition of the theory of reasoned action (Fishbein & Ajzen, 1975) and the technology acceptance model (TAM) (Davis, 1989). Accordingly, the influence of individual characteristics on individuals' intentions and behaviors are thought to be mediated by their beliefs and attitudes. For example, Phang, Sutanto, Li, and Kankanhalli (2005) found that perceived usefulness of Web sites was the most significant predictor of senior citizens' intention to adopt them. Contrary to Doellman, Allen, and Powell (2006), Phang et al. (2005) and Gilbert, Balestrini, and Littleboy (2004) who did not find support for the influence of citizen's perceived ease of use on adoption, Carter and Bélanger (2005) found that perceived ease of use had a significant effect on citizens' intention to use. They also found a significant relationship between compatibility and intention to use, and between perceived trustworthiness and intention to use. Similar to Carter and Bélanger (2005), Hung, Chang, and Yu (2006) found that perceived ease of use had a significant influence on tax payers' attitude towards usage. Furthermore, several researchers have studied the construct of trust as an antecedent of e-government adoption by individuals. For example, Bélanger and Carter's (2005) field survey finds that "institution-based trust" and "characteristic-based trust" had a significant influence on citizens' intention to use "government online." Similarly, Lee, Braynov, and Rao (1993) found that "trusting beliefs in e-government" had a significant effect on citizens' "intention to use," "intention to provide personal information," as well as on "intention to depend on information" provided by e-government services. Moreover, Lee, Kim, and Rao (2005) also found that "Internet competence belief" had a significant indirect effect on intention to use, and that "trust in government" had a significant influence on "e-government authority goodwill." Gefen, Pavlou, Warkentin, and Gregory (2002) conceptualize trust's influence on intention to use by citizens to be mediated by perceived usefulness and perceived ease of use, and found that trust had a significant effect on both perceived usefulness and ease of use.

Moreover, studying e-government adoption at a national level, Srivastava and Teo (2006a, 2006b) found that ICT infrastructure, technology development, and the quality of human capital had a significant effect on e-government development. Finally, some studies adopted an interpretive approach to tackle the complex phenomena underlying e-government adoption. For example, Sorrentino (2005) argues that by taking into account overlooked factors such as "the degree of autonomy/heteronomy of actors, their levels of discretionary power and the coordination arrangements among them" (p. 2), a process-oriented perspective provides a richer understanding of e-government implementation and adoption. In the same vein, Scatolini and Cordella (2005) found, through an action research study, that the "defense of political bonds" was the most salient resistance factor to IT adoption in a government setting. They also found that "organizational climate" and "decision making and responsibility assumption" were strong determinants of organizational innovation.

In sum, the importance of organizational and individual characteristics on e-government adoption appears to have been clearly established. However, future research related to the influence of these factors would probably gain much explanatory power if more longitudinal studies were conducted and if institutional factors (Gasco, 2003) were simultaneously considered as possible salient influences affecting organizational or individual intention to adopt e-government systems.

Topic 3. The Influence of Subcultures

Studies related to the cultural characteristics of public administration (e.g., Drake, Stecklem, & Koch, 2004; Schedler & Scharf, 2000) focus on explaining how the artifacts, values, symbols, and basic beliefs in the public sector influence the nature and the consequences of e-government adoption and acceptance. For example, Drake et al. (2004) shows the coexistence and coevolution of three principal subcultures in public administration: (1) a scientific culture, (2) a political culture, and (3) a bureaucratic culture. According to Drake et al. (2004), the differences between these three governmental subcultures can help explain the different design and information sharing modes that are found in governmental administrations. Whereas the members of a scientific culture tend to see information as a means of connectivity that binds them to bodies of knowledge or communities of practice aiming at resolving problems, members of a political culture are essentially interested in knowing how information could help them influence political and legislative processes. On the other hand, members of a bureaucratic culture tend to see information as a convenience that constitutes the foundation of effectively managing public administration.

As such, the existence of cultural differences regarding the adoption and use of information and data within public administration points to two important considerations. First, it suggests that it is important to take into account task-technology fit (Goodhue, 1995), that is, the fit between the various tasks of the different subcultures and the IT being implemented. Second, it shows the importance of carefully assessing the interrelationships between cultural variables and other salient factors influencing e-government adoption and use.

Topic 4. The Influence of IT Characteristics

Studies grouped within this stream of research investigated the influence of IT design features on individuals' acceptance and use of e-government applications. For example, several authors have shown that data security, accessibility, and perceived confidentiality significantly influenced individuals' adoption of e-government services (Jaeger, 2003, 2006; Lee & Rao 2003; Warkentin et al., 2002) and that government Web sites generally neglected Web site accessibility for citizens with cognitive imparement and learning disabilities (Jaeger, 2006).

Other researcher within this stream includes studies of the influence of specific application models and algorithms on public managers' and politicians' decision-making process (Henderson & Schilling, 1985; Lakshmi, Holstein, & Adams, 1990), and research that investigates the relationship between IT characteristics and IT diffusion in the public sector. For example, Northrop (2003) found that very few applications had interactive or transactional characteristics, thus hindering extensive participation of the citizens to the political life.

Topic 5. Assessing the Impacts of E-Government

Studies related to this stream focus on assessing the consequences of e-government adoption and use. While there is agreement among researchers regarding the importance of measuring e-government impacts systematically, some discord remains about which methods to employ and which metrics to use (Chircu & Lee, 2003; Gupta & Jana, 2003; Lee, 2005). Several researchers argue that the relationship between the adoption of e-government systems and their consequences is very complex and should be understood as emergent and context-dependent (Robey & Holmström, 2001; Robey & Sahay, 1996; Waddell & Borning, 2004). For example, several studies of the implementation of specific IT in the public sector (e.g., OLAP in 2001, GIS in 1996, and UrbanSim in 2004) found that the anticipated results of adoption did not materialize. Similarly, a survey of municipalities found that the cost reduction and downsizing benefits expected from e-government adoption did not materialize due to structural, legal, human, and organizational barriers (Moon, 2002). Along the same vein, other researchers found that IT enabled municipality downsizing only when the technology was aligned with implementation strategy, and was well integrated with organizational processes (Pinsonneault & Kraemer, 2002). Likewise, Tolbert and Mossberger (2006) found that perceived government transparency, accessibility, and responsiveness were significantly influenced by citizens' use of e-government systems. Furthermore, other researchers have suggested that the assessment of e-government impacts should take into account both tangible and intangible benefits, thereby combining both "hard and soft" performance measures (Gupta & Jana, 2003). Consistent with this line of thinking, Saxton, Naumer, and Fisher (2007) propose a logic model for identifying e-government benefits at the individual, organizational, and societal levels. Finally, some researchers have argued that e-government benefits can only be captured when linkages are made between the benefits of e-government systems and the stage of evolution of e-government (Gupta & Jana, 2003; Layne & Lee, 2001; Moon, 2002).

A Research Framework of
E-Government Adoption and Acceptance

Our literature search identified 99 articles published between January 1990 and February 2007 on e-government adoption and acceptance. Compared to previous literature reviews on e-government (Andersen & Henriksen, 2005; Grönlund, 2005b; Norris & Lloyd, 2006), the present search adopted a drill down approach by specifically focusing on findings related to e-government adoption within two contextual e-government research domains identified by Andersen and Henriksen (2005): (1) diffusion management; and (2) administrative e-services. Contrary to Grönlund (2005b), but consistent with Andersen and Henriksen (2005) and Norris and Lloyd (2006), we found that theory testing papers represented a large portion of e-government adoption research (59% of the 99 papers) with 31% having conducted field surveys and 28% case studies. Conceptual papers were also significant in that they represented 22% of the 99 papers. As our sampling frame, time period and focus differ from the literature reviews mentioned above, the present review complements and extends these earlier studies by providing a synthesis of the factors that enable or inhibit e-government adoption and acceptance.

More specifically, the present chapter identifies four main categories of factors that influence e-government adoption and acceptance, and one category of factors related to the consequences of e-government adoption. The studies of the first category (Table 1) aim at identifying and measuring specific management strategies and actions that can influence e-government adoption and acceptance. The most significant factors identified within this category include top management/political support and the use of a clear and well-executed process reengineering strategy. The second category (Table 2) includes research aimed at identifying specific organizational or individual characteristics affecting e-government adoption and acceptance. Within this research stream, process integration, political issues, financial resources, size, perceived usefulness, and trust were found to be the most significant antecedents. The studies in the third category (Table 3) focus on examining how cultural differences affected e-government acceptance (and finding that the existence of governmental subcultures resulted in different motivations and patterns of adoption). The fourth category of research (Table 4) investigate the influence of IT design characteristics on e-government adoption and acceptance, identifying perceived security, privacy, accessibility, usability, and confidentiality as the most significant antecedents. Finally, the fifth category of studies (Table 5) focus on the assessment of the consequences of e-government adoption and acceptance, generally finding that the measurement of adoption outcomes was tightly linked with the extent of process reengineering induced by e-government implementation, as well as with the type of measures used to assess the benefits of e-government adoption (i.e., hard vs. soft measures, outcome-based, service specific, and agency specific measures).

Several researchers have pointed out that the complex interdependencies and interactions that exist between organizational, managerial, technical, political, and individual factors are key to understanding e-government adoption and acceptance (Andersen & Henriksen, 2005; Dawes et al. 2003; Gasco, 2003; Grönlund, 2005a; Kraemer & King, 2003; Pardo et al. 2004; Roy, 2005; Scholl, 2005). However, in the 99 articles that were identified, none were found to conceptualize the multidimensional and multilevel nature of e-government adoption and acceptance or to systematically theorize and measure these interactions and complex relationships. As many empirical studies have been based on strict replications of established frameworks related to the IS literature (eg. TAM, or unified theory of acceptance and use of technology [UTAUT] models with extensions such as trust or self-efficay, etc.), or to the change management literature (eg. business process reengineering (BPR) models and maturity stage models), their explanatory power remains limited. In particular, past e-government adoption and acceptance research has not been able to explain the significant discrepancies in the levels of adoption and effective usage that have been observed among public agencies (Andersen & Henriksen, 2006; Grönlund, 2005a; Norris, 2005).

In order to overcome the limitations of past approaches, we recommend that an e-government adoption and acceptance model not only identify the factors that influence the net-enablement of public administrations, but conceptualize the interdependencies and nonlinear relationships that exist between these factors as well.

We also believe that a framework that combines dynamic capability theory (DCT) (Eisenhardt & Martin, 2000; Pentland & Rueter, 1994; Teece, Pisano, & Shuen, 1997) and the theory of complementarities (TC) (Barua, Lee, & Whinston, 1996; Levina & Ross, 2003; Milgrom & Roberts, 1995a, 1995b; Samuelson, 1974, Whittington & Pettigrew, 2003) can provide a useful starting point for that purpose. First, DCT may help fully conceptualize and take into account the overlooked implications of the net-enabled customer focus of actual e-government initiatives (Ho, 2002). Net-enablement refers to an organization's ability to electronically "execute transactions, rapidly exchange information, and innovate at an unprecedented pace" by means of digital networks (Wheeler, 2002, p. 125). For governments, net-enablement entails significant changes to their structure and processes, as it calls them to "ask a new set of questions, to draw on new technical and commercial skills, and to employ new problem solving approaches" (Henderson & Clark, 1990, p. 9), also requiring them to execute "timely and ongoing reconfiguration of firm resources" (Wheeler, 2002) and capabilities. Capability[2] reconfiguration is particularly relevant in this context since bureaucratic routines and processes have been documented to be the main source of structural inertia within public administrations (Hannan & Freeman, 1984; Perrow, 1986). However, while routines may indeed represent an important source of organizational rigidity (Leonard-Barton, 1992), they have also been shown to be a major source of "flexibility and change" (Feldman & Pentland, 2003). Organizational routines have in effect been shown to be both a key determinant of organizational behavior (Becker, Knudsen, & March, 2006), and a "major source of the reliability and speed of organizational performance" (Cohen & Bacdayan, 1994, p. 554). Therefore, understanding the mechanisms by which actual bureaucratic routines and capabilities are modified and reconfigured to produce new net-enabled delivery service competencies could provide key insights regarding the process of e-government acceptance, effective usage, and performance.

Second, because organizational capabilities are likely to be formed by complementary factors (Tranfield, Duberley, Smith, Musson, & Stokes, 2000, p. 253), the theory of complementarities can also provide a useful approach for conceptualizing and measuring their complex relationships (Barua et al., 1996). In the context of e-government adoption and acceptance, a research model that is based on the concept of complementarities could be useful for three reasons: (1) It is likely to provide a means to capture the continuous and contextual character of e-government acceptance and the need for its apprehension as a process (Categories 1 and 5); (2) It can help highlight the role of managers and strategic leadership in e-government adoption (Categories 1 and 2); and (3) It can allow the capturing of the "interaction effects" that are likely to exist between various complementary (or substitutive) factors that influence e-government adoption and acceptance (Categories 1, 2, 3, and 4). The concept of complementarities can also allow researchers to take into account the complexity of integrating business processes in the public sector by more specifically identifying key integration enabling or inhibiting factors and their relationships (Barki & Pinsonneault, 2005).

Conclusion

In summary, our review of prior research related to e-government adoption and acceptance points to considerable diversity in the topics, constructs, and relationships considered by different studies. While the present chapter has identified and categorized the key antecedents of e-government adoption and acceptance investigated in past research, much work remains to be done. In particular, given the multilevel nature and scope of e-government adoption and acceptance, future research is needed to investigate the influence of different stakeholders (internal and external constituencies) (Grönlund, 2005a) on e-government design, adoption, and acceptance, the mechanisms that enable integrations of a complex nature (Barki & Pinsonneault, 2005), and the interaction effects that exist between different antecedents of e-government adoption and acceptance.

Table 1. E-government "managerial practices" research

Authors	Theoretical framework	Methodology	Level of analysis	Technology	Variables or key concepts	Main results or arguments
Andersen and Henriksen (2006)	▪ E-government maturity models literature.	▪ Secondary data analysis ▪ N= 110 ▪ Conceptual	▪ Organizational	▪ N/A	▪ Public sector process rebuilding maturity model	▪ Proposes a public sector process rebuilding (PPR) maturity model as an extension to the Layne and Lee (2001) model. ▪ Argues that the PPR model allows the capture of the strategic use of e-government systems by taking account all external users when performing the core activities of government.
Bygstad, Lanestedt, and Choudrie (2007)	▪ Broadband diffusion literature ▪ IS project management literature	▪ Field survey ▪ N= 130	▪ Organizational	▪ N/A	▪ Service innovation ▪ Project management ▪ Broadband diffusion	▪ Argues that broadband service innovation in the public sector should focus more on the organizational rather than on the technical aspects of implementation. ▪ Posits that project management techniques are not suited to understand and manage service innovation.
Cahill (2006)	▪ BPR literature	▪ Action research ▪ N= 1	▪ Organizational	▪ N/A	▪ BPR ▪ Organizational change	▪ Argues that the success of BPR activities is significantly enhanced when the potential of organizational actors is fully utilized, and when change is delivered through people instead of method.
Caudle, Gorr, and Newcomer (1991)	▪ N/A	▪ Field survey ▪ N= 353	▪ Individual	▪ N/A	▪ Middle managers ▪ Red tape ▪ Local government	▪ "Linking the IS budgeting process and long-range IS planning is unique to the public sector, as is the technology transfer issue." ▪ Top level public managers "are less inclined to implement new IT than middle-level public managers." ▪ The "more red tape, the more flexible the IT employed." ▪ Small government agencies "are more interested in technology transfer than large ones." ▪ Local government IS issues "are driven by transaction processing while state and federal government IS are more suitable for their oversight mission."

Table 1. continued

Authors	Theoretical framework	Methodology	Level of analysis	Technology	Variables or key concepts	Main results or arguments
Chan and Pan (2006)	• Resource based view • Enactment concept	• Case study • N=1	• Organizational	• E-File system	• Resource enactment • Knowledge resource • Leadership resource • Social resource	• Proposes a process model of resource enactment during three phases of e-government system implementation (planning, developing, and operating). • Argues that the three key complementary resources in e-government implementation are the leadership, knowledge, and social resources. • Posits that the capability to be innovative, the capability to be adaptive, and the capability to be responsive represent the focal capabilities during the planning, developing, and operating phases of implementation respectively.
Chan et al. (2003)	• Stakeholder theory	• Action research • N=1	• Organizational	• N/A	• Project management • Relationship management	• Proposes a typology of relationships between stakeholders and e-government projects.
Chircu and Hae-Dong Lee (2003)	• IT investments literature	• Case study • N=3	• Organizational	• e-grants application and processing system	• IT value • IT risk • IT investment decision • Political mission • Power-shifting	• Proposes a value-oriented framework for IT investment decisions.
Cohen and Eimicke (2003)	• N/A	• Conceptual	• Organizational	• N/A	• Digital divide • Procurement and information policies and processes • Politics of information • Professional skills • Information overload	• Proposes guidelines to overcome five obstacles related to e-government adoption (see preceding column).
Davison, Wagner, and Ma (2005)	• Transition stage models literature	• Conceptual	• Organizational	• N/A	• Transition paths • Strategic alignment	• Proposes a five stage transition model for e-government.
Ebrahim, Irani, and Al Shawi (2004)	• Adoption literature • Stage development models literature	• Conceptual	• Organizational	• N/A	• Stages of growth model • Technological, organizational, and environmental factors • Benefits and barriers	• Proposes a strategic framework for e-government adoption.

Table 1. continued

Authors	Theoretical framework	Methodology	Level of analysis	Technology	Variables or key concepts	Main results or arguments
Esteves and Joseph (2006)	▪ N/A	▪ Conceptual	▪ Organizational	▪ N/A	▪ Maturity stages ▪ e-government assessment ▪ Stakeholders	▪ Proposes a framework for assessing e-government initiatives by taking into account the influence of the stakeholders and the maturity stages of e-government deployment.
Gauld (2007)	▪ N/A	▪ Case study ▪ N= 1	▪ Organizational	▪ Shared medical system (SMS)	▪ IS implementation failure	▪ Argues that the SMS implementation failure in a large public Hospital was due to 14 ill managed elements: "Large and multifaceted project; IS needs not defined; IS project objectives not defined; No certainty that SMS product appropriate; Discontinuity of key management staff; No CIO through entire project; Ad-hoc reliance on external consultants for advice; Board views differ from management and front-line staff; Expectation of organizational reengineering; Lack of front-line staff involvement in decision-making; Ill-constructed purchase contract; Front-line staff resistance; Political interference in decision-making; High-level of politicization: external reviews, media, and political attention" (p.108).
Golden et al. (2003)	▪ BPR literature	▪ Case study ▪ N= 3	▪ Organizational	▪ PSB (public service broker)	▪ BPR ▪ Evolutionary change ▪ Revolutionary change	▪ E-government adoption was found to be enhanced by top level management support and the creation of a central specific entity to supervise the implementation process.
Homburg and Beckers (2002)	▪ Resource dependency theory ▪ Property rights theory	▪ Case study ▪ N=2	▪ Organizational	▪ GBA (Dutch Municipal Register of Citizens' Residential Data) ▪ NKR (Dutch Vehicle Registration)	▪ Back-office IS ▪ Political economies ▪ Integration ▪ Information exchange	▪ Contrasts project management and process management characteristics, and argues that intraorganizational e-government acceptance may be enhanced by process management methods (rather than project management methods) which emphasize consensus building, goal seeking, identifying win-win situations, creating shared meanings, and coupling issues in various arenas (eg., system design, data ownership, and legislation).

Table 1. continued

Authors	Theoretical framework	Methodology	Level of analysis	Technology	Variables or key concepts	Main results or arguments
Jain and Patnayakuni (2003)	▪ N/A	▪ Conceptual	▪ Organizational	▪ N/A	▪ Public expectations ▪ Public scrutiny	▪ Call for research into "public expectations" and "public scrutiny" in the context of e-government. ▪ E-government initiatives are not adequately addressing "public expectations." ▪ Proposes an adaptation of the Servqual approach to measure public expectations. ▪ Proposes a framework to measure public scrutiny.
Janssen and Joha (2006)	▪ Resource-based view ▪ Dynamic capability view	▪ Case study ▪ N= 2	▪ Organizational	▪ N/A	▪ Decision making structures ▪ Alignment processes ▪ Formal communications ▪ Organizational and managerial processes ▪ Asset position ▪ Path dependency ▪ Value ▪ Rareness ▪ Nonsubstitutability ▪ Imperfectly imitable	▪ Governance mechanisms (decision-making structure, alignment processes, and formal communication) were found to significantly influence the ability to share services, and attain objectives among centralized and decentralized organizations.
Kawalek and Wastall (2005)	▪ BPR literature	▪ Case study ▪ N= 3	▪ Project	▪ Case 1: CIR (comprehensive information repository) ▪ Case 2: E-mail + call center support ▪ Case 3: Internet sourcing and maintenance	▪ Radical change ▪ Change methodology ▪ Strategic alignment	▪ Description and application of the Salford Process Reengineering Involving New Technology (SPRINT) methodology for process reengineering. ▪ E-government impacts are positive but limited in scope. ▪ Call for discontinued strategies of change. ▪ Participation may be a barrier to the success of the bureaucratic model.
Ke and Wei (2004)	▪ CSF and stage models development literature	▪ Case study ▪ N= 1	▪ Organizational	▪ Portal	▪ Change Process ▪ Critical success factors	▪ Top management support was found to be a major enabling factor of e-government adoption at the infusion stage. ▪ Presence of a champion, change management, resources, mindset changes, bridging digital divide, usability, and strong leadership were found to be critical success factors of portal acceptance.

Table 1. continued

Authors	Theoretical framework	Methodology	Level of analysis	Technology	Variables or key concepts	Main results or arguments
Layne and Lee (2001)	▪ N/A	▪ Conceptual	▪ Organizational	▪ N/A	▪ Cataloguing ▪ Transaction ▪ Vertical integration ▪ Horizontal integration	▪ Proposes a four stage developmental model of e-government implementation and their associated technological and organizational challenges. ▪ "Universal access," "privacy and confidentiality," and "citizen focus in government management" are posited to be key factors for "efficient and effective" e-government.
Lee and Kim (2007)	▪ Grounded theory	▪ Field interviews ▪ N= 26	▪ Organizational	▪ N/A	▪ Growing systems ▪ Vertical integration ▪ Horizontal integration ▪ Management of emerging specialists ▪ Reward of risk takers ▪ Differentiated training programs ▪ Flexible budgetary cycle ▪ Accommodation of various viewpoints ▪ Fast technological development	▪ E-government initiatives were found to be hindered by five main categories of factors: 1) financial (resource limitation, funding, and change of technology); 2) organizational (smokestack phenomenon and scattered efforts); 3) technical (synchronization); 4) human resources (retention); and 5) expectation (escalating commitment, project delay).
Melitski, Holzer, Kim, Kim, and Rho (2005)	▪ Stage models development literature	▪ Content analysis ▪ N=84 municipality Web sites	▪ Web site	▪ Web site	▪ Security/privacy ▪ Usability ▪ Content ▪ Service ▪ Participation	▪ Develops an instrument to measure e-government practices in municipalities worldwide. ▪ Results suggest that security and privacy issues should be taken into account more to enhance citizens' acceptance.
Ni and Bretschneider (2005)	▪ Principal agent theory	▪ Secondary data ▪ N= 644 observations	▪ Governmental services	▪ Multiple	▪ E-government services ▪ Contracting-out	▪ Contrary to what occurs at the local level, outsourcing decisions at the national level are politically oriented.

Table 1. continued

Authors	Theoretical framework	Methodology	Level of analysis	Technology	Variables or key concepts	Main results or arguments
Pardo and Scholl (2002)	▪ Infromation system development literature	▪ Action research ▪ N=1	▪ Project	▪ Central accounting system (CAS)	▪ Large-scale projects ▪ Risk ▪ Failure	▪ Proposes a system development and maintenance framework comprising 13 cyclical activities that are posited to help avoid 7 identified shortcuts to failure. ▪ Stakeholder involvement and prototyping are posited to be critical success factors.
Pardo et al. (2004)	▪ Organizational integration literature	▪ Conceptual	▪ Organizational	▪ N/A	▪ Interorganizational information integration ▪ Social processes ▪ Resources ▪ Organizational artifacts ▪ Technology artifacts	▪ Proposes a process model of interorganizational information integration. Posits that effective interpretation and use of integrated information requires "the development and use of IT artifacts, which are embedded in a social process. The artifacts are developed jointly, through emerging social and technical processes...[These] processes are embedded in four different but related contexts: technology, business process, interorganizational, and political" (p. 4).
Park (2005)	▪ Cost-benefit analysis literature	▪ Case study ▪ N= 1	▪ Project	▪ Seoul Open System	▪ Efficiency ▪ Public goods ▪ Corruption ▪ Privacy and security ▪ System characteristics ▪ Maintenance ▪ Distributional and equity issues	▪ Cost-benefit analyses of government spenders were found to inflate the benefits of the project, while downplaying (or ignoring) major intangible costs. ▪ Maintenance and upgrading costs, as well as opportunity costs of government held assets were found to be the most underestimated costs of the project. ▪ Power issues should be taken into account in future research.
Roy (2005)	▪ Public administration literature ▪ Trust literature	▪ Conceptual ▪ Illustration	▪ Organizational	▪ N/A	▪ Trust ▪ Transparency ▪ Security ▪ Service ▪ Governance	▪ Argues that public confidence and public trust are key determinants of e-government and e-governance reforms (p. 50). ▪ Posits that successful e-government and e-governance requires more integration between the technical design work of technology deployment and the broader governance design/redesign work overseeing it (p. 52).

Table 1. continued

Authors	Theoretical framework	Methodology	Level of analysis	Technology	Variables or key concepts	Main results or arguments
Schildt, Beaumaster, and Edwards (2005)	▪ Strategic management model	▪ Case study ▪ N= 1	▪ Organizational	▪ MOPUS (municipally operated public utility systems)	▪ Change management	▪ Proposes a strategic management model of change for IT implementation. ▪ The complex nature of IT "poses political risks for the organization attempting to manage the IT infrastructure" (p. 1). ▪ Successful strategies for managing IT "must take into account the differing value sets among [the] organizational and political members" (p. 1)
Schildt and Beaumaster (2004)	▪ Strategic planning literature	▪ Case study ▪ N=1 municipal public utility department	▪ Organizational	▪ Various (e.g., SCADA, [System control and data acquisition], inventory bar code system, wireless meter reading, 800 MHz radios, blackberries, kiosks)	▪ Change management ▪ IT Strategic planning	▪ Proposes a strategic information technology management framework highlighting the interactions between organizational, technological and political factors. ▪ Argues that internal and external driving forces for IT-led organizational transformation enhance the complexity of IT planning and management processes.
Scholl (2003)	▪ BPR literature	▪ Conceptual	▪ Organizational	▪ N/A	▪ Business process change	▪ Argues that e-government should be viewed as a special case of IT-enabled business process change, and draws 18 propositions to reflect the multidimensional nature of e-government.
Scholl (2005)	▪ BPR literature	▪ Case study? ▪ N=2	▪ Project	▪ N/A	▪ Stakehoder involvement ▪ Culture/change readiness ▪ Process and resource inventory ▪ Workflow analysis ▪ Internal competency and learning ▪ Consensus among officials and citizens ▪ Senior leadership support ▪ Challenges in record keeping	▪ Stakeholder involvement and senior executive commitment were found to be the most significant issues affecting e-government change processes. ▪ Challenges in record keeping, workflow analysis and culture/change readiness assessment were found to be important issues affecting e-government change processes. ▪ Process and resource inventorying, as well as internal competency and learning were found to have little influence on e-government change processes. ▪ Consensus between officials and citizens was found to have no effect on e-government change processes.

Table 1. continued

Authors	Theoretical framework	Methodology	Level of analysis	Technology	Variables or key concepts	Main results or arguments
Shackelton, Fisher, and Dawson (2004)	• Maturity models literature	• Content analysis • N= 20 Web sites • Case study • N=1	• Web site	• Web site	• Local government • E-management • E-service • E-commerce • E-decion making/ e-democracy	• Suggests that e-government linear maturity models may not fit the local government context since it was found that most municipalities had relatively immature Web sites while at the same time offering electronic participatory functions that were more advanced than higher government levels.
Tan et al. (2005)	• Organizational change literature	• Conceptual • Case study • N=1	• Organizational	• CORENET	• Barriers to adoption • Change intervention	• Proposes a three stage framework linking change interventions (commanding, engineering, teaching, and socializing) to adoption barriers.
Thong et al. (2000)	• BPR literature	• Case study • N=1	• Project	• N/A	• Radical change • Change methodology • Differences between public and private sector	• Public organizations are "highly resistant to change" (p. 265). • Mass-media communication plays an important role in informing public managers about the necessity of change as well as its challenges. • A neutral reengineering team facilitates the change process. • Management support facilitates the implementation process • The use of pilot sites is an important success factor for e-government adoption.
Williams and Beynon-Davies (2004)	• Value chain literature	• Text analysis • N=22	• Organizational	• N/A	• Implementation enablers	• Proposes a value chain model positing that supply chain (e.g., extranets and tele-working), internal value chain (e.g., integration), customer chain (e.g., customer relationship management or CRM), informatics planning, informatics management, informatics development, and e-community represent key enabling factors of implementation success.

Table 2. E-government "organizational and individual characteristics" research

Authors	Theoretical framework	Methodology	Level of analysis	Technology	Variables or key concepts	Main results or arguments
Bélanger and Carter (2005)	▪ TAM ▪ Trust literature	▪ Field survey ▪ N= 214	▪ Individual	▪ Government online (not specified)	▪ Disposition to trust ▪ Institution-based trust ▪ Characteristic-based trust ▪ Perceived risk ▪ Intention to use	▪ Institution-based trust and characteristic-based trust were found to have a significant influence on intention to use. ▪ Disposition to trust had a significant influence on Institution-based and characteristic-based trust. ▪ Perceived risk had a significant influence on intention to use but not in the hypothesized direction. ▪ Institution-based trust had no impact on perceived risk. ▪ Characteristic-based trust had a significant and negative impact on perceived risk.
Bretschneider and Wittmer (1993)	▪ Innovation diffusion theory	▪ Field survey ▪ N= 1005	▪ Organizational	▪ Microcomputers	▪ Adoption ▪ Diffusion ▪ Environmental factors ▪ Facilitating and inhibiting adoption factors ▪ Prior experience ▪ Slack resources ▪ Red tape and bureaucracy	▪ After controlling for "organizational size, experience with computer technology, current investment in computer technology, procurement practices, and the task environment, the sector an organization operates in has a major influence on the adoption of microcomputer technology" (p. 88). ▪ Public organizations have more computers per employee, which can be due to their information intensive environment, as well as the use of IT as a side payment in lieu of salary, compared to private organizations.
Carter and Bélanger (2004)	▪ TAM ▪ Innovation diffusion theory ▪ Trust literature	▪ Field survey ▪ N= 136 students	▪ Individual	▪ State e-government services (not specified)	▪ Perceived usefulness ▪ Compatibility ▪ Relative advantage ▪ Image ▪ Complexity ▪ Perceived ease of use (PEOU) ▪ Intention to use	▪ Perceived usefulness, relative advantage, and compatibility were found to significantly influence intention to use. ▪ No support was found for the link between PEOU, image, and complexity on intention to use.

Table 2. continued

Authors	Theoretical framework	Methodology	Level of analysis	Technology	Variables or key concepts	Main results or arguments
Carter and Bélanger (2005)	• Technology acceptance model • Innovation diffusion theory • Trust literature	• Field survey • N= 105	• Individual	• Department of Motor Vehicle (DMV) on-line system • Department of Taxation (TAX) on-line system	• Compatibility • Relative advantage • Image • Complexity • PEOU • Perceived Usefullness (PU) • Trust of Internet • Trust of Government • Intention to use	• Compatibility, PEOU, and perceived trustworthiness were found to significantly influence citizens' intention to use. • Image and relative advantage did not have a significant influence on intention to use.
Chen, Fan, and Fam (2007)	• Transaction cost theory	• Field survey • N=255	• Individual	• Electronic Toll Collection System (ETC)	• Uncertainty • Asset specificity • Perceived risk • Transaction frequency • Intention to adopt	• Uncertainty and asset specificity were found to have a significant effect on perceived risk. • Perceived risk was found to have a significant and negative effect on intention to adopt and so forth. • Transaction frequency was found to have a significant effect on intention to adopt and so forth.
Conklin (2007)	• TAM • Theory of reasoned action (TRA) • Change management literature • Innovation diffusion literature	• Conceptual	• Individual	• N/A	• Attitude • Subjective norm • Behavioral intention • Senior leadership • Constituent desires • Bureaucratic rules • Usage behavior • PEOU • PU • Intention to use	• Proposes an extension to TRA and TAM models in the context of e-government adoption. • Proposes the following moderating effects. For TRA: 1) leadership moderates the relationship between attitude and intention; 2) constituent desires moderate the relationship between subjective norm and intention; and 3) bureaucratic rules moderates the relationship between intention and use. For TAM: 1) leadership and constituent desires moderate the relationship between PU and intention; and 2) bureaucratic rules moderate the relationship between PEOU and intention, and between intention and use.

Table 2. continued

Authors	Theoretical framework	Methodology	Level of analysis	Technology	Variables or key concepts	Main results or arguments
Dawes et al. (2003)	• Public administration literature • IS use literature (not specified)	• Field interviews • N= 22 administrators od data repositories • Prototype evaluation • N= 3 prototypes	• Application	• NYS-GIS (New York State Geographic Information System) • HIMS (Homeless Information Management System) • KWIC (Kids' Well-being indicator Clearinghouse)	• Characteristics of users • Predictability of uses • Sensitivity of content • Frame of reference • Status of meta data • Uniformity of information sources • Degree of integration among information sources • Usefulness of content over time • Structure of relationships with information suppliers and users • Involvement of access provider • Extent of data analysis conducted by access provider • Nature of data flows • Suitability of existing IT • Relationship of the access program to overall organizational mission	• Design, implementation and operation of government access systems were found to be influenced by 15 dimensions related to information users, suppliers, content, or use, and to aspects of the access program and its organizational context (see preceding column). • Interactions among the dimensions are posited to be crucial implementation factors. Three specific interaction groups were identified: a) interaction between nature of users and uses and nature of available data and metadata; b) interaction between size and nature of data repository and relationships among players, organizational structures, and business processes; and c) interactions between IT investments and the place of the investment in the mission of the provider organization (p.7).
Doellman et al. (2006)	• Unified theory of acceptance and use of technology (UTAUT)	• Field survey • N= 76 students	• Individual	• Online voting	• Performance expectancy • Effort expectancy • Social influence • Computer anxiety • Trust	• Performance expectancy, social influence, and trust in the Internet were found to have a significant influence on intention to use online voting. • Experience was found to moderate the relationship between performance expectancy and intention to use.
Fulla and Welch (2002)	• Interactivity literature	• Case study • N= 1	• Relationship	• ICAM	• Communicative interaction model • Relationships	• Proposes a four stage model of interactive communication between citizens and governments that develops upon virtual feedback.

Table 2. continued

Authors	Theoretical framework	Methodology	Level of analysis	Technology	Variables or key concepts	Main results or arguments
Gallat, Culnan, and McLoughlin (2007)	• Adoption literature	• Field survey • N= 953	• Individual	• Electronic Tax Filing system	• E-Filing • Convenience • Expensive • Ease of use • Risk	• People who e-filed were found to perceive e-filing as less useful (measured as convenience) and less expensive than non e-filers.
Gefen et al. (2002)	• TAM • Trust literature	• Field survey • N= 243 MBA students	• Individual	• Online tax service	• PU • PEOU • Social influence • Perceived risk • Belief in Humanity • Disposition to trust • Predictability • Integrity • Benevolence • Ability • Intention to use • Perceived social characteristics • Institutional guarantees • Process-mode trust • Nature of expected interaction	• PU and social influence had a significant impact on intention to use and explained 33% of its variance. • PEOU had a significant impact on PU. • Social influence and trust were found to have a significant impact on PU. • Perceived risk had a significant and negative impact on PU. • Trust had a significant and negative impact on Risk. • Trust had a significant influence on PEOU. • Trust was found to be significantly influenced by belief in humanity, the nature of expected interaction, the perceived social characteristics, and by the Institutional guarantees. • Disposition to trust had no influence on trust.
Gilbert et al. (2004)	• Innovation diffusion theory • TAM • Service quality literature	• Field survey • N= 111	• Individual	• Online public service delivery	• Perceived relative benefits • Avoid personal interaction • Cost • Time • Perceived barriers • Visual appeal • Experience • Financial security • Information quality • Low stress • Trust • Willingness to use	• Time, cost, financial security, trust, and information quality were found to significantly influence willingness to use. • Ease of use was not found to be a significant determinant of willingness to use. • Older respondents (55+) were found to be less willing to use online public services than younger ones.

Table 2. continued

Authors	Theoretical framework	Methodology	Level of analysis	Technology	Variables or key concepts	Main results or arguments
Grönlund (2003)	• Actor network theory	• Case study • N= 4	• Organizational	• E-mail • Discussion forums • Web site • Electronic search tools • E-voting	• Translation • Inscription • Negotiation • Emerging electronic infrastructures • E-democracy	• Politics "as design" (top-down strategy) and politics "as evolution" (bottom-up strategy) constitute two conflicting perspectives in the development of e-democracy. • The "increasing use of IT in administrative processes, [...] restricts the action space of the political sphere, as this infrastructure becomes hard to change" (p. 69). • The "civil society cultures, [...] contain strong social elements but less of the characteristics of formal politics" (p. 69). • The "official e-democracy initiatives, [...] generally endorse information rather than participation" (p. 69).
Henriksen et al. (2004)	• N/A	• Conceptual	• Organizational	• PePP (Public eProcurement Portal)	• Public procurement adoption • Economic rationality • Political rationality	• Argues that economic rationalities are a necessary but insufficient condition for adopting public procurement systems. • Pricinpal barriers to adoption are posited to stem from structural-political issues related to widespread decentralization among government levels in Denmark. • Suggests that a split between task and responsibility may decrease adoption barriers.
Hinnant and Welch (2002)	• Adoption literature	• Field survey • N= 856 program managers	• Individual	• N/A	• Self-efficacy • Use • Training • Education level • Work experience • IT strategy • IT activities • IT quality	• Computer self-efficay was found to be significantly influenced by the level of IT training and the extent of IS usage. • Computer self-efficay was found to significantly influence managers' perceptions regarding the effects of IT usage.

Table 2. continued

Authors	Theoretical framework	Methodology	Level of analysis	Technology	Variables or key concepts	Main results or arguments
Ho (2002)	▪ N/A	▪ Content analysis ▪ N= 46 cities	▪ Organizational	▪ WWW	▪ Local government reinvention	▪ The e-government paradigm, which emphasizes coordinated network building, external collaboration, and one-stop customer services, contradicts the traditional bureaucratic paradigm, which emphasizes standardization, departmentalization, and division of labor. ▪ "Insufficient staff, lack of funding and the problem of digital divide among racial groups are major hindering factors" (p. 440) to the paradigm shift.
Holden, Norris, and Fletcher (2003)	▪ Adoption literature	▪ Field survey ▪ N= 1881 (municipalities and counties)	▪ Organizational	▪ Web sites	▪ Local government adoption ▪ E-government barriers	▪ Web site adoption was found to be related to size of government, level and form of government, region and metro status (p. 4). ▪ Lack of technology/Web staff, financial resources, technology/Web expertise, information about e-government applications, as well as security and privacy issues, the need to upgrade technologies, convenience fees for online transactions issues, and lack of support from elected officials were found to be the major barriers to e-government adoption at the local level.
Hung et al. (2006)	▪ Theory of Planned Behavior (TPB)	▪ Field study ▪ N= 1099	▪ Individual	▪ Online tax filing and payment system	▪ PEOU ▪ PU ▪ Perceived risk ▪ Trust ▪ Personal innovativeness ▪ Compatibility ▪ Attitude ▪ External influence ▪ Interpersonal influence ▪ Subjective norms ▪ Self-efficacy ▪ Facilitating conditions ▪ Perceived behavioral control ▪ Behavioral intention	▪ PEOU, PU, perceived risk, trust and compatibility were found to have a significant influence on attitude. ▪ External and interpersonal influence were found to have a significant influence on subjective norms. ▪ Self-efficacy and facilitating conditions were found to have a significant effect on Perceived behavioral control. ▪ Attitude, subjective norms, and perceived behavioral control were found to have a significant influence on behavioral intention and explained 72% of its variance. ▪ Sub-group comparisons between adopters (N=1008) and nonadopters (N=91) are also provided.

Table 2. continued

Authors	Theoretical framework	Methodology	Level of analysis	Technology	Variables or key concepts	Main results or arguments
Kim and Bretschneider (2004)	• Innovation and IT innovation literature	• Case study • N= 7 municipalities	• Organizational	• Multiple (e.g., PCs, office applications, wireless devices, payroll systems, HR systems, etc.)	• IT capacity • Managerial capability of IT manager • Administrative authorities support • Financial support	• IT capacity (defined as the ability of the local government to effectively apply IT to achieve desired ends) was found to be influenced by the managerial capability of IT manager through interactions with administrative support and financial support.
Lee and Rao (2007)	• Social exchange theory • Transaction cost theory • IT acceptance literature.	• Conceptual • Field survey (pilot) • N=25	• Organizational	• Interagency anti/counter terrorism information sharing systems.	• Information sensitivity • Perceived mutual benefit • Other's info assurance • Subjective organizational norm • Ease of systems integration • Internal systems utilization • Institutional pressure • Info sharing standards • Info sharing systems acceptance.	• Perceived information assurance of others, and information sensitivity were found to have a positive correlation with information sharing systems acceptance. • Subjective organizational norm and institutional pressure were found to have a positive correlation with information sharing systems acceptance and with interorganizational information sharing. • Subjective organizational norm was found to have a positive correlation with Information sensitivity and perceived mutual benefits from information sharing.

Table 2. continued

Authors	Theoretical framework	Methodology	Level of analysis	Technology	Variables or key concepts	Main results or arguments
Lee, Braynov and Rao (2005)	▪ TAM ▪ Trust literature	▪ Field survey ▪ N= 158	▪ Individual	▪ NS	▪ Trust in the Government ▪ Perceived public emergency ▪ Trusting beliefs in e-Government ▪ Perceived riskiness ▪ PU ▪ Intention to depend on information ▪ Intention to provide personal information ▪ Intention to use	▪ Citizens' trust in the government and perceived public scrutiny were found to have marginal effects on individual trusting beliefs in e-government, perceived riskiness of the Internet, and perceived usefulness of e-government services. ▪ Trusting beliefs in e-government and PU had a significant effect on intention to use, on intention to provide personal information, and on intention to depend on information. ▪ Perceived riskiness had a significant and negative effect on intention to use, and on intention to provide personal information.
Lee and Rao (2003)	▪ Trust literature	▪ Conceptual + pilot experiment (N= 48 students)	▪ Individual	▪ Department of Natural Resources Web sites	▪ Web site attributes ▪ Domain of authority ▪ Authority ▪ Structural assurance belief ▪ Competence belief ▪ Benevolence belief ▪ Integrity belief ▪ Trusting intention	▪ Proposes a conceptual model predicting intention to transact with online government services. ▪ The preliminary experiment found that "not all government sites command the same level of trust and that they cannot sorely rely on their authorities expecting successful online services" (p. 825).
Lee et al. (2005)	▪ IT acceptance literature ▪ Trust literature	▪ Field survey ▪ N= 84	▪ Individual	▪ IRS e-file service	▪ E-file experience ▪ Perceived potential benefit ▪ Trust in e-government ▪ Belief in goodwill ▪ Domain competence ▪ Internet competence ▪ Trust in government and businesses ▪ Disposition to trust ▪ Internet risk ▪ Internet self-efficacy ▪ Intention to use	▪ Belief in IRS goodwill did not have a significant direct or indirect effect on intention to use. ▪ Internet competence belief was found to have a significant indirect effect, through potential benefit, on intention to use. ▪ The interaction of relational risk and goodwill of third party was found to be a "possible determinant" of intention to use. ▪ Trust in government was found to influence the belief in the goodwill of e-government authority. ▪ Direct positive experience was found to have a significant effect on trusting beliefs.

Table 2. continued

Authors	Theoretical framework	Methodology	Level of analysis	Technology	Variables or key concepts	Main results or arguments
Luna-Reyes, Gil-Garcia, and Cruz (2006)	▪ N/A	▪ Semistructured interviews (N= 18) ▪ Documentation analysis	▪ Organizational	▪ N/A	▪ Collaboration ▪ Trust ▪ Benefits ▪ Risk ▪ Institutional arrangements ▪ Organizational structures ▪ integration	▪ Proposes a framework explaining how institutions affect cross-organizational collaboration and interorganizational information integration. ▪ The framework proposes that cross-organizational collaboration is the result of initial trust, which in turn is the result of perceived risk and perceived benefits of the project.
Moon (2002)	▪ E-government developmental stages literature.	▪ Survey ▪ N= 1471	▪ Organizational	▪ Web site, Intranet	▪ E-government adoption ▪ E-government evolution ▪ Information stage ▪ Two-way communication stage ▪ Service and financial transaction ▪ Vertical and horizontal integration ▪ Political participation	▪ 85.3% of the responding municipal governments had a Web site, and 57.4% of them had an Intranet. ▪ 8.2% of the responding municipal governments were found to have a "comprehensive strategy or master plan to guide their future e-government initiatives." ▪ Adoption and longevity of municipal government Web sites were found to be positively associated with their size. ▪ Lack of financial resources, lack of technology staff and expertise, technological upgrades, security, and privacy issues were found to hinder e-government adoption and evolution.
Norris and Moon (2005)	▪ IT adoption literature	▪ Field survey ▪ N= 1881 local governments in 2000, and N= 4125 local governments in 2002.	▪ Organizational	▪ Web sites	▪ Adoption ▪ Organizational characteristics ▪ Organizational output and outcomes	▪ Local governments in the US "continue to make incremental progress in adopting and deploying e-government systems" (p. 72). ▪ Adoption of Web sites by public administrations "is strongly related to local government size (measured in terms of population)" (p. 72). ▪ "Not all reported impacts of e-government are positive" (p. 72). ▪ The most significant barriers to e-government adoption include lack of technology, Web staff, and financial resources, as well as privacy and security issues.

Table 2. continued

Authors	Theoretical framework	Methodology	Level of analysis	Technology	Variables or key concepts	Main results or arguments
Norris (2005)	▪ N/A	▪ Field survey (2) ▪ N= 1881 local governments in 2000, and N= 4125 local governments in 2002.Focus group ▪ N= 37	▪ Organizational	▪ Web sites	▪ Local government adoption ▪ Nonfinancial transactions ▪ Financial transactions	▪ Argues that while local governments were found to plan enhancements to their e-government service offerings, the pace of adoption would be slow. ▪ Shows that future e-government adoption at the local level involves more difficult implementation issues such as "integration with back office systems, integrating Web applications horizontally across the "silos" within governments, and integrating vertically among levels of government…" (p.4).
Phang et al. (2005)	▪ TAM	▪ Field survey ▪ N= 99	▪ Individual	▪ Central provident fund (CPF) e-Withdrawal	▪ Compatibility ▪ Image ▪ Internet safety perceptions ▪ PEOU ▪ PU ▪ Intention to Use	▪ Contrary to Morris and Venkatesh (2000), perceived usefulness was found to be the most significant predictor of use intention in the context of senior citizens' adoption intention in non-working workplace settings. ▪ Compatibility and image had no significant effect on perceived usefulness. Internet safety perceptions and perceived ease of use had a significant effect on perceived usefulness.
Phang and Kankanhalli (2005)	▪ Participation theories	▪ Conceptual	▪ Individual	▪ N/A	▪ Incentives-related factors ▪ Resource-related factors ▪ Political institution factors ▪ Social capital factors ▪ Personal belief factors ▪ IT factors ▪ Participation	▪ Proposes a research framework for citizen participation via e-consultation.
Pieterson, Ebbers, and van Dijk (2007)	▪ Implementation literature ▪ TAM	▪ Conceptual	▪ Organizational ▪ Individual	▪ N/A	▪ Personalization of electronic services ▪ Organizational obstacles ▪ User obstacles	▪ Proposes that implementation and use of personalized electronic services are hindered by five organizational obstacles (i.e., process-based, financial, governance based, legal, and technical) and five user obstacles (i.e., access, trust, privacy, control, and acceptance).

Table 2. continued

Authors	Theoretical framework	Methodology	Level of analysis	Technology	Variables or key concepts	Main results or arguments
Scatolini and Cordella (2005)	▪ Interpretive perspective	▪ Action research ▪ N= 1 project	▪ Organizational	▪ "onlining project": various hardware and software.	▪ IT adoption ▪ IT sensemaking ▪ IT as a social object	▪ "Management capacity of the direction," "Personal and professional training" and "sharing responsibility for change" were found to be the most significant issues affecting IT implementation and adoption. ▪ The "defence of political bonds" was found to be the most salient resistance factor to IT adoption. ▪ "Human resource management," "Organizational climate" and "decision making and responsibility assumption" were found to be strong determinants of organizational innovation.
Sorrentino (2005)	▪ Organizational change literature	▪ Case study ▪ N=1	▪ Organizational process	▪ Automatic filing system	▪ Resistance ▪ Process analysis	▪ Proposes a process-oriented perspective for understanding resistance to change and IT adoption.
Srivastava and Teo (2006a)	▪ Technology-organization-environment framework (Tomatzky and Fleisher)	▪ Secondary data analysis ▪ N= 115	▪ National	▪ N/A	▪ ICT infrastructure ▪ Technology development ▪ Human capital ▪ Public institutions ▪ Macro-economy ▪ E-government development	▪ ICT infrastructure, technology development, and human capital were found to have a significant relationship on e-government development. ▪ In post-hoc analysis, public institutions were found to be significantly, but negatively, related to e-government development.

Table 2. continued

Authors	Theoretical framework	Methodology	Level of analysis	Technology	Variables or key concepts	Main results or arguments
Srivastava and Teo (2006b)	• Technology-organization-environment framework (Tomatzky and Fleisher) • IT impact literature	• Secondary data analysis • N=113	• National	• N/A	• ICT infrastructure • Human capital • Public institutions • Macro-economy • E-government development • E-business development • Business competitiveness	• ICT infrastructure was found to have a significant influence on e-government development. • Quality of human capital was found to have a significant effect on e-government development. • No support was found regarding the effect of public institutions and the macr-economy on e-government development.
Tan et al. (2005)	• Trust literature	• Case study • N=1	• Individual	• E-filing system	• Process-based trust • Characteristic-based trust • Institution-based trust	• Each trust mode can only be restored through a blend of sociopolitical strategies and IT
Treiblmaier, Pinterits, and Floh (2004)	• Theory of planned behavior	• Field survey • N=631	• Individual	• Electronic payment systems	• Frictionless use • Trust in e-payment security • Experience • Attitude toward e-payment • Intention to use e-payment	• Experience with online payment was found to significantly influence frictionless use and trust in e-payment security. • Attitude toward e-payment was found to be significantly influenced by frictionless use and trust in e-payment security. • Attitude had a significant impact on intention to use e-payment.
Ventura (1995)	• Innovation diffusion theory	• Case study • N=1 • "Participant observation" (multiple agencies, number not specified)	• Organizational	• GIS	• Adoption • Use • Technical factors • Organizational factors • Institutional factors	• Barriers to adoption include technical, organizational and institutional factors. • Technical factors affecting adoption include system components, system design and technical expertise (p. 461). • Organizational factors affecting adoption include "how well the staff of the organization understands the technology and its role, and how the organization adapts to new sources and types of information" (p. 461). • Institutional factors affecting adoption include: "intergovernmental relations, the economic and legal environment… the mandates and budgets under which (the agency) operates, and the perceptions of other organizations and the public" (p. 465).

Table 2. continued

Authors	Theoretical framework	Methodology	Level of analysis	Technology	Variables or key concepts	Main results or arguments
Warkentin et al. (2002)	• Technology acceptance model • Theory of planned behavior • Trust literature	• Conceptual	• Individual	• N/A	• Institutional structures • Disposition to trust • Characteristics-based trust • Experience • PEOU • PU • Perceived behavioral control • Perceived risk • Degree of intrusiveness • Culture (uncertainty avoidance) • Culture (power distance acceptance) • Intention to engage in e-government	• Proposes a conceptual model of key factors affecting individual e-government adoption.
Weerakkod, Choudrie, and Currie (2004)	• Stage development models literature	• Case study • N=1	• Multiple	• Web site	• Adoption barriers	• Accessibility of Web sites, paradigm shift, financial constraints, political constraints, technological constraints, data protection and security constraints, trust, awareness, usability, computer knowledge, and language were found to be key barriers to adoption.

Table 3. E-government "subculture" research

Authors	Theoretical framework	Methodology	Level of analysis	Technology	Variables or key concepts	Main results or arguments
Coursey, Welch, and Pandey (2005)	• Web site effectiveness	• Filed survey • N= 274	• Individual	• Web sites	• Web help • Centralization • Records • Goal ambiguity • Internal communication • Bureaucratic culture • Innovation culture • Red tape • External communication • Political influence • Customer orientation • Budget • Program • Client groups pressure • State pressure • National political influence • Regulatory pressure	• Web site effectiveness was positively related to external political and business pressures, internal communication characteristics, innovative organizational culture, and size. • External pressures positively affected Web site adoption by legitimating internal managerial actions. • Web site adoption is effective when organizations are entrepreneurial, innovative, and open to external influence.
Drake et al. (2004)	• Archival documents analysis • Critical incident interviews	• Conceptual • Case study • N= 2	• Organizational	• N/A	• Information sharing • Public management context • Political context • Science context • Bureaucrat subculture • Political subculture • Scientist subculture	• Choices "about data and data systems are predicated on a political stance and create political consequences" (p. 78). • Information sharing systems "need to account for the downstream implications of choices people make, upstream requirements for information people need to make these choices, and tributary contributions and expectations regarding information from outside constituencies" (p. 79). • The three subcultures "have different pressures, mandates, and goals for their work and, as a result, have developed differences in their bodies of knowledge and practices" (p. 80).

Table 3. continued

Authors	Theoretical framework	Methodology	Level of analysis	Technology	Variables or key concepts	Main results or arguments
Dubauskas (2005)	▪ Privacy protection	▪ Literature review ▪ Web site evaluation (replication)	▪ Application	▪ Web sites	▪ Self-regulation ▪ Legislation	▪ Citizens' expectations are not taken into consideration during the elaboration of confidentiality policies. ▪ Public agencies do not consider consumer privacy concerns
Siau and Long (2004)	▪ Growth theory ▪ Human capital theory	▪ Secondary data analysis ▪ E-government Reports (2003) ▪ Human development report (2003)	▪ Project	▪ Web sites	▪ Information and computer technology ▪ Human development indicator (HDI) ▪ E-government development	▪ Technological and social factors affect the adoption of e-government by public administrations ▪ E-government development for countries with high HDI is significantly different from countries with medium or low HDI.

Table 4. E-government "IT characteristics" research

Authors	Theoretical framework	Methodology	Level of analysis	Technology	Variables or key concepts	Main results or arguments
Barnes and Vigden (2003)	▪ N/A	▪ Field survey ▪ N= 65 (T1) and 59 (T2)	▪ Web site	▪ FSMKE (Strategic Management Knowledge Exchange) Web site	▪ Usability ▪ Infromation quality ▪ Service interaction	▪ Ease of use was found to be a major factor of Web site usability. ▪ Argues that evaluation and use of transnational e-government Web sites varies across cultures.
Fedorowicz, Gogan, Gelinas, and Williams (2004)	▪ Adoption literature	▪ Case study ▪ N= 1	▪ Organizational	▪ IPP (Internet payment platform)	▪ Data technical issues ▪ Data utility issues ▪ Data security issues	▪ The appreciating database (i.e., a database where data is retained and available for inquiry at any time) was found to be a key enabling factor of IPP adoption. Data technical issues (e.g., handling of orders), utility issues (e.g., error reduction), and security issues (e.g., access control) were found to influence IPP adoption.
Gant and Gant (2001)	▪ N/A	▪ Content analysis ▪ N= 50 State Web sites	▪ Web site	▪ Web sites	▪ Openness ▪ Customization ▪ Usability ▪ Transparency ▪ Accesibility	▪ Scroll down menu for information access is posited to facilitate Web site use as well as Web site maintenance and upgrade. ▪ Only three states were found to provide customization features for their Web sites. ▪ Intuitive menu system, site map, new information indicators, search tools, common state logo, uniform masterhead, and dynamically generated list boxes were found to be key features of Web site usability. ▪ User help, online training, and assistance focused on new users were found to enhance usability. ▪ User ability to generate transactional receipts, absence of advertising, and security and privacy features were found to enhance Web site transparency

Table 4. continued

Authors	Theoretical framework	Methodology	Level of analysis	Technology	Variables or key concepts	Main results or arguments
Huang (2003)	▪ W3C Web content accessibility guidelines	▪ Content analysis ▪ N=35 Web sites	▪ Web site	▪ Web sites	▪ Accessibility indicators	▪ Posits that Web site accessibility is enhanced when a strategic planning team is formed to apply the W3C guidelines. ▪ Use of "alt" attributes, simplicity and clarity of the interface, incorporation of new technologies (e.g., flash), and the existence of formal accessibility rules and regulations were found to enhance usability for citizens with disabilities.
Jaeger (2006)	▪ Section 508 Rehabilitation Act compliance.	▪ Policy analysis ▪ User testing (N=10) ▪ Expert testing ▪ Field survey (N=4)	▪ Web site	▪ Web sites	▪ Accessibility indicators	▪ Compliance with section 508 was found to significantly vary between Web sites, thus hindering use of e-government sites by people with disabilities. ▪ Failure of text or buttons on sites to enlarge, the lack of sufficient space between lines of text, and the use of colors that were hard to distinguish were found to inhibit Web sites use (p. 184). ▪ Web site design for users with cognitive impairement, and users with learning disabilities were found to be neglected among government Web sites.

Table 4. continued

Authors	Theoretical framework	Methodology	Level of analysis	Technology	Variables or key concepts	Main results or arguments
Northrop (2003)	▪ N/A	▪ Secondary data analysis ▪ N= 42 cities	▪ Organizational	▪ WWW	▪ Diffusion	▪ Many city Web sites are not frequently updated: 1/3 of the Urbis cities waited more than a month before any changes were made. 1/8 updated weekly and 50% updated daily. There were "no absolutely common features on city web pages" (p. 12). ▪ Online transaction features "are still very rare across the board except in the cutting edge Best of Web cities" (p. 12). ▪ "Budget and privacy constraints are critical to how fast cities can move" to the transactional phase
Waddell and Broning (2004)	▪ N/A	▪ Case study ▪ N= 1	▪ Project	▪ UrbanSim	▪ Project management ▪ Agile software development	▪ Proposes an approach to identify real, unmet needs of local and regional governments ▪ Proposes a model specification process for developing e-government systems.
Wang, Bretschneider, and Gant (2005)	▪ Web site evaluation standards	▪ Case study N= 1 ▪ Lab experiment N= 1	▪ Individual	▪ Web sites	▪ Task characteristics ▪ Process outcome ▪ Site characteristics ▪ Individual characteristics	▪ Develops a client centric Web design methodology.

Table 5. E-government "impact measurement" research

Authors	Theoretical framework	Methodology	Level of analysis	Technology	Variables or key concepts	Main results or arguments
Abhichandani and Horan (2006)	▪ User satisfaction literature	▪ Field survey ▪ N1= 155 ▪ N2= 246	▪ individual	▪ Online advanced transportation information services	▪ Utility ▪ Reliability ▪ Efficiency ▪ Customization ▪ Flexibility ▪ E-gov satisfaction	▪ Proposes and tests a scale of 15 items for the measurement of e-government satisfaction.
Danziger (2004)	▪ Innovation theory	▪ Critical book review	▪ Multiple	▪ Internet	▪ Technology enactment	▪ IT allows for "levels of integration and cooperation that far exceed those possible with earlier modes of mainframe and desktop computing. The potential for such deeper structural changes raises the stakes for bureaucratic actors" (p. 108). ▪ Both the "bureaucratic structure and the behavior of key actors will determine the nature of IT use and its impacts" (p. 109). ▪ The manner in which "IT will be enacted is dependent on the interplay of bureaucracy, networks, and institutional arrangements" (p. 109). ▪ Bureaucratic actors in the public sector are "driven by certain embedded imperatives and calculations that are possibly at risk or even incompatible with the likely effects of Web-based systems on behavior, incentives and information flows."

Table 5. continued

Authors	Theoretical framework	Methodology	Level of analysis	Technology	Variables or key concepts	Main results or arguments
Gasco (2003)	▪ New institutionalism	▪ Conceptual	▪ Organizational	▪ N/A	▪ Institutional change	▪ E-government projects "are being implemented considering the type of institution they are inserted into" (p. 13). ▪ E-government projects "will cause institutional change when they give rise to the adjustments of the whole set of technological, managerial, and political variables affected by ICT implementations" (p. 13). ▪ E-government projects "do not determine whether institutional change, when it occurs, takes a positive or a negative direction" (p. 13). ▪ E-government projects "do not necessarily alter that type of institution for greater efficiency and transparency or lead to culture and actors' mental models transformations" (p. 13). ▪ There is a need for further research regarding the 'specific institutional constraints government agencies have to face when implementing e-government systems, [as well as] the strategies needed to facilitate a positive institutional change leading to a sustainable, successful e-government project implementation" (p. 13).
Gupta and Jana (2003)	▪ Performance measurement literature	▪ Case study ▪ N=1	▪ Project	▪ NDMC E-government infrastructure	▪ Cost benefit analysis ▪ Benchmarking ▪ Scoring method ▪ Stages of e-government ▪ Sociological angle ▪ Hierarchy of performance measures	▪ Proposes a framework to measure e-government tangible and intangible benefits by combining hard and soft performance measures.

Table 5. continued

Authors	Theoretical framework	Methodology	Level of analysis	Technology	Variables or key concepts	Main results or arguments
Grönlund (2005a)	▪ Actor network theory ▪ Structuration theory ▪ Institutional theory	▪ Conceptual	▪ Organizational	▪ NA	▪ Political sphere ▪ Administrative sphere ▪ Civil society ▪ Motivation ▪ Interest ▪ Mode of operation	▪ E-government systems "will only achieve long-term success when they sufficiently well implement interests and modes of operation of all three spheres of a governance system: formal politics, administration, and civil society" (p. 7).
Hae-Dong Lee (2005)	▪ IT business value	▪ Literature review ▪ Meta-analysis ▪ N= 39 articles	▪ Project	▪ NA	▪ IT value ▪ Public vs. private sector differences	▪ The public sector is inclined to use "soft" metrics to measure IT business value. ▪ E-government initiatives have a distinct set of business value sources different from those of e-business projects.

Table 5. continued

Authors	Theoretical framework	Methodology	Level of analysis	Technology	Variables or key concepts	Main results or arguments
Kraemer and King (2003)	▪ N/A	▪ Conceptual	▪ Organizational	▪ N/A	▪ Integration ▪ Radical change ▪ IT impact ▪ IT use	▪ Administrative reform "involves the making of dramatic, fundamental or radical change in form, and not just a change in degree as implied by the phrase 'continuous improvement.' Reform can be fast and disruptive or slow and incremental" (p. 4). ▪ There is "greater 'readiness' for administrative reform and for approaches such as reengineering than ever before" (p. 5). ▪ "Experience with IT and administrative reform has shown technology to be useful in some cases of administrative reform, but only when reform expectations are already well established. IT applications do not cause reform" (p. 8). ▪ "IT applications have brought relatively little change to organizational structures, and seem to reinforce existing structures" (p. 9). ▪ "The benefits of IT have not been evenly distributed within government organizational functions: the primary beneficiaries have been functions favored by the dominant political-administrative coalitions in public administrations, and not those of technical elites, middle managers, clerical staff, or ordinary citizens" (p. 10). ▪ Government organizations "are driven by political/institutional forces that are not and cannot be subjected to destructive change without severe consequences for their constituents" (p.13).

Table 5. continued

Authors	Theoretical framework	Methodology	Level of analysis	Technology	Variables or key concepts	Main results or arguments
Moon et al. (2005)	▪ N/A	▪ Conceptual	▪ National	▪ Not specified	▪ Web presence index ▪ E-government index ▪ Openness, transparency and interactivity index ▪ E-government score ▪ Macroeconomic stability ▪ HDI ▪ Internet penetration ▪ Democratic Government expenditures ▪ Public institutions	▪ Argues that although there have been multiple attempts to develop global e-government measures, there is still a lack of rigorous measures to comparatively assess e-government performance among nations. ▪ Suggests that future research should focus on developing more intermediate, ultimate outcome-based, agency-specific, and service-specific measures to capture e-government impact.
Reddick (2006)	▪ Information resource management literature ▪ E-government literature	▪ Feld survey ▪ N=75	▪ Individual	▪ N/A	▪ Reinventing government ▪ External environment ▪ Resource capacity ▪ Demographic factors	▪ Information resource managers' (IRM) e-government effectiveness was found to be significantly influenced by four categories of variables: 1) Reinventing government variables (employee's empowerment and teamwork increase); 2) External environment variables (business and citizen interaction increase, effectiveness in dealing with customers, and greater need for e-government); 3) Resource capacity variables (job easiness, elimination of manual processes); and 4) Demographic variables (gender).

Table 5. continued

Authors	Theoretical framework	Methodology	Level of analysis	Technology	Variables or key concepts	Main results or arguments
Robey and Holmström (2001)	• Institutional theory • Organizational politics	• Case study • N=1	• Multilevel	• Powerplay (OLAP tool)	• Organizational transformation • IT implementation social consequences • Globalization	• A "logic of opposition" involving forces promoting both change and persistence was found to help "problematize the transformational agenda" of public agencies. • IT may "enhance public participation in the democratic process" depending on the organizational and institutional processes in place.
Robey and Sahay (1996)	• Social interpretation perspective	• Case study • N= 2	• Organizational	• GIS	• Social consequences of IT • Organizational transformation • Organizational learning	• The same IT was found to be experienced differently in two similar settings (counties). • IT consequences are "socially constructed" and "depend upon its social meanings more than its material properties" (p. 106). • The differences in consequences were found to be related to the differences in the implementation.
Saxton et al. (2007)	• 2-1-1 Information and referral services literature.	• Case study • N=1	• Individual • Organizational • Societal	• 2-1-1 information and referral (I&R) services system	• information and referral services • Benefits • Costs	• Proposes a logic model identifying the benefits and costs of the 2-1-1 information and referral services system at the individual, organizational, and societal levels. • At the individual level, 2-1-1 system was found to provide value in terms of immediate answers, saved time, correct information, comprehensive solving problems, more time to focus on deeper issues, and fewer people in need of resources. • At the organizational level, 2-1-1 was found to induce outcomes such as saved resources, knowledgeable clients, less time wasted, and stronger and more focused organizations. • At the societal level, 2-1-1 was found to induce outcomes such as better informed users of services, knowlageable public, increased social capital, better services, and a better disaster infrastructure.

Table 5. continued

Authors	Theoretical framework	Methodology	Level of analysis	Technology	Variables or key concepts	Main results or arguments
Srivastava and Teo (2006b)	▪ Technology-organization-environment framework (Tornatzky and Fleisher) ▪ IT impact literature	▪ Secondary data analysis ▪ N= 113		▪ N/A	▪ ICT infrastructure ▪ Human capital ▪ Public institutions ▪ Macroeconomy ▪ E-government development ▪ E-business development ▪ Business competitiveness	▪ E-government development was found to have a significant influence on e-business development. ▪ No support was found regarding the relationship between e-government development and national business competitiveness. ▪ Posits that the impact of e-government development on national business competitiveness is mediated through e-business development.
Tolbert and Mossberger (2006)	▪ Trust literature	▪ Field survey ▪ N= 815		▪ Web sites	▪ Transaparency and effectiveness of government ▪ Accessibility of government ▪ Responsiveness of government ▪ Trust in government	▪ After controlling for demographic, economic, and attitudinal factors, use of federal government Web sites was found to significantly influence user's perceptions of government transparency. ▪ After controlling for demographic, economic, and attitudinal factors, use of federal government Web sites was found to significantly influence user's perceptions of government accessibility (measured by the ease of finding information). ▪ After controlling for demographic, economic, and attitudinal factors, perceptions of local government responsiveness (through use of local government Web sites) were found to significantly influence user's trust in government.

Acknowledgment

The authors wish to thank the participants at the International Conference on eGovernment (ICEG) 2005 mini-track on e-government adoption for their useful comments on earlier versions of this chapter. They also wish to thank the Editor-In-Chief, the Guest Editor and the three anonymous reviewers of the *International Journal of Electronic Government Research* (*IJEGR*, 2006, Vol. 2, Issue 3) for their insightful comments and suggestions. They finally wish to thank Professors Suzanne Rivard and Alain Pinsonneault for their valuable input and recommendations.

References

Abhichandani, T., & Horan, T.A. (2006). Toward a new evaluation model of e-government satisfaction: Results of structural equation modeling. In *Proceedings of the Twelfth Americas Conference on Information Systems* (pp. 249-257).

Allard-Poesi, F. (2003). Coder les données in *Conduire un projet de recherche, Une perspective qualitative,* Coordonné par Y. Giordano, Éditions EMS.

Andersen, K.V., & Henriksen, H.Z. (2005). The first leg of e-government research: Domains and applications areas 1998-2003. *International Journal of Electronic Government Research, 1*(4), 26-44.

Andersen, K.V., & Henriksen, H.Z. (2006). E-government maturity models: Extension of the Layne and Lee model. *Government Information Quarterly, 23,* 236-248.

Barki, H., & Pinsonneault, A. (2005). A model of organizational integration, implementation effort, and performance. *Organization Science, 16*(2), 165-179.

Barnes, S.J., & Vigden, R.T. (2003). Assessing the quality of a cross-national e-government Web site: A case study of the forum on strategic management knowledge exchange. In *Proceedings of the 36th Hawaii International Conference on System Sciences* (pp. 1-10).

Barua, A., Lee, C.H.S., & Whinston, A.B. (1996). The calculus of reengineering. *Information System Research, 7*(4) 409-428.

Becker, M.C., Knudsen, T., & March, J.G. (2006). Schumpeter, winter, and the sources of novelty. *Industrial and Corporate Change, 15*(2), 353-371.

Bélanger, F., & Carter, L. (2005). Trust and risk in e-government adoption. In *Proceedings of the Eleventh Americas Conference on Information Systems,* Omaha, Nebraska, (pp. 1955-1964).

Boynton, A.C., Zmud, R.W., & Jacobs, G.C. (1994). The influence of IT management practice on IT use in large organizationa. *MIS Quarterly, 18*(3), 299-318.

Bretschneider, S., & Wittmer, D. (1993). Organizational adoption of microcomputer technology: The role of sector. *Information Systems Research, 4*(1), 88-108.

Bygstad, B., Lanestedt, G., & Choudrie, J. (2007). Successful broadband projects in the public sector: A service innovation perspective. In *Proceedings of the 40th Hawaii International Conference on System Sciences* (pp. 103b-109).

Cahill, M. (2006). Establishing a new vision for BPR in a large, complex, public sector organisation. In *Proceedings of the Twelfth Americas Conference on Information Systems* (pp. 2371-2374).

Carter, L., & Bélanger, F. (2004). Citizen adoption of electronic government initiatives. In *Proceedings of the 37th Hawaii International Conference on System Sciences* (p. 50119c-501129).

Carter, L., & Bélanger, F. (2005). The utilization of e-government services: Citizen trust, innovation and acceptance. *Information Systems Journal, 15*(1), 5-25.

Caudle, S.L., Gorr, W.L., & Newcomer, K.E. (1991). Key information systems management issues for the public sector. *MIS Quarterly, 15*(2), 171-188.

Chan, C. M. L. & Pan, S.-L. (2006). Resource enactment in the e-government systems implementation: A case study on the e-file system. In *Proceedings of the 27th International Conference on Information Systems* (pp. 483-498).

Chan, C. M. L., Pan, S.-L., & Tan, C. (2003). Managing stakeholder relationships in an e-government project. In *Proceedings of the 9th Americas Conference on Information Systems* (pp. 783-791).

Chan, C.M.L., & Pan, S.L. (2003). *Managing stakeholder relationships in an e-government project.* Paper presented at the Ninth Americas Conference on Information Systems (pp. 783-791).

Chen, C.D., Fan, Y.W., & Farn, C.K. (2007). Investigating factors affecting the adoption of electronic toll collection: A transaction cost economics perspective. In *Proceedings of the 40th Hawaii International Conference on System Sciences* (pp. 107a-116).

Chircu, A.M., & Hae-Dong Lee, D. (2003). *Understanding IT investments in the public sector: The case of e-government.* Paper presented at the Ninth Americas Conference on Information Systems (pp. 792-800).

Ciborra, C. (2005). Interpreting e-government and development. Efficiency, transparency or governance at a distance? *Information Technology and People, 18*(3), 260-279.

Cohen, M.D., & Bacdayan, P. (1994). Organizational routines are stored as procedural memory: Evidence from a laboratory study. *Organization Science, 5*(4), 554-568.

Cohen, S., & Eimicke, W. (2003). The future of e-government: A project of potential trends and issues. In *Proceedings of the 36th Hawaii International Conference on System Sciences* (pp. 146-156).

Conklin, W.A. (2007). Barriers to adoption of e-government. In *Proceedings of the 40th Hawaii International Conference on System Sciences* (pp. 98-105).

Coursey, D.H., Welch, E.W., & Pandey, S.K. (2005). Organizational determinants of internally perceived Website effectiveness in state health and human service agencies. In *Proceedings of the 38th Hawaii International Conference on System Sciences* (pp. 135-145).

Danziger, J.M. (2004). Innovation in innovation? The technology enactment framework. *Social Science Computer Review, 22*(1), 100-110.

Davis, F.D. (1989). Perceived usefulness, perceived ease of use, and user acceptance of information technology. *MIS Quarterly, 13*(3), 319-340.

Davison, R.M., Wagner, C., & Ma, L.C.K. (2005). From government to e-government: A transition model. *Information Technology & People, 18*(3), 280-299.

Dawes, S. S., Pardo, T. A., & Creswell, A. M. (2003). Designing government information access programs: A holistic approach. In *Proceedings of the 36th Hawaii International Conference on System Sciences* (pp. 146-154).

Dawes, S.S., Pardo, T.A., & Creswell, A. M. (2003). Designing government information access programs: A holistic approach. In *Proceedings of the 36th Hawaii International Conference on System Sciences* (pp. 146-154).

Doellman, T., Allen. J., & Powell, A. (2006). Perceptions of online voting: New voters and senior citizens. In *Proceedings of the Twelfth Americas Conference on Information Systems* (pp. 2352-2356).

Drake, D.B., Stecklem, N.A., & Koch, M.J. (2004). Information sharing in and across government agencies. The role and influence of scientist, politician and bureaucratic subcultures. *Social Science Computer Review, 22*(1), 67-84.

Du Gay, P. (2003). The tyranny of the epochal: Change, epochalism and organizational reform. *Organization, 10*(4), 663-684.

Du Gay, P. (2004). Against 'enterprise' (but not against 'enterprise,' for that would make no sense). *Organization, 11*(1), 37-57.

Dubauskas, N. (2005). Business compliance to changing privacy protections. In *Proceedings of the 38th Hawaii International Conference on System Sciences* (pp. 134-143).

Dunleavy, P., & Margets, H. (2000). *The advent of digital government: Public bureaucracy and the state in the Internet age.* Paper presented at the Annual Conference of the American Political Science Association, Washington.

Ebrahim, Z., Irani, Z., & Al Shawi, S. (2004). A strategic framework for e-government adoption in public sector organisations. In *Proceedings of the Tenth Americas Conference on Information Systems* (pp. 1116-1125).

Eisenhardt, K.M., & Martin, J.A. (2000). Dynamic capabilities: What are they? *Strategic Management Journal, 21*, 1105-1121.

Esteves, J., & Joseph, R. (2006). Developing a framework for the assessment of egovernment initiatives. In *Proceedings of the Twelfth Americas Conference on Information Systems*, (pp. 2325-2332).

Fedorowicz, J., Gogan, J. L., Gelinas, U.J., Jr., & Williams, C. (2004). E-government, e-procurement, and e-payments: Data sharing issues associated with an appreciating database. In *Proceedings of the Tenth Americas Conference on Information Systems* (pp. 995-1002).

Feldman, M.S., & Pentland, B.T. (2003). Reconceptualizing organizational routines as a source of flexibility and change. *Administrative Science Quarterly, 48*(1), 94-118.

Fishbein, M., & Ajzen, I. (1975). *Belief, attitude, intentions and behavior: An introduction to theory and research.* Boston: Addison-Wesley.

Fulla, S., & Welch, E. (2002). Framing virtual interactivity between government and citizens: A study of feedback systems in the Chicago police department. In *Proceedings of the 35th Hawaii International Conference on System Sciences* (pp. 125-135).

Gallant, L.M., Culnan, M.J., & McLoughlin, P. (2007). Why people e-file (or don't e-file) their income taxes. In *Proceedings of the 40th Hawaii International Conference on System Sciences* (pp. 107b-112).

Gant, J.P., & Burley Gant, D. (2001). Web portals and their role in e-government. In *Proceedings of the Seventh Americas Conference on Information Systems* (pp. 1617-1623).

Gasco, M. (2003). New technologies and institutional change in public administration. *Social Science Computer Review, 21*(1), 6-14.

Gauld, R. (2007). Public sector information system project failures: Lessons from a New Zealand hospital organization. *Government Information Quarterly, 24*, 102-114.

Gefen, D., Pavlou P.A., Warkentin, M., & Gregory, M.R. (2002). Egovernment adoption. In *Proceedings of the Eighth Americas Conference on Information Systems* (pp. 569-576).

Gilbert, D., Balestrini, P., & Littleboy, D. (2004). Barriers and benefits in the adoption of e-government. *The International Journal of Public Sector Management, 14*(4), 286-301.

Golden, W., Hughes, M., & Scott, M. (2003). The role of process evolution in achieving citizen centered e-government. In *Proceedings of the Ninth Americas Conference on Information Systems* (pp. 801-810).

Goodhue, D.L. (1995). Understanding user evaluations of information systems. *Management Science, 41*(12), 1827-1844.

Grönlund, A. (2003). Emerging electronic infrastructures. *Social Science Computer Review, 21*(1), 55-72.

Grönlund, A. (2005a). What's in a field: Exploring the egovernment domain. In *Proceedings of the 38th Hawaii International Conference on System Sciences* (pp. 125-132).

Grönlund, A. (2005b). State of the art in e-gov research: Surveying conference publications. *International Journal of Electronic Government Research, 1*(4), 1-25.

Gupta, M.P., & Jana, D. (2003). E-government evaluation: A framework and case study. *Government Information Quarterly, 20*, 365-387.

Hannan, M.T., & Freeman, J. (1984). Structural inertia and organizational change. *American Sociological Review, 49*, 149-164.

Henderson, J.C., & Schilling, D.A. (1985). Design and implementation of decision support systems in the public sector. *MIS Quarterly, 9*(2), 157-169.

Henderson, R.M., & Clark, K.B. (1990). Architectural innovation: The reconfiguration of existing product technologies and the failure of established firms. *Administrative Science Quarterly, 35*, 9-30.

Henriksen, H. Z., Mahnke, V., & Meiland, J. H. (2004). Public e-procurement: Economic and political rationality. In *Proceedings of the 37th Hawaii International Conference on System Sciences* (pp. 50124-50132).

Hinnant, C. C. & Welch, E. W. (2003). Managerial capacity and digital government in the States: Examining the link between self-efficacy and perceived impacts of IT in public organizations. In *Proceedings of the 36th Hawaii International Conference on System Sciences* (pp. 1-9).

Hinnant, C.C., & Welch, E.W. (2003). Managerial capacity and digital government in the states: Examining the link between self-efficacy and perceived impacts of IT in public organizations. In *Proceedings of the 35th Hawaii International Conference on System Sciences* (pp. 1-9).

Ho, A.T.K. (2002). Reinventing local governments and the e-government initiative. *Public Administration Review, 62*(4), 434-444.

Holden, S.H., Norris, D.F., & Fletcher, P.D. (2003). Electronic government at the grass roots: Contemporary evidence and future trends. In *Proceedings of the 36th Hawaii International Conference on System Sciences* (pp. 134-140).

Homburg, V., & Bekkers, V. (2002). The back-office of e-government (managing information domains as political economies). In *Proceedings of the 35th Hawaii International Conference on System Sciences.*

Huang, J.C. (2003). Usability of e-government Web-sites for people with disabilities. In *Proceedings of the 36th Hawaii International Conference on System Sciences.*

Hung, S.Y., Chang, C.M., & Yu, T.Y. (2006). Determinants of user acceptance of the e-government services: The case of online tax filing and payment system. *Government Information Quarterly, 23,* 97–122.

Jaeger, P.T. (2003). The endless wire: E-government as global phenomenon. *Government Information Quarterly, 20,* 323-331.

Jaeger, P.T. (2006). Assessing section 508 compliance on federal e-government Web sites: A multi-method, user-centered evaluation of accessibility for persons with disabilities. *Government Information Quarterly, 23,* 169-190.

Jain, A., & Patnayakuni, R. (2003). *Public expectations and public dcrutiny: An sgenda for tesearch in the context of e-government.* Paper presented at the Ninth Americas Conference on Information Systems (pp. 811-820).

Jansse, M., & Joha, A. (2006). Governance of shared services in public administration. In *Proceedings of the Twelfth Americas Conference on Information Systems* (pp. 2306-2314).

Kallinikos, J. (2003). Work, human agency and organizational forms: An anatomy of fragmentation. *Organization Studies, 24*(4), 595-618.

Kallinikos, J. (2004). The social foundations of the bureaucratic order. *Organization, 11*(1), 13-36.

Kawalek, P., & Wastall, D. (2005). Pursuing radical transformation in information age government: case studies using the sprint methodology. *Journal of Global Information Management, 13*(1), 79-101.

Ke, W., & Wei, K.K. (2004). Understanding of e-government development: A case study of Singapore e-government. In *Proceedings of the Tenth Americas Conference on Information Systems* (pp. 617-625).

Kim, H. J. & Bretschneider, S. (2004). Local government information technology capacity: An exploratory theory. In *Proceedings of the 37ʰ Hawaii International Conference on System Science* (pp. 1-10).

Kraemer, K.L., & Leslie King, J. (2003). Information technology and administrative reform: Will the time after e-government be different? *CRITO, Center for research on information technology and organizations.* Retrieved August 27, 2007, from http://www.crito.uci.edu.

Lakshmi, M., Holstein, W.K., & Adams, R.B. (1990). EIS: It can work in the public sector. *MIS Quarterly, 14*(4), 435.

Layne, K., & Lee, J. (2001). Developing fully functional e-government: A four stage model. *Government Information Quarterly, 18*, 122-136.

Lee, D.H.-D. (2005). Contextual IT business value and barriers: An e-government and e-business perspective. In *Proceedings of the 38th Hawaii International Conference on System Sciences* (pp. 221-234).

Lee, J., & Kim, J. (2007). Grounded theory analysis of e-government initiatives: Exploring perceptions of government authorities. *Government Information Quarterly, 24*, 135-147

Lee, J.K., & Rao, H.R. (2003). *A study of customer's trusting beliefs in government-to-customer online services.* Paper presented at the Ninth Americas Conference on Information Systems (pp. 821-826).

Lee, J.K., & Rao, H.R. (2007). Understanding socio-technical environments for acceptance of inter-agency anti/counter-terrorism information sharing systems. In *Proceedings of the 38th Hawaii International Conference on System Sciences* (pp. 98-106).

Lee, J.K., Braynov, S., & Rao, H.R. (1993). Effects of a public emergency on citizens' usage intention toward e-government: A study in the context of war in Iraq. In *Proceedings of the Twenty Fourth Internationl Conference on Information Systems* (pp. 896-902).

Lee, J.K., Kim, D.J., & Rao, H.R. (2005). An examination of trust effects and pre-existing relational risks in e-government services. In *Proceedings of the Eleventh Americas Conference on Information Systems,* Omaha, Nebraska, (pp. 1949-1954).

Leonard-Barton, D. (1992). Core capabilities and core rigidities: A paradox in managing new product development. *Strategic Management Journal, 13*, 111-125.

Levina, N., & Ross, J.W. (2003). From the vendor's perspective: Exploring the value proposition in information technology outsourcing. *MIS Quarterly, 27*(3), 331-364.

Luna-Reyes, L.F., Gil-Garcia. J.R., & Cruz, C.B. (2006). Collaborative digital government in Mexico: Some lessons from federal Web-based inter-organizational information integration initiatives. In *Proceedings of the Twelfth Americas Conference on Information Systems* (pp. 2375-2384).

Marche, S., & McNiven, J.D. (2003). E-government and e-governance: The future isn't what it used to be. *Canadian Journal of Administrative Sciences, 20*(1), 74-86.

Margetts, H., & Dunleavy, P. (2002). Cultural barriers to e-government. *National Audit Office (HC 704-III) in conjunction with the Value for Money report "Better Services Through E-Government" (HC 704).*

Melitski, J., Holzer, M., Kim, S.-T., Kim, C.-G., & Rho, S.-Y. (2005). Digital government worldwide: An e-government assessment of municipal Web sites. *International Journal of Electronic Government Research, 1*(1), 1-19.

Milgrom, P., & Roberts, J. (1995a). Complementarities and fit: Strategy, structure, and organizational change in manufacturing. *Journal of Accounting and Economics, 19*, 179-208.

Milgrom, P., & Roberts, J. (1995b). The economics of modern manufacturing: Reply. *The American Economic Review, 85*(4), 997-999.

Moon, M. J., Welch, E. W., & Wong, W. (2005). Wha drives global e-governance? An exploratory study at a macro level. In *Proceedings of the 38th Hawaii International Conference on System Sciences* (pp. 131-139).

Moon, M.J. (2002). The evolution of e-government among municipalities: Rhetoric or reality. *Public Administration Review, 62*(4), 424-433.

Moon, M.J., & Bretschneider, S. (2002). Does the perception of red tape constrain IT innovation in organizations? Unexpected results from simultaneous equation model and implications. *Journal of Public Administration Research and Theory, 12*(2), 273-291.

Ni, A.Y., & Bretschneider, S. (2005). Why does state government contract out their e-government services? In *Proceedings of the 38th Hawaii International Conference on System Sciences* (pp. 130c-140).

Norris, D. F. (2005). E-government at the American grassroots: Future trajectory. In *Proceedings of the 37th Hawaii International Conference on System Sciences* (pp. 125b-129).

Norris, D.F., & Lloyd, D.A. (2006). The scholarly literature on e-government: Characterizing a nascent field. *International Journal of Electronic Government Research, 2*(4), 40-56.

Norris, D.F., & Moon, M.J. (2005). Advancing e-government at the grassroots: Tortoise or hare? *Public Administration Review, 65*(1), 64-75.

Northrop, A. (2003). E-government: The URBIS cities revisited? *CRITO, Center for Research on Information Technology and Organizations*. Retrieved August 27, 2007, from http://www.crito.uci.edu

Pardo, T. A., Cresswell, A. M., Dawes, S. S., & Burke, G. B. (2004). Modeling the social and technical processes of interorganizational information integration. In *Proceedings of the 37th Hawaii International Conference on System Sciences* (pp. 50120-10127).

Pardo, T., & Scholl, H.J. (2002). Walking atop the cliffs: Avoiding failure and reducing risk in large scale e-government projects. In *Proceedings of the 35th Hawaii International Conference on System Sciences* (pp. 1656-1665).

Park, H.M. (2005). A cost-benefit analysis of the Seoul OPEN system: Policy lessons for electronic government projects. In *Proceedings of the 38th Hawaii International Conference on System Sciences* (pp. 126b-135).

Pentland, B.T., & Rueter, H.H. (1994). Organizational routines as grammars of action. *Administrative Science Quarterly, 39*(3), 484-510.

Perrow, C. (1986). *Complex organizations: A critical essay* (3rd ed.). McGraw-Hill Publishing Company.

Phang, C.W., & Kankanhalli, A. (2005). A research framework for citizen participation via e-consultation. In *Proceedings of the Eleventh Americas Conference on Information Systems,* Omaha, Nebraska, (pp. 2003-2010).

Phang, C.W., Sutanto J., Li, Y., & Kankanhalli, A. (2005). Senior citizens' adoption of e-government: In quest of the antecedents of perceived usefulness. In *Proceedings of the 38th Hawaii International Conference on System Sciences* (p. 130a).

Pieterson, W., Ebbers, W., & van Dijk, J. (2007). Personalization in the public sector an inventory of organizational and user obstacles towards personalization of electronic services in the public sector. *Government Information Quarterly, 24,* 148–164.

Pinsonneault, A., & Kraemer, K.L. (2002). Exploring the role of information technology in organizational downsizing: A tale of two American cities. *Organization Science, 13*(2), 191-208.

Radio Canada. (2003). *Québec met fin au projet Gires.* Retrieved August 27, 2007, from http://radio-canada.ca/nouvelles/Index/nouvelles/200309/30/012-gires-abandon-rb.shtml.

Reddick, C.G. (2006). Information resource managers and E-government effectiveness: A survey of Texas state agencies. *Government Information Quarterly, 23,* 249–266.

Robey, D., & Holmström, J. (2001). Transforming municipal governance in global context: A case study of the dialectics of social change. *Journal of Global Information Technology Management, 4*(4), 19-31.

Robey, D., & Sahay, S. (1996). Transforming work through information technology: A comparative case study of geographic information systems in county government. *Information Systems Research, 7*(1), 93-110.

Roy, J. (2005). Service, security, transparency & trust: Government online or governance renewal in Canada? *International Journal of Electronic Government Research, 1*(1), 40-58.

Samuelson, P.A. (1974). Complementarity: An essay on the 40th anniversary of the Hicks-Allen revolution in demand theory. *Journal of Economic Literature, 12*(4), 1255-1289.

Saxton, M.L., Naumer, C.M., & Fisher, K.E. (2007). 2-1-1 information services: Outcomes assessment, benefit-cost analysis, and policy issues. *Government Information Quarterly, 24,* 186-215.

Scatolini, E., & Cordella, A. (2005). *Technological artifacts and sense making in an Italian public administration.* Paper presented at the 21st European Group for Organisational Studies (EGOS) Colloquium, Berlin.

Schedler, K., & Scharf, M.C. (2000). *Exploring the interrelations between electronic government and the new public management. A managerial framework for electronic government.* Switzerland: Institute for Public Services and Tourism at the University of St. Gallen.

Schildt, K. & Beaumaster, S. (2004) Strategic information technology management: The city of Anaheim technological initiatives. In *Proceedings of the 37th Hawaii International Conference on System Science* (pp. 50121a-50130a).

Schildt, K., Beaumaster, S., & Edwards, M. (2005). Strategic information technology man-agement: Managing organizational, political, and technological forces. In *Proceedings of the 38th Hawaii International Conference on System Sciences* (pp. 126-135).

Scholl, H.J. (2003). E-government: A special case of ICT-enabled business process change. In *Proceedings of the 36th Hawaii International Conference on System Sciences* (pp. 136-147).

Scholl, H.J. (2005). E-government-induced business process change (BPC): An empirical study of current practices. *International Journal of Electronic Government Research, 1*(2), 27-49.

Shackleton, P., Fisher, J., & Dawson, L. (2004). Evolution of local government e-services: The applicability of e-business maturity models. In *Proceedings of the 37th Hawaii International Conference on System Sciences* (pp. 50120-50128).

Siau, K., & Long, Y. (2004). *Factors impacting e-government development.* Paper presented at the Twenty-Fifth International Conference on Information Systems (pp. 221-234).

Sorrentino, M. (2005). *Reconceptualizing resistance to change: A case of IT implementation in a local authority.* Paper presented at the 21st European Group for Organisational Studies (EGOS) Colloquium, Berlin.

Srivastava, S.C., & Teo, T.S.H. (2006a). Facilitators for e-government development: An application of the technology-organization-environment framework. In *Proceedings of the Twelfth Americas Conference on Information Systems* (pp. 2315-2324).

Srivastava, S.C., & Teo, T.S.H. (2006b). *Determinants and impact of e-government and e-business devlopment: A glabal perspective.* Paper presented at the Twenty-Seventh International Conference on Information Systems (pp. 1-18).

Stokes, J., & Clegg, S. (2003). Once upon a time in the bureaucracy: Power and public sector management. *Organization, 9*(2), 225-247.

Tan, C.W., Pan, S.L, & Lim, E.T.K. (2005). Towards the restoration of public trust in elec-tronic governments: A case study of the e-filing system in Singapore. In *Proceedings of the 38th Hawaii International Conference on System Sciences* (pp. 126-135).

Teece, D.J., Pisano, G., & Shuen, A. (1997). Dynamic capabilities and strategic manage-ment. *Strategic Management Journal, 18*(7), 509-533.

Thong, J.Y.L., Yap, C.S., & Seah, K.L. (2000). Business process reengineering in the public sector: The case of the housing development board in Singapore. *Journal of Manage-ment Information Systems, 17*(1), 245-270.

Tolbert, C.J., & Mossberger, K. (2006). The effects of e-government on trust and confidence in government. *Public Administration Review, 3*, 354-369.

Tranfield, D., Duberley, J., Smith, S., Musson, G., & Stokes, P. (2000). Organizational learning: It's just routine. *Management Decision, 38*(4), 253-260.

Treiblmaier, H., Pinterits, A., & Floh, A. (2004). *Antecedents of the adoption of e-payment services in the publicsSector.* Paper presented at the Twenty-Fifth International Con-ference on Information Systems (pp. 65-76).

UNDP (2001). *Human development report 2001: Making new technologies work for human development.* Retrieved October 5, 2007, from http://hdr.undp.org/reports/global/2001/en

Ventura, S.J. (1995). The use of geographic information systems in local government. *Public Administration Review, 55*(5), 461-467.

Waddel, P., & Borning, A. (2004). A case study in digital government: Developing and applying UrbanSim, a system for simulating urban land use, transportation, and environmental impacts. *Social Science Computer Review, 22*(1), 37-51.

Wang, L., Bretschneider, S., & Gant, J. (2005). Evaluating Web-based e-government services with a citizen-centric approach. In *Proceedings of the 38th Hawaii International Conference on System Sciences* (pp. 129-137).

Warkentin, M, Gefen, D., Pavlou, P.A., & Rose, G.M. (2002). Encouraging citizen adoption of e-governement by building trust. *Electronic Markets, 12*(3), 157-162.

Webster, J., & Watson, R.T. (2002). Analyzing the past to prepare for the future: Writing a literature review. *MIS Quarterly, 26*(2), 13-23.

Weerakkody, V., Choudrie, J., & Currie, W. (2004). Realising e-government in the UK: Local and national challenges. In *Proceedings of the Tenth Americas Conference on Information Systems* (pp. 972-980).

Welch, E. W. & Pandey, S. (2005). E-Government and network technologies: Does bureaucratic red tape inhibit, promote or fall victim to intranet technology implementation? In *Proceedigns of the 38th Hawaii International Conference on System Sciences* (pp. 1-10).

Wheeler, B.C. (2002). NEBIC: A dynamic capabilities theory for assessing net-enablement. *Information Systems Research, 13*(2), 125-146.

Whittington, R., & Pettigrew, A.M. (2003). Complementarities thinking. In A.M. Pettigrew, R. Whittington, L. Melin, C. Sanchez-Runde, F. Van den Bosch, W. Ruigrock, et al. (Eds.), *Innovative forms of organizing: International perspectives* (pp. 125-132). London: Sage Publications.

Williams, M. D., & Beynon-Davies, P. (2004). Implementing e-government in the UK: An analysis of local-level strategies. In *Proceedings of the Tenth Americas Conference on Information Systems* (pp. 1008-1015).

World Bank (2007). *World Bank.* Retrieved October 5, 2007, from http://web.worldbank.org

Zahra, S.A., & George G. (2002). Absorptive capacity: A review, reconceptualization, and extention. *Academy of Management Review, 27*(2), 185-203.

Endnotes

¹ The other two contextual research domains identified by Andersen and Henriksen (2005) are: a) conceptualization of e-government, which refers to broad and conceptual aspects on, or related to, e-government; and b) e-democracy.

² An organizational capability refers to "a high level routine (or collection of routines)" (Winter, 2002, p. 3).

Chapter IV

Worldwide E-Governance:
A Longitudinal Assessment of Municipal Web Sites and the Digital Divide

Tony Carrizales, Marist College, USA

Marc Holzer, Rutgers University – Newark, USA

Aroon Manoharan, Rutgers University – Newark, USA

Abstract

This following chapter highlights the research findings of a digital governance survey conducted in the fall of 2005. The study replicates a 2003 survey of large municipalities worldwide. This longitudinal assessment, based on the Rutgers-SKKU E-Governance Performance Index, focused on the evaluation of current practices in government, with emphasis on the evaluation of each Web site in terms of digital governance. Specifically, we analyzed security, usability, content of Web sites, the type of online services currently being offered, and citizen response and participation through Web sites established by city governments. Based on the 2005 evaluation of 81 cities, Seoul, New York, Shanghai, Hong Kong, and Sydney represent the highest performing cities in digital governance. There were only slight changes in the top five cities when compared to the 2003 study. Moreover, there continues to be a divide in terms of digital governance throughout the world among the 30 developed nations belonging to the Organization for Economic Cooperation and Development (OECD) and non-OECD member nations. This divide is highlighted by the change in average scores among the municipalities when comparing municipalities from OECD and non-OECD member nations.

Introduction

The following research highlights the results of an international survey conducted in the fall of 2005 evaluating the practice of digital governance in large municipalities. A similar study was conducted in 2003 (Holzer & Kim 2004; Melitski, Holzer, Kim, Kim, & Rho, 2005) which provided one of the most exhaustive studies of municipal e-governance ever conducted. The research was replicated two years later through a collaboration between the E-Governance Institute at Rutgers-Newark and the Global e-Policy e-Government Institute at Sungkyunkwan University in Seoul. The joint study again produced a wealth of information that contributes to the growing field of digital government. In particular, we focus on the changes over two years in this longitudinal assessment of municipal Web sites.

Literature Review

A review of digital governance literature includes numerous areas of research, all highlighting the potential of technology under terms such as e-government, e-democracy, e-participation, and digital democracy. In particular, the literature below indicates potential for improved government services and online democratic practices. Our survey research evaluates municipal Web sites in these areas and the data presented reflect the current practice of e-governance throughout the world.

Numerous researchers have highlighted the potential for e-governance. In order for good governance to be achieved, Cloete (2003) argues for an acceptance of technological innovations, suggesting that Internet-based services and other technological service delivery applications will be the only way governments can meet their own service delivery goals. A 2003 survey by the Pew Internet & American Life Project attempted to determine how Americans contact government. Their study found that e-government is an increasingly popular tool for Internet users, with a primary purpose of getting information and sending messages to the government (Horrigan, 2004). West (2004) highlights a study of chief information officers, where the respondents felt positive about the capacity for the Internet to transform government, however, argues that e-government "has fallen short of its potential to transform government" in the areas of service delivery and trust in government (p. 16).

E-government initiatives, specifically the Internet, must go beyond the static listing of information to more "intentions-based" design so that citizens can more effectively utilize Web portals (Howard, 2001). Recent advances in e-services include the personalization of government Web pages. Virginia's "MyGov" allows an individual to format Web pages around their interests from options such as public meeting announcements, interactive government services, legislative sites, local government, local media, public schools, lottery numbers, press releases, state government, and traffic information (Eggers, 2005). These developments in e-services are well intentioned, but misdirected suggests Eggers (2005), because they are underutilized and rarely involve transactions, adding little to no value for individuals and businesses. Individuals still do not visit government Web sites enough to make services such as personalized Web pages a common locus for e-government initiatives.

Moreover, a relatively new aspect of digital governance, e-democracy, is in reality a concept with a history dating to the 1960s in which scholars, activists, and politicians were forecasting technological utopias (Bryan, Tsagarousianou, & Tambini, 1998). The current interest in e-democracy can in part be attributed to the lack of performance in old technologies used for democracy (Shane, 2002). Early discussions of the technology-democracy relationship highlighted the potential of telecommunications, with emphasis on cable television and telephone conferencing (Arterton, 1987, 1988; Becker, 1993; Christopher, 1987, McLean, 1989). However, the focus has now significantly shifted to the Internet (Bellamy & Taylor, 1998; Browning, 2002; Gattiker, 2001; Kamarck & Nye, 1999, 2003; Loader, 1997; Westen, 1998, 2000; Wilhelm, 1998; Witschge, 2002).

Unlike other mediums, citizens are now able to demand and obtain content when going online (Browning, 2002). Korac-Kakabadse and Korac-Kakabadse (1999) point out that ICTs provide the possibility for direct-democracy on a larger scale. They define e-democracy as the capacity for ICTs to enhance the degree and quality of public participation in government. Proponents argue that e-democracy will allow for greater government transparency and openness, which leads to a better-informed citizenry. The openness of government can lead to increased accountability and reduced government corruption. The case of Seoul's Online Procedures Enhancement for Civil Application (OPEN) system has demonstrated a successful practice of transparency and decreased corruption in government via the use of the Internet (Holzer & Kim, 2004).

Online discussion boards are another example of an opportunistic use of technology for developing e-democracy. Online discussion boards allow for political discussions without requiring participants to share space and time, leading to increased access to political debate (Malina, 1999). The potential for citizen participation in decision and policy-making is growing, albeit slowly, through initiatives such as regulations.gov (Skrzycki, 2003a, 2003b). Some municipalities have already begun to practice aspects of e-democracy, which include information disclosure pertinent to government decision making as well as mediums for two-way communication.

The following data will also reflect the changes in online citizen participation among municipalities worldwide.

Scholars have outlined the potential of digital governance, but little can be said about the state of current e-government's practices in municipalities worldwide. International studies, as this research is, are critical contributions to the overall literature of digital governance. To better understand how various regions of the world differ in the area of e-governance, comprehensive studies of regions throughout the world are necessary for a basis of comparison. More importantly, regional studies provide regional benchmarks and best practices that allow for increased performance in digital governance overtime for those municipalities still in the earliest developments.

A review of the literature also suggests that our survey instrument is one of the most thorough in practice for e-governance research today. With 98 measures and five distinct categorical areas of e-governance research, the survey instrument is unlike any other. In studies of e-governance practices worldwide, our Performance Index differs quite significantly from other survey instruments. The following section reviews four of the most prominent and encompassing longitudinal worldwide e-governance surveys. The critiques of the Annual Global Survey at Brown University's Taubman Center for Public Policy (West 2001-2005), the United Nations Global E-government Report (UNPAN 2003, 2004, 2005), the Accenture E-government Leadership Survey (Accenture, 2002, 2004) and Capgemini's European Commission Report (Capgemini, 2005) are intended to highlight the distinct differences between the survey instruments and results. The findings and rankings of e-governance worldwide can best be understood by highlighting the distinct differences among the survey instruments.

The Taubman Center's Global E-government Survey is one of the only international e-government studies that have been conducted on an annual basis for the past five years (e.g., West 2001, 2004, 2005). Since 2001, the researchers at the Taubman Center have utilized an index instrument that measures the presence of Web site features. That instrument is geared toward specific Web functions, with limited attention to addressing privacy/security or usability. The e-governance area of citizen participation is only measured by one item. Moreover, their survey instrument has changed substantially from year to year. One of the problems with a rapidly evolving instrument is in the applicability of comparisons over the years. Our survey instrument has also changed with the inclusion of new questions, specifically in the citizen participation section. However, the Taubman Center's survey instrument has decreased its measurement criteria over the years. In 2001 and 2002, the number of measures were 24 and 25, respectively. In 2003, 2004, and 2005 the number of measures decreased to 20, 19, and 19, respectively. For 2005, its measures are broken down into two groups, with 18 primary measures and one bonus measure encompassing 28 possible points. The final overall scores are converted for a possible total score of 100. We also use a final possible score of 100, with each of our five categories allowing for a possible score of 20.

In all, the number of measures in the Taubman survey is limited, with only 19 metrics. A final score of e-governance performance is reflective of the specific questions focused on Web features that are captured by those 19 measures. One of the consequences of this methodology is the limited differentiation in performance of e-governance among countries. As a result, many of the countries received the same scores. In addition, there is an inconsistency in the annual rankings, specifically in the non-English Web sites. For example, the Republic of Korea has fluctuated in rankings as follows: 45th in 2001, 2nd in 2002, 87th in 2003, 32nd in 2004, and 86th in 2005. In other international findings, however, such as the United Nations Global E-government Survey, the Republic of Korea has consistently been recognized as one of the best in e-governance performance (4th in 2004 and 2005). One other example is Bolivia, which has also significantly fluctuated over the years in rankings. Bolivia was ranked 18th in 2001, 164th in 2002, 119th in 2003, 20th in 2004, and 225th in 2005. These significant variations in rankings can, in part, be attributed to the limited number of measures, allowing for shifting variations in overall scores. However, this can also be attributed to the method of not using native speakers when evaluating all the Web sites. In some cases, researchers at the Taubman Center have utilized language translation software available online, such as http://babelfish.altavista.com. Online translation software, however, can misinterpret specific languages and phrases.

The United Nations Global E-government Report is also one of the few longitudinal studies of Web presence throughout the world (e.g., UNPAN, 2004, 2005). The UN has two specific studies that it produces: an e-government readiness index and an e-participation index. The e-government readiness index incorporates Web measures, telecommunication infrastructure, and human capital. Their Web measure index is a quantitative measure, evaluating national Web sites. Their evaluation is based on binary values (presence/absence of a service). Their e-participation index is a qualitative study, with 21 measures used to assess the quality, relevance, usefulness, and willingness of government Web sites in providing online information and service/participation tools for citizens. The UN Global E-government Report takes methodological precautions to ensure accuracy and fairness. The surveying of Web sites is done within a 60-day "window" and Web sites are reevaluated by senior researchers for purposes of consistency. In addition, the survey incorporates native language speakers when necessary in an effort to review every Web site in the official language. However, this survey does differ from our research in that the UN studies central government Web sites, while we focus on large municipal Web sites throughout the world.

Accenture conducts a third global e-government study. Accenture's annual E-government Leadership report highlights the performance of 22 selected countries (e.g., Accenture 2002, 2004). The most recent report (2004) measured 206 services when assessing national government Web sites. The 206 national government services were divided between 12 service sectors: eDemocracy, education, human services, immigration, justice and security, postal, procurement, regulation, participation, revenue and customs, and transport. As an effort toward reliability, the research was conducted in a two-week period. The Accenture report, however, only focuses on 22 countries. The Accenture study omits numerous countries throughout the world, as well as many of the top performing governments in e-governance. Similarly, a study conducted by Capgemini, on behalf of the European Commission, is limited in international focus (Capgemini, 2005). This study is limited to nations in the European Union and only utilizes 20 basic public services as measures in the research study. The methodology is split between studying services to citizens (12) and services to businesses (8). An additional worldwide e-government survey is conducted by the Waseda University Institute of E-Government in Japan. There methodology includes 26 indicators as well as a component for surveying the Chief Information Officer of each country (World E-Gov Forum, 2007). Similar to the UN and Taubman Center studies, the Accenture, Capgemini, and Waseda University studies focus on national government Web sites, a distinguishing aspect from our research.

Design and Methodology

As stated above, previous e-governance research varies in the use of scales to evaluate government Web sites. For example, one researcher uses an index consisting of 25 dichotomous (yes or no) measures (West, 2001); other assessments use a more sophisticated four-point scale (Kaylor, 2001) for assessing each measure. We have developed the Rutgers-SKKU E-Governance Performance Index for evaluating city and municipal Web sites, consisting of five components: 1.) Security and Privacy; 2.) Usability; 3.) Content; 4.) Services; and 5. Citizen Participation. Our 2005 survey instrument utilizes 98 measures, of which 43 are dichotomous. For each of the five e-governance components, our research applies 18 to 20 measures, and for questions which were not dichotomous, each measure was coded on a four-point scale (0, 1, 2, 3; see Table 1). Furthermore, in developing an overall score for

Table 1. E-governance scale

Scale	Description
0	Information about a given topic does not exist on the Web site
1	Information about a given topic exists on the Web site (including links to other information and e-mail addresses)
2	Downloadable items are available on the Web site (forms, audio, video, and other one-way transactions, popup boxes)
3	Services, transactions, or interactions can take place completely online (credit card transactions, applications for permits, searchable databases, use of cookies, digital signatures, restricted access)

each municipality, we have equally weighted each of the five categories so as not to skew the research in favor of a particular category (regardless of the number of questions in each category). The dichotomous measures in the "service" and "citizen participation" categories correspond with values on our four point scale of "0" or "3"; dichotomous measures in "security/ privacy" or "usability" correspond to ratings of "0" or "1" on the scale.

In this research, the main city homepage is defined as the official Web site where information about city administration and online services are provided by the city. The city Web site includes Web sites about the city council, mayor, and executive branch of the city. Based on the concept above, this research evaluated the official Web sites of each city selected. Nineteen of 100 cities, however, do not have official city Web sites or were not accessible during the survey period: ten in Africa (71%), seven in Asia (22%), and two in North America (20%). As a result, this research evaluated only 81 cities of the 100 cities initially selected. Our research examined local government services using an e-governance model of increasingly sophisticated e-government services. Moon (2002) developed a framework for categorizing e-government models based on the following components: information dissemination, two-way communication, services, integration, and political participation. Our methodology for evaluating e-government services includes such components; however, we have added an additional factor of security.

That additional e-governance factor was grounded in recent calls for increased security, particularly of our public information infrastructure. Concern over the security of the information systems underlying government applications has led some researchers to the conclusion that e-governance must be built on a secure infrastructure that respects the privacy of its users (Kaylor, 2001).

The 2005 E-Governance Performance Index differs slightly from the one used in 2003. The most significant change was in the citizen participation component, where six new research questions were added. These new questions are, in part, recognition of the growing literature focusing on the various methods for more digitally-based democracy. These new questions survey the presence and functions of municipal forums, online decision making (e.g., e-petitions and e-referenda), and online surveys and polls. The new questions for the citizen participation component bring the total number of questions to 20, with a total possible raw score of 55. In addition, one question was removed from the security and privacy component. That question focused on the scanning of viruses during downloadable files from the municipal Web site. This aspect was found to be more dependent on personal computers than as a function of a municipal Web site. The removal of the question for the security and privacy component brings the total number of questions to 18, with a total possible raw score of 25. The final change to the E-Governance Performance Index was a question added to the content component. The additional question focuses on the number of possible downloadable documents from a municipal Web site. The

Table 2. E-governance performance measures

E-governance Category	Key Concepts	Raw Score	Weighted Score	Keywords
Security/ Privacy	18	25	20	Privacy policies, authentication, encryption, data management, and use of cookies
Usability	20	32	20	User-friendly design, branding, length of homepage, targeted audience links or channels, and site search capabilities
Content	20	48	20	Access to current accurate information, public documents, reports, publications, and multimedia materials
Service	20	59	20	Transactional services involving purchase or register, interaction between citizens, businesses, and government
Citizen Participation	20	55	20	Online civic engagement, internet based policy deliberation, and citizen based performance measurement
Total	98	219	100	

new question for content brings the total number of questions to 20, with a total possible raw score of 48.

The changes to the E-Governance Performance Index have helped make this ongoing survey of municipal Web sites one of the most thorough in the field of e-governance research. The Index now has a total of 98 questions, with a total possible raw score of 219. Given the changes to the survey instrument between 2003 and 2005, the method of weighting each component for a possible score of 20 and a total score of 100 allows for a consistency in comparisons over time. Table 2, which features e-governance performance measures, summarizes the 2005 survey instrument, and in Appendix A we present an overview of the criteria used during the evaluation.

Similar to our 2003 study, to ensure reliability each municipal Web site was assessed in the official language by two evaluators. Many of our evaluators were either doctoral students or researchers in the area of digital governance. In addition, all of the evaluators were provided comprehensive written instructions for assessing Web sites. The instructions and survey instrument itself included detailed examples for associated scores for each question. The two adjusted scores for each Web site were then compared and evaluated for consistency in evaluation. The evaluations were done via a preset spreadsheet instrument that alerted researchers when errors were made. Also, the instrument allowed for specific comments associated with each question, so that researchers can review in cases of evaluator discrepancy. Each Web site evaluation was done independent of one another and in cases where significant variation (+ or − 10%) existed on the weighted score between evaluators,

Web sites were analyzed a third time. The only Web site requiring a third evaluator for the 2005 survey was Brussels, Belgium. The three evaluations for Brussels were then reviewed and scores averaged to represent a municipal score. A framework of the survey instrument utilized is included in Appendix A.

International Municipalities

Both the 2003 and 2005 studies focused on the evaluation of current practices in government, and the emphasis in the research was on the evaluation of each Web site in terms of digital governance. Simply stated, digital governance includes both digital government (delivery of public service) and digital democracy (citizen participation in governance). Specifically, we analyzed security, usability, content of Web sites, the type of online services offered, and citizen response and participation through Web sites established by city governments.

This research examines cities throughout the world based on their population size, and the total number of individuals using the Internet. In the 2003 survey, data from the International Telecommunication Union (ITU), an organization affiliated with the United Nations (UN), were used to determine the 100 municipalities studied. Of 196 countries for which telecommunications data were reported, those with a total online population over 100,000 were identified. As a result, the most populated cities in 98 countries were selected to be surveyed (along with Hong Kong and Macao). For the 2005 worldwide survey, the most recent available ITU-UN data were used. These updated figures produced slightly different results from the previous survey in 2003. Countries with an online population over 100,000 increased to 119. Therefore, we set a new cut-off mark at countries with an online population over 160,000. This resulted in 98 countries which met the new mark. With the inclusion of Hong Kong and Macao, as in 2003, a total of 100 cities were identified for the 2005 survey. Hong Kong and Macao were added to the 98 cities selected, since they have been considered as independent countries for many years and have high percentages of Internet users.

The rationale for selecting the largest municipalities stems from the e-governance literature, which continues to suggest a positive relationship between population and e-governance capacity at the local level (Moon, 2002; Moon & deLeon, 2001; Musso, Weare, & Hale, 2000; Weare, Musso, & Hale 1999). In 2003, the most populated city in each country was identified using various data sources. In cases where the city population data that were obtained utilized a source dated before 2000, a new search was done for the most recent population figures. All city population data were updated to reference 2000-2005 figures.

Six countries that were identified in 2003 do not have online populations of over 160,000. These countries and their most populated cities are: Manama, Bahrain; Port Louis, Mauritius; Port-of-Spain, Trinidad & Tobago; Asuncion, Paraguay;

Sarajevo, Bosnia; and Havana, Cuba. Of these six cities, only five were surveyed, with Havana having an unidentified official government Web site. As none of the five surveyed cities listed above was ranked in the top 25th percentile of rankings, their exclusion from the 2005 worldwide survey was not found to be significant enough to retain. The six new cities are: Abidjan, Cote d'Ivoire; Accra, Ghana; Chisinau, Moldova; Omdurman, Sudan; Halab, Syria; and Libya, Tripoli. In 2003, 80 of the 100 cities identified were surveyed (by two surveyors) and were included in the overall rankings. For the 2005 data, 81 of the 100 cities were included in the overall rankings, excluding municipalities where no official Web site was obtainable. Table 3 is a list of the 100 cities selected.

Table 3. One-hundred cities selected by continent (2005)

Africa (14)		
Abidjan (Cote d'Ivoire)*	Casablanca (Morocco)*	Lome (Togo)*
Accra (Ghana)*	Dakar (Senegal)*	Nairobi (Kenya)
Algiers (Algeria)*	Dar-es-Salaam (Tanzania)*	Omdurman (Sudan)*
Cairo (Egypt)	Harare (Zimbabwe)*	Tunis (Tunisia)*
Cape Town (South Africa)	Lagos (Nigeria)	
Asia (31)		
Almaty (Kazakhstan)*	Hong Kong SAR (Hong Kong)	Quezon City (Philippines)
Amman (Jordan)	Istanbul (Turkey)	Riyadh (Saudi Arabia)
Baku (Azerbaijan)*	Jakarta (Indonesia)	Seoul (Republic of Korea)
Bangkok (Thailand)	Jerusalem (Israel)	Shanghai (China)
Beirut (Lebanon)	Karachi (Pakistan)	Singapore (Singapore)
Bishkek (Kyrgyzstan)*	Kuala Lumpur (Malaysia)	Tashkent (Uzbekistan)
Colombo (Sri Lanka)	Kuwait City (Kuwait)*	Tehran (Iran)
Dhaka (Bangladesh)	Macao SAR (Macao)	Tripoli (Libya)*
Dubai (United Arab Emirates)	Mumbai (India)	Tokyo (Japan)
Halab (Syria)*	Muscat (Oman)*	
Ho Chi Minh (Vietnam)	Nicosia (Cyprus)	
Europe (34)		
Amsterdam (Netherlands)	Kiev (Ukraine)	Rome (Italy)
Athens (Greece)	Lisbon (Portugal)	Sofia (Bulgaria)
Belgrade (Serbia and Montenegro)	Ljubljana (Slovenia)	Stockholm (Sweden)
Berlin (Germany)	London (United Kingdom)	Tallinn (Estonia)
Bratislava (Slovak Republic)	Luxembourg City (Luxembourg)	Vienna (Austria)
Brussels (Belgium)	Madrid (Spain)	Vilnius (Lithuania)
Bucharest (Romania)	Minsk (Belarus)	Warsaw (Poland)
Budapest (Hungary)	Moscow (Russian Federation)	Zagreb (Croatia)
Chisinau (Moldova)	Oslo (Norway)	Zurich (Switzerland)
Copenhagen (Denmark)	Paris (France)	
Dublin (Ireland)	Prague (Czech Republic)	
Helsinki (Finland)	Reykjavik (Iceland)	
	Riga (Latvia)	

continued on following page

Table 3. continued

North America (10)		
Mexico City (Mexico) Guatemala City (Guatemala) Kingston (Jamaica)* New York (United States)	Panama City (Panama) San Jose (Costa Rica) San Salvador (El Salvador) Santo Domingo (Dominican Republic)*	Tegucigalpa (Honduras) Toronto (Canada)
South America (9)		
Buenos Aires (Argentina) Caracas (Venezuela) Guayaquil (Ecuador)	La Paz (Bolivia) Lima (Peru) Montevideo (Uruguay)	Santa Fe De Bogota (Colombia) Santiago (Chile) Sao Paulo (Brazil)
Oceania (2)		
Auckland (New Zealand)	Sydney (Australia)	

* Official city Web sites unavailable

Findings and Longitudinal Assessment

The rankings in Table 4 reflect the top twenty municipalities in overall score based on the five e-governance component categories. The highest possible score for any one city Web site is 100. Seoul received a score of 81.70, the highest ranked city Web site for 2005. Seoul's Web site was also the highest ranked in 2003, with a score of 73.48. New York City had the second highest ranked municipal Web site, with a score of 72.71. New York City moved up two places from its fourth place ranking in 2003. Similarly, Shanghai, China moved up two places in ranking since 2003, with the third ranked score of 63.93 in 2005. Hong Kong and Sydney, Australia complete the top five ranked municipal Web sites with scores of 61.51 and 60.82, respectively. Hong Kong was also ranked in the top five in 2003; however, Sydney significantly increased its score and ranking from 2003 (ranked 19th with a score of 37.41).

Privacy and security results indicate that Seoul, Sydney, Zurich, New York, and Hong Kong are top ranked cities in the category of privacy and security. New to the top five are Sydney and Zurich. Sydney was ranked 11th in 2003 with a score of 6.79, but has improved to 2nd overall with a score of 16.80 in 2005. Zurich was ranked 20th in 2003 with a score of 3.57, but has improved to 3rd overall with a score of 16.40 in 2005. The average score in this category is 4.17, an increase from a score of 2.53 in 2003. Thirty-one cities evaluated earned 0 points in this category, a decrease in the total number of municipalities that earned 0 points in 2003 (36). Many cities still have not properly understood the importance of a privacy and security policy, a very important deficiency in the development of digital governance.

Usability results indicate that New York, Shanghai, Seoul, Sydney and Riga are top ranked cities in the category of usability. New to the top five are New York, Sydney and Riga. New York was ranked 11th in 2003 with a score of 15.63, but has improved to 1st overall with a score of 19.06 in 2005. Sydney was ranked 34th in 2003 with a score of 12.19, but has improved to 4th overall with a score of 17.81 in 2005. Riga was ranked 51st in 2003 with a score of 10.00, but has improved to 5th overall with a score of 17.50 in 2005. The average score in this category is 12.42, an increase from a score of 11.45 in 2003. One of the best practices in the category of usability is New York, scoring 19.06. The Web sites for New York are very "user-friendly." For example, all pages use consistent color, formatting, "default colors," and underlined text to indicate links. There are consistent uses of navigation bars and links to the homepage on every page. The Web sites contain very advanced forms, allowing citizens to submit pertinent information.

Results for content indicate that Seoul, New York, Tallinn, Zurich, Hong Kong, and Riga are top ranked cities in the category of content. New to the top five are Tallinn, Zurich, and Riga. Tallinn was ranked 6th in 2003 with a score of 12.55, but has improved to 3rd overall with a score of 14.79 in 2005. Zurich was ranked 28th in 2003 with a score of 7.66, but has improved to 4th overall with a score of 13.96 in 2005. Riga was ranked 51st in 2003 with a score of 4.26, but has improved to 5th overall with a score of 13.75 in 2005. The average score for the top five cities has only slightly increased from 2003. The average score for the top five ranked cities in 2005 is 14.66, while the average score for the top five ranked cities in 2003 was 14.08. However the overall average increase for this category is second largest of the five categories. The average score in this category is 7.63, an increase from a score of 6.43 in 2003.

The results for online services indicate that Seoul, New York, Singapore, Hong Kong, and Warsaw are the top ranked cities in the category of online services. New to the top five are New York and Warsaw. New York was ranked 6th in 2003 with a score of 12.28, but has improved to 2nd overall with a score of 15.76 in 2005. Warsaw was ranked 62nd in 2003 with a score of 1.93, but has improved to 5th overall with a score of 11.86 in 2005. The average score in this category is 5.32, an increase from a score of 4.82 in 2003. Only two cities evaluated earned 0 points in this category, a decrease from the three municipalities that earned 0 points in 2003. The average score for the top five ranked cities in 2005 is 14.51, while the average score for the top five ranked cities in 2003 was 13.69.

The results for citizen participation indicate that Seoul, Warsaw, Bratislava, London, and Prague are the top ranked cities in the category of privacy and security. New to the top five are all of those cities except Seoul, which repeats as the top ranked city in the category. Warsaw was ranked 74th in 2003 with a score of 0.00, but has improved to 2nd overall with a score of 12.55 in 2005. Bratislava was not ranked in 2003, but has received a 3rd overall ranking with a score of 10.91 in 2005. London was ranked 51st in 2003 with a score of 1.54, but has improved to 4th overall with a score of 10.55 in 2005. Prague was not ranked in 2003 but has received a 5th overall ranking with a score of 10.18 in 2005. The average score in this category is 3.57, an increase from a score of 3.26 in 2003. The category of citizen participation resulted in the smallest overall increase in performance. This can be attributed in part to the additional questions added to the survey instrument to better survey citizen participation online. However, the results can also be attributed, in part, to the lack of support for such online practices.

Table 4. Top 20 cities in digital governance (2005)

Ranking	City	Score	Privacy	Usability	Content	Service	Participation
1	Seoul	**81.70**	17.60	17.81	16.04	16.61	13.64
2	New York	**72.71**	16.00	19.06	14.79	15.76	7.09
3	Shanghai	**63.93**	12.00	18.75	13.13	11.69	8.36
4	Hong Kong	**61.51**	15.60	16.25	13.75	13.73	2.18
5	Sydney	**60.82**	16.80	17.81	12.50	8.98	4.73
6	Singapore	**60.22**	10.40	15.94	11.67	14.58	7.64
7	Tokyo	**59.24**	12.00	16.25	12.29	10.34	8.36
8	Zurich	**55.99**	16.40	14.69	13.96	9.49	1.45
9	Toronto	**55.10**	11.20	14.06	11.46	9.83	8.55
10	Riga	**53.95**	6.80	17.50	13.75	6.44	9.45
11	Warsaw	**53.26**	0.00	15.31	13.54	11.86	12.55
12	Reykjavik	**52.24**	11.60	13.13	13.54	10.34	3.64
13	Sofia	**49.11**	8.00	13.44	11.67	7.46	8.55
14	Prague	**47.27**	0.00	16.88	10.21	10.00	10.18
15	Luxembourg	**46.58**	7.20	15.31	11.88	7.29	4.91
16	Amsterdam	**46.44**	10.40	12.50	9.79	5.93	7.82
17	Paris	**45.49**	8.80	15.94	11.46	4.75	4.55
18	Macao	**45.48**	10.40	13.44	13.13	5.42	3.09
19	Dublin	**44.10**	8.00	16.88	11.04	4.92	3.27
20	Bratislava	**43.65**	0.00	15.94	11.04	5.76	10.91

Table 5. Top 10 cities in privacy and security (2005)

Rank	City	Country	Score
1	Seoul	Republic of Korea	17.60
1	Sydney	Australia	16.80
3	Zurich	Switzerland	16.40
4	New York	United States	16.00
5	Hong Kong	Hong Kong	15.60
6	Rome	Italy	13.20
7	Berlin	Germany	12.80
8	Shanghai	China	12.00
8	Tokyo	Japan	12.00
10	Reykjavik	Iceland	11.60

Table 6. Top 10 cities in usability (2005)

Rank	City	Country	Score
1	New York	United States	19.06
2	Shanghai	China	18.75
3	Seoul	Republic of Korea	17.81
3	Sydney	Australia	17.81
5	Riga	Latvia	17.50
6	Oslo	Norway	17.19
7	Dublin	Ireland	16.88
7	Prague	Czech Rep.	16.88
7	Jerusalem	Israel	16.88
10	Hong Kong	Hong Kong	16.25

Table 7. Top 10 cities in content (2005)

Rank	City	Country	Score
1	Seoul	Republic of Korea	16.04
2	New York	United States	14.79
2	Tallinn	Estonia	14.79
4	Zurich	Switzerland	13.96
5	Riga	Latvia	13.75
5	Hong Kong	Hong Kong	13.75
7	Warsaw	Poland	13.54
7	Reykjavik	Iceland	13.54
9	Shanghai	China	13.13
9	Macao	Macao	13.13

Table 8. Top 10 cities in service delivery (2005)

Rank	City	Country	Score
1	Seoul	Republic of Korea	16.61
2	New York	United States	15.76
3	Singapore	Singapore	14.58
4	Hong Kong	Hong Kong	13.73
5	Warsaw	Poland	11.86
6	Shanghai	China	11.69
7	Tokyo	Japan	10.34
7	Reykjavik	Iceland	10.34
9	Prague	Czech Rep.	10.00
10	Toronto	Canada	9.83

Table 9. Top 10 cities in citizen participation (2005)

Rank	City	Country	Score
1	Seoul	Republic of Korea	13.64
2	Warsaw	Poland	12.55
3	Bratislava	Slovak Republic	10.91
4	London	United Kingdom	10.55
5	Prague	Czech Rep.	10.18
6	Riga	Latvia	9.45
7	Toronto	Canada	8.55
7	Sofia	Bulgaria	8.55
9	Shanghai	China	8.36
9	Tokyo	Japan	8.36

The comparisons between the findings from the 2003 evaluation and the findings of the 2005 evaluation indicate an overall average score increase from 28.49 in 2003 to 33.11 in 2005. This would be the expectation for municipalities increasingly seeking ways to utilize technology to increase effectiveness and efficiency. The Internet is an ideal medium for meeting such goals. Table 10 highlights these increases by continent. All six identified regions have collectively improved in their e-governance performance.

The results, when analyzed by Organization for Economic Cooperation and Development (OECD) and non-OECD member countries, highlight a growing gap between the two groups. In all, 30 countries represent OECD member countries, and the

Table 10. Average score by continent for 2005 and 2003

	Oceania	Europe	Average	Asia	North America	Africa	South America
2005 Overall Averages	49.94	37.17	33.11	33.05	30.21	24.87	20.45
2003 Overall Averages	46.01	30.23	28.49	30.38	27.42	17.66	20.05

largest municipality for each of these countries was evaluated and included in the results. Fifty-one non-OECD member countries are also included in the evaluations. Seoul, Korea was the highest ranked municipality for OECD member countries and Shanghai, China was the highest ranked municipality for non-OECD member countries. OECD member countries have a combined average of 44.35, well above the overall average for all municipalities, 33.11. Non-OECD member countries have an overall average of 26.50. The increase for OECD member countries from 2003 was 8.01 points, and for non-OECD member countries there was an increase of only 2.24 from 2003. More importantly, the gap between OECD and non-OECD member countries increased since the 2003 evaluation. The difference in 2003 between the average scores of OECD and non-OECD member countries was 12.08. Based on the 2005 evaluations, the gap has increased to 17.85. The increase in the overall average of scores has been predominately a result of OECD member countries improving overall municipal Web site performance. The following Figure 1 reflects the average scores of OECD member and nonmember countries, as well as the average score

Figure 1. Average score by e-governance categories in OECD member and non-member countries (2005)

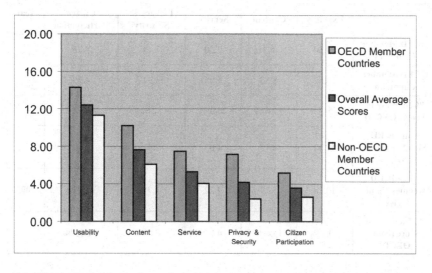

for each of the five e-governance categories. The figure highlights the gap between OECD member and nonmember countries across all categories.

On further research, it has been found that the digital divide between the OCED and non-OCED member countries varies across the five established criteria as shown in Table 11. The most significant gap has been recorded in the areas of service, privacy, and citizen participation. Overall, OCED member countries have shown a higher percentage of increase in all areas except usability. In the area of usability, non-OCED member countries increased 10.1% in average score, while OCED member countries had a minimal increase of 5%. However, the OCED member countries showed significant increase in scores in the areas of privacy and service with 82% and 26% change, respectively. The percent change for non-OECD member countries in the same e-government categories were only 36.4% and -4.5 %. This comparison sheds light on the significance of investment in e-government infrastructure involving privacy and security to sustain the e-government mechanisms in OCED countries, while the need for increased investment in non-OECD member countries. Moreover the negative average score changes for citizen participation (-2.95%) and services (-4.5 %) among non-OCED member countries signify that Web presence alone will not indicate an increase in performance, but rather non-OCED member countries may need to develop a comprehensive policy that addresses the unique e-government requirements of individual countries and help in bridging the digital divide.

Specific increases in the five e-governance categories have been discussed above, but it is important to note that the most significant improvement in average score is in the area of privacy and security. Municipalities have recognized Web site security and

Table 11. Variations in OCED and non-OCED member countries

	Usability	Content	Service	Privacy & Security	Citizen Participation	Year
OCED Member Countries	14.30	10.21	7.50	7.17	5.18	**2005**
OCED Member Countries	13.62	8.55	5.95	3.94	4.29	**2003**
% Increase in Score (OECD)	5 %	19.4 %	26.0 %	82 %	20.7 %	
Non-OCED Member Countries	11.32	6.12	4.03	2.41	2.63	**2005**
Non-OCED Member Countries	10.28	5.29	4.22	1.77	2.71	**2003**
% Increase in Score (Non-OECD)	10.1 %	15.6 %	- 4.5 %	36.4 %	- 2.95 %	

Table 12. Average score by e-governance categories in 2005 and 2003

	Usability	Content	Service	Privacy & Security	Citizen Partici-pation
2005 Average Scores	12.42	7.63	5.32	4.17	3.57
2003 Average Scores	11.45	6.43	4.82	2.53	3.26

Table 13. Change in rank between 2003 and 2005 evaluations

Ranking	City	Country	2003	2005	Rank (2003)	Rank 2005	Change in Rank
1	Seoul	Korea	73.48	81.70	1	1	**0**
2	New York	United States	61.35	72.71	4	2	**+2**
3	Shanghai	China	58.00	63.93	5	3	**+2**
4	Hong Kong	Hong Kong	66.57	61.51	2	4	**-2**
5	Sydney	Australia	37.41	60.82	19	5	**+14**
6	Singapore	Singapore	62.97	60.22	3	6	**-3**
7	Tokyo	Japan	46.52	59.24	9	7	**+2**
8	Zurich	Switzerland	28.59	55.99	35	8	**+27**
9	Toronto	Canada	46.35	55.10	10	9	**+1**
10	Riga	Latvia	17.12	53.95	62	10	**+52**

citizen privacy as key components to effective and efficient Web sites. The category with the smallest increase in average score is citizen participation. Municipalities still have not found that citizen participation in government is a critical component for online functions. Table 12 highlights these findings.

In addition, some of the changes in the individual municipal rankings from 2003 to 2005 are of note. Table 13 shows the rankings of the top 10 municipalities based on the 2005 evaluations, as well as their change in ranking position. In general, Web sites would not be expected to decrease in score or ranking significantly, as a reduction or elimination in Web site services and functions is not common practice. For the most part, ranking changes were three places or less; however, there are significant changes in a few Web sites that have improved over the two years between evaluations. Those Web sites that have improved their Web sites significantly, as is apparent by their increase in overall ranking, are Sydney, Zurich, and

Riga. Sydney moved up 14 places in ranking to a 5th place ranking in 2005. Zurich moved up 27 places to 8th overall. Riga represented the most significant increase in rankings from those municipal Web sites evaluated in 2003. Riga moved up 52 places to 10th overall in the 2005 evaluation.

Conclusion

The study of municipal e-governance practices throughout the world is an area that clearly requires ongoing research. Our studies in 2003 and 2005 have produced findings that contribute to the e-governance literature, in particular in the areas of Web site privacy/security, usability, content, services, and citizen participation. The 2005 study highlights the increased attention spent on privacy and security and the need for further attention in the area of citizen participation via municipal Web sites.

In addition, the gap between OECD and non-OECD member countries in average scores has increased since 2003. Although overall average scores have improved for non-OECD member countries, they have not done so at the rate of OECD member countries. As we concluded in 2003, since there is a gap between developed and less-developed countries, it is very important for international organizations such as the UN and cities in advanced countries to attempt to bridge the digital divide. We recommend developing a comprehensive policy for bridging that divide. That comprehensive policy should include capacity building for municipalities, including information infrastructure, content, and applications and access for individuals.

With the growing research and development of e-governance emerging throughout the world, as well as the importance of information and communication technologies, we expect that the gap discussed above will be begin to close. The continued study of municipalities worldwide, with a third evaluation planned in 2007, will further provide insight into the direction of e-governance and the performance of e-governance throughout regions of the world. This second study of worldwide digital governance has allowed for initial assessments in the direction of e-governance performance via a two-year comparison. With forthcoming studies, already in the planning, the data will become critical in evaluating whether the gaps highlighted hear continue to increase. Moreover, every region has examples of best practices for overall performance and in each specific e-governance category. As municipalities seek to increase their municipal Web site performance, searching within their region offers opportunities to identify e-governance benchmarks. Those municipalities that serve as top performers in their respective regions can then look at the top-ranked cities in municipalities throughout the world. Although the 2005 study highlights increases in e-governance performance throughout the world, continuous improvement should be the norm for every municipality.

Acknowledgment

We are grateful for the work and assistance of research staffs in the E-Governance Institute/ National Center for Public Productivity at Rutgers, the State University of New Jersey, Campus at Newark, and the Global e-Policy e-Government Institute at Sungkyunkwan University. We would also like to express our deepest thanks for their contributions to the evaluators who participated in this project. A complete listing of names can be found at http://www.andromeda.rutgers.edu/~egovinst/Website/

References

Accenture. (2002). eGovernment leadership: Realizing the vision. *The Government Executive Series*. Retrieved September 9, 2006, from http://www.accenture.com/Global/Services/By_Industry/Government/R_and_I/EGovVision.htm

Accenture (2004). eGovernment leadership: High performance, maximum value. *The Government Executive Series*. Retrieved September 9, 2006, from http://www.accenture.com/Global/Services/By_Industry/Government/R_and_I/

Arterton, F. C. (1987). *Can technology protect democracy?* Newbury Park: SAGE Publications.

Arterton, F. C. (1988). Political participation and teledemocracy. *PS: Political Science and Politics, 21*(3), 620-626.

Becker, T. (1993). Teledemocracy: Gathering momentum in state and local governance. *Spectrum: The Journal of State and Government, 66*(2), 14-19.

Bellamy, C., & Taylor, J. A. (1998). *Governing in the information age*. Buckingham: Open University Press.

Browning, G. (2002). *Electronic democracy: Using the internet to transform American politics*. Medford: CyberAge Books.

Bryan, C., Tsagarousianou, R., & Tambini, D. (1998). Electronic democracy and the civic networking movement in context. In R. Tsagarousianou, D. Tambini, & C. Bryan, *Cyber democracy: Technology, cities, and civic networks* (pp. 1-17). New York: Routledge.

Capgemini. (2005) Online availability of public services: How is Europe progressing? *European Commission Report*. Retrieved September 7, 2006, from http://www.capgemini.com/news/2005/Online_availibility_of_public_services_5th_measurement.pdf

Christopher, A. F. (1987). *Teledemocracy: Can technology protect democracy?* Newbury Park: SAGE Publications.

Cloete, F. (2003). Assessing governance with electronic policy management tools. *Public Performance & Management Review, 26*(3), 276-290.

Eggers, W. D. (2005). *Government 2.0: Using technology to improve education, cut red tape, reduce gridlock, and enhance democracy.* New York: Rowan & Littlefield Publishers, Inc.

Gattiker, U. E. (2001). *The Internet as a diverse community: Cultural, organizational, and political issues.* Mahwah, NJ: Lawrence Erlbaum.

Giga Consulting. (2000). *Scorecard analysis of the New Jersey department of treasury.* Unpublished report to the NJ Department of Treasury.

Holzer, M., & Kim, S.-T. (2004). *Digital governance in municipalities worldwide.* Newark, NJ: National Center for Public Productivity. Retrieved July 5, 2006, from http://www.andromeda.rutgers.edu/~egovinst/Website/Report%20-%20Egov.pdf

Horrigan, J. B. (2004). *How Americans get in touch with government: Internet users benefit from the efficiency of e-government, but multiple channels are still needed for citizens to reach agencies and solve problems.* Washington, DC: Pew Internet & American Life Project.

Howard, M. (2001, August). e-Government across the globe: How will "e" change Government? *Government Finance Review,* 6-9.

Kamarck, E. C., & Nye, J. S., Jr. (Eds.). (1999). *Democracy.com? Governance in a networked world.* Hollis: Hollis Publishing.

Kamarck, E. C., & Nye, J. S., Jr. (Eds.), (2003). *Governance.com: Democracy in the information age.* Washington, DC: Brookings Institution Press.

Kaylor, C., Deshazo, R., & Van Eck, D. (2001). Gauging e-government: A report on implementing services among American cities. *Government Information Quarterly, 18,* 293-307.

Korac-Kakabadse, A., & Korac-Kakabadse, N. (1999). Information technology's impact on the quality of democracy: Reinventing the 'democratic vessel.' In R. Heeks (Ed.), *Reinventing government in the information age: International practice in IT-enabled public sector reform.* London: Routledge.

Loader, B. D. (Ed.). (1997). *The governance of cyberspace: Politics, technology and global restructuring.* London: Routledge.

Malina, A. (1999). Perspectives on citizen democratisatin and alienation in the virtual public sphere. In B. N. Hague & B. D. Loader (Eds.), *Digital democracy: Discourse and decision making in the information age.* London: Routledge.

McLean, I. (1989). *Democracy and the new technology.* Cambridge: Polity Press.

Melitski, J., Holzer, M., Kim, S.-T., Kim, C.-G.., & Rho, S. Y. (2005). Digital government worldwide: An e-government assessment of municipal Web-sites. *International Journal of E-Government Research, 1*(1), 1-19.

Moon, M. J. (2002). The evolution of e-government among municipalities: Rhetoric or reality? *Public Administration Review, 62*(4), 424-433.

Moon, M. J., & deLeon, P. (2001). Municipal reinvention: Municipal values and diffusion among municipalities. *Journal of Public Administration Research and Theory, 11*(3), 327-352.

Musso, J., Weare, C., & Hale, M. (2000). Designing Web technologies for local governance reform: Good management or good democracy. *Political Communication, 17*(l), 1-19.

Skrzycki, C. (2003a, January 23). U.S. opens online portal to rulemaking; Web site invites wider participation in the regulatory process. *The Washington Post*, p. E01.

Skrzycki, C. (2003b, October 28). Idea of electronic rulemaking boots up slowly. *The Washington Post*, p. E01.

Shane, P. M. (2002, September 20-22). *The electronic federalist: The internet and the eclectic institutionalization of democratic legitimacy.* Paper Presented at the Prospects for Electronic Democracy Conference, Carnegie Mellon University, Pittsburgh, Pennsylvania.

United Nations Online Network in Public Administration (UNPAN). (2003). *United Nations global e-government survey.* Retrieved September 7, 2006, from http://www.unpan.org/egovernment3.asp

United Nations Online Network in Public Administration (UNPAN). (2004). *United Nations global e-government readiness report.* Retrieved September 7, 2006, from http://www.unpan.org/egovernment4.asp

United Nations Online Network in Public Administration (UNPAN). (2005). *United Nations global e-government readiness report.* Retrieved September 7, 2006, from http://www.unpan.org/dpepa-egovernment%20readiness%20report.asp

Weare, C. J., Musso, & Hale, M. (1999). Electronic democracy and the diffusion of municipal Web pages in California. *Administration and Society, 31*(1), 3-27.

West, D.M. (2001). *WMRC e-government survey.* Retrieved March 16, 2006, from http://www.insidepolitics.org/egovt01int.html

West, D. M. (2004). *Global e-government survey.* Retrieved March 16, 2006, from http://www.insidepolitics.org/egovt04int.html

West, D. M. (2005). *Global e-government survey.* Retrieved March 16, 2006, from http://www.insidepolitics.org/egovt05int.pdf

Westen, T. (1998). Can technology save democracy? *National Civic Review, 87*(1), 47-56.

Westen, T. (2000). E-democracy: Ready or not, here it comes. *National Civic Review, 89*(3), 217-227.

Wilhelm, A. G. (1998). Virtual sounding boards: How deliberative is on-line political discussion. *Information, Communication & Society, 1*(3), 313-338.

Witschge, T. (2002, September 22-22). *Online deliberation: Possibilities of the internet for deliberation.* Paper Presented at the Prospects for Electronic Democracy Conference, Carnegie Mellon University, Pittsburgh, Pennsylvania.

World E-Gov Forum. (2007) *Top ten e-government countries 2007.* Retrieved February 28, 2007, from http://www.worldegovforum.com/article.php3?id_article=1367

Chapter V

Local Democracy Online:
An Analysis of Local Government Web Sites in England and Wales*

Lawrence Pratchett, De Montfort University, UK

Melvin Wingfield, De Montfort University, UK

Rabia Karakaya Polat, Isik University, Istanbul

Abstract

This report from the field analyzes the extent to which local authorities in England and Wales have responded to the e-democracy agenda by examining their Web sites and assessing their potential to deliver democracy. The analysis of Web sites provides a powerful insight into how local government is using the Internet to promote democracy. Two aspects of Web site use are particularly significant. First, the analysis reveals the overall commitment to e-democracy in local government, as it is a measure of actual behavior rather than simply an attitudinal survey. Second, it highlights the types of democratic structure being supported and the values being emphasized in the implementation of e-democracy. The research demonstrated that the potential of the Internet for enhancing democracy is not fully exploited by local authorities and there remain considerable variations between different authorities.

Introduction

The idea that information and communication technologies (ICTs) have the capacity to greatly enhance democracy is hardly new. As long ago as 1970, researchers were examining the possibilities and problems of technology-mediated democracy and arguing that democratic engagement could be enhanced through ICTs (Martin & Norman, 1970). It was only in the 1990s, however, with the commercial development of the Internet and its associated technologies, that the possibilities started to translate into reality. Initiatives from as far afield as Canada (Lyon, 1993) and the Netherlands (Schalken & Tops, 1995) experimented with different forms of citizen engagement in local government based primarily on the innovative application of new technologies. For the first time, new technologies were being taken seriously as a potential solution for some of democracy's contemporary problems (cf. Arterton, 1987; Abrahamson, Arterton, & Orren, 1988).[1]

Despite the existence of a range of e-democracy tools and some significant experience of using them in different contexts, the penetration and take-up of e-democracy in England and Wales, as elsewhere, remain limited. It is this gap between the existence of a variety of tools and their take-up that is the main focus of the research reported here. This paper reports on the results of a survey of local government Web sites in England and Wales. The results of a second phase of the project—in-depth interviews with a range of people who have responsibility for or an impact on local government's approach to e-democracy—is described in more detail elsewhere (see Pratchett, Wingfield, & Karakaya-Polat, 2005).

Local government in the United Kingdom has made a significant investment in e-government over the last few years. Supported by the Office of the Deputy Prime Minister through a range of 'national projects' and other devices, e-enabled local government is now considered to be a reality across all local authorities in England and Wales. Among these national projects has been a £4.5 million, 2-year local e-democracy program aimed at "harnessing the power of new technology to encourage citizen participation in local decision-making between election times" (cited in MORI, 2005, p. 9). This research analyzes the extent to which local authorities have responded to the e-democracy agenda by examining their Web sites and assessing their potential to deliver democracy. Consequently, it provides an analysis of e-democracy practice in England and Wales.

E-Democracy Online: A Framework for Analysis

The Web site is a core strategic tool for local authorities. It is a unique medium for communicating information and providing services. In the context of e-democracy, it is also a medium that can be used for encouraging political participation and democratic engagement. The Web site, hence, has a key role in providing channels for political participation and bringing life to the rhetoric of democratic renewal. In this research, the Web site analysis aimed to produce an e-democracy baseline and a first indication of the gap between rhetoric and reality in the e-democracy practices of local government.

Although the analysis of media sources and political documents has a long tradition (Berelson, 1952; Holsti, 1969), analysis of Web sites is a recent area of study within various disciplines. The research interests and specific research questions have differed across disciplines and depending on the purposes of the study. However, many of them start from the properties of the Internet and ask whether or not the examined Web sites exploit these properties. For example, Gibson and Ward (2000), in their analysis of political party Web sites, first identify the properties of the Internet and then ask, "*given* these distinctive properties, what are the particular ways in which we would expect parties to be using the WWW (emphasis added, p. 304)?" This leads to a technology-led evaluation of Web sites. We think that taking the properties of the Internet as "given" is a form of technological determinism. Instead, in this research we asked the following: "Given the importance of participation and democracy in the current political climate and the role of elected local government to engender participation and democracy, how do local authorities use the Internet for democratic purposes?"

Accordingly, the main interest has been to evaluate the capacity of the Web sites to provide opportunities for citizen participation and the extent to which the Web sites provide information about the working of the local democratic system, such as information on elections, elected members, political management and so on. The framework also evaluated their ease of use by looking at features such as search facility or site map.

The Web site analysis is based on a quantitative approach. Although initial Web site analyses were descriptive and anecdotal, more recent studies have taken a more systematic approach. This requires identification of indicators to measure various aspects of Web sites, such as ease of use, information content and interactivity (Gibson & Ward, 2000; Musso et al., 2000). Quantitative studies allow for systematic analyses of political sites. They also enable the researcher to identify trends across time and different cases. The Society of Information Technology Managers (SOCITM), for example, has been conducting a Web survey of all local authorities in the UK since 2000 using more or less similar tools. In this research, we aimed to develop a framework that would enable us to conduct a systematic analysis of local authority Web sites that can be used in the future for the same purpose. What distinguishes this framework from that developed and deployed by SOCITM is its specific emphasis on the democratic devices available (or not) in these Web sites. Therefore, we have not been interested in the capacity of these Web sites in providing services electronically.

Research into local authority Web sites was undertaken using a data collection tool designed to test various elements of what facilitated democratic engagement. The data collection tool consisted of 141 factors which, taken together, represented aspects of democratic practice. The aim of the research was to replicate the experience from the perspective of the average user. Consequently, a research assistant with only a general knowledge of local government was employed to analyze all local authority (i.e., council) Web sites in England and Wales. Using a fast Internet connection within the University, the researcher was asked to spend no longer than 1 minute attempting to find the answer to each question. Our assumption here was that a member of the public, probably using a slower connection than that available within a university, should not be expected to spend longer than 1 minute searching a local government Web site for information that supports the democratic process. The reliability of the research tool was validated by cross-sampling with two other researchers on 10% of the Web sites analyzed. The research was conducted from November to December 2004. All local authorities in England and Wales were included in the sample; therefore, the sample and population was equal (N = 408). There were no questions of an ethical nature to consider given the public access of Web sites.

The research tool was divided into a number of sections, each of which investigates a different component of democracy as it might be offered through a Web site:

- *Maintenance and navigability* is concerned with the general look and feel of the Web site and its accessibility. Questions such as how easily the Web site can be found from a "Google" search and when it was last updated are all standard points of Web site investigation that clarify the value of the Web site to users. From a democratic point of view, citizens should expect a Web site to be easily found and navigated, and for the information on it to be up to date.

- *Information* is a key role of any Web site. From an e-democracy perspective, however, we can expect a good local government Web site to provide basic information on what the council's roles and responsibilities are and how they are organized. Beyond this obvious information, there are also some core documents that might be expected to be available, such as the Council's constitution and so on. These questions test for a selection of core documents rather than for comprehensiveness.

- *Elected members* are clearly central to the way democracy works in local government, so it seems reasonable to expect Web sites to provide extensive information about them. As democracy is an inherently political process, it seems reasonable for the council's Web site to state clearly the political allegiance of council members and the overall political balance of the council: Otherwise, the mechanism of political accountability is severely limited in the online world.

- *Information about elections* is also an important component of the democratic process, so the Web site survey tests for how much information is available on this topic.

- *Political management* processes are clearly central to the day-to-day operation of local democracy. The survey tool asks a number of questions about the way in which political management processes are communicated through the Web site. The rationale behind these questions is to test the transparency of the new political management systems (introduced by the Local Government Act 2000) and the extent to which Web sites are being used to enhance the accountability of these new policy and decision-making structures.

- *Links to other bodies* are important insofar as local democracy is no longer just about elected local government but also about much wider patterns of local governance (cf. Sullivan & Skelcher, 2002; Stoker, 2004). It seems plausible to argue, therefore, that if local authorities are to fulfil their community leadership role and lead on democratizing governance structures, then their Web sites should provide at least some links to key partner organizations.

- *Consultations* are a significant means of ensuring responsiveness to the public. The survey tests the Web sites, therefore, for the range and accessibility of both online and off-line consultation activities that local authorities might be engaged in. While these consultations are not necessarily about democracy, they are, nevertheless, a good proxy for the openness of the council towards public engagement.

- *Online discussion* forums are a widely recognized form of providing a greater voice for the public. While opinion is divided on their value to the democratic process (see, e.g., Wilhelm, 2000), again, they provide a good measure of councils' willingness to engage with the public.

Chart 1. Maintenance and navigability

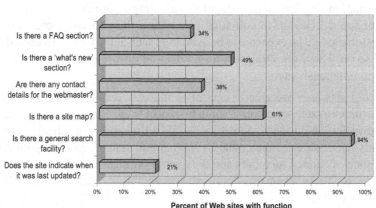

The analysis of Web sites provides a powerful insight into how local government is using the Internet to promote democracy. Two aspects of Web site use are particularly significant. First, the analysis can reveal the overall commitment to e-democracy in local government, as it is a measure of actual behavior rather than simply an attitudinal survey. Second, it can highlight the types of democratic structures being supported and the values being emphasized in the implementation of e-democracy. Although some of the questions offered in this framework are specific to UK local government, the overarching framework is of more generic value to the analysis of e-democracy in any local government context.

Findings From the Analysis

The analysis of Web sites reveals a sophisticated picture of how e-democracy is developing among local authorities in England and Wales. This main section reports the findings from the analysis, organized around the key features of the framework.

Maintenance and Navigability

Maintenance and navigability are important from a democratic perspective because they indicate how much emphasis is put on accessibility to the Web site across the community. Thus, the existence of a site map, an indication of when the site was last updated and so on (all of which are "good practice" on Web design) all provide some idea of how serious the local authority is about using the Web site as a tool for community engagement.

Even at the most basic level, many local government Web sites failed to meet these expectations. As Chart 1 shows, only 21% of Web sites indicated when the site had last been updated. This indicator might not be directly related to democratic practice, but it is related to ease of use of sites which, in turn, it could be argued, is necessary for democratic engagement. Only 38% provided contact details for the Webmaster, while less than half offered a "what's new" section as part of the Web site. In terms of maintenance, therefore, many local government Web sites remain poor. However, on a more positive note, a significant majority of Web sites provided good navigability. More than 60% offered a site map, while 94% of Web sites had a general search facility allowing users to search for their area of interest.

In many respects, these findings match earlier analyses of local government Web sites (see e.g., SOCITM, 2004), which show that the degree of "professionalization" and quality of Web sites vary considerably. This finding is not only true of local government Web sites in the UK, but is also repeated in relation to local government Web sites in other European countries and, indeed, even in relation to some national

Chart 2. Basic information

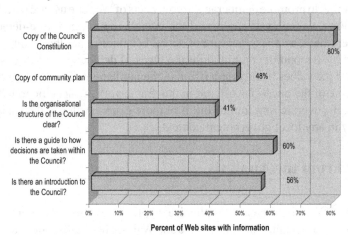

parliamentary Web sites within the European Union (Trechsel, Kies, Mendez, & Schmitter, 2002).

Basic Information

Maintenance and navigability, of course, provide only partial insight into how councils are attempting to communicate with the public. The basic information the Web site makes available is another and, arguably more significant, means of assessing the democratic intentions of the Council. The questions in this section were designed particularly to take account of the way in which local authorities would try to inform citizens of the basic roles and responsibilities they perform and the fundamentals of the political decision-making structures that exist. This type of information is important because, as the British Social Attitudes (BSA) Survey found, knowledge of local government is, at best, partial among large sections of the community. Nearly half of respondents to the BSA's 1998 survey (admittedly before most local authorities had a Web presence) agreed that the council did not keep them well informed about the services it provides (DETR, 1999). This finding is backed up by research for the Scottish Executive in 1999, which found that citizens in Scotland do not feel well informed about local services or local government more generally (Scottish Executive, 1999). Furthermore, the BSA survey found worryingly low levels of knowledge about local politics among citizens: Only 14% of respondents claimed to know the name of the leader of their local council and only one-third of these respondents were actually able to name that leader correctly (DETR, 1998). This knowledge gap translates into wider political inefficacy at the local level (Rao & Young, 1999).

Chart 3. Political balance

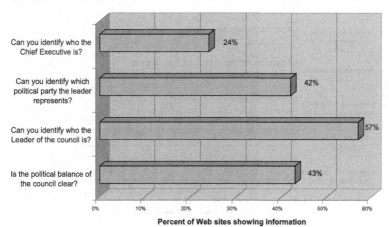

The potential for local government Web sites to narrow this information gap and, thereby, enhance potential engagement in politics is obvious. For them to achieve this goal, however, there is some fundamental information that might be expected to have emerged on local government Web sites as they have been developed over the last few years. As Chart 2 shows, however, much of this information is surprisingly absent from local government Web sites. Only 56% of local authority Web sites included a general introduction to the council. Some 59% of Web sites failed to clearly outline the structure of the council, while 40% failed to include a guide on how decisions were made within the authority. Even the most basic information that might be expected is missing (or is hard to find) in a significant number of cases.

Of more concern, however, was the finding that 57% of authorities failed to show basic information on the political control and balance of the council: that is, which party had control and how many seats each party had. This information seems to be a fundamental component of any democratic institution. Party politics in local government has become a major feature of local democracy, with more local authorities being formally controlled by political parties than ever before (Rallings & Thrasher, 2003). It seems counter intuitive, therefore, that councils should not want to highlight the political features of council members and afford them some prominence on their Web sites—especially in a climate of declining political engagement and concomitant attempts to reinvigorate local politics. As Chart 3 shows, however, there is an absence of clear information on political control and allegiance on many Web sites. The implications of this gap for effective e-democracy are significant. If even the most basic political information is excluded from local government Web sites, or buried to the extent that it is difficult to find for average citizens, then it seems that Web sites not only are failing to rise to the e-democracy challenge but that they may also, in some instances, be militating against effective democratic

Chart 4. Information on elected members

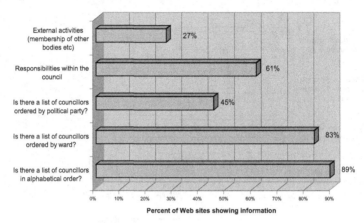

engagement. Failure to provide this basic information on a Web site may not only reflect an information gap but may actively discourage interested citizens from becoming more engaged when they discover that they cannot find the information they feel they need on the Web site.

It should be noted that in some instances the information on political balance could be obtained by looking at a list of council members and then counting the number of seats each party held. From our perspective, however, we discounted this information from the analysis because it does not specifically indicate political balance and its implications. For example, in hung councils it is not always clear what the coalition is (if it exists at all) simply by counting seats. Furthermore, it should not be assumed that all citizens will know that the majority of seats equates with political control.

Elected Members

The issue of information on elected members follows from the previous point about keeping citizens informed about the political processes of the council. Citizens not only need to know the political balance and leadership of the council but also who their council member is, their political allegiance and political activities on the council. Indeed, the ability to examine and monitor the political behavior of elected members is one of the big advantages predicted by many in relation to the development of e-democracy (Trechsel et al., 2002). It is somewhat disappointing, therefore, that in many cases identifying elected members was as far as councils appeared willing to go. As Chart 4 shows, on most Web sites there was a list of councillors by name (89%) or by ward (83%). However, on only 45% of Web sites were councillors

Chart 5. Councillors online

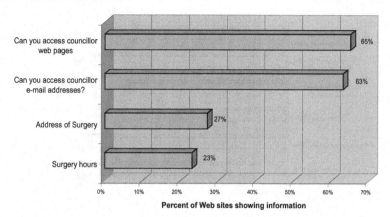

ordered by political party. Of course, this finding is not surprising, given the evidence from Chart 3. However, it does pose some challenging questions about how local authorities are seeking to develop e-democracy if, at the same time, many of them are ignoring or, at best, downplaying the political aspects of the council. What distinguishes local government from other elements of the governance structure is its elected nature based on party politics. Hence, it is difficult to understand why party identities are so weakly represented in local government Web sites.

One of the ways in which the Internet could be used to enhance local democracy is by supporting the relationship between elected members and citizens. This relationship could be enhanced through frequent use of e-mail, online surgeries, councillor Web sites and so on. Chart 5 analyzes the extent to which local authorities are exploiting these features. Two surprising features of the chart are worth emphasizing. First, an encouragingly high number of Web sites offer links to councillor e-mail addresses and councillor Web sites. Some 63% link to councillors' e-mail addresses and 65% to their Web sites. However, it should be noted that a significant proportion of these are personal Web accounts rather than those provided by the council. This difference is significant, because it means that councillor Web sites and e-mail addresses lack both the legitimacy and clarity of council-owned addresses (i.e., with domain names that end with councilname.gov.uk). Members of the public cannot easily predict the name of a councillor's e-mail address or Web site that is not in the council's domain and cannot be certain that their e-mails will be directed exclusively to their councillor when e-mailing a non-council-owned address. Second, very few local government Web sites take the opportunity to provide information on councillor surgeries. Only 27% show surgery locations and even less (23%) provide surgery hours. This finding needs to be matched against the Office of the Deputy Prime Minister (ODPM)'s priority outcomes for local e-government (ODPM, 2004),

Chart 6. Election information

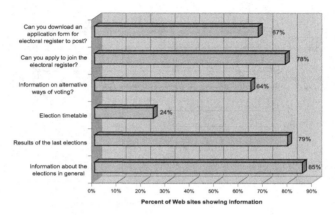

which encourage online surgeries to be developed. Of course, the lack of interest in either of these forms of communication with citizens reflects the fact that many councillors do not hold surgeries, preferring other means of keeping in contact with their ward constituents (cf. Copus, 2004; Rao, 2000).

Elections

If information on party politics and councillors is limited, what about information on formal political processes? As Chart 6 shows, councils make extensive use of their Web sites in transmitting the results from previous elections (79%) and discussing elections in general terms (85%). Less use is made, however, of the facility Web sites offer in informing users of the forthcoming election cycle (24%). The research was conducted outside any election period; therefore, there was no imperative on local authorities to discuss the electoral process. An important element of the discussions on e-democracy focuses on the provision of alternative ways of voting, including e-voting. Some 64% of Web sites provided information about alternative ways of voting. The Web sites were also commonly used for electoral registration purposes (78%).

Overall, therefore, we conclude that local authorities are generally good at using their Web sites to provide election information.

Chart 7. Cabinet and scrutiny

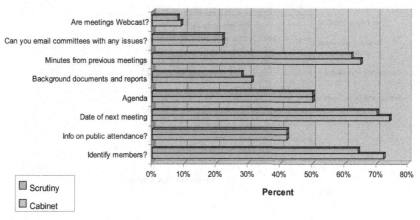

Political Management

The other aspect of local democracy is the extent to which the formal decision-making processes of the council are made more transparent through the Web site. One of the main reasons for reforming the political management processes of local government into a clearer separation of executive and assembly functions was to enhance such transparency (Armstrong, 1999). In exploiting Web sites, it can be expected that good councils will provide detailed information on cabinet and scrutiny functions.[2]

There was evidence of what could be considered good practice in informing Web users of both the time and access to cabinet and scrutiny meetings in many authorities. There was some variability, however, between cabinet and scrutiny. While it was possible to identify cabinet members in 72% of authorities, the corresponding figure for members of scrutiny panels dropped to 64%. Authorities were generally more reticent to use their Web site to inform users of the possibility of attending either cabinet or scrutiny meetings. In both cases, only 42% of authorities used the medium offered by the Web site to inform Web users whether access was possible.

There is obviously scope for authorities to increase the channels of communication by adding e-mail links to members of cabinet/scrutiny, thereby improving communication. Currently, 78% of authorities fail to provide a service whereby cabinet/scrutiny members can be contacted to discuss issues relating to their position.

Chart 8. External links

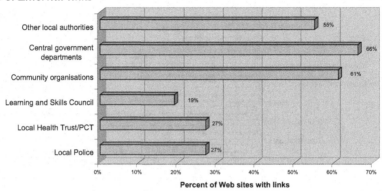

Percent of Web sites with links

Links to Other Bodies

So far, the analysis has concentrated on the internal features of representative democracy in local government. However, as most councillors and officers recognize, local policy-making and decisions are increasingly a feature of a wider process of local governance in which a broad range of partners are necessary to effect changes in the locality. One of the main features of the Internet is its potential for Web sites to help "join up" disparate aspects of local governance (Perri 6, Leat, Seltzer, & Stoker, 2002). However, the reality of this joining up is much more limited. Almost three-quarters of authorities fail to link to either the local Police Authority or the local Health/Primary Care Trust (PCT), even though these bodies are key partners in most local strategic partnerships. Web sites are much more likely to have links to other elected local authorities (especially neighboring) and central government departments than they are to other service providers in the locality.

Consultation

Public engagement through consultation has become a significant part of local government over the last decade and continues to grow in significance, encouraged by best-value performance reviews and the responsiveness components of the Comprehensive Performance Assessment (Lowndes & Wilson, 2001). It seems logical, therefore, that councils should make use of e-democracy tools to support consultation, not least because by 2001, some 52% of local authorities claimed to use an interactive aspect of their Web site to support consultation (Birch, 2002). Our Web site analysis, therefore, applies hard measures to this claim.

Chart 9. Consultation

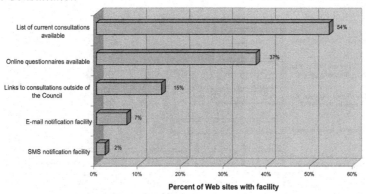

Percent of Web sites with facility

Chart 9 reveals some significant insights into the way local authorities are actually using online consultation, especially when compared with claims they have made to surveys. While 54% of local authorities provide an online list of "live" consultations, online questionnaires were used by just more than one-third of authorities (37%). It must be recognized that authorities may well have used this tool in the past, but during the period of our research none were in use. Consequently, this evidence does not necessarily contradict the Bristol/MORI survey of local authority 'consultation leads' (MORI, 2005), which found that online surveys were conducted by 47% of their respondents, but it does suggest the need to reflect on the limited number of authorities using such tools.

The other interesting feature of Chart 9 is that 15% of Web sites have links to consultations outside of the council. These links include consultations undertaken by other agencies in the area (police, health trusts, learning and skills councils, other local authorities and so on) or in collaboration with them. However, it is difficult to know how to interpret this figure. On the one hand, 15% seems a surprisingly low level of linkage, given that consultation is a key feature of most local agencies' daily life and that almost all local authorities "claim to be working in collaboration with other organizations on schemes to enhance public participation" (Birch, 2002). On the other hand, the fact that some local authorities are making such links is encouraging, suggesting that there is significant scope for local government to act as community leaders in citizen engagement through the effective use of Web sites.

Finally, only a small number of local authorities are actively using new technologies to provoke or promote participation. Only 7% of Web sites offered an option for individuals to be notified of future consultation exercises by e-mail and only 2% offered a similar system by SMS text message. Even among those offering such facilities, the level of innovation was limited: Only half of those offering alert

Chart 10. Online discussion

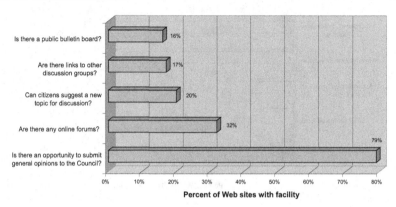

Percent of Web sites with facility

systems allowed citizens to customize the consultation alert according to whether it had significance for their postcode or was in a policy area in which they had a specific interest. Given that such facilities are specified as one of the "good" priority outcomes by the ODPM and are products that the Local e-Democracy National Project are now supporting, it can be expected that this type of facility will expand quickly in local government.

Online Discussion

The final area of interest from the Web survey is the development of discussion forums as a means of providing citizens with an equal opportunity for "voice." For many, the development of various forms of discussion forums is the most promising feature of e-democracy insofar as they provide the opportunity for citizens to engage on their own terms. However, there is also critical literature on such forums, which demonstrates that, in many instances, they do not lead to any form of deliberative engagement but merely provide another opportunity for those with strong views to "talk past each other" (cf. Wilhelm, 2000; Wright, 2004).

Despite the apparent limitations of various discussion forums, Chart 10 shows that a significant number of local authorities do provide such facilities. In 32% of Web sites, there were online discussion forums, some of which provided the opportunity for people to suggest new topics for discussion (20%). The existence of public bulletin boards in 16% of Web sites also supported this trend. However, what is not clear from this analysis is the extent to which these various forums are being used, the degree of moderation involved (if any) and the range of issues being discussed.

Of possibly even greater significance is the extent to which they are being listened to by councillors or officers.

Conclusion

This analysis shows that local government Web sites are already providing many functions that can be deemed a feature of e-democracy. However, there remains much more that they could do. The potential of the Internet for enhancing democracy is not fully exploited by local authorities and there remain considerable variations between different authorities. This conclusion does not necessarily mean that local authorities are not aware of the ways they can use the Internet for democratic purposes. They may be encountering many barriers, such as lack of resources both in terms of human resources and finances.

It is important to recognize the limitations of data collected in this way. The Web site analysis by itself does not tell the full story about the attitudes of local authorities towards using the Internet for democratic purposes. Limited use of the Internet could be related to certain normative arguments against the use of the Internet. Previous research shows that concerns about social exclusion and overrepresentation of certain groups, worries about losing the personal and face-to-face relation with citizens and a *perceived* lack of demand from citizens for e-democracy are important barriers to implementing e-democracy in local authorities (Karakaya, 2005).

Likewise, the Web site analysis by itself cannot reveal whether the available information is made use of by citizens or whether the participation opportunities are used by them. In other words, the research did not examine the extent to which citizens had been using the council Web sites. Local authorities may be abstaining from using their Web sites for democratic purposes if they believe citizens would not be interested anyway.

Despite these limitations, this research provides important insights into the scale and depth of e-democracy in local government. By investigating practice rather than attitudes, the Web site analysis provides a first benchmark of how seriously local authorities in England and Wales are taking e-democracy and where their main strengths and weaknesses lie. The absence of political information on local authority Web sites is particularly instructive and raises significant questions over how serious local governments are about supporting existing institutions of democracy: Much of the e-democracy emphasis appears to seek alternative and individualistic forms of engagement. Of course, this position may change over time as e-democracy matures.

References

Abrahamson, J., Arterton, F.C., & Orren, G.R. (1988). *The electronic commonwealth: The impact of new media technologies on democratic politics.* New York: Basic Books.

Armstrong, H. (2000). The key themes of democratic renewal. In L. Pratchett (Ed.), *Renewing local democracy? The modernisation agenda in British local government.* London: Frank Cass.

Arterton, F.C. (1987). *Teledemocracy: Can technology protect democracy?* New York: Sage.

Barber, B. (1984). *Strong democracy: Participatory politics for a new age.* Berkeley: University of California Press.

Beetham, D. (1996). Theorising democracy and local government. In D. King, & G. Stoker (Eds.), *Rethinking local democracy.* Basingstoke: Macmillan.

Birch, D. (2002). *Public participation in local government: A survey of local authorities.* London: ODPM.

Blair, T. (1998). *Leading the way: A new vision for local government.* London: Institute of Public Policy Research.

Blears, H. (2003). *Communities in control: Public services and local socialism.* London: Fabian Society.

Cochrane, A. (1996). From theories to practice: Looking for local democracy in Britain. In D. King, & G. Stoker (Eds.), *Rethinking local democracy.* Basingstoke: Macmillan.

Coleman, S. (2002). *Hearing voices: The experience of online public consultations and discussions in UK governance.* London: Hansard Society.

Copus, C. (2004). *Party politics and local government.* Manchester: Manchester University Press.

Department of the Environment, Transport and the Regions. (1998). *Modern local government: In touch with the people.* London: DETR.

Department of the Environment, Transport and the Regions. (1999). *1998 British social attitudes survey: Secondary data analysis of the local government module.* Retrieved from http://www.local.dtlr.gov.uk/research/surv1998/04.htm#0301

Department for Transport, Local Government and the Regions. (2001). *Strong local leadership: Quality public services.* London: The Stationery Office.

Hacker K.L., & Dijk, J. (Eds.). (2000). *Digital democracy: Issues of theory and practice.* London: Sage.

Hague, B., & Loader, B. (1999). *Digital democracy: Discourse and decision making in the information age.* London: Routledge.

Held, D. (1996). *Models of democracy: Second edition.* Cambridge: Polity Press.

Horrocks, I., & Pratchett, L. (1995). Electronic democracy: Central themes and issues. In J. Lovenduski, & J. Stanyer (Eds.), *Contemporary political studies 1995.* Newcastle: Political Studies Association.

Horrocks, I., & Webb, J. (1994). Electronic democracy: A policy issue for UK local government? *Local Government Policy Making, 21*(3).

Karakaya, R. (2005). The Internet and democratic local governance: The context of Britain. *International Information and Library Review, 37*(2), 87-97.

Laudon, K. (1977). *Communication technology and democratic participation.* London: Praeger.

Leach, S., & Pratchett, L. (2005). Local government: A new vision, rhetoric or reality? *Parliamentary Affairs, 58*(2), 318-334.

Leigh, I. (2000). *Law, politics and local democracy.* Oxford: Oxford University Press.

Lowndes, V., Pratchett, L., & Stoker, G. (2001). Trends in public participation: Part 1—Local government perspectives. *Public Administration, 79*(1), 205-222.

Lowndes, V., & Wilson, D. (2001). Social capital and local governance: Exploring the institutional design variable. *Political Studies, 49,* 629-647.

Maloney, W., Smith, G., & Stoker, G. (2000). Social capital and urban governance: Adding a more contextualised "top-down" perspective. *Political Studies, 48,* 802-820.

Lyon, D. (1993). *The electronic eye: The rise of the surveillance society.* Cambridge: Polity Press.

Martin, J., & Norman, R.D. (1970). *The computerised society.* London: Prentice Hall.

MORI. (2005). *'What works': Key lessons from recent e-democracy literature.* Retrieved from http://www.e-Democracy.gov.uk

ODPM. (2004). *Defining e-government outcomes for 2005 to support the delivery of priority services & national strategy transformation agenda for local authorities in England.* Retrieved from http://www.odpm.gov.uk/pns/pnattach/20040112/1.doc

Pattie, C., Seyd, P., & Whiteley, P. (2004). *Citizenship in Britain: Values, participation and democracy.* Cambridge: Cambridge University Press.

Perri 6, Leat, D., Seltzer, K., & Stoker, G. (2002). *Towards holistic governance.* Basingstoke: Palgrave Macmillan.

Pratchett, L. (Ed). (2000). *Renewing local democracy? The modernisation agenda in British local government.* London: Frank Cass.

Pratchett, L., & Leach, S. (2003). Local government: Selectivity and diversity. *Parliamentary Affairs, 56*(2), 255-269.

Pratchett, L., & Lowndes, V. (2004). *Developing democracy in Europe: An analytical summary of the Council of Europe's Acquis.* Strasbourg: Council of Europe Publishing.

Pratchett, L., & Wingfield, M. (1996). Petty bureaucracy and woolly-minded liberalism? The changing ethos of local government officers. *Public Administration, 74*(4), 639-656.

Pratchett, L., Wingfield, M., & Karakaya-Polat, R. (2005). *Barriers to e-democracy: Local government experiences and responses.* Retrieved from http://www.dmu.ac.uk/faculties/business_and_law/business/lgru/lgru_research_edemocracy.jsp

Rao, N. (2000). *Reviving local democracy?* Bristol: Policy Press.

Rao, N., & Young, K. (1999). Revitalising local democracy. In R. Jowell, J. Curtice, A. Park, & K. Thomson (Eds.), *British social attitudes: The 16ᵗʰ report—Who shares new labour's values?* Aldershot: Ashgate.

Rallings, C., & Thrasher, M. (2003, September 5). I don't even get out of bed for that. *Local Government Chronicle.*

Saward, M. (2003). Enacting democracy. *Political Studies, 51*(1), 161-179.

Scottish Executive. (1999). *Perceptions of local government: A report of focus group research.* Edinburgh: Scottish Executive Central Research Unit. Retrieved from http://www.scotland.gov.uk/cru/kd01/local-gov-01.htm

Schalken, K., & Tops, P. (1995). Democracy and virtual communities: An empirical exploration of the Amsterdam digital city. In W.B.H.J. van de Donk, I. Snellen, & P. Tops (Eds.), *Orwell in Athens: A perspective on informatization and democracy.* Amsterdam: IOS Press.

Sullivan, H., & Skelcher, C. (2002). *Working across boundaries.* Basingstoke: Palgrave Macmillan.

Stanyer, J. (1976). *Understanding local government.* London: Fontana.

Stoker, G. (2004). *Transforming local governance.* Basingstoke: Palgrave Macmillan.

Stoker, G., & Wilson, D. (2004). *British local government into the 21st century.* Basingstoke: Palgrave Macmillan.

Toffler, A. (1980). *Future shock.* New York: Bantam.

Trechsel, A.H., Kies, R., Mendez, F., & Schmitter, P.C. (2002). *Evaluation of the use of technologies in order to facilitate democracy in Europe: E-democratising the parliaments and parties of Europe.* Retrieved from http://www.cies.iscte.pt/destaques/pdf/1.pdf

van de Donk, W.B.H.J., & Tops, P. (1995). Orwell or Athens? In W. B.H.J. van de Donk, I. Snellen, & P. Tops (Eds.), *Orwell in Athens: A perspective on informatization and democracy.* Amsterdam: IOS Press.

Wilhelm, A. (2000). *Democracy in the digital age.* London: Routledge.

Wilson, D., & Game, C. (2002). *Local government in the United Kingdom.* Basingstoke: Palgrave Macmillan.

Wright, S. (2004). Unpublished thesis, University of East Anglia.

Endnotes

*   This research was sponsored by the UK Office of the Deputy Prime Minister (ODPM) through its Local e-Democracy National Project. We are grateful for permission to use the findings of the research here. We are also grateful to James Waterton for his efforts on Web analysis and to Anne V. Roland for editing the original document.

[1]   For detailed reviews of the early literature on e-democracy (sometimes referred to as digital or tele-democracy) see van de Donk and Tops (1995), Horrocks and Web (1994), Horrocks and Pratchett (1995) *inter alia*. For a summary of some of the recent literature, see MORI (2005).

[2]   The research recognized that there are some exceptions to the cabinet and scrutiny systems.

This work was previously published in International Journal of Electronic Government Research, Vol. 2, Issue 3, edited by D. F. Norris, pp. 75-92, copyright 2006 by IGI Publishing, formerly known as Idea Group Publishing (an imprint of IGI Global).

Chapter VI

User Help and Service Navigation Features in Government Web Sites

Genie N.L. Stowers, San Francisco State University, USA

Abstract

This chapter examines user help and service navigation features in government Web sites and compares them across levels of government. These features are critical to ensuring that users unfamiliar with government are able to successfully and easily access e-government services and information. The research finds clear patterns in the use of similar help and navigation features across governments, leading to a conclusion that these features are diffusing in the public sector Web development field. The chapter concludes by stating that Web developers should work to overcome a second digital divide, one with a lack of knowledge of Web site organization and government structure. Users need to be actively assisted to find information by Web developers.

Introduction

This chapter reports on efforts to make American state, local, and federal e-government portals more user-friendly by providing user help, service navigation, and organizational structures to assist potentially novice users in finding e-government information and services.

Once users have access to the Internet and learn how to use computers, they still have to understand how to navigate Web sites and find the information or services they need. Then, they have to understand how to interact with the Web site so that they can access those services. Governments need to provide more proactive user help features, service navigation features, and organizational structures to actively assist users in finding information and services they desire; otherwise, they create a second digital divide, one between those who understand Web site structure and organization structure and those, who do not. As Hargittai (2003, p. 3) puts it:

many a Web developer wrongly assumes that gaining access to the Internet obliterates any potential inequality that may result from lack of access to the new medium. There are factors beyond mere connectivity that need to be considered when discussing the potential implications of the Internet for inequality. In addition to relying on basic measures of access to a medium, one needs to consider more nuanced measures of use such as user 'skill.' 'Skill' is defined as the ability to locate content online effectively and efficiently.

Usability in Public Sector Web Sites

Today, West (2005) suggests that there is a great degree of variation among the organization and structure of current public sector Web sites and that not all sites are organized in a user-friendly fashion. Indeed, there is little formal focus on these elements and their importance sometimes goes unheeded. Many government portals and Web sites are designed with government workers in mind, not the ordinary users without experience in government or with the use of Internet services.

Bridging the "digital divide" does not mean just making computers themselves accessible but also involves making the Web sites themselves more user-friendly and easy to use by removing barriers due to lack of experience with the Internet (Nielsen, 2000; Rosenfeld & Morville, 1998). Designers and developers of public sector Web sites must assume that those using their sites have limited training and experience and will need sites that are easy to use and designed with usability and effective information architecture in mind. They must also consider that the design lessons developed for private sector e-commerce sites might not necessarily work for public sector sites.

User help, service navigation, and organizational structure are critical features of any public sector main portal that is dedicated to having users find its services and information. The presence or absence of these features on public sector sites can greatly affect the ability of a user to find information and services that might be available on the site and to effectively use those services.

The usability of the e-government portal interface is an important feature of human-computer interaction. To many users, the interface of the main portal is in fact the only important part (Singh & Kotze, 2002). Usability is typically defined as:

The measure of the quality of a user's experience when interacting with a product or system—whether a Web site, a software application, mobile technology, or any user-operated device. Usability is a combination of factors that affects the user's experience with the product or system, including: ease of learning, efficiency of use, memorability, error frequency and severity, and subjective satisfaction. (U.S. Department of Health and Human Services, 2005)

Other factors that can be incorporated into usability include effectiveness, a match between the system and the real world, user control, safety, utility, flexibility, robustness, and consistency and usefulness of navigation (Nielsen, 2000; Singh & Kotze, 2002). We also argue that usability includes adequate help features (including embedded help, interactive help, or manuals) and an information architecture that is descriptive, broad, and shallow enough for users to "click through" rather than relying upon a deep structure (Kitajima, Blackmon, & Polson, 2005, 2000; Nielsen, 2000).

Since the beginning of the World Wide Web, empirical studies have reported variations in usability for government Web sites (Harrison & Petrie, 2007), including low rates of successful information and retrieval (Nielsen, 2000) and wide variation in the lengths of time taken for success (Hargittai, 2003). When Hargittai (2003) tested user ability to find the IRS 1040 tax form (given an unlimited amount of time), 93% could find the form but the time required varied from 30 seconds to almost nine minutes. Of those participating, 60% used a search engine and 40% tried a specific URL. Among the problems encountered, particularly by those who were significantly older and by more recent users, were confusion about URLs and about page design layout.

Jenkins, Corritore, and Wiedenbeck (2003) identify four groups of users who utilized different search strategies based upon their level of expertise in subject matter and with the World Wide Web. Those who were domain, or content, and Web novices searched broadly first but did little evaluations of their findings. Domain experts who were Web novices searched broadly first but were able to evaluate their results more thoroughly for accuracy. Domain and Web experts first looked deeply, utilizing their expertise, and were able to follow those deep trails and evaluate their findings. Those who were experts on both domain and the Web were able to quickly find and identify the information needed.

As Kitajima, Blackmon and Polson (2000) describe it, if a user has a 90% chance of finding and selecting the correct link at each level and there are five levels to go before they can access their desired services or content, the chance of successfully finding that information falls to .53 ($.9^6$) or 53%, rather than the 81% chance of success if there are only two levels to move through.

Users typically seek to improve these odds by being goal driven and focused upon descriptions of content and links that match with their understanding of reality, rather than necessarily utilizing search facilities or navigation aids (Kitajima, Blackmon, & Polson, 2005, 2000). They seek out "information scent," defined as "the imperfect, subjective, perception of the value, cost or access path of information sources obtained from proximal cues, such as Web links, or icons representing the content sources" (Chi, Pirolli, & Pitkow, 2000, p. 2).

Typically, users perform this through a two stage process. The first is an "attention" process where the user seeks to separate a Web page into sections based on labels, layout, and information on the page. To be effective in laying out information scent to guide user behavior, the layout and labels have to be able to direct the user to the appropriate section with labels that make sense for them. The second step is the "action selection" stage where the user decides upon which link to choose. Clearly, here the appropriate labels are crucial to user success. Successful navigation thus requires gaining the user's attention and leading them to the correct selection of the appropriate link at each hierarchical level of the Web site (Blackmon, Kitajima, & Polson, 2005).

For many users seeking online government information, conducting a successful search for information means solving an unfamiliar problem (Blackmon, Kitajima, & Polson, 2005). In essence, they know too little about government and how it is structured to be able to successfully navigate and make link choices on many government Web sites.

There are numerous difficulties with the Web search task, some of them based upon the knowledge of and familiarity with Web site labels themselves. Takeuchi and Kitajima (2002) effectively illustrate that, at the very least, there are gender differences in the understanding of many technical words. These differences are further accentuated when viewed across cultural divisions. Given that there are many other differences in levels of understanding of information and a wide variety of quality in labeling and the laying of information scents, it is clear that government Web designers have a daunting task.

To overcome these many differences in abilities and understanding of how to use the technology and content, Web developers must develop effective site structures that reflect the users' views of the content at that site, not just the organization's own view of itself (such as one based upon the Web designers' own organizational chart) (Nielsen, 2000). In addition, many gaps in user knowledge can also be filled with effective help systems like live chat, online learning and tutorials, online manuals, and well-structured designs which seek to define choices in terms that inexperienced users might know (Shneiderman & Hochheiser, 2001).

Usability features include those which assist the user in finding information, finding services, and in finding their way around the Web site. They include:

- Navigation (features that assist the user in moving around the site).
- Labeling (how the content is labeled, again so that the user knows how to find information).
- Searching systems (the usefulness of the search features) (Rosenfeld & Morville, 1998).
- Visible help features, including a help page, frequently asked questions (FAQs) about the site, site maps (pages that literally provide a map of the entire site), and tutorials on using the site.

This previous research is important in understanding the project reported on here but is still not sufficient to allow us to generate meaningful hypotheses of the more specific topic explored here, user help features. Therefore, the research reported here will be structured around research questions.

Structuring Research Questions about User Help Features

Before we can identify research questions about user help features, we must identify these features. Initially, standard content analysis techniques were used to identify existing user help, navigation, and information architecture features on the Web portals. Agency and government portals were visited, features were identified and categorized, and a comprehensive list was developed. Once the list was developed, each portal in the study was coded as to the presence or absence of each feature.

Table 1 presents the types of user help features identified on government portal sites as well as a brief explanation of each. These include information about the site, an explicit Help section, FAQs, information in other languages, and sitemaps. These features are organized into two sections according to whether or not they would be relatively easy to implement or require few resources. Thus, simple e-mail linkages for contacting the agency, an additional help feature, a feature with more informa-

Table 1. User help features

Feature	Explanation
Easiest and Requires Fewest Resources To Implement	
About the Site	Link to information about the site
Contact Us	Information and links to allow the user to contact the agency for more information or for help with the site
FAQs	Includes answers to Frequently Asked Questions
Feedback	Invites users to give them feedback about the site
Help	Explicit agency- provided help with the site
Index	An index of information, data, and agencies available
Search	Search engine to allow users to search the site
Sitemap	Visual representation of the entire Web site
User Tips	Helpful hints on how users can use the site
More Technically Difficult or Resource-Heavy To Implement	
Live Help	Links to live chat with agency representative to provide assistance
Other Languages	Site provides information in other languages
Text Version	An alternate site is provided in text

tion about the site, user tips, and an e-mail or comment section to provide feedback about the site would be easy to implement. Indices, sitemaps, FAQs, and search engines also would require minimally more work but little technical expertise to implement.

The most reasonable explanation for widespread user help features is that the features which are easiest and cheapest to produce will be utilized most frequently. There is no reason to believe that this pattern would differ across levels of government. Therefore, the first research question is:

R1: User help features requiring the least technical abilities and fewest resources to implement will be found more frequently across all levels of government. The features requiring the most technical abilities and greatest levels of resources to implement will be found least often.

Table 2 provides a listing of the various portal features used to provide users assistance in finding agency online services. These features are not as common as the user help features listed above. They include agency or government calendars leading to information as well as various ways to link to services (e.g., Answers A to Z, Do You Know?, Facilities Locators, Frequently Requested Site, Featured Links, Quick Links, and What's New).

Table 2. Service navigation aid features

Feature	Explanation
Agency information	Listings of all agencies in directory form
Answers A to Z	Alphabetized listings of answers to questions
Calendars	Calendars of government activities and events
Contact Information	Linkages to direct contact information for agencies
Do You Know How I Do ___ ...?	List of questions organized according to major service areas from the citizen's point of view, stating "how do I do x or y?"
E-Government Services	Direct link from home page to all e-government services
Events	Link to information on major events
Facilities Locator	Direct linkage to way to locate government offices
Featured Link/Spotlight	Many sites have featured programs or linkages
Hot Topics	Link to information on what are considered currently important issues
Most Visited/Frequently Requested Site	Links to or listings of the most frequently visited sites, indicating the importance of that information
Popular Services/Major Programs	Highlighting of popular services or major programs
Quick Links	Listing of the commonly asked questions in prominent format
Special Initiatives	Current, new, or special initiatives from the agency
What's new	Listing of new items posted on the site

We already know that well-planned formatting leads to success in finding sought-after information or services (Blackmon, Kitajima, & Polson, 2005) since users seek "information scent," or clues to the information they want (Chi, Pirolli, & Pitkow, 2000). Further, Web site developers can structure a site's portal entryway to separate users into knowledgeable consumers or users who might not know much about government. Thus, they are able to take advantage of the fact that users with experience and expertise typically utilize different strategies to find information (Jenkins, Corritore, & Wiedenbeck, 2003). Different agencies have used these principles to structure entry into their Web sites in different ways. This information can be used to structure service navigation schemes or the overall information organization of the entire Web portal.

This research is clearly exploratory and there are few theoretical or practical reasons to distinguish one type of service navigation scheme from another. In fact, there is no clear difference in the amount of level of technical expertise or resources needed to develop each scheme; they are just different ways of conceptualizing services and setting up the information scent discussed above. However, the simplest service navigation schemes are the ones which provide only basic description and require no reconceptualization (e.g., E-Government Services linkages and Links to Agencies); therefore, we would suggest that these would be most popular. There would be no expectation that the usage of these labeling systems would differ from one level to another level of government.

R2: The E-Government Services/Links to Agencies service navigation labeling systems would be found most commonly among government agency Web portals, no matter the level of government.

Table 3 identifies the information architecture, or structure, of systems of various Web site portals; in other words, how access to the information is organized. The various possible ways in which the Web portal can be organized include an audience/market orientation (the now familiar citizen/visitor/business/government) according to the types of services or tasks available, the kinds of topics or issues, or a hybrid of several types.

The audience/market orientation is one in which the Web portal's navigation scheme is segmented into a separate set of linkages for each potential audience. For example, the audience-oriented FirstGov.gov site has four tabs leading to four different sets of site features: For Citizens, For Businesses and Non-Profits, For Federal Employees, and Government-to-Government. States with audience/market orientations will often have their sites segmented according to the purpose of a visitor (Access Washington's Living in Washington, Working/Employment, Doing Business, Education/Learning, and Visiting/Recreation).

A portal guiding its visitors according to the types of services or tasks available will have navigation features listing the types of services provided by the agency and providing links to information or services on those areas. Portals guiding users according to topics or issues sets up navigation according to subject matter dealt with within the agency or government.

Table 3. Types of information and service organization on government Web portals

Type of Information Architecture	Description.. Site is Organized Around:
Audience/Market	The needs of particular audiences or markets. For example, Firstgov.gov has information organized around Online Services for Citizens, for Businesses, and for Governments.
E-Government Services/ Links to Agencies	The services, tasks, or functions offered by the agency
Topics/Issues	Various topics, often just miscellaneous listings of topics
Hybrid site	Combinations of all of the above

One of the few theoretical suggestions as to how these features would be clustered is by Ho (2002), who suggests that the system of information architecture used is a function of whether an agency is traditionally organized with a bureaucratic paradigm (in which case the information architecture would be structured according to a traditional listing of agencies) or whether it has moved to the more efficient e-government paradigm emphasizing a customer service orientation (with a structure according to the Web site audience or market).

However, Ho's (2002) hypothesis also suggests that there is necessarily a direct and strong linkage between design ideas within an agency's technology branch and the organizational sophistication of the overall agency, which is unlikely. Indeed, staff from these two areas are unlikely to communicate often (this is, in fact, one of the most commonly cited breakdowns of technological systems, the lack of communication between technology developers and end users). Therefore, no research question is posited for these site features.

As discussed in the research methodology section, the components of these features on each government's main Web portal were identified for this project, their presence or absence on the portal was coded, and basic analysis was conducted.

Project Methodology

The research project discussed here utilized a cross-sectional comparison that focused upon a review of federal, state, and local e-government portals and comparisons between them. All federal agency portals from executive agencies, cabinet agencies (including subagencies with their own domain name), and independent agencies were included in the study. Federal boards and commissions were not included. All 50 states plus Washington, D.C. were included in the analysis along with all cities over 100,000 in population. This resulted in 43 federal sites, 51 state sites, and 47 urban sites. The data were collected during the summer of 2005.

The first stage of this analysis was to identify the user help features, service navigation features, and types of information architecture, or organization and presentation of information, that are currently being used on public sector Web sites all the while focusing upon the home portal of each portal. (While accessibility is also a crucial aspect of usability, it was not part of this overall project and is not reported here.)

Portals were the initial points of entry for users, as they define the usability and information architecture features for the entire site. Therefore, they are the most crucial part of an agency or government's entire Web site. The identification of help or navigation features was accomplished by content analysis of federal, state, and local home pages and the construction of coding sheets including the identified features. The presence of various features was determined through the examination of the site's portal, as this is the main entryway and where users would need these features.

All coding was conducted by one individual, the author, which is a shortcoming of this research. To attempt to overcome this issue, the author double-checked the results and of course a simple yes or no check-off for each feature is a much less complex coding task than having to code an arbitrary scale of the effectiveness of a feature. All features were working at the time of the coding. Sixty-four variables were coded, along with three additive indices.

The author recognizes that a simple count does not address the issue of whether or not a feature is well-designed or not; however, this research is the first step in investigating this phenomena and the first step should be whether a feature exists or not. Later, additional research should be conducted on the effectiveness of these features across jurisdictions.

Usability and Help Features

The research reported here explores the simple research questions discussed above and is descriptive and exploratory in nature.

Descriptive Results

Table 4 presents basic descriptive data on user help features. As can be seen, most governments utilize more than one help feature up to a maximum of six different features on the same portal, with state governments utilizing the most user help features. One federal and one local agency utilized none.

Table 5 reports descriptive data on service navigation features. An average of 5.1 features per government Web portal were used, with federal agencies utilizing an average of 4.3 and state agencies utilizing the highest average number with 5.6 service navigation features per site. The minimum number on a site was one for federal and local and two for state. The maximum number utilized was quite high with seven features for federal agencies, eleven for state, and ten for local agencies.

Exploration of Research Questions

The next part of the analysis is the exploration of the research questions and then more exploratory analysis. Clearly, the first research question can be supported, as the easiest and least resource-intensive types of user help features were found much more frequently (Table 6). Among all levels of government, the most commonly seen

Table 4. Distribution of user help features across level of government

	Total	Federal	State	Local
N	141	43	51	47
Mean Number of Features	3.7 features	3.7 features	4.3 features	3.1 features
Standard Deviation	1.36	1.35	1.30	1.17
Minimum Number of Features	0	0	2	0
Maximum Number of Features	6	6	6	6

Table 5. Distribution of service navigation features across level of government

	Total	Federal	State	Local
N	141	43	51	47
Mean Number of Features	5.1 features	4.3 features	5.6 features	5.3 features
Standard Deviation	1.78	1.59	1.62	1.85
Minimum Number of Features	1	1	2	1
Maximum Number of Features	11	7	11	10

help feature was a search engine (found in 97.9% of all sites investigated, with no significant differences among levels of government). This was followed by invitations to Contact Us, found in 70.2% of sites, also with no significant differences across types of government. Sitemaps and Help areas were also found very commonly but exhibited different patterns across governments. Sitemaps were used most frequently by federal agencies and only by less than one-quarter of local agencies. Help areas were created most frequently by state agencies (58.8%), followed by one-quarter of federal agencies, and only 12.8% of local agencies. User tips were very seldom utilized as user help features by any level of government.

Also as suggested in Research Question 1, those user help features that would require more resources or more technical sophistication were found less frequently on government Web portals. However, two of them—the site presented in Other Languages and an alternate Text Version, both very resource intensive features—were available in 25.5% and 18.4% of all sites, respectively, and there were significant differences across types of governments. Federal agencies were much more likely to have sites available in other languages and text versions were more frequently found at state sites.

Table 7 presents the distribution of service navigation features by level of government. As suggested, the very basic E-Government Services was present in 60.3% of all government sites, but more surprisingly, was seldom found on federal sites

Table 6. Distribution of help features by level of government (ranked by most frequently used by all jurisdictions)

User Help Feature	Total	Federal (% Sites With Feature)	State (% Sites with Feature)	Local (% Sites with Feature)	Chi-Square	Probability
Easiest and Requires Fewest Resources To Implement						
Search	97.9%	97.7%	100%	95.7%	2.139	0.343
Contact Us	70.2	65.1	72.5	72.3	0.769	0.681
Sitemap	*48.2*	*69.8*	*52.9*	*23.4*	*20.043 ****	*0.000*
Help	*33.3*	*25.6*	*58.8*	*12.8*	*25.021 ****	*0.000*
FAQs	19.9	27.9	21.6	10.6	4.355	0.113
About the Site	*18.4*	*11.6*	*31.4*	*10.6*	*8.901 ***	*0.012*
Feedback on Site	15.6	4.7	21.6	19.1	5.744	0.057
Index	12.8	20.9	5.9	12.8	4.744	0.093
User Tips	2.8	2.3	2	4.3	0.526	0.769
More Technically Difficult or Resource-Heavy To Implement						
Other Languages	*25.5%*	*41.9*	*11.8*	*25.5*	*11.11 ***	*0.004*
Text Version	*18.4%*	*4.7*	*31.4*	*17*	*11.17 ***	*0.004*
Live Help	*9.2%*	*0*	*19.6*	*6.4*	*11.39 ***	*0.003*

Help features which are present at significantly different levels across government levels are bolded.
*   Statistically different and significant at the .05 level
**   Statistically different and significant at the .01 level
***   Statistically different and significant at the .000 level

(16.3% only). It was very common on state and local sites (72.5% and 87.2%); however and the differences between all three levels of government was statistically significant.

Featured Links, Links to Agencies, and Popular Services were the next most commonly found across all levels of government but again there were significant differences across those levels in where it was used. Featured Links were found on two-thirds of state and local sites, and Agency Links were found in three-quarters of local sites, approximately one-half of the state sites, but on only one third of the federal sites.

Table 7. Distribution of service navigation features by level of government (ranked by most frequently used by all jurisdictions)

Service Navigation Feature	Total	Federal (% Sites With Feature)	State (% Sites with Feature)	Local (% Sites with Feature)	Chi-Square Statistic	Probability Level
E-Government Services	*60.3%*	*16.3%*	*72.5%*	*87.2%*	*52.2 ****	*0.000*
Featured Links	*60.3*	*44.2*	*66.7*	*68.1*	*6.7 **	*0.035*
Link to Agencies	*51.8*	*25.6*	*52.9*	*74.5*	*21.5 ****	*0.000*
Popular Services	*35.5*	*32.6*	*54.9*	*17.0*	*15.6 ****	*0.000*
Do You Know/= How I Do ___?	31.9	18.6	37.3	38.3	5.1	0.080
Calendars	*27.0*	*7*	*33.3*	*38.3*	*12.8 ***	*0.002*
Link to Contacts	27.0	20.9	27.5	31.9	1.4	0.500
Events	*23.4*	*18.6*	*15.7*	*36.2*	*6.5 **	*0.038*
What's New	22.7	27.9	17.6	23.4	1.4	0.492
Quick Links	19.1	16.3	27.5	12.8	3.7	0.154
Special Initiatives	14.9	16.3	15.7	12.8	0.3	0.879
Most Visited	*12.8*	*2.3*	*15.7*	*19.1*	*6.3 **	*0.042*
Facilities Locator	*10.6*	*30.2*	*3.9*	*0.0*	*25.4 ****	*0.000*
Hot Topics	9.2	4.7	11.8	10.6	1.6	0.454
Answers A to Z	3.5	4.7	3.9	2.1	0.5	0.798

Service navigation features which are present at significantly different levels across government levels are bolded.
* *Statistically different and significant at the .05 level*
** *Statistically different and significant at the .01 level*
*** *Statistically different and significant at the .000 level*

Features like Calendars and Events were most commonly found on state and local sites while Facilities Locators, not surprisingly, were most often found on federal sites but very seldom on state or local sites (governments evidently presume that their residents know where these government facilities are located).

Finally, Table 8 presents the distribution of information organization types across levels of government. The most commonly utilized organizational scheme is the audience/market scheme, but that is because it is used by practically one-half of all states and 40% of all large cities in their Web portals. Federal agencies utilize this type only 14% of the time. A structure breaking down information by the types of services or processes offered is utilized far more often by federal agencies (44.2%)

Table 8. Distribution of information or service organization available by level of government (ranked by most frequently used by all jurisdictions)

Type of Organization Available	Total	Federal (% Sites With Feature)	State (% Sites with Feature)	Local (% Sites with Feature)	Chi-Square Statistic	Probability Level
Audience	35.5	14.0	49.0	40.4		
Services, Processes	34.8	44.2	43.1	17.0		
Hybrid	17.7	7.0	5.9	40.4		
Topics or Issues	11.3	34.9	2.0	2.1		
					67.7	.0000

and by most of the rest of the states not using the audience scheme (43.1%). Only 17% of the large cities used this type. Cities most frequently used a hybrid type of portal (in 40.4% of the cases) while states and federal agencies seldom used this. Finally, another third (34.9%) of federal agencies organized their information around topics or issues, a scheme avoided by states and local governments.

Clearly, the differences here are statistically and substantively significant. The types of information organization schemes utilized are a function of the types of services provided and the site managers' perceptions of their audiences. Federal agencies seem to focus on what they can offer users rather than be organized according to any anecdotal perception of their audience's identity (FirstGov.gov is a significant exception). State agencies focus on the services they offer or provide a user perspective. Cities, on the other hand, have fewer resources with which to work, which might explain the high number of hybrid sites, which are of course less well-organized. Still, 40% of local portals have taken the audience approach.

These initial results focus upon identifying user help, service navigation, and information architecture features used by the public sector. This is the first step in identifying which of these features ultimately are effective and really are helpful in assisting the general public in understanding these public sector portals and their services, and how to navigate and use them.

Conclusion

From the results, it appears that similar patterns do exist across levels of government in the types of user help and information organizational structure utilized. More technically difficult features appear to be utilized by larger levels of government so financial and staff resources are clearly determining patterns. However, there are many user help features that require little technical expertise so it is hard to explain their usage by the simple existence of resources in larger governments or agencies. In addition, it appears that states are leading the way in offering multiple types of features (see Tables 4 and 5) and in offering the arguably more user-friendly audience-based type of information and service organizational structure.

Given the patterns found for some features, it appears that diffusion of these innovations and features is occurring across jurisdictions and within level of government. Local government IT professionals meet and know one another through conferences, professional associations, and other informal networks, as do those at the federal and state levels. Certain features are discussed and popularized among IT professionals as important and useful for assisting users. Then, other governments in a network follow up and develop that feature for their own Web site. Or, Web managers visit the Web portals of their sister governments, see a feature they like that works well for their own level of government, and move to adopt it. However, there is no sense, from these results, that there is any systematic usability testing being utilized in the Web development process.

The development of user help and service navigation features—as well as systematic usability testing on Web portals—is crucial if governments really intend to effectively utilize e-government and provide electronic services. Deservedly, much focus is put upon the differences still existing between classes of users due to their access to computers and the Internet. Obviously, the inability of some groups of users to access e-government services reduces the equity of these services.

However, it should be recognized that another digital divide exists. Even if users have access to computers and the Internet, in order to fully utilize e-government services, they need government agency Web sites that can be understood and navigated successfully by everyone, not just by those who have knowledge and understanding about how government agencies and services work and are organized.

Effective user help and service navigation features can remove this second divide by allowing novice users or users unused to contacting government to understand and fully utilize e-government services and information. We should not create the "other digital divide." We should work to ensure that all can access government services in an online context.

References

Blackmon, M. H., Kitajima, M., & Polson, P. G. (2005.) Tool for accurately predicting Website navigation problems, non-problems, problem severity and effectiveness of repairs. In *Proceedings of the Conference on Human Factors in Computing Systems* (pp. 31-40). Retrieved July 29, 2005, from http://staff.aist.go.jp/kitajima.muneo/English/PAPERS(E)/CHI2005.pdf

Blackmon, M. H., Polson, P. G., Kitajima, M., & Lewis, C. (2002). *Cognitive walkthrough for the Web.* Retrieved July 29, 2005, from http://staff.aist.go.jp/kitajima.muneo/English/PAPERS(E)/CHI2002.pdf

Chi, E. H., Pirolli, P., & Pitkow, J. (2000). The scent of a site: A system for analyzing and predicting information scent, usage, and usability of a Web site. In *Proceedings of CHI 2000.* ACM Press. Retrieved July 29, 2005, from http://www-users.cs.umn.edu/~echi/papers/chi2000/scent.pdf

Cohen, S. A., & Eimecke, W.B. (2001). The use of the Internet in government service delivery. *PricewaterhouseCoopers foundation for the business of government.* Retrieved August 22, 2002, from http://endowment.pwcglobal.com/pdfs/CohenReport.pdf

Daabaj, Y. (2002). An evaluation of the usability of human-computer interaction methods in support of the development of interactive systems. In *Proceedings of the 35ᵗʰ Hawaii International Conference on System Sciences.*

Daily Internet Activities. (2002). Retrieved August 30, 2005, from http://www.pewinternet.org/reports/chart.asp?img=Daily_Internet_Activities.jpg

Dillon, A. (2001). Beyond usability: Process, outcome and affect in human computer interactions. *Canadian Journal of Information and Library Science, 26*(4), 57-69.

Falling Through the Net: Toward Digital Inclusion. (2000). Retrieved February 21, 2001, from http://www.esa.doc.gov/fttn00.pdf

Hargittai, E. (2003, Winter). Serving citizens' needs: Minimizing online hurdles to accessing government information. *IT and Society, 1*(3), 27-41. Retrieved July 29, 2005, from http://www.ITandSociety.org

Harrison, C., & Petrie, H. (2007). Severity of usability and accessibility problems in ecommerce and egovernment Websites. *People and Computers, (EDIT20),* 255-262.

Ho, A. T.-K. (2002). Reinventing local governments and the e-government initiative. *Public Administration Review, 62*(4), 434-444.

Huang, C. J. (2003). Usability of e-government Web-sites for people with disabilities. In *Proceedings of the 36ᵗʰ Hawaii International Conference on System Sciences.*

Internet Activities. (2002). Retrieved August 30, 2005, from http://www.pewinternet.org/reports/chart.asp?img=Internet_Activities.jpg

Jansen, B. J., & Pooch, U. (2000). Web user studies: A review and framework for future work. *Journal of the American Society of Information Science and Technology, 52*(3), 235-246. Retrieved August 1, 2005, from http://jimjansen.tripod.com/academic/pubs/wus.pdf

Jenkins, C., Corritore, C. L., & Wiedenbeck, S. (2003, Winter). Patterns of information seeking on the Web: A qualitative study of domain expertise and Web expertise. *IT and Society, 1*(3), 64-89. Retrieved July 29, 2005, from http://www.ITandSociety.org

Jones, C. P. (2003). Usability and information design. In *Proceedings of the Annual Conference for the Society for Technical Community* (Vol. 50, pp. 333-338).

Kitajima, M., Blackmon, M. H., & Polson, P. G. (2000). A comprehension-based model of Web navigation and its application to Web usability analysis. In S. McDonald, Y. Waern, & G. Cockton (Eds.), *People and computers XIV: Usability or else! (Proceedings of HCI 2000)* (pp. 357-373). Springer. Retrieved July 29, 2005, from http://staff. aist.go.jp/kitajima.muneo/English/PAPERS(E)/HCI2000.pdf

Kitajima, M., Blackmon, M. H., & Polson, P. G. (2005). *Cognitive architecture for Website design and usability evaluation: Comprehension and information scent in performing by exploration.* Paper presented at the HCI International 2005. Retrieved July 30, 2005, from http://staff.aist.go.jp/kitajima.muneo/English/PAPERS(E)/HCII2005-CoLiDeS.html on

Lazar, J., Bessiere, K., Ceaparu, I., Robinson, J., & Shneiderman, B. (2003, Winter). Help! I'm lost: User frustration in Web navigation. *IT & Society, 1*(3), 18-26. Retrieved July 29, 2005, from http://www.ITandSociety.org

Nielsen, J. (2000). *Designing Web usability: The practice of simplicity.* Indianapolis: New Riders Publishing.

Norris, P. (2001). *Digital divide: Civic engagement, information poverty, and the Internet worldwide.* New York: Cambridge Press.

Paciello, M. G. (2000a). *Web accessibility for people with disabilities.* Lawrence, KA: CMP Books.

Pearrow, M. (2000b). *Web site usability handbook.* Rockland, MA: Charles River Media, Inc.

Pew Research Center. (2002). Getting serious online. *Pew Internet and American life project.* Retrieved August 30, 2005, from http://www.pewinternet.org/reports/pdfs/PIP_Getting_Serious_Online3ng.pdf

Reiss, E. L. (2000). *Practical information architecture.* New York: Addison Wesley.

Rosenfeld, L. (2000). Special report: Design usability--seven pitfalls to avoid in information architecture. *Internet World Magazine.* Retrieved July 29, 2005, from http://www. internetworld.com/magazine.php?inc=121500/12.15.00feature3long.html

Rosenfeld, L., & Morville, P. (1998). *Information architecture for the World Wide Web.* Sebastopol, CA: O'Reilly and Associates.

Shneiderman, B., & Hochheiser, H. (2001). Universal usability as a stimulus to advanced interface design. *Human-computer interaction lab, University of Maryland.* Retrieved from August 1, 2005http://www.cs.umd.edu/hcil/pubs/tech-reports.shtml

Singh, S., & Kotze, P. (2002). Towards a framework for e-commerce usability. In *Proceedings of the 2002 Annual Research Conference of the South African Institute of Computer Scientists and Information Technologist on Enablement Through Technology.* Retrieved July 29, 2005, from http://portal.acm.org/citation.cfm?id=581508&CFID=51211042 &CFTOKEN=76008125

State and Federal E-Government. (2005). Retrieved October 15, 2005, from http://www. insidepolitics.org/egovt05us.pdf

Takeuchi, H., & Kitajima, M. (2002). *Web contents evaluation based on human knowledge of words.* Paper presented at the International Conference on Soft Computing and

Intelligent Systems. Retrieved July 29, 2005, from http://staff.aist.go.jp/kitajima. muneo/English/PAPERS(E)/SCIS2002Takeuchi.pdf

U.S. Department of Commerce. (2002). *A nation online: How Americans are expanding their use of the Internet.* Retrieved February 15, 2002, from http://www.ntia.doc. gov/ntiahome/dn/index.html

U.S. Department of Health and Human Services. (2005). *Usability basics at usability.gov.* Retrieved August 4, 2005, from http://www.usability.gov/basics/index.html

U.S. Office of Management and Budget E-Government Task Force. (2002). *E-Government strategy: Simplified delivery of service to citizens.* Retrieved September 1, 2007, from http://www.whitehouse.gov/omb/inforeg/egovstrategy.pdf

West, D. M. (2005). *Global e-government.* Retrieved October 28, 2005, from http://www. insidepolitics.org/egovt05int.pdf

Chapter VII

Repeated Use of E-Gov Web Sites:
A Satisfaction and Confidentiality Perspective

Sangmi Chai, State University of New York at Buffalo, USA*

T. C. Herath, State University of New York at Buffalo, USA

I. Park, State University of New York at Buffalo, USA

H. R. Rao, State University of New York at Buffalo, USA

Abstract

The potential success of e-government depends on its citizens adopting online services and the security of those services. However, despite the development and diffusion of a variety of government services on the Internet, little research has been carried out regarding: (1) the impact of perceived confidentiality of a user's information on his or her intention to use the service; (2) the relationship between intention towards repeated use and satisfaction derived from service performance of government; and

Author names are listed alphabetically.

*(3) the moderating effect of demographic characteristics (gender and race differ-
ence) on the relationship between a user's satisfaction, confidentiality and repeated
use intention. This paper develops an integrated framework of intentions towards
repeated use with a level of confidential information shared by a user as one factor
and e-government satisfaction derived from service performance as another factor.
The results suggest that a user's intention to continue using government Web sites
is related to the user's satisfaction, perceived performance of the Web site and the
requirement for confidential information. This research also confirms that gender
difference does moderate the relationship between users' satisfaction levels and
repeated use intention. Race difference has an effect on the strength of the relationship
between the user's perceived confidentiality and repeated use intention.*

Introduction

In recent years, we have seen tremendous growth in the use of the Internet. As the
use of the Web by the private sector has grown, the public sector has followed closely
behind. According to United Nations (UN) estimates, more than 173 countries have
developed government Web sites. More than 17 nations are now well beyond Web
publishing and have begun to implement interactive transaction capabilities. The
development and increasing use of information technology (IT) in the government
(e-government) can result in more efficient processes by improving the quality and
speed of government services toward citizens.

Many citizens who previously would visit or call government offices, often only
to wait in line or on hold, increasingly choose to contact the government online to
request information, register complaints or communicate their opinions on current
issues. A July 2003 survey by the Pew Internet & American Life Project mentions
that nearly 97 million adult Americans, or 77% of Internet users, took advantage of
online government services in 2003, which included going to government. Users
can seek information using Web sites and can contact government officials through
e-mail. Internet facilities can be very cost effective for providers of high-volume,
standardized services, and may also improve service and convenience levels to
their users.

E-government can be defined broadly as the use of information and communication
technologies (ICT) to improve the activities of government organizations. According to Prattipati (2003), there are three main domains of e-government: Improving government processes (e-administration), connecting citizens (e-citizens and
e-services), and building external interactions (e-society). According to the World
Bank definition, e-government refers to the use of ICT to improve the efficiency,
effectiveness, transparency, and accountability of government by providing better

service delivery to citizens, providing better services to businesses, and empowering through information and efficient government purchasing (2005). E-government can leverage the capabilities and power of IT to deliver services provided by governments at local, municipal, state, and national levels. But implementing e-government can be a major effort (Grant & Chau, 2005) making it necessary to understand the factors that influence the use of e-government.

Government cannot realize the potential benefits of e-government unless people use them. Despite the development and diffusion of a variety of government services on the Internet, little research has been carried out focusing on factors affecting repeated use. We contribute to current research by attempting to fill this gap.

Since the emergence of the Internet, a great deal of research has been conducted in the areas of marketing and information systems (electronic commerce), among others, that study the success factors that lead to the continued adoption of commercial Web sites by customers. Theories and lessons learned from these studies can effectively be adopted in e-government to see what factors may lead citizens to use government services through the Web. This paper focuses on citizen-centric applications and investigates whether the perceived performance of the government Web site and satisfaction of the user influences the intention of repeated use of the government Web sites. We also identify perceived confidentiality as one of the factors influencing users' intention to use government Web sites repeatedly.

This paper is organized as follows: First, we provide a brief background explaining the theories and constructs considered in this study. We consider not only the SERVPERF theory, explaining the constructs "satisfaction" and "performance," but also "confidentiality," which is a crucial element of information security. Next, we discuss the methodology used to empirically test the research model. Finally, we discuss the results of the empirical analysis and conclude with a discussion of theoretical and managerial implications.

Theoretical Background

Service Performance and Satisfaction

One of the strongest driving factors to construct e-government is customer-friendly government. According to Timonen, O'Donnell, and Humphreys (2003), the main motivation to develop e-government in Ireland is not a cost savings, but a desire to make efficient, citizen-oriented, and customer-friendly government. More importantly, based on survey results of 250 state-level government departments in Australia, Canada, and the United States, Breen (2000) found that governments think about their interaction with their citizens as they begin to realize that an enterprise approach to customer service yields the best results in starting e-government service. From these research findings, we strongly imply that success of e-government depends on how governments provide high-quality and customer-centric e-government services to the citizen.

One of the critical factors in the success of e-government is government Web sites.

To attract more citizens to government Web sites, government should provide high-quality Web sites.

Bruno et al. (1997) and Agarwal, Ghosh, Banerjee, and Kishore (2000) present major components of quality Web sites. These include well-structured databases; well-presented multimedia, such as streaming video; audio; and quick and error-free navigation. To make users stay on the Web site, a server has to have short response time and be reliable in allowing many users on the Web site simultaneously.

The relationship between the quality of a Web site and the success of a Web site has been discussed in some papers. According to Palmer (2002), Web site-quality indicators leading to Web site success can be measured by connection speed, navigability, interactivity, responsiveness, and quality content. A study by Bateson (1984) found that efficiency and speed are the attributes highly important to a user. Web site quality has also been found to have a positive effect on developing customers' trusting intentions toward an e-commerce Web site (McKnight, Choudhury, & Kacmar, 2000). Thus, Web site service quality can be assumed as one of the strong predictors of e-government success and a user's intention to repeatedly use an e-government Web sites. To study the relationship between Web site service quality and a user's intention to use e-government Web site, we introduce the SERVPERF model. A performance-based service quality measurement scale, SERVPERF, developed by Cronin and Taylor (1992), measures the quality of a service perceived by a consumer based on his or her perception of the performance of a service provider. They find that consumers' satisfaction with the service is positively related to their perception of the performance. Similarly, Alford (1996), Chenet, Tynan, and Money (1999), and Ennew (1999) also find a focal relationship between the perceived performance of a service and satisfaction based on the SERVPERF scale.

Consumers are thought to have a positive perception of technology-based service attributes since they believe technology will deliver faster and more efficient services than that of an employee (Weatherall, Ledingham, &Worell, 1984; Angur et al., 1999). Furthermore, performance of the Web site has a direct impact on online consumers' satisfaction (Kohli, Devaraj, & Mahmood, 2004). From prior research findings, we can expect that users, who think e-government Web sites perform well, will have a tendency to have a higher level of satisfaction with a Web site. Thus, a user's perception of performance of an e-government Web site may increase the user's level of satisfaction with the Web site. We therefore hypothesize the following:

Hypothesis 1: *Perceived performance of an e-gov Web site will positively affect a user's level of satisfaction.*

Cronin (1992) points out that increased satisfaction with service enhances customers' repurchasing intentions towards that product or service. Similarly, Anderson, and Sullivan (1993) found that a customer's repurchase intention was increased when they are more satisfied with products. In an online context, a study by Kim, Ferrin, and Rao (2003) supports this relationship, where they find that satisfaction is a strong predictor of the consumer's repurchase intention. Bearden and Jessie (1983) and Churchill and Carol (1982) also confirm that the customer's satisfaction leads to a repurchase intention on e-commerce Web sites. In the Web site context, Loiacono, Chen, and Goodhue (2002) found that Web site quality, such as usefulness, entertainment and response time, is a major factor that aids in predicting a Web consumer's intention to reuse a Web site. This means that a user's satisfaction about e-commerce Web site quality is one of the factors that influences increase in users' continuous use of a Web site.

Based on previous research, we expect a positive relationship between a user's satisfaction and a user's intention to continue to use an e-gov Web site. If users are satisfied, they will have more of an inclination to use the e-gov Web site repeatedly when they need to contact or get a service. Therefore:

Hypothesis 2: *The user's level of satisfaction with an e-gov Web site will positively affect a user's intention to continue to use the e-gov Web site.*

Previous research indicates that a user's perceived performance toward products or a Web site can be another strong factor that indicates a user's intention of repeated purchase, along with customer's satisfactions of products (Cronin et al., 2000). Brady, Cronin, and Brand (2002) analyzed this relationship and found that both perceived performance and service quality positively influence consumers' repurchase intentions. From these research findings, we can hypothesize that users who have a high level of perceived performance of an e-government Web site will have more inclination towards usage of an e-government Web site. If users think that the e-government Web sites perform well, they will be more satisfied, which will result in an increased intention to repeatedly and continually use the Web site. In this study, we assume that there is a positive relationship between the user's perceived performance of an e-gov Web site and the user's intention to continue to use the Web site. Therefore:

Hypothesis 3: *The user's perceived performance of an e-gov Web site will positively affect a user's intention to continue to use an e-gov Web site.*

Moderating Effects of Gender and Race

Gender differences in technology adoption, usage behavior and perception has been extensively studied in various literatures. Several studies suggest that gender difference is a strong predicator of a user's usage behavior and perception of technology. Gefen and Straub (1997) found that women and men show difference in perceptions and usage of e-mail. Their study confirms that women and men differ in their perception of the social presence of e-mail. Women also perceive a higher value of usefulness than men do. Their research supports the notion that men feel more at ease with computers than women do. Other studies point out that that gender differences play a significant role in a user's online purchase intention (Kim & Kim, 2004; Larsen & Oystein, 2005; Slyke, Comunale, & Belanger, 2002). Male employees have a tendency to use the internet more frequently then female workers in an organization (Larsen & Oystein, 2005). In contrast to gender differences on technology adoption research, studies researching racial differences with the intention of using technology or usage behavior are few. However, Kolodinsky, Hogarth, and Hilgert (2004) found that there is no significant difference between various races while considering the utilization of e-banking.

Based on these previous research findings, we propose the next two hypotheses.

Hypothesis 4: *Gender difference will have a moderating effect on the relationship between the user's level of satisfaction with an e-gov Web site and the user's intention to continue to use the e-gov Web site.*

Hypothesis 5: *Race difference will have a moderating effect on the relationship between the user's level of satisfaction with the e-gov Web site and the user's intention to continue to use the e-Gov Web site.*

Perceived Confidentiality

Since the last decade, information privacy has been widely acknowledged as a major concern that has a profound effect on users' adoption of the Internet. In recent years, sharing or loss of personal and sometimes confidential information among different agencies, organizations and even businesses has caused quite a concern.

The advances in IT that continue to increase capabilities and decrease cost allow us to capture and use information with ease. Ironically, the same practice that provides value to organizations and their customers also raises privacy concerns (Culnan et al., 1999). Technology advances have been accompanied by growing concerns over ethical and legal issues as related to the loss of private confidential information (Al-

Fedaghi, 2005; Stalder, 2002). Currently, one of the major concerns is information security. This is primarily due to the fact that a user's private information obtained by an unauthorized individual, whether internal or external to an organization, can be harmful (Hexmoor, Bhattaram, & Wilson, 2004).

Government agencies have taken steps toward implementing policies that regulate and direct the sharing of information to protect the privacy and security of personal data. The federal government plays an important role in many existing regulation efforts. Among the federal government regulations, The Gramm-Leach-Bliley Act (GLBA), also known as the Financial Service Modernization Act, is supported and enforced by numerous national agencies, such as the Federal Trade Commission (FTC), Office of the Comptroller of the Currency (OCC), Federal Reserve (FED), Federal Deposit Insurance Corporation (FDIC) and Office of Thrift Supervision (OTS). Another important federal regulation enacted by the FTC, "Fair Information Practices" in the area of electronic markets encourages Web sites to notify online customers about privacy policies in practice, provide customers with access to their personal information collected by the electronic banks, and secure customer information from leaks. In the health sector, implementation of the Health Insurance Portability and Accountability Act of 1996 (HIPAA), which was designed to stream-line the health industry's inefficiencies, had the primary objective of guaranteeing security and privacy of health information.

Besides government attention to this issue, many researchers have studied the impact of privacy concerns on businesses in privacy, trust, confidentiality-related studies in information systems, electronic commerce, or marketing research. Researchers have found that a substantial percentage of the population is, to some degree, concerned about threats to privacy. Such threats to privacy may stem from new digital technolo-gies, free markets and the virtually unlimited exchange of electronic information (Lester, 2001). Risk can be defined as "a consumer's perceptions of the uncertainty and adverse consequences of engaging in an activity" (Dowling & Staelin, 1994, p. 119). Hoffman, Novak, and Peralta (1999) reported that consumers fear to provide credit card information to commercial Web vendors, simply because they lack enough trust to engage in business relationships involving financial transactions.

A study carried out by Ribbink, Riel, Liljander, and Streukens (2004) shows that e-trust has a significant positive effect on loyalty. Furthermore, assurance is shown to affect continued use positively both via customer satisfaction and e-trust. Without trust, the relationship between online buyers and sellers on the Internet will neither take place nor continue (Ambrose, 1998). Users are unlikely to trust a Web site if they perceive their online experience as not sufficiently secure (Vatanasombut, Stylianou, & Igbaria, 2004). Results of a survey study conducted by Brown and Muchira (2004) indicated that both errors in handling personal information and invasion of privacy have a significant inverse relationship with online purchase behavior. That is, the way in which personal data is handled appears to be critical. This may be partly due to the risk perceived by the consumer. The direct influence of perceived risk on intention is related to the notion of perceived behavioral control in the theory of planned behavior (Ajzen, 1991, 1985). Individuals are likely to hold beliefs of high personal control when they feel assured of the privacy of their personal information. Although many of these studies focus on the commercial Web sites and customer relations, the theories and lessons can be similarly applied to e-government.

Privacy is defined in several ways in different contexts. Privacy is the ability of an individual to control the terms under which personal information is acquired and used (Culnan et al., 1999). It can be the expectation of anonymity, the expectation of fairness and control over personal information, or the expectation of confidentiality (Berman & Mulligan, 1999). Compared to the concept of privacy, confidentiality refers to the ways in which the information is handled and used (Commission, 2001), a tool for protecting privacy (NILAC, 1995). In general, confidential information refers to any information kept in confidence such that its revelation requires the consent of its owner (Al-Fedaghi, 2005). For this reason, the notion of confidentiality is usually applied to private information, government secrets and trade secrets (Coleman, 1993).

Thus, confidentiality can be perceived in terms of the user's perception regarding how their personal information will be handled by the government and to what level it will be protected. In the absence of direct knowledge of the process of how their personal information is handled, confidentiality may be perceived by a user in terms of how much personal information a particular service needs. Therefore, if users use a government Web site for purposes of searching for information such as tax, election date, and so forth, they may perceive the risk to be low, since they do not provide the government Web site any private information for such a simple search. However, if they use the Web site for paying taxes, updating licenses or getting permits, where they have to provide personal information on the Web site, they may perceive the risk to be high and, hence, the perceived confidentiality to be low. For this rationale, we hypothesize:

Hypothesis 6: *The need for confidential information for a particular task by an e-gov Web site will negatively affect the user's intention to continue to use the e-gov Web site.*

Customer satisfaction has been studied in the context of physical environments and human interactions. A SERVQUAL dimension used in an online context includes reliable/prompt responses, access, ease of use, attentiveness, security and credibility. Balasubramanian, Konana, and Meon (2003) suggested that dimensions such as tangibles, empathy and responsiveness—which are important in a traditional environment—are less applicable in an online environment. However, they found that in an online investment market where potential transactions may contain sensitive information, perceived security has considerable effect on consumer satisfaction mediated through trustworthiness. Based on this, we propose:

Hypothesis 7: *The need for confidential information for a particular task by an e-gov Web site will negatively effect the user's satisfaction towards the e-gov Web site.*

Moderating Effects of Gender and Race

Many studies have discussed trust and perception of risk in great detail. A general norm seems to be that disposition to trust may affect the perception of risk in addition to various environmental factors, such as the nature of the situation or task. Prior literature suggests that the presence of privacy concerns leads to suspicion, which subsequently leads to active behavior. People who are concerned with privacy and take action to protect it are also less likely to continue online behavior, such as subscribing and purchasing (Dommeyer & Gross, 2003). On the opposite spectrum, Salisbury, Pearson, Pearson, and Miller (2001) found that perceived Web security enhances intent to purchase online in that customers who feel secure enough to give sensitive information such as a credit card number will engage in online activity, such as purchases.

Although the results of the studies considering the relationship between demographic variables (such as gender) and privacy have been mixed, available literature discusses many demographic factors that may impact trust or disposition to trust, including gender, race, age, education, income and prior experience. To date, existing literature has considered e-mail usage pattern, communication as well as networking differences between men and women. Researchers have investigated whether gender affects privacy concerns, but several of these investigations have not revealed any gender effects. Phelps et al. (2000) examined a number of demographic variables—sex, income, marital status, education and employment status—and found only education to have a statistically significant relationship with privacy concern. Nonetheless, women have been found to process information in more detail and, thus, are more aware of and sensitive to changes in their environments (Meyers-Levy & Maheshwaram, 1991). Several surveys conducted in the 1990s as well as a 2002 survey by Harrison Interactive confirms that women conveyed more concerns about the potential misuse of their personal information. Flynn et al. (1994) suggested an explanation in the role of gender or race in perceived risk in terms of sociopolitical factors. Based on prior literature and results of their own study, Finucane et al. (2000) found that risks tend to be judged lower by men than by women and by white people than by people of color. This leads us to hypothesize:

Hypothesis 8: *Gender will moderate the relationship between the need for confidential information and the user's intention to continue to use the e-gov Web site; and females will show higher negative impact than males.*

In a health information-related study, Brodie, Flournoy, Altman, and Blendon (2000) found that blacks are more likely than whites to have concerns about Internet privacy. Most claimed that they were "very worried" about the probability of an unauthorized person gaining access to their personal data. In their study, Finucane et al. (2000) found that white people tend to judge the risks as lower than people of color. Based on this, we hypothesize:

Hypothesis 9: *Race will moderate the relationship between the need for confidential information and the user's intention to continue to use the e-gov Web site; and whites will show reduced negative impact of the relationship than their non-white counterparts.*

Method

Sample

This study analyzes the "E-Government Survey 2003" data collected by Pew Research Center. A random digit-dial telephone survey was administered to adult (18 years or older) Americans by Princeton Survey Research Association between June 25 and August 3, 2003. The main aim of surveys carried out by Pew Internet is to explore the impact of the Internet on families, communities and life in general. This survey was specific to e-government, and questioned Internet users about their experiences with regard to government.

The dataset available on the Pew Internet Web site contained 4,933 responses. No information could be obtained regarding how many people were initially contacted in order to understand the response rate. Among the 4,933 respondents, approximately 23.4% (1,154) had access to the Internet and had used e-government services, and were considered as a sample for further analysis. Fifty percent of the remaining 1,154 users of e-government were males. The average age for the Internet user sample was 41.16 years.

Figure 1. Research model

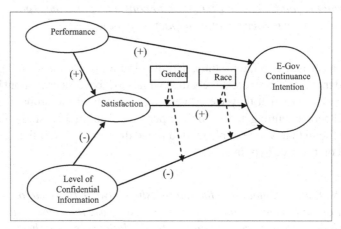

Measurement

The analysis uses a subset of the original questionnaire items to test our hypotheses.

Intention towards repeat use (E-Gov Continuance Intention)*:* the dependent variable measured on a dichotomous scale, refers to the respondents' intent to continue to use the Internet for contacting government.

Performance: This independent variable was measured by the combination of two factors that compose the government's performance: outcome perceived by the user and performance related to expected time. Perceived outcome was captured by a four-point scale question—"The outcome of your last contact with the government?" that attempts to find the outcome in terms of success in accomplishing the task. Performance related to expected time was measured with another four-point scale question—"Did your last contact with the government take about the amount of time you expected, more time than you expected, or less time than you expected?" The responses for these two questions were added to get the overall measure for performance.

Satisfaction: A four-point interval scale question—"How satisfied were you with your LAST experience contacting the government?"—was used as a measure of this second independent variable. Although satisfaction is a single-item scale, previous research has shown considerable precedence for using single-item measures in the context of large-scale satisfaction studies (e.g., LaBarbera & Mazursky, 1983;

Kekre, Krishnan, & Srinivasan, 1995). For example, Yi's research (1990) compared reliabilities between several multi- and single-item scales and showed that the reliability of single-item scales is acceptable.

Confidentiality: The level of confidential information was measured based on the amount of personal information shared by the user; a low level of personal or confidential information shared and a high level of personal information shared. This was measured by proxy based on responses to the question—"When you made contact with the government last time, what was the purpose of that contact?"—on a dichotomous scale. Categories such as getting information and expressing opinion were considered "low level of confidential information shared," since they require a small amount of personal information to be given out during a transaction. On the other hand, responses to actions such as filing taxes or registering a car were used to measure "high level of confidential information shared," since these transactions needed a higher level of personal information to be filled out.

Demographics: We used gender and race as moderators of the relationship between independent and dependent variables. It is important that gender has a critical role when considering e-gov usage in both the organization and household contexts, because they may have different styles for using the Internet and Web sites. Race was also included as a moderator for similar reasons. Race was divided into "white" and "non-white."

Analysis and Results

SPSS 11.5 was used for testing relationships of satisfaction, performance and perceived confidentiality on intention to continue to use e-gov. Since the dependent variable "intention to use" is dichotomous, this study was based on logistic regression analysis. For testing moderating effect of demographic variables "gender" and "race," we followed Jaccard's method on interaction effect in logistic regression (Jaccard, 2001). This method has been frequently cited as robust way in social science fields for testing the interaction effect. In the model, we also have a second-order dependent variable, "satisfaction," for hypothesis.

In addition, we conducted linear regression for testing the effect of performance of an e-gov Web site where satisfaction is the continuous variable as described earlier.

The Effect of Independent Variables on Intention to Repeat Use

To test the effect of independent variables on Intention to repeat use, we conducted logistic regression analysis. This model was found to be significant (χ^2= 27.216, $P<0.000$) and is reported in Table 1. Table 1 also summarizes the results that show a significant effect of satisfaction, performance, and level of confidential information on intention towards repeated use. The results indicate that intention to continue to use e-government increases as a user's satisfaction increases. For every unit increase in satisfaction, the intention to continue to use increases by 1.2 times.

As previous research in various fields, including information systems, marketing and organization, have argued (Anderson & Sullivan, 1993; Gupta, Guimaraes, & Raghunathan, 1992; Bhattacherjee, 2001), the significant results imply that the positive relationship that exists between satisfaction and intention to use is robust.

Performance (0.491, P<0.001) and level of confidential information (-0.549, P<0.01) were also found to affect the continuance intention significantly. The result shows that a unit increase in performance increases the likelihood of continuous use by 1.634 times. Users who need to share higher levels of personal information use government Web sites less than users who need to share lower levels of personal information. These results are consistent with the study carried out by Ribbink, Riel, Liljander, and Streukens (2004) where assurance was shown to affect loyalty.

An interesting find in this analysis is that satisfaction is a weaker predictor of persistent intention than confidentiality. In other words, confidentiality was found to be a more important factor for e-government users to use the service repeatedly. These findings show that users who use government Web sites are more concerned about the security of their personal information than satisfaction or perceived performance of the e-government site.

Table 1. Logistic regression results

Effect of Satisfaction, Performance and Level of Confidential Information on Intention Towards Repeat Use						
Variable	B	S.E.	Wald	df	Sig.	Exp(B)
Satisfaction	0.183*		6.064	1	0.014	1.201
Performance	0.491**		19.248	1	0.000	1.634
Level of Confidential Information Shared	-0.549**		9.391	1	0.002	0.577
Chi-square= 27.216, *df*=3, *P*<0.000; Accuracy=65%, sample size=1,474						

Table 2. Linear regression results

Effect of Performance and Level of Confidential Information on Satisfaction					
Variable	Std. Coefficient	Std. Error	T	*p*-value	Model
Intercept	1.95	-.001	10.987	.000	$R^2 = .297$
Level of Confidential Information Shared	-.001	.297	-.016	.987	$F_{2,549} = 26.477***$
Performance	.297	.058	7.263	.000	
Dependent Variable: Satisfaction					

The Effect of Exogenous Variables on E-Government Satisfaction

This analysis was conducted by linear regression. Due to different dependent variables from the first part of the analysis, the sample size was changed. Table 2 tabulates the results of the effect of confidentiality and performance on satisfaction using linear regression. Unlike confirmation-expectation theory (Oliver, 1980), where satisfaction is determined by disconfirmation between expectation and perceived performance, we apply perceived performance of service quality as an antecedent of satisfaction according to SERVPERF (Cronin & Taylor, 1994, 1992). That is, satisfaction is determined by "performance-only measures," which means that *the user's perceptions of the performance of e-government services*, as opposed to the difference between the consumers' perceptions about the performance and their performance expectations. We follow this method since it provides a useful tool for measuring overall service quality attitudes in a simple way (Cronin & Taylor, 1994).

For the baseline model, $R^2 = 0.297$ and $F_{2, 549} = 26.477$ shows a decent fit. Our results indicate that performance of e-government's services as perceived by users is an antecedent of satisfaction, even in the e-government context (b=.297, P< 0.01) and shows significant effect on satisfaction. However, the level of confidential information shared by the user does not act as an antecedent for satisfaction but directly affects the continuance intention (*b*=-0.001, *P*>0.1).

The Moderating Effect of Demographics on Intention to Re-Use

One of the important issues is the moderating effect of demographics on the intention to repeatedly use e-gov Web sites. According to Baron and Kenny (1986), a moderator is defined as a qualitative (e.g., sex, race, class) or quantitative (e.g., level

Table 3. Testing moderating effects of gender using logistic regression

Testing Steps in Mediation Model	B	S.E.	Wald	df	Sig.	Exp(B)
Satisfaction	.408	.113	12.999	1	.000	1.504
Gender (1)*	1.626	.519	9.798	1	.002	5.082
Race (1)	-.352	.652	.292	1	.589	.703
Satisfaction × Gender (1)	-.455	.159	8.208	1	.004	.635
Satisfaction × Race (1)	-.098	.208	.224	1	.636	.906
Constant	-.728	.369	3.897	1	.048	.483

Model Chi-square= 30.237, *df* =5, *P*<0 .001; accuracy=65%, sample size=708
*Reference: : male=1, female=0; white=0, non-white=1

of reward) variable that affects the direction and/or strength of the relation between an independent or predictor variable and a dependent or criterion variable.

In our research, we propose that gender and ethnicity affects strength of relationship between satisfaction and intention to re-use. For testing this effect, we considered gender and race regarding the moderating role of demographics. Results are reported in Table 3. The result on satisfaction was statistically significant, which indicates that gender has considerable effect on the relationship between satisfaction and intention to re-use. Effect of satisfaction was significant after considering the gender effect (b=0.408, p<0.001). Regarding Hypotheses 4 and 5, Table 3 showed that gender interacts in the relationship between satisfaction and intention (b= -0.352, p<0.01). Race, however, did not have any impact on intention; neither did it have an effect on moderating the relationship between satisfaction and intention to re-use.

Specific interaction effect of gender has been shown in Figure 2, with predicted log odd values of intention, which are the predicted values of logistic regression

Figure 2. Interaction effect of gender

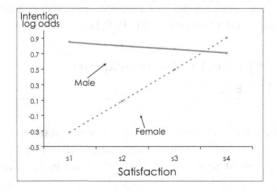

Table 4. Testing moderating effects of race using logistic regression

Testing Steps in Mediation Model	B	S.E.	Wald	df	Sig.	Exp(B)
Level of Confidential Information Shared	-.576	.264	4.752	1	.029	.562
Race	-1.465	.395	13.731	1	.000	.231
Gender	.563	.285	3.899	1	.048	1.756
Level of CI × Race	1.371	.506	7.338	1	.007	3.940
Level of CI × Gender	-.377	.375	1.011	1	.315	.686
Constant	.861	.200	18.572	1	.000	2.364
Model Chi-square= 27.876, df=5, $P<0$ .000; accuracy=65.9%, sample size=346						

represented in Table 3 (Jaccard, 2001). Figure 2 indicates that for males, the intention to re-use slightly decreased as satisfaction increased. Other incentives may be required to make males' intentions to re-use higher. On the other hand, females had a steeper slope than males, indicating that intention to re-use increased as satisfaction increased. This trend indicates that females focus more on satisfaction than males do for the decision to use e-gov sites repeatedly.

For Hypothesis 9, Table 4 shows the moderating effect of race. When the interaction effect term is included in the model, results show that the impacts of each level of confidential information shared, race and gender on Intention were significant (b= -.576, -1.465, and .563). Furthermore, significant interaction exists between level of confidential information shared and race on Intention to re-use e-gov (b= 1.371, $p<0.01$). However, the interaction effect of gender was not statistically significant (.b=-.377, $p>0.1$).

Figure 3 indicates that whites have higher probability of intention to re-use even in the case where a higher amount of confidential information is required (*prob.*= 70.3%) than tasks that require very little to no personal information (*prob.*= 57.1%). For non-whites, the results show that higher possibility of intention to re-use in lower levels of personal information requirements (*prob.* = 54.78%). This result shows that different races may have different points of view with regard to confidentiality. That is, whites may consider using government Web sites to perform tasks that require higher levels of personal information. This is consistent with our hypothesis. This may be due to the ease that online services provide. On the other hand, it is shown that non-whites usually think of requirement of confidential information as a barrier to using e-gov Web sites. For this reason, they have low intention to re-use when the amount of personal information required is high.

Figure 3. Interaction effect of race

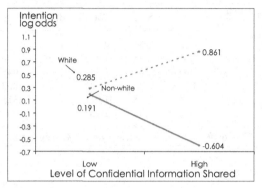

Figure 4. Direct and moderating effects on e-gov continuance intention

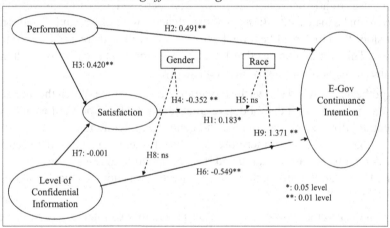

Figure 4 shows the results of our conceptual model for all hypotheses. According to the test results, Hypotheses 1 2, 3, 4, 6 and 9 are supported by this data. However, the data did not support Hypothesis 7, which examines the effect of level of confidential information shared on satisfaction. Moderating effect of race on the relationship between satisfaction and intention, as well as moderating effect of gender on the relationship between confidentiality and intention, were also not supported.

Discussion

This study attempts to examine the role of three factors—namely, e-government's service performance, satisfaction resulting from the performance and the level of confidential information shared—on users' intention to repeatedly use e-gov services, using the survey data from Princeton Survey Research center. More specifically, we argue that the amount of personal information shared is a deterministic factor for users to use a government Web site repeatedly. Service performance and satisfaction also play a role as an antecedent of repeated use intention. In addition, we have tried to determine whether e-government satisfaction is affected by performance and confidentiality. The empirical results of this study reveal that, as demonstrated by previous studies, performance is a predictor of satisfaction. However, perceived confidentiality does not directly effect a user's satisfaction towards the service. This indicates that the level of confidential information plays a role, not as an antecedent of satisfaction but as the same level of satisfaction. Our findings are consistent with previous research, thus revealing the effect of satisfaction and confidentiality on intention to use. Confidentiality was considered more by users for using e-government than satisfaction.

Our results of the effect of satisfaction and performance on intention towards repeated usage suggest that satisfaction and performance play a role as an antecedent of the intention to repeated usage as revealed by previous research. We found that performance has a more direct effect on repeated usage than satisfaction, which results from performance. In addition, the relationship between the amount of confidential information needed for a task and the intention of repeated use of the service indicates that users are critically concerned about exposing or sharing their personal information through the government Web site. They regard it as a determining factor in repeating use of the site more than other factors, such as satisfaction or performance.

Finally, this study showed that users' demographics, gender and race act as a moderator on the relationship between reuse intention and satisfaction (confidentiality) by providing the interaction effect. Specifically, gender (race) played as a moderator on the relationship between intention to reuse and satisfaction (level of confidential information). Interestingly, in the relationship between intention to reuse and satisfaction, male users tended to slightly decrease their intention to reuse as satisfaction increased, whereas female users' intentions drastically increased. According to marketing literature, satisfaction is a major antecedent of repurchase intention or retention (Bearden & Teel, 1983; Hellier, Geursen, Carr, & Rickard, 2003; Oliver, 1980, 1981), which implies that a high satisfaction level leads to high intention of reuse. However, when compared to previous studies on satisfaction, our study showed different results on government Web sites for male users, although the impact on the relationship between intention and satisfaction was insignificant.

This result indicates that users' attitudes might be different depending on the contexts they face. In a recent study, Jolley, Mizerski, and Olaru (2006) showed that satisfaction does not play a primary role for enhancing retention in online gambling contexts; rather, users' habits play a major role for the retention. In a similar vein, the results from this study provide a question for further research on e-government in the online Web site context with regard to the moderating effect of gender on the relationship between reuse intention and satisfaction.

This study offers important practical and academic contributions. First, we provide empirical evidence that users are still reserved in participating in online activities that need personal information. Their participation can be encouraged by increasing trust. Salam, Rao, and Pegels (2003) found that consumer-perceived risk is reduced with the increase in institutional trust. Although it can be assumed that users may have a high level of trust in the government as an institution, the trust also has to be developed in terms of technology and process. Therefore, to ensure the perception of security, users must be convinced that the Web is a secure place to engage in the exchange, and it must be proven to them that interacting with the site is safe and secure. The former can be done by implementing and informing users about security features available on the Web; for example, digital certificates, secure servers or third-party trusting agencies. Government must communicate that they have implemented technologies and procedures that prevent computer crimes; they always adhere to privacy principles; and their system is reliable because they always allocate sufficient resources to effectively correct any occurrence of errors. Thus, assurance is a service quality dimension that can be controlled by the service provider, which may aid in increasing citizen trust.

Second, this study showed important cues about how reuse intentions regarding e-gov Web sites could be affected by different factors from commercial Web sites. Researchers have devoted little attention to assessing intention to use e-government Web sites. By revealing factors that influence reuse intention of e-gov Web sites, this study has extended research in e-government. For example, the likelihood to reuse e-gov Web sites decreased despite increase of satisfaction with Web sites, and satisfaction has less effect than confidentiality. This is consistent with another recent study that shows that satisfaction was not a critical factor for reusing online gambling Web sites and online shopping (Jiang, 2005; Jolley et al., 2006).

Avenues for Future Research

In this study, we used a secondary data set. Secondary data analysis can allow for the validation of prevalent theories. The main advantages of secondary data include: the availability of data without gathering it, which overcomes the obstacles of gathering data, such as peoples' and organizations' willingness to participate and cost to conduct the study. However, since the data is not collected though the protocols of scientific research with a specific study in mind, it can have drawbacks. The survey was designed to measure public opinion. The original research was not driven by a theoretical model. This may impact the validity and reliability of the measures. Individual questionnaire items may be unbiased but may not necessarily pass psychometric properties, such as the need to use multiple items. In this study, most of the variables were represented by one question each (except perceived performance, which was measured with two questions); hence, validity was based on expert opinion.

The data has to be available for all the concepts that must be considered, which may not always be possible. Several other quality indicators mentioned earlier in the study can also be considered to consider satisfaction. But lack of items capturing such indicators posed limitations in considering any additional variables. We had to use different methods (logistic and linear regression) for analysis due to differing scales of the variables (i.e., dichotomous scale for dependent variable and all independent variables being continuous). For this reason, we could not test the causal relationship among those constructs statistically, but test only the effects (relationship) of each variable on endogenous variables.

In the light of these limitations, a more detailed analysis of each construct using a proper design methodology is recommended. Despite some limitations, this study is among the first studies measuring the impact of perceived confidentiality on the intention of repeated usage of a government's site. More importantly, the strength of the research is that the data represents a national random sample of the US adult population rather than a convenience sample, and that the results are consistent with theory. We believe the findings from our research could shed meaningful light regarding e-government.

Acknowledgment

We appreciate the comments made by anonymous reviewers and attendees at the ICEG 2005 conference, which have enhanced this paper. The research of the fourth author is funded by NSF under grant #0420448. The usual disclaimer applies.

References

Agarwal, R., Ghosh, B., Banerjee, S., & Kishore, P. (2000). Ensuring Web site quality: A case study. In *Proceedings of Management of Innovation and Technology, ICMIT 2000* (pp. 664-670).

Ajzen, I. (1985). From intentions to actions: A theory of planned behavior. In J. Kuhl, & J. Beckman (Eds.), *Action control: From cognition to behavior*. Berlin: Springer-Verlag.

Ajzen, I. (1991). The theory of planned behavior. *Organizational Behavior and Human Decision Processes*, *50,* 179-211.

Al-Fedaghi, S.S. (2005). Privacy as a base for confidentiality. In *Proceedings of WEIS05*, Boston, Massachusetts, USA.

Alford, B.L., & Sherrell, D.L. (1996). The role of affect in consumer satisfaction judgments of credence-based services. *Journal of Business Research, 37,* 71-84.

Ambrose, P.J., & Johnson, G.J. (1998). A trust-based model of buying behavior in electronic retailing. In *Proceedings of the 4th Americas Conference on Information Systems*, Baltimore, Maryland, USA.

Anderson, E.W., & Sullivan, M.W. (1993). The antecedents and consequences of customer satisfaction for firms. *Marketing Science (1986-1998)*, *12,* 125-143.

Angur, M.G., Natarajan, R., & Jahera, J.S., Jr. (1999). Service quality in the banking industry: An assessment in a developing economy. *The International Journal of Bank Marketing, 17*(3), 116-123.

Anol, B. (2001). Understanding information systems continuance: An expectation-confirmation model. *MIS Quarterly, 25,* 351-370.

Balasubramanian, S., Konana, P., & Meon, N. (2003). Customer satisfaction in virtual environments: A study of online investing. *Management Science, 49*(7), 871-889.

Baron, R.M., & Kenny, D.A. (1986). The moderator-mediator variable distinction in social psychological research: Conceptual, strategic, and statistical considerations. *Journal of Personality and Social Psychology, 51,* 1173-1182.

Bateson, J.E. (1984). *Perceived control and service encounter*.

Bearden, W.O., & Teel, J.E. (1983). Selected determinants of consumer satisfaction and complaint reports. *Journal of Marketing Research, 20,* 21-28.

Berman, J., & Mulligan, D. (1999). Privacy in the digital age: Work in progress. *Nova Law Review, 23*(2), 551-582.

Bhattacherjee, A. (2001). Understanding information systems continuance: An expectation-confirmation model. *MIS Quarterly, 25*(3), 351-370.

Brady, M.K., Cronin, J.J., & Brand, R.R. (2002). Performance-only measurement of service quality: A replication and extension. *Journal of Business Research, 55,* 17-31.

Breen, J. (2000). At the dawn of e-government: The citizen as customer. *Government Finance Review,16*(5), 15-20.

Brodie, M., Flournoy, R.E., Altman, D.E., & Blendon, R.J. (2000). Health information, the Internet, and the digital divide. *Health Affair, 19*(6), 255-265.

Brown, M., & Muchira, R. (2004). Investigating the relationship between Internet privacy concerns and online purchase behavior. *Journal of Electronic Commerce Research, 5,* 62-70.

Bruno, G., & Agarwal, R. (1997). Modeling the engineering environment. *IEEE Transactions on Engineering Management, 44*(1), 20-30.

Chenet, P., Tynan, C., & Money, A. (1999). Service performance gap: Re-evaluation and redevelopment. *Journal of Business Research, 46*, 133-147.

Churchill, G.A., Jr., & Surpernant, C. (1982). An investigation into the determinants of customer satisfaction. *Journal of Marketing Research, 19*, 491-504.

Coleman, A. (1993). Protecting confidential information. In C. Reed (Ed.), *Computer law* (2nd ed.). London: Blackstone Press.

Cronin, J.J., Brady, M.K., & Hult, G.T.M. (2000). Assessing the effects of quality, value, and consumer satisfaction on consumer behavioral intentions in service environments. *Journal of Retailing, 76*(2), 193-218.

Cronin, J.J., Jr., & Taylor, S.A. (1992). Measuring service quality: A reexamination and extension. *Journal of Marketing, 56*, 55-68.

Cronin, J.J., & Taylor, S.A. (1994). SERVPERF versus SERVQUAL; Reconciling performance-based and perceptions-minus-expectations measurement of quality. *Journal of Marketing, 58*, 125-131.

Culnan, M.J., & Armstrong, P.K. (1999). Information privacy concerns, procedural fairness, and impersonal trust: An empirical investigation. *Organization Science, 10*(1), 104-115.

Dommeyer, C.J., & Gross, B.L. (2003). What consumers know and what they do: An investigation of consumer knowledge, awareness, and use of privacy protection strategies. *Journal of Interactive Marketing, 17*(2), 34-51.

Dowling, G.R., & Staelin, R. (1994). A model of perceived risk and intended risk-handling activity. *Journal of Consumer Research, 21*, 119-134.

Ennew, C.T., & Binks, M.R. (1999). Impact of participate service relationships on quality, satisfaction and retention: An exploratory study. *Journal of Business Research, 46*, 121-132.

Finucane, M.L., Slovic, P., Mertz, C.K., Flynn, J., & Satterfield, T.A. (2000). Gender, race, and perceived risk: The 'white male' effect. *Health, Risk & Society, 2*(2), 159-172.

Flynn, J., Slovic, P., & Mertz, C.K. (1994). Gender, race, and perception of environmental health risks. *Risk Analysis, 14*(6), 1101-1108.

Gefen, D., & Straub, D.W. (1997). Gender differences in the perception and use of e-mail: An extension to the technology acceptance model. *MIS Quarterly, 21*, 389-400.

Gupta, Y.P., Guimaraes, T., & Raghunathan, T.S. (1992). Attitudes and intentions of information center personnel. *Information & Management, 22*, 151-160.

Harris Interactive. (2002, February 7). *Privacy on and off the Internet: What consumers want*. Retrieved January 11, 2006, from http://www.aicpa.org/download/webtrust/priv_rpt_21mar02.pdf

Hellier, P.K., Geursen, G.M., Carr, R.A., & Rickard, J.A. (2003). Customer repurchase intention: A general structural equation model. *European Journal of Marketing, 37*, 1762.

Hexmoor, H., Bhattaram, S., & Wilson, S.L. (2004). Trust-based security policies. In *Proceedings of the Secure Knowledge Management Workshops*, Buffalo, New York, USA.

Holmes, M.C. (1998). Comparison of gender differences among information systems professionals: A cultural perspective. *The Journal of Computer Information Systems*, *38*(4), 78-87.

Huberman, B.A., Adar, E., & Fine, L.R. (2005). Valuating privacy. In *Proceedings of WEIS05*, Boston, Massachusetts, USA.

Jaccard, J. (2001). *Interaction effects in logistic regression.* Thousand Oaks: Sage Publications.

Jiang, P., & Rosenbloom, B. (2005) Customer intention to return online: Price perception, attribute-level performance, and satisfaction unfolding over time. *European Journal of Marketing 39*(1/2), 150.

Jolley, B., Mizerski, R., & Olaru, D. (2006). How habit and satisfaction affects player retention for online gambling, *Journal of Business Research, 59*, 770.

Jyoti, C., & Heejin, L. (2004). Broadband development in South Korea: Institutional and cultural factors. *European Journal of Information Systems*, *13*(2), 103-114.

Jyoti, C., & Yogesh, K.D. (2005). The demographics of broadband residential consumers in a British local community: The London Borough of Hillingdon. *Journal of Computer Information Systems*, *45*(4), 93-102.

Kekre, S., Krishnan, M.S., & Srinivasan, K. (1995). Drivers of customer satisfaction for software products: Implications for design and service support. *Management Science*, *41*(9), 1456-1470.

Kim, D.J., Ferrin, D.L., & Rao, H.R. (2003). A study of the effect of consumer trust on consumer expectations and satisfaction: The Korean experience. In *Proceedings of the 5th International Conference on Electronic Commerce*, Pittsburgh, Pennsylvania, USA.

Kim, E.Y., & Kim, Y.-K. (2004). Predicting online purchase intentions for clothing products. *European Journal of Marketing*, *38*, 883-897.

Kohli, R., Devaraj, S., & Mahmood, M.A. (2004). Understanding determinants of online consumer satisfaction: A decision process perspective. *Journal of Management Information Systems*, *21*, 115-136.

Kolodinsky, J.M, Hogarth, J.M., & Hilgert, M.A. (2004). The adoption of electronic banking technologies by US consumers. *International Journal of Bank Marketing*, *22*(4), 238-259.

Labarbera, P.A., & Mazursky, D. (1983). A longitudinal assessment of consumer satisfaction/dissatisfaction: The dynamic aspect of the cognitive process. *Journal of Marketing Research*, *20*, 393-404.

Larsen, T.J., & Sorebo, O. (2005). Impact of personal innovativeness on the use of the Internet among employees at work. *Journal of Organizational and End User Computing*, *17*, 43-63.

Lester, T. (2001). The reinvention of privacy. *The Atlantic Monthly*, 27-39.

Loiacono, ET, Chen, D.O., & Goodhue, D. (2002). WEBQUAL revised: Predicting the intent to reuse a Web site. In *Proceedings of the 8th Americas Conference on Information Systems*, Barcelona, Spain.

Longstaff, T.A., Ellis, J.T., Herman, S.V., Lipson, H.F., McMillan, R.D., Pesante, L.H., et al. (1997). *Security of the Internet*. Pittsburgh: Carnegie Mellon University, Software Engineering Institute.

McKnight, D.H., Choudhury, V., & Kacmar, C. (2000). Trust in e-commerce vendors: A two-stage model. In *Proceedings of the 21st International Conference on Information Systems*, Brisbane, Queensland, Australia.

Meyers-Levy, J., & Maheshwaram, D. (1991). Exploring differences in males and females processing strategies. *Journal of Consumer Research, 18*, 63-70.

National Bioethics Advisory Commission. (2001). *Ethical and policy issues in research involving human participants: Report and recommendations of the National Bioethics Advisory Commission.* Retrieved from http://www.georgetown.edu/research/nrcbl/nbac/pubs.html

NIIAC. (1995). *Common ground: Fundamental principles for the national information infrastructure.* The National Information Infrastructure Advisory Council (NIIAC).

Oliver, R.L. (1980). A cognitive model of the antecedents and consequences of satisfaction decisions. *Journal of Marketing Research, 17*, 460-469.

Oliver, R.L. (1981). Measurement and evaluation of satisfaction processes in retail settings. *Journal of Retailing, 57*, 25.

Palmer, J.W. (2002). Web site usability, design, and performance metrics. *Information Systems Research, 13*(2), 151-167.

Phelps, J., Nowak, G., & Ferrell, E. (2000). Privacy concerns and consumer willingness to provide personal information. *Journal of Public Policy & Marketing, 19*(11), 27-41.

Pratippati, S.N. (2003). Adoption of e-governance: Differences between countries in the use of online government service. *Journal of American Academy of Business, 3*, 386-391.

Ribbink, D., van Riel, A.C.R., Liljander, V., & Streukens, S. (2004). Comfort your online customer: Quality, trust and loyalty on the Internet. *Managing Service Quality, 14*, 446-456.

Salam, A., Rao, H., & Pegels, C. (2003). Consumer-perceived risk in e-commerce transactions. *Communications of ACM, 46*, 325-331.

Salisbury, W.D., Pearson, R.A., Pearson, A.W., & Miller, D.W. (2001). Perceived security and World Wide Web purchase intention. *Industrial Management + Data Systems, 101*(3/4), 165-176.

Slyke, C.V., Comunale, C.L., & Belanger, F. (2002). Gender differences in perceptions of Web-based shopping. *Communications of the ACM, 45*, 82-86.

Stalder, F. (2002). The voiding of privacy. *Sociological Research Online, 7*.

Timonen, V., O'Donnell, O., & Humphreys, P. (2003). *E-government and the decentralization of service delivery, to achieve seamless client-centred service* (CPMR Discussion Paper, 25). Dublin: IPA.

Vatanasombut, B., Stylianou, A.C., & Igbaria, M. (2004). How to retain online customers. *Communications of ACM, 47*, 65-69.

Weatherall, D.J., Ledingham, J.G.G., & Worell, D.A. (1984). *Oxford textbook of medicine.* Oxford: Oxford University Press.

Yi, Y. (1990). A critical review of consumer satisfaction. In V. Zeithaml (Ed.), *Review of marketing.* American Marketing Association.

This work was previously published in International Journal of Electronic Government Research, Vol. 2, Issue 3, edited by D. F. Norris, pp. 1-22, copyright 2006 by IGI Publishing, formerly known as Idea Group Publishing (an imprint of IGI Global).

Chapter VIII

If You Build a Political Web Site, Will They Come?
The Internet and Political Activism in Britain

Pippa Norris, Harvard University, USA

John Curtice, Strathclyde University, UK

Abstract

This study focuses on the capacity of the Internet for strengthening political activism. The first part summarizes debates about these issues in the previous literature. This study starts from the premise that political activism is a multidimensional phenomenon and that we need to understand how different channels of participation relate to the social and political characteristics of the online population. We predict that certain dimensions of activism will probably be strengthened by the rise of the knowledge society, particularly cause-oriented forms of political participation, reflecting the prior social and political characteristics of the online population. By contrast, we expect the Internet to have far less impact upon conventional channels of political participation, exemplified by election campaigns. The second part summarizes the sources of data and the key measures of political activism used in this study, drawing upon the British Social Attitudes Survey from 2003. The third part examines the evidence for the relationship between use of the Internet and patterns of civic engagement in the British context. The conclusion summarizes the results and considers their broader implications.

Introduction

The rise of knowledge societies represents one of the most profound transformations that have occurred in recent decades. This phenomenon, characterized by the widespread diffusion of information and communication technologies (ICTs) across society, promises to have major consequences by expanding access to education and training, broadening channels of expression and social networks, as well as revolutionizing the nature of work and the economy. The primary impact of this development has been evident in affluent nations such as the United States, Sweden, and Britain, but the Internet has also been widely regarded as an important instrument for social change in poorer countries with relatively high levels of ICTs, such as Malaysia and Brazil (U.N., 2002; Franda, 2002). The core issue for this study concerns the social and political consequences of the rise of knowledge societies, in particular the capacity of the Internet for strengthening civic engagement.

To consider these issues, the first part summarizes debates about the impact of the Internet on civic engagement. This study assumes that political activism is a multidimensional phenomenon. The impact of the Internet on each of these dimensions, in turn, is assumed to be heavily dependent upon the social and political characteristics of Internet users. Given this framework, the study predicts that the primary impact of using the Internet will be upon facilitating cause-oriented forms of political activism, thereby strengthening social movements, voluntary associations, and interest groups, more than upon conventional channels of political participation, exemplified by election campaigns. To test these propositions in the British context, the second part summarizes the sources of data and the key measures of political activism used in this study, drawing upon the British Social Attitudes Survey of 2003. The third part examines the evidence for the relationship between use of the Internet and indicators of civic engagement. The conclusion in the final part summarizes the empirical results and considers their broader implications.

Theories of the Impact of
Knowledge Societies on Democracy

Multiple theories exist about how the growth of knowledge societies could potentially influence political participation and civic engagement in contemporary democracies. Three main perspectives can be identified in the previous literature.

The Internet as a Virtual Agora

The most positive view is held by cyber-optimists, who emphasize the Panglossian possibilities of the Internet for the involvement of ordinary citizens in direct, deliberative, or "strong" democracy. Digital technologies are thought to hold promise as a mechanism facilitating alternative channels of civic engagement, exemplified by political chat-rooms, remote electronic voting in elections, referenda, and plebiscites, and the mobilization of virtual communities, thereby revitalizing levels of mass participation in public affairs (Barber, 1998; Budge, 1996, Rash, 1997; Rheingold, 1993; Schwartz, 1996). This view was popular as the Internet initially rapidly expanded in the United States during the mid-1990s, and this perspective continues to be expressed by enthusiasts today (Gilder, 2000). For example, Hauben and Hauben (1997) argue that by bringing people together, the Internet can help rebuild a sense of community and trust (see also Wellman & Guilia, 1999). Empirical backing for this view has come from analysis of the Pew Internet and American Life Project, which suggests that Internet users have wider social networks than non-users (Ranney, 2000; Robinson et al., 2000; Pew 2001; Uslaner, 2004), a result replicated in Britain (Gardner & Oswald, 2001).

The Knowledge Elite and Social Inequalities

Yet these claims remain highly controversial. Cyber-pessimists regard the knowledge society as a Pandora's box reinforcing existing inequalities of power and wealth, generating deeper divisions between the information rich and poor. In this perspective, the global and social divides in Internet access mean that, far from encouraging mass participation, the growth of ICTs will disproportionately benefit the most affluent sectors in the developed world (Golding, 1996; Hayward, 1995; Murdock & Golding, 1989; Weber, Loumakis, & Bergman, 2003). Observers suggests that traditional interest groups, major parties, and governments have the capacity to reassert their control in the virtual political sphere, just as traditional multinational corporations have the ability to reestablish their predominance in the world of e-commerce (Hill & Hughes, 1998; McChesney, 1999; Selnow, 1998;

Toulouse & Luke, 1998). If political resources on the Internet reflect the voice and influence of the more affluent sectors and dominant groups, this could reinforce existing political disparities and class biases commonly found in political activism within democratic societies.

Politics as Usual

An alternative skeptical perspective suggests that so far the potential of the knowledge society has failed to have a dramatic impact on the practical reality of "politics as usual," for good or ill, even in countries such as the United States at the forefront of digital technologies (Margolis & Resnick, 2000). This view stresses the embedded status quo and the difficulties of achieving radical change to political systems through technological mechanisms. During the 2000 American election campaign, for example, commentators suggest that George W. Bush and Al Gore used their Web pages essentially as glossy shop-windows, as fundraising tools, and as campaign ads, rather than as interactive "bottom up" formats facilitating public comment and discussion (Foot & Schneider, 2002; Media Metrix, 2000). Elsewhere, content analysis of political party Web sites in countries as diverse as the UK, France, Mexico, and the Republic of Korea have found that their primary purpose has been the provision of standard information about party organizations and policies that was also widely available off-line, providing more of the same rather than anything new, still less interactive facilities:

Party presence on the Internet seems to represent largely an additional element to a party's repertoire of action along with more traditional communication forms rather than a transformation of the fundamental relationship between political parties and the public, as some earlier advocates of cyber democracy hoped. (Gibson, Nixon, & Ward, 2003)

Studies of the contents of government department Web sites have also found that these are often primarily used for the dissemination of information and the provision of routine administrative services. The Internet thereby serves as an aid to good governance and transparency, but it does not necessarily function so effectively as a medium expanding opportunities for citizen consultation, policy discussion, or other public inputs into the policymaking process (Allen, Juillet, Paquet, & Roy, 2001; Chadwick & May, 2003; Fountain, 2001; Haque, 2002; Stowers, 1999; Thomas & Streib, 2003).

The Multidimensional Nature of Political Activism

In contrast to these perspectives, this study follows the convention established by Verba and his colleagues (Verba, Nie, & Kim, 1978; Verba, Schlozman, & Brady 1995) in assuming that political activism is multidimensional with many distinct forms of involvement, each associated with differing costs and benefits. The impact of the Internet can be expected to differ in each of these, mainly due to the prior social and political characteristics of the online population. Four main categories can be distinguished, each with different costs and benefits: voting, campaign-oriented activism, cause-oriented activism, and civic-oriented activism.

Voting in regular elections is one of the most ubiquitous forms of citizen-oriented participation, requiring some initiative and awareness for an informed choice but making fairly minimal demands of time, knowledge, and effort. Through the ballot box, voting exerts diffuse pressure over parties and elected officials, and the outcomes of elections affect all citizens. Participating at the ballot box is central to citizenship in representative democracy but due to its relatively low costs the act is atypical of other, more demanding forms of participation. The Internet can be expected to encourage voting participation mainly by lowering some of the information hurdles to making an informed choice, although the provision of remote electronic voting through a variety of new technologies can be expected to have a more radical impact upon turnout (Tolbert & McNeal, 2003; Norris, 2004).

Campaign-oriented forms of participation concern acts focused primarily upon how people can influence parliament and government in representative democracy, primarily through political parties in British politics. Verba, Nie, and Kim focus on this aspect when they defined political participation as "those legal activities by private citizens that are more or less directly aimed at influencing the selection of governmental personnel and/or the actions they take" (Verba et al., 1978, p. 46). Work for parties or candidates, including party membership and volunteer work, election leafleting, financial donations to parties or candidates, attending local party meetings, and get-out-the-vote drives, all typify this category. Parties serve multiple functions in representative democracies: notably simplifying and structuring electoral choices; organizing and mobilizing campaigns; aggregating disparate interests; channeling political debate; selecting candidates; structuring parliamentary divisions; acting as policy think tanks; and organizing government. Not only are parties one of the main conduits of political participation, they also serve to boost and strengthen electoral turnout. If mass party membership is under threat, as many indicators suggest, this could have serious implications for representative democracy (Mair & van Biezen 2001; Scarrow, 2001). Campaigning and party work typically generates collective rather than individual benefits but requires greater initiative, time, and effort (and sometimes expenditure) than merely casting a ballot. The Internet can be expected to provide new opportunities for activism in parties and election campaigns, for example, through downloading information, joining parties or donating funds, or participating in discussion groups hosted on party or candidate Web sites (Gibson, Nixon, & Ward, 2003; Hague & Loader, 1999; Norris, 2001). At the same time, the online population is usually younger than average, while party members and activists are typically drawn from middle-aged and older sectors of society. The social characteristics of online users mean that they are unlikely to be drawn toward party Web sites and thus traditional forms of campaign activism.

Cause-oriented activities are focused primarily upon influencing specific issues and policies. These acts are exemplified by whether respondents have actual experience in taking part in demonstrations and protests, signing a petition, or raising an issue in the news media. The distinction is not water-tight; for example, political parties can organize mass demonstrations, and social movements often adopt mixed action strategies that combine traditional repertoires, such as lobbying representatives, with a variety of alternative modes such as online networking, street protests, and consumer boycotts. Nevertheless, compared with campaign-oriented actions, the distinctive aspect of cause-oriented repertoires is that these are most commonly used to pursue specific issues and policy concerns among diverse targets, both within and also well beyond the electoral arena. These acts seek to influence representative democracies within the nation-state through the conventional channels of contacting elected officials, ministers, civil servants, and government departments, but their target is often broader and more diffuse, possibly in the non-profit or private sectors, whether directed at shaping public opinion and "life-styles," publicizing certain issues through the news media, mobilizing a networked coalition with other groups or non-profit agencies, influencing the practices of international bodies such as the World Trade Organization or the United Nations, or impacting public policy in other countries. The proliferation of cause-oriented Web sites, combined with the typical age and educational profile of the online population, makes this a particularly rich area of activism that can be expected to be reinforced through the Internet.

Lastly **civic-oriented** activities, by contrast, involve membership and working together in voluntary associations, as well as collaborating with community groups to solve a local problem. The core claim of "Toquevillian" theories of social capital is that typical face-to-face deliberative activities and horizontal collaboration within voluntary organizations far removed from the political sphere—exemplified by trade unions, social clubs, and philanthropic groups—promote interpersonal trust, social tolerance and cooperative behavior. In turn, these norms are regarded as cementing the bonds of social life, creating the foundation for building local communities, civil society, and democratic governance. In a "win-win" situation, participation in associational life is thought to generate individual rewards, such as career opportunities and personal support networks, as well as facilitating community goods, by fostering the capacity of people to work together on local problems. Civic organizations such as unions, churches, and community groups, Putnam suggests, play a vital role in the production of social capital where they succeed in bridging divisive social cleavages, integrating people from diverse backgrounds and values, promoting "habits of the heart" such as tolerance, cooperation, and reciprocity, thereby contributing toward a dense, rich, and vibrant social infrastructure (Putnam, 1993, 1996, 2000, 2002; Pharr & Putnam, 2000). This dimension involves direct action within local communities, such as raising funds for a local hospital or school, where the precise dividing line between the "social" and "political" breaks down. Trade unions and churches, in particular, have long been regarded as central pillars of civic society, which have traditionally served the function of drawing European citizens into public life. For a variety of reasons, including the way that voluntary associations can strengthen social networks, foster leadership skills, heighten political awareness, create party linkages, and facilitate campaign work, people affiliated with church-based or union organizations can be expected to participate more fully in public life. (Cassel, 1999; Radcliff & Davis, 2000) Access to the knowledge society can be expected to expand social networks and information, facilitating membership in civic associations and social groups, although the evidence whether the Internet strengthens or weakens social capital remains under debate (Bimber, 1998; Horrigan, Rainie, & Fox 2001).

Therefore the argument developed in this study rejects the view that everything will change as the Internet facilitates radical forms of direct democracy that come to replace the traditional channels of representative governance (as optimists originally hoped). Nor do we accept that the digital divide will inevitably reinforce existing socio-economic and demographic disparities in political activism (as pessimists predicted). The alternative view that nothing will change as the digital world merely replicates "politics as usual" (as the skeptics suggest) also seems implausible. Instead the argument developed here suggests that we need to understand the multidimensional nature of political activism and how this interacts with the characteristics of Internet users. We predict that certain dimensions of activism will probably be strengthened by the rise of the knowledge society, particularly cause-oriented forms of political participation, reflecting the prior social and political characteristics of the online population.

Conceptual Framework, Evidence, and Survey Data

Interpretations of the results of the existing empirical studies about the role of ICTs on civic engagement remain divided in part because the outcome may be conditional upon the characteristics of early Internet adopters, the location of individuals within society, and the particular types of society under comparison. It remains unclear how far the patterns uncovered in much of the existing U.S. research on these issues are conditioned by the particular characteristics of American politics and society, or how far the findings hold more generally elsewhere. One way to explore this issue is to consider the evidence for the uses and functions of the Internet in Britain. Both

Britain and America are affluent post-industrial service economies, sharing strong cultural links. Yet significant contrasts are also evident, including in general levels of electoral turnout, party activism, and associational membership (Norris 2003).

To explore the impact of Internet use upon political activism in the British context, this paper draws upon the results of a multi-wave research project based on a special battery of items, contained in the British Social Attitudes (BSA) 2003. The BSA is a representative national survey that has been conducted every year since 1983. Each survey is conducted using more than 3,000 interviews with a representative random sample of people in Britain. The 2003 survey monitored use of the Internet, social capital, and civic engagement. The core items are being repeated in two subsequent waves of the BSA surveys, allowing the evolution of the Internet to be monitored over time.

The 2003 survey gauged contemporary Internet access at home and at work, as well as measuring a variety of ways of using new communication and information technologies. To illustrate the baseline population, Figure 1 shows how far people use the Internet in the British sample. Overall, almost half (47%) of respondents never used the Internet, so that 53% went online in Britain, either at home, at work, or somewhere else. This proportion is about 8-10% less than the comparable figure in America during the equivalent period, as monitored by the Pew Internet & American Life Project[1]. Among the online population in Britain, just over one quarter (28%) had access only at home, while about one quarter had access both at home and at work, and a few (4%) only accessed the Internet at work. These estimates confirm, as expected, that Internet access currently remains lower in Britain than in the United States. Nevertheless the Pew surveys suggest that for the last few years

Figure 1. Access to the Internet in Britain, 2003

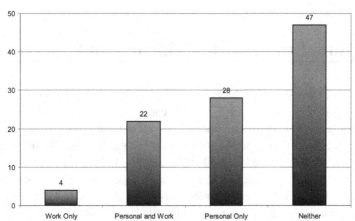

Figure 2. Growing home use of the Internet in Britain, 1999-2003

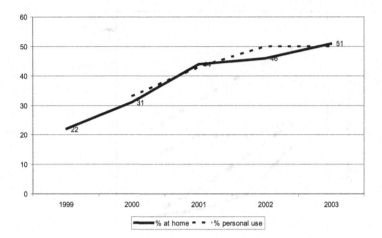

American Internet access appears to have stabilized at around two-thirds of the U.S. population, while by contrast Figure 2 indicates that in Britain personal use of the Internet has not yet hit a ceiling and indeed continues to expand slightly in recent years, albeit at a slower rate than earlier. The 2005 BSA suggests that use has now spread slightly further, to 56% of respondents.

As Internet use has diffused more widely in Britain, the social composition of the online population has become less distinctive in its higher educational background and its younger age profile, although analysis of the social characteristics of the online population by Bromley (2004) confirms that important digital divides in Internet access remain in Britain, as commonly found elsewhere (Norris, 2001; Wilhelm, 1999). This means that any multivariate analysis of the impact of Internet use needs to control for the prior social and demographic characteristics of users, including their age, sex, race, education, and social class.

Nevertheless, with only cross-sectional survey data it remains difficult to isolate and disentangle the impact of access to the Internet from the social background of users. The BSA-2003 does provide a proxy indicator, however, by monitoring when people reported that they first went online. This makes it possible to compare the groups who are and are not online, as well as to compare the group who only recently started to use the Internet against the early adopters, who commenced using the Internet five or more years ago (i.e., prior to 1998). Any effect from the cumulative experience of using the Internet should be apparent if we find some significantly different political attitudes and behavior among these groups, for example, if more experienced users acquire civic skills and social networks online that encourage them to become more

Figure 3. Uses of the Internet by length of experience

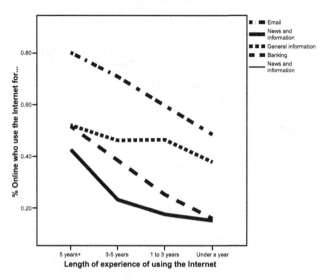

active in community affairs. Figure 3 illustrates some of these common contrasts, for example, how the most experienced users were significantly more likely to use the Internet for email, banking, and news. At the same time caution is needed when drawing inferences based on length of Internet experience, because over time the online population has gradually "normalized" in its characteristics, becoming more representative of the general public. As a result, it remains unclear whether any contrasts between the more and less experienced user groups can be attributed to Internet exposure per se, or to the "normalization" of the online population.

If we establish that levels of civic engagement are significantly associated with use of the Internet, we still need to establish a suitable benchmark to evaluate the strength of this relationship. This study therefore compares Internet use with the role of regular newspaper readership. Studies have commonly found that those who habitually use and pay attention to newspapers are significantly more knowledgeable than the average citizen about party policies, civics, and candidates, as well as being more interested in public affairs and more likely to turnout to vote (Miller, 1991; Newton, 1997; Norris et al., 1999, p. 113). Similar patterns are commonly found elsewhere, with regular newspaper readers more informed and engaged than average (Norris 2000). The models in this study therefore compare the relationship between Internet use and civic engagement with that between regular newspaper readership and civic engagement. Controlling for newspaper readership also provides a way to monitor prior political predispositions.

The design of the items measuring civic engagement are based upon the assumption that involvement is multidimensional, with many distinct forms, each associated with differing costs and benefits (Verba et al., 1978, 1995). This study compares the impact of Internet use and newspaper readership on the four main dimensions of activism already discussed, namely: voting, campaign-oriented, cause-oriented, and civic-oriented. These are summarized into a Political Activism Index combining all dimensions[2]. The basic items used to develop the measures are listed in Appendix A.

Voting participation is measured in the BSA 2003 by whether respondents reported that they recalled voting in the 2001 British general election.

Experience of *campaign-oriented* activism is gauged in this study by a three-item scale including whether people are members of a party[3], whether they express a "fairly" or "very" strong party identification, and whether they have ever contacted their MP or MSP. Admittedly, these measures are far from ideal. Party identification is a psychological attitude, rather than form of behavior. Many people contact their MP for reasons that have nothing to do with campaigning per se. Better measures of campaign activism would also gauge typical activities, such as canvassing, donating funds to parties, or attending party meetings. These will be monitored in subsequent BSA surveys, but the measures used here can be regarded as at least general, if far from perfect, proxies for campaign activism that are available in the 2003 survey.

Cause-oriented activism is measured in this study by a seven-battery item including whether, in response to an unjust or harmful government action, people have signed a petition, spoken to an influential person, contacted a government department, raised the issue in an organization, formed a group of like-minded people, contacted radio, TV, or a newspaper about the issue, or gone on a protest or demonstration.

Lastly, experience of civic activism is gauged here by a 14-point scale summarizing membership in a series of different types of voluntary organization and associations, focusing mainly upon traditional sectors such as parent-teacher associations, charitable organizations, church groups, and social clubs (excluding party membership), although also including some "new" social movements, exemplified by groups concerned about the environment and about international issues.

The summary Political Activism Index, providing an overview, is constructed simply by adding together experience of each of these different types of acts (each coded 0/1). The study has therefore formed additive indices of each item within each of the four groups and also created an additive index across all four groups. It should be noted that the resulting summary index is currently heavily dominated by the civic-oriented scale, as this has the most items. It should also be noted that in this conceptual framework, with the important exception of partisan identification, this study focuses upon political *activity*; we are concerned with *doing* politics rather than being attentive to public affairs or having psychological attitudes thought conducive to civic engagement, such as trust in parliament or a sense of political efficacy, explored elsewhere (Curtice & Norris, 2004). The study therefore does not regard exposure or attention to mass communications, exemplified by following political events in newspapers, as indicators of political activism per se. These factors may indeed plausibly contribute toward participation, and thereby help explain this phenomenon, as prior pre-conditions, but they are not, in themselves, channels that citizens can use for expressing political concerns or mobilizing group interests.

Analysis of the Results

We can start by examining the simple bivariate relationships between Internet use and these multidimensional indicators of political activism, with the important proviso that the background of online users in Britain continues to be skewed to-

Table 1. Mean scores on the indicator of political activism scales by experience of Internet use, without any controls

Uses Internet	Political activism scale	Voted	Campaign-oriented activism	Cause-oriented activism	Civic-oriented activism
Non-users	2.15	.69	.48	.43	.55
All Internet users	2.65	.65	.51	.65	.83
Difference	*+0.50*	*-.04*	*+.03*	*+.22*	*+.28*
Sig.	.000	.004	.149	.000	.000
Eta	.117	.044	.022	.129	.129
SD Non-users	1.83	.46	.48	.74	.55
SD all Internet users	2.36	.48	.51	1.01	1.21
Used the Internet...					
Under a year	2.79	.66	.49	.75	.93
1-3 years	2.94	.67	.56	.74	.98
3-5 years	3.39	.63	.66	.92	1.14
5 years+	3.74	.65	.65	1.07	1.39
Difference	*+0.95*	*-0.01*	*+0.16*	*+0.32*	*0.46*
Sig.	.000	.486	.009	.000	.000
Eta	.147	.039	.084	.126	.133
Total sample	2.38	.67	.50	.53	.68

Notes: *The significance of the mean difference between Internet users and non-users is measured by ANOVA. See the text for details of the construction of the scales.*

Source: *The British Social Attitudes survey, 2003*

Figure 4. Civic engagement by length of experience of using the Internet

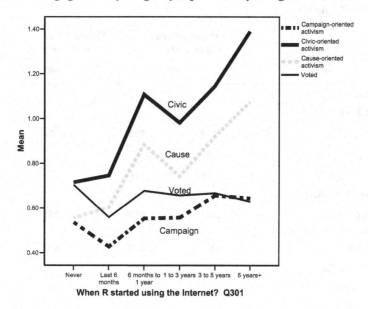

ward the well-educated and more affluent social sectors, which are both resources closely associated with political activism, so that multivariate analysis is required controlling for these factors.

Table 1 presents the mean score on these indicators for the group of all Internet users compared with all non-users, the standard deviation, and the significance of the difference (estimated by ANOVA). In line with our initial expectations, the results confirm that Internet users in Britain proved significantly more politically engaged than non-users across the indicators of cause-oriented and civic-oriented participation, as well as in the total activism scale. This pattern suggests that the forms of political involvement that are most likely to benefit through the development of the Internet are through single-issue politics, voluntary associations, and community groups, as expected given the prior characteristics of the online population. By contrast, if we compare more traditional forms of engagement, Internet users were slightly less likely to vote than non-users, and there were no significant differences between users and non-users in their levels of campaign activism.

The comparison of activism by length of Internet use displays a slightly different pattern, illustrated in Figure 4, where early adopters with the longest experience of going online proved significantly more politically active across all dimensions except voting turnout (where there was no difference) when compared against those who

Table 2: The impact of Internet use on the overall Political Activism scale, with controls (full model)

	Unstandardized Coefficients		Standardized Coefficients	Sig.
	B	Std. Error	Beta	P.
(Constant)	-.580	.137		.000
DEMOGRAPHIC				
Age (in years)	**.032**	**.002**	**.271**	**.000**
Sex (Male=1/Female=0)	-.008	.062	-.002	.902
Ethnic minority (1)	.000	.116	.000	.998
SOCIO-ECONOMIC				
Education (Highest qualification on 7-point scale)	**.242**	**.019**	**.251**	**.000**
Managerial	**.433**	**.088**	**.097**	**.000**
Lower white collar	-.007	.052	-.002	.895
Petit bourgeoisie	.037	.041	.014	.360
Foremen and technicians	.032	.025	.020	.199
MEDIA USE				
Regular newspaper reader (Normally reads paper at least 3 times a week)	**.273**	**.061**	**.065**	**.000**
Uses Internet (Yes=1/No=0)	**.323**	**.074**	**.076**	**.000**
Adjusted R²	**.135**			

Notes: *The model presents the results of OLS regression analysis where the dependent variable is the overall Political Activism scale. Class is categorized by the respondent's occupation where the 'working class' functions as the contrast category in the model. The significant variables are highlighted in* **bold**.

Source: *The British Social Attitudes survey, 2003*

had first ventured online more recently. Yet without any controls it is not possible to determine whether this pattern is due to the effects of length of exposure to the Internet per se or whether this reflected the gradual changes in the social composition and political attitudes of the Internet population.

The multivariate regression analysis presented in Table 2 displays the results of the full model predicting overall levels of political activism, including the range of social and demographic controls as well as the impact of regular newspaper reading and use of the Internet. The results show that, as expected, age had a significant and strong effect upon political participation, with people becoming more active as they enter middle age, with a slight fall in a curvilinear pattern in the over-70s. Interestingly, gender and race appear to be insignificant predictors of activism in this model, although women and men in Britain have been found to have different patterns of participation in other studies (Norris, Lovenduski, & Campbell 2004). As numerous studies have reported, by providing civic skills and boosting a sense of internal efficacy, education is one of the strongest influences upon activism (Verba et al., 1978, 1995). Graduates and those with higher educational qualifications are consistently the most politically engaged. Social class also plays a significant role in participation, with managers and professionals the most engaged, in part because occupational status is so closely related to educational qualifications. Even with this battery of controls, both regular newspaper readership and Internet use remain significant predictors of political activism. This relationship may obviously be reciprocal, with knowledge and engagement encouraging media habits, as well as vice versa (Norris, 2000). The way in which the Internet serves as a source of general information about news, current affairs, and political events may help provide the knowledge and confidence that are strongly associated with active engagement in public affairs. And patterns of activism that develop may well encourage greater use of the Internet as a way to find out about current affairs, government services, or events in the news. In this regard, the Internet may appear to function in a similar

Table 3: Summary models of the impact of media use on the activism indicators, with demographic and social controls (not presented)

	Voted			Campaign-oriented activism			Cause-oriented activism			Civic-oriented activism		
	B	se	sig	B	se	sig	B	se	sig	B	se	sig
Regular newspaper reader (Normally reads paper at least 3 times a week)	**.280**	**.020**	**.000**	**.117**	**.020**	**.000**	.036	.027	.172	**.067**	**.032**	**.036**
Uses Internet (Yes=1/ No=0)	**.216**	**.086**	**.012**	.043	.024	.071	**.073**	**.033**	**.026**	**.158**	**.039**	**.000**

Notes: The table presents the results of regression analysis models, including the unstandardized betas (B), the standard error (s.e.), and their significance, where the dependent variables are the indicators of the four main dimensions of political activism. The full model presented in Table 2 is used, controlling for the respondent's age, sex, race, education, and occupational class, although these coefficients are not reported here. A binary logistic model is used for voting participation and OLS linear models for the other scales. The significant variables are highlighted in bold.

Source: The British Social Attitudes survey, 2003

way to newspapers, while also providing social networks and reinforcing contacts that can help mobilize citizens in the public sphere.

Similar models were run with the battery of controls for all the four separate indicators of political activism. The results in Table 3 confirm that Internet users remain more active than non-users in cause-oriented and civic-oriented forms of participation, suggesting that this is not simply a product of their distinctive social profile in terms of their age, gender, race, education, and class. The difference among users and non-users remains insignificant in the more traditional campaign-oriented forms of activism. And contrary to expectations, after applying these controls, Internet users became significantly more likely to vote, not less. It may be that the ubiquity and particular characteristics of this activity, with the lowest demands of time and energy, mean that voting participation is associated with both media. When the effects of Internet use are compared with those associated with regular newspaper readership, the patterns show the strongest contrast between traditional forms of campaign activism (which are significantly related to regular newspaper readership) and cause-oriented activism (which are significantly related to Internet use). The implications of these patterns for the political participation in democracy are considered next.

Conclusion and Discussion

The rise of the Internet has generated considerable interest and concern about its possible consequences for government and democracy. The bursting of the Internet economic bubble dampened the more utopian political hopes as well, and the conventional wisdom shifted in a more skeptical direction. Yet in reality both the many hopes and fears may well prove to have been exaggerated, although this does not mean that there are no significant political consequences flowing from the development of new communication and information technologies.

The conclusion from this study is that any analysis of the impact of using the Internet needs to take into account the distinct dimensions by which people channel their activism into public affairs. We need to understand how the types of Internet activism interact with the social profile of the online population. This account suggests that the most popular forms of online activism are likely to reflect the preponderance of younger and well-educated populations using the Internet, in Britain and elsewhere, until such a time as the online population eventually "normalizes" to reflect a cross-section of the general electorate.

The conclusion from the British survey evidence is that the potential impact of the Internet on democratic participation depends heavily upon the type of activism under comparison. The online population is most predisposed to engage in cause-oriented forms of activism, characteristic of petitioning, demonstrating, and contacting the media over single-issue politics and civic-oriented activities, such as belonging to voluntary associations and community organizations. By contrast, traditional campaign-oriented forms of political activism are associated more strongly with newspaper readership. The patterns by voting participation suggest that without any controls, Internet users are less likely to turnout than non-users, although this pattern is reversed once controls are introduced for the age, education, gender, and class of the online population. Subsequent surveys will monitor how far this pattern persists or evolves with newer developments in the Internet. The implications of these findings are not simply about whether use of the Internet will mobilize citizens at individual level but also for the type of political practices that the rise of the Internet might encourage in the political system. What seems apparent is that use of the Internet by political parties seems unlikely to stem any erosion in traditional campaign-oriented activities. At the same time, the new technologies will probably prove to be of greatest benefit to engaging supporters in social movements, transnational policy networks, and single-issue causes, encouraging their expansion in many democracies.

Acknowledgment

The special battery of items on Internet use was part of the E-society research program funded by the Economic and Social Research Council of the UK. The authors are most grateful to the ESRC for supporting this project and to all the staff of The National Centre for Social Research (NatCen) for administering and conducting the BSA 2003 survey. For more details, see http://www.natcen.ac.uk.

References

Allen, B. A., Juillet, L., Paquet, G., & Roy, J. (2001). E-governance & government on-line in Canada: Partnerships, people & prospects. *Government Information Quarterly, 18*(2), 93-104.

Barber, B. R. (1998). Three scenarios for the future of technology and strong democracy. *Political Science Quarterly, 113*(4), 573-589.

Bimber, B. (1998). The Internet and political transformation: populism, community and accelerated pluralism. *Polity, XXXI*(1), 133-160.

Bimber, B. (2000). The study of information technology and civic engagement. *Political Communication, 17*(4), 329-333.

Bimber, B. (2001). Information and political engagement in America: The search for effects of information technology at the individual level. *Political Research Quarterly, 54*(1), 53-67.

Boas, T. C. (2000). The dictator's dilemma? The Internet and U.S. policy toward Cuba. *The Washington Quarterly, 23*(3), 57-67.

Bonfadelli, H. (2002). The Internet and knowledge gaps: a theoretical and empirical investigation. *European Journal of Communication, 17*(1), 65-84.

Bromley, C. (2004). Can Britain close the digital divide? In A. Park (Ed.), *British social attitudes, 21st report*. London: Sage.

Budge, I. (1996). *The new challenge of direct democracy*. Oxford: Polity Press.

Carpini, M. X. D. (2000). Gen.com: Youth, civic engagement, and the new information environment. *Political Communication, 17*(4), 341-349.

Cassel, C. A. (1999). Voluntary associations, churches, and social participation theories of turnout. *Social Science Quarterly, 80*(3), 504-517.

Chadwick, A., & May, C. (2003). Interactions between states and citizens in the age of the Internet: 'E-government' in the United States, Britain and the European Union. *Governance, 16*(2), 271-300.

David, R. (1999). *The web of politics*. Oxford: Oxford University Press.

Davis, R., & Owen, D. (1998). *New media and American politics*. New York: Oxford University Press.

Drake, W. J., Kalathil, S., & Boas, T. C. (2000). Dictatorships in the digital age: Some considerations on the Internet in China and Cuba. *iMP: The Magazine on Information Impacts*. Retrieved October from www.cisp.org/imp

Foot, K. A., & Schneider, S. M. (2002). Online action in campaign 2000: An exploratory analysis of the US political web sphere. *Journal of Broadcasting & Electronic Media, 46*(2), 222-244.

Fountain, J. E. (2001). *Building the virtual state: Information technology and institutional change*. Washington, DC: Brookings Institution Press.

Franda, M. (2002). *Launching into cyberspace: Internet development and politics in five world regions*. Boulder, CO: Lynne Rienner.

Gibson, R., Nixon, P., & Ward, S. (Eds.). (2003). *Political parties and the Internet: Net gain?* London: Routledge.

Gilder, G. (2000). *Telecosm: How infinite bandwidth will revolutionize our world*. New York: Free Press.

Golding, P. (1996). World wide wedge: division and contradiction in the global information infrastructure. *Monthly Review, 48*(3), 70-85.

Hague, B. N., & Loader, B. D. (Eds.). (1999). *Digital democracy: Discourse and decision making in the information age*. New York: Routledge.

Haque, M. S. (2002). E-governance in India: Its impacts on relations among citizens, politicians and public servants. *International Review of Administrative Sciences, 68*(2), 231-250.

Hayward, T. (1995). *Info-rich, info-poor: Access and exchange in the global information society*. K.G. Saur.

Hill, K. A., & Hughes, J. E. (1998). *Cyberpolitics: Citizen activism in the age of the Internet*. Lanham, MD: Rowan & Littlefield.

Horrigan, J., Rainie, L., & Fox, S. (2001). *Online communities: Networks that nurture long-distance relationships and local ties*. Pew Internet & American Life Project. Retrieved from http://www.pewinternet.org

Jennings, M. K., & Zeitner, V. (2003). Internet use and civic engagement—A longitudinal analysis. *Public Opinion Quarterly, 67*(3), 311-334.

Johnson, T. J., & Kaye, B. K. (2003). Around the World Wide Web in 80 ways—How motives for going online are linked to Internet activities among politically interested Internet users. *Social Science Computer Review, 21*(3), 304-325.

Kalathil, S., & Boas, T. C. (2003). *Open networks closed regimes: The impact of the Internet on authoritarian rule*. Washington, D.C.: Carnegie Endowment for International Peace.

Kamarck, E. C., & Nye, J. S., Jr. (1999). *Democracy.com? Governance in a networked world*. Hollis, NH: Hollis Publishing.

Keck, M. E., & Sikkink, K. (1998). *Activists beyond borders—Advocacy networks in international politics*. Ithaca, NY: Cornell University Press.

Kent Jennings, M., & Zeitner, V. (2003). Internet use and civic engagement—A longitudinal analysis. *Public Opinion Quarterly, 67*(3), 311-334.

Mair, P., & van Biezen, I. (2001). Party membership in twenty European democracies 1980-2000. *Party Politics, 7*(1), 7-22.

Margolis, M., & Resnick, D. (2000). *Politics as usual: The cyberspace 'revolution'*. Thousand Oaks, CA: Sage.

McChesney, R. W. (1999). *Rich media, poor democracy*. Champaign, IL: University of Illinois Press.

Media Metrix. (October 2000). *Campaign 2000: Party politics on the World Wide Web*. Retrieved from http://www.mediametrix.com

Murdock, G., & Golding, P. (1989). Information poverty and political inequality: Citizenship in the age of privatised communications. *Journal of Communication, 39*, 180-195.

Norris, P. (2000). *A virtuous circle*. New York: Cambridge University Press.

Norris, P. (2001). *Digital divide*. New York: Cambridge University Press.

Norris, P. (2002). *Democratic phoenix: Reinventing political activism*. New York: Cambridge University Press.

Norris, P. (2003). The bridging and bonding role of online communities. In P. N. Howard, & S. Jones (Eds.), *Society online: The Internet in context*. Thousand Oaks, CA: Sage.

Norris, P. (2004). Will new technology boost turnout? In N. Kersting, & H. Baldersheim (Eds.), *Electronic voting and democracy: A comparative analysis* (pp. 193-225), London: Palgrave.

Norris, P. (2005). The impact of the Internet on political activism: Evidence from Europe. *International Journal of Electronic Governance, 1*(1), 20-39.

Norris, P., Lovenduski, J., & Campbell, R. (2004). *Gender and political participation* (Report for the UK Electoral Commission).

Norris, P., & Sanders, D. (2003). Medium or message? *Political Communications*.

Pharr, S., & Putnam, R. (Eds.). (2000). *Disaffected democracies: What's troubling the trilateral countries?* Princeton, NJ: Princeton University Press.

Putnam, R. D. (1993). *Making democracy work: Civic traditions in modern Italy.* Princeton, NJ: Princeton University Press.

Putnam, R. D. (1996). The strange disappearance of civic America. *The American Prospect, 24*.

Putnam, R. D. (2000). *Bowling alone: The collapse and revival of American community.* New York: Simon and Schuster.

Putnam, R. D. (Ed.). (2002). *Democracies in flux.* Oxford: Oxford University Press.

Radcliff, B., & Davis, P. (2000). Labor organization and electoral participation in industrial democracies. *American Journal of Political Science, 44*(1), 132-141.

Rash, W., Jr. (1997). *Politics on the net: Wiring the political process.* New York: W.H. Freeman.

Rheingold, H. (1993). *The virtual community: Homesteading on the electronic frontier.* Reading, MA: Addison Wesley.

Scammell, M. (2000). The Internet and civic engagement: The age of the citizen-consumer. *Political Communication, 17*(4), 351-355.

Scarrow, S. (2001). Parties without members? In R. Dalton, & M. Wattenberg (Eds.), *Parties without partisans*. New York: Oxford University Press.

Schwartz, E. (1996). *Netactivism: How citizens use the Internet.* Sebastapol, CA: Songline Studios.

Selnow, G. W. (1998). *Electronic whistle-stops: The impact of the Internet on American politics.* Westport, CT: Praeger.

Shah, D. V., Kwak, N., & Holbert, R. L. (2001). "Connecting" and "disconnecting" with civic life: Patterns of Internet use and the production of social capital. *Political Communication, 18*(2), 141-162.

Shah, D. V., McLeod, J. M., & Yoon, S. H. (2001). Communication, context, and community: An exploration of print, broadcast, and Internet influences. *Communication Research, 28*(4), 464-506.

Stowers, G. N. L. (1999). Becoming cyberactive: State and local governments on the World Wide Web. *Government Information Quarterly, 16*(2), 111-127.

Thomas, J. C., & Streib, G. (2003). The new face of government: Citizen-initiated contacts in the era of e-government. *Journal of Public Administration Research and Theory, 13*(1), 83-101.

Tolbert, C. J., & McNeal, R. S. (2003). Unraveling the effects of the Internet on political participation? *Political Research Quarterly, 56*(2), 175-185.

Toulouse, C., & Luke, T. W. (Eds.). (1998). *The politics of cyberspace*. London: Rout-ledge.

United Nations/ American Society for Public Administration. (2002). *Benchmarking e-gov-ernment: A global perspective*. New York: United Nations/DPEPA.

Uslaner, E. M. (2004). Trust, civic engagement, and the Internet. *Political Communication, 21*(2), 223-242.

Verba, S., Nie, N., & Kim, J. (1978). *Participation and political equality: A seven-nation comparison*. New York: Cambridge University Press.

Verba, S., Schlozman, K., & Brady, H. E. (1995). *Voice and equality: Civic voluntarism in American politics*. Cambridge, MA: Harvard University Press.

Weber, L. M., Loumakis, A., & Bergman, J. (2003). Who participates and why? An analy-sis of citizens on the Internet and the mass public. *Social Science Computer Review, 21*(1), 26-42.

Wilhelm, A. (2000). *Democracy in the digital age: Challenges to political life in cyberspace*. New York: Routledge.

Endnotes

1   See www.pewinternet.org

2   Since the dimensions are theoretically defined and constructed, based on understand-ing the role of different forms of participation in representative democracy, the study did not use factor analysis to generate the classification or measurement.

3   It should be noted that the BSA survey monitored "party and trade union" membership, but the latter was also measured separately, so in the recoded measure, the residual group remains only the party members.

This work was previously published in International Journal of Electronic Government Research, Vol. 2, Issue 2, edited by D. F. Norris, pp. 1-21, copyright 2006 by IGI Publishing, formerly known as Idea Group Publishing (an imprint of IGI Global).

Appendix A

Scales	Question wording
Voted	*May I just check, thinking back to the last general election - that is the one in 2001 - do you remember which party you voted for then, or perhaps you didn't vote in that election?* Yes/No

Campaign-oriented activism	*And have you ever done any of the things on this card about a government action which you thought was unjust and harmful?...*
	  • *Contact my MP or MSP*
	
	Are you currently a member of, or do you regularly join in the activities of, any of the organisations on this card?
	  • *Political parties or trade unions (inc student unions)*
	
	Do you think of yourself as a little closer to one political party than to the others?
	(IF 'yes'), Would you call yourself very strong *(party)*, fairly strong, or not very strong? ('very'+'fairly').

Cause-oriented activism	*And have you ever done any of the things on this card about a government action which you thought was unjust and harmful?*
	  • *Contact a government department*
	  • *Contact radio, TV or a newspaper*
	  • *Sign a petition*
	  • *Raise the issue in an organization I already belong to*
	  • *Go on a protest or demonstration*
	  • *Form a group of like-minded people*

Civic-oriented activism	*Are you currently a member of, or do you regularly join in the activities of, any of the organisations on this card?*
	  • *An environmental or conservation group*
	  • *A pressure group or campaigning organisation*
	  • *Parent-teachers' / school parents association / Board of Governors etc*
	  • *Youth groups (e.g. scouts, guides, youth clubs etc)*
	  • *Education, arts, drama, reading or music group / evening class*
	  • *Religious group or church organisation*
	  • *A sports or recreation club*
	  • *Tenants' / Residents' group / Neighbourhood watch*
	  • *Social club / working men's club*
	  • *Women's group / Women's Institute*
	  • *Group for older people (e.g. lunch clubs)*
	  • *Local groups which raise money for charity (e.g. The Rotary Club)*
	  • *Other local community or voluntary group*
	  • *Other national or international group*

Chapter IX

Civic Engagement via E-Government Portals:
Information, Transactions, and Policy Making*

Yu-Che Chen, Northern Illinois University, USA

Daniela V. Dimitrova, Iowa State University, USA

Abstract

This exploratory study examines civic engagement with e-government via Web sites. It provides an analytical framework that integrates both the supply and demand sides of citizen interaction with e-government. In modeling three dimensions of online civic engagement (government information access, service transactions, and contributing to government policy-making processes), the study framework incorporates a number of variables, including political activism, civic involvement, perceived benefits and difficulties, information channels, and demographic characteristics. Based on a national sample of Internet users, the study highlights the importance of the supply side (availability of e-government) for promoting civic engagement. Furthermore, political activism is found to be positively related to accessing gov-

This study was funded by an internal grant from the Institute of Science and Society (ISS) at Iowa State University. An earlier version of this manuscript was published in the International Journal of Electronic Government Research.

ernment policy information and contributing to policy-making processes. The study results also confirm the significant impact of perceived benefits in fostering online civic engagement. Future research can benefit from this study by utilizing a more comprehensive model, treating various dimensions of online engagement separately, and conducting an in-depth analysis of the elements of perceived benefits.

Introduction

Electronic government services have gradually evolved from simply providing information on Web portals to offering citizens opportunities to communicate and conduct online transactions. Engaging citizens online to improve governance and facilitate e-democracy remains one of the key challenges of the next generation of electronic government (Pratchett & Krimmer, 2005). Norris and Moon (2005) report, however, that there is little progress made at the local level in adopting interactive services (Norris & Moon, 2005). A study of local government officials also suggests that e-democracy is not high on their agenda for future deployment of electronic government (Norris, 2005). Surveys of government Web sites indicate that even, when available, interactive features to engage citizens in formulating public policy are rarely used (West, 2004). Although with the introduction of Internet technologies, governments are shifting away from the traditional bureaucratic paradigm, providing customer services rather than enhancing citizen participation in policy making remains the primary focus (Ho, 2002). This seems to be a missed opportunity when recent evidence has shown a positive link between visiting local government Web sites and trust in government (Tolbert & Mossberger, 2006).

Learning from experience and building on the information and communication infrastructure, government can introduce meaningful ways to engage citizens in the policy making process. One of the main criticisms of current e-government concerns the top-down bias impacting decisions on what type and nature of information and services are to be provided (McNeal, Tolbert, Mossberger, & Dotterweich, 2003). Thus, e-government tends to either ignore the citizen's perspective or misunderstand it. Moreover, existing scholarly literature on e-government seems to pay limited attention to the citizen's perspective. Studies of transparency (Pandey & Bretschneider, 1997), information and service delivery (Holden et al, 2003), online public involvement (Scott, 2006), and reforms (Ho, 2002) are mostly based on surveys of either government Web sites and/or government officials. Although some popular studies take a more citizen-centric approach in trying to understand the demand side (e.g., Graafland-Essers & Ettedgui, 2003; Horrigan, 2004), such studies have limited analytical methodologies for understanding the impact of individual factors. One exception is the investigation of the factors leading to e-government adoption by Carter and Belanger (2004), who tested the impact of several variables on intent to adopt e-government services. However, using college students as the sample limits the generalizability of their findings. Finally, current e-government studies tend to ignore opportunities for integrating insights from relevant bodies of literature. For example, public administration and political science researchers often overlook literature on information management systems, and rarely integrate social and network dimensions into the study of e-government (Norris & Lloyd, 2004).

To fill these gaps in existing research, this book chapter proposes a framework that takes into account both the supply and demand sides of civic involvement in e-government. This study sheds light on how making online services available impacts the willingness of citizens to use e-government and their actual utilization of e-government information and services. Moreover, the study integrates insights from allied fields of research, examining the social aspects of civic engagement and analyzing the importance of information channels and perceived benefits of e-government services. Lastly, this study employs regression analysis to ascertain both the direction and significance of various factors impacting online civic engagement, thus moving beyond mere descriptive studies.

We begin by introducing the proposed analytical framework and formulating hypotheses based on relevant theoretical insights. Next, we discuss the models and measures used and explain the data collection and data analysis process. The discussion of the results includes theoretical and policy implications of the key findings. Finally, we conclude with a summary of the findings and suggestions for future research.

Analytical Framework

The proposed conceptual framework aims for comprehensiveness by addressing both the supply and demand sides of e-government as they impact the level of civic engagement. Supply side refers to the availability of e-government services. Demand side refers to citizen willingness to interact with government online. This supply-demand approach is analogous to Pippa Norris's (2005b) political market model. Graafland-Essers and Ettedgui (2003) also provide some important insights into the dynamics of supply and demand. Supply and demand are seen as jointly determining the levels of engagement and satisfaction. The framework is illustrated in Figure 1.

The other main goal of the framework is to make a clear distinction between willingness to adopt and actual utilization of electronic government information and services. Willingness to adopt does not necessarily translate into actual adoption. It is particularly the case when the interactive features citizens may demand are not made available to them. As a result, the percentage of citizens using transactional services

Figure 1. A conceptual framework for online civic engagement

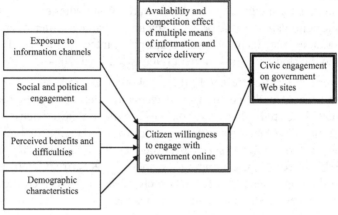

is relatively low. For example, online renewal of driver licenses and recreational licenses are at 12% and 4%, respectively (Larsen & Rainie, 2002, p. 3).

Several theoretical models are relevant for understanding how citizens behave when they interact with government online. The technology acceptance model (TAM) developed and modified by Davis (1986, 1989) and Venkatesh and Davis (2000) shows the importance of the perception of benefits and the perception of task complexity in determining the actual use of information technology. Roger's (2003) diffusion of innovations approach puts emphasis on how social systems impact diffusion and adoption decisions. These models are relevant because engaging government online can be conceptualized either as acceptance of new technology (i.e., Web-based technologies) or innovation adoption (using online functions as adopting innovation).

In a 2005 white paper, Titah and Barki offer a comprehensive review of literature on e-government adoption. They categorize all published articles on this topic into the following broad categories: (1) e-government "managerial practices" research; (2) e-government "organizational and individual characteristics" research; and (3) e-government "subculture" research. Our research fits well under the individual characteristics of e-government users category. Common theoretical approaches within this category of research are the TAM model and diffusion theory insights from which are used in our proposed model.

Literature on social capital also provides certain insights (Lin, 2001). Social capital is conducive to traditional civic engagement (Skocpol & Fiorina, 1999, p. 13) and it impacts cyber engagement as well (Brainard, 2003). Literature from mass communication also proves relevant, reinforcing the notion that initial exposure to multiple information and communication channels creates awareness and may lead to shifting opinions about an issue (Andreasen, 1995; Rice & Atkin, 2001). Individuals who are exposed to multiple information and communication channels are more likely to learn about innovations such as new e-government functions (Rogers, 2003; Whitehead, 2000). Reviewing e-government research, we can identify factors affecting the use of government Web sites, particularly demographic characteristics emphasized in studies on the "digital divide" (Mossberger, Tolbert, & Stansbury, 2003; Norris, 2005b). These studies also provide some potential classifications of dimensions of citizen online engagement (Ho, 2002; West, 2004).

Below, we incorporate these theoretical insights into the key components of the framework, while hypothesizing the relationships among the components. We shall begin by defining online civic engagement as the main dependent variable in the conceptual framework.

Defining Online Civic Engagement with Government

In a broad sense, civic engagement refers to "the participation of individual citizens in the association of civil and political society" (Brint & Levy, 1999, p. 164). The present study focuses on government Web sites as the vehicle for civic engagement. This approach complements, without duplicating, the efforts of political scientists to understand political mobilization via the Internet in elections.[1] This study aims to analyze the factors affecting the willingness and actual utilization of e-government services that help engage citizens in public governance. Thus, in this study, "civic engagement" is limited to interactions with government online via Web portals.

Further, this study draws from Ho's (2002) scheme classifying various activities in online civic engagement. Ho (2002) argues that there is a hierarchy of activities. At the most basic level, citizens conduct passive search for government information, such as information on council meetings, community calendars, and schedules for rule making. This basic level of engagement is important because citizens can use the information as resources. Above this level of interaction, citizens conduct relevant transactions with the government by downloading forms, paying taxes, and so forth. At yet another higher level, citizens participate in government policy making by providing online comments and using other types of input mechanisms. At the highest level, according to Ho (2002), citizens participate in government in real-time.

The present study views such online activities as interlocked dimensions, not as a hierarchy of levels. Online transactions such as paying taxes and processing permits are rather different from getting public policy information and providing input. There is probably no hierarchical progression in such participation.

Nevertheless, we must make an important distinction, differentiating between the mere willingness to interact and the actual level of interaction with government online. This distinction may prove particularly critical when what government offers through their Web portals lags behind citizen demands and expectations.

Demographic Characteristics

Citizens who tend to interact with government online share several common demographic characteristics. First, users of government Web sites tend to be middle age (GAO, 2001; Horrigan, 2004; Thomas & Streib, 2003). Second, these users tend to be affluent, as evident in Internet voting patterns (Gibson, 2002), and as suggested by patterns in searches for government information and getting services online (GAO, 2001; Hart-Teeter, 2003; Horrigan, 2004; Mossberger et al., 2003). Third, education is positively correlated to sending comments to government (Larsen & Rainie, 2002, p. 16) and holding a positive view of engaging government via the Internet (Shelley, Trane, Shulman, Lang, Beiser, Larson, et al., 2004). A fourth factor involves race. Minorities are under-represented in Internet voting (Gibson, 2002) and they conduct less online searches for government information (Mossberger et al., 2003).

The relationships suggested by these studies are based on analyses of both Internet and non-Internet users. Following the insights of these studies, we formulate Hypothesis 1:

Hypothesis 1:

H1a: *A high level of education and income is positively related to engagement with government online.*

H1b: *Middle-age and nonminority citizens are more likely to exhibit willingness to interact with government online.*

It should be noted that the present study is focused on a broad set of factors determining online engagement with government and the inclusion of demographic characteristics is mostly for control. There is already extensive literature focusing on these variables. We will instead concentrate on less-researched, nondemographic factors.

Social and Political Involvement

All else being equal, one might expect politically active citizens to be more likely to engage government online. Indeed, there is positive correlation between Internet use and political participation (Weber, Loumakis, & Bergman, 2003). Such political participation would include attending public meetings, writing letters to elected officials, and participating in political rallies and speeches (Weber et al., 2003, p. 32). Internet use includes surfing the Internet for recreation and accessing digital libraries, newspapers, and magazines, for example. Moreover, based on European Social Survey data, Pippa Norris (2005b) shows the importance of prior political orientation in shaping the demand for electronic information on government and politics. Dimitrova and Chen (2006) also found that prior interest in government is a significant predictor of e-government adoption. Thus, we can expect that a citizen who is more active in politics is more likely to engage government online.

Hypothesis 2: *A higher level of political activism is positively related to engagement with government online.*

In addition to political activism, community involvement is also likely to be positively associated with engaging government online. Community involvement refers the level of citizen participation in community groups such as church or school organizations. A relationship between community involvement and online engagement with government probably stems from two complementary factors: the positive role of social influence in shaping innovation adoption decisions (Lin, 2003; Lynch, Kent, & Srinivasan, 2001; Rogers, 2003), and the need for involved citizens to engage government to foster communities. In terms of the first factor, when citizens are active in a community, they are more likely to be exposed to innovative ideas, or are more likely to be innovators themselves. As a result, these community activists are more likely to utilize online information and services that help further build a sense of community. For instance, the electronic village at Blacksburg, Virginia, has seen church groups and clubs actively utilize the online community network to facilitate communication and collaboration with their existing and potential members (Carrroll & Rosson, 1996).

In terms of the second factor, engaging government to foster community may include, for example, applying for a community development grant to construct a community center, or participating in public meetings. Online networks can further facilitate citizens' involvement in discussing about and mobilizing around community issues (Rogers, Collins-Jarvis, & Schmitz, 1994). The use of the Public Electronic Network (PEN), an interactive communication system, in Santa Monica facilitates the involvement of disadvantaged segments of population (i.e., the homeless) in deliberation of public policy. The experience of PEN demonstrates the association between community involvement and the use of online government services. As government puts more and more information and services online, the citizens with high community involvement will be more likely to access these services. Hence, we arrive at Hypothesis 3.

Hypothesis 3: *A higher level of community involvement is positively related to engagement with government online.*

Information Channels

One basic theme of electronic government is the utilization of information and communication channels. As posited by the literature on innovation diffusion, early adopters of innovations tend to utilize more information channels than nonadopters (Rogers, 2003). Mass media channels are particularly important in creating awareness of new services such as e-government transactions (Andreasen, 1995; Rice & Atkin, 2001). These channels include newspapers, TV, radios, billboards, printed materials such as government newsletters, electronic mails, and Web sites. An individual who utilizes many channels of communication is probably more likely to use government Web portals. Mass media information channels are effective not only in creating awareness, but also in changing the attitudes of potential adopters (ITPC, 2002; Whitehead, 2000).

Existing e-government research neglects to assess the relationship between the use of multiple information and communication channels and the propensity for engaging government online. Diffusion literature shows that individuals with a high level of utilization are more likely to receive information about e-government information and service offerings (Andreasen, 1995; Rogers, 2003). As a result, we expect that those who are exposed to multiple information and communication channels would be more likely to show a willingness to engage government online.

Hypothesis 4: *High level utilization of information channels is positively related to engagement with government online.*

Perceived Usefulness and Complexity

Perceived usefulness is important for the adoption of new technologies. Based on the technology acceptance model (TAM) (Davis, 1986, 1989; Venkatesh & Davis, 2000), perceived usefulness is empirically asserted to be an important determinant of adoption. Perceived usefulness refers to "the extent to which a person believes that using the system will enhance his or her job performance" (Venkatesh & Davis, 2000, p. 187).

Perceived usefulness is a concept broad enough that it can be applied to citizen interaction with government. Nedovic-Budic and Godschalk (1996), utilizing TAM, studied the willingness to adopt geographic information systems at government agencies. For individuals, perceived usefulness in comparison with the old system is an important factor in their willingness to use that system. Perceived benefits could include improvement in job performance and convenience. Extending the argument to the context of online civic engagement, perceived usefulness refers to the belief that interacting with government online benefits participating citizens. These benefits may include the convenience of no waiting in line, avoidance of mail delay, and the convenience of accessing information and services 24/7. If citizens believe they could benefit significantly from obtaining online information or from conducting online transactions on government Web sites, they would more likely to use them. Therefore, we expect that perceived usefulness is positively associated with willingness to interact with government online.

Hypothesis 5: *Perceived usefulness is positively related to engagement with government online.*

On the other hand, perceived problems are likely to reduce the willingness of citizens to interact with government online. Individuals may lack the needed comfort level to conduct online transactions. This may stem from personal attitudes or beliefs (Lin, 2003; Ajzen & Fishbein, 1980). For example, citizens may not wish to conduct transactions with government because of a lack of trust due to perceived security problems or privacy concerns. Moreover, it may stem from the lack of technological expertise, or perceptions of low self-efficacy (Bandura, 1997).

Technical expertise of individuals shapes their perception of the severity of the problems and difficulties associated with adopting a new piece of technology. Northrop, Dunkle, Kraemer, and King (1994) show that people's computer background affects their use of a computer. If software is easy-to-use, users are more likely to adopt the application. Previous computer experience and exposure to technology are also favorable conditions for individual adoption of geographic information systems in a local government (Nedovic-Budick & Godshalk, 1996).

In terms of engaging government online, there are several sources of potential problems, such as, the quality and accessibility of information (Horrigan, 2004), and privacy and security (West, 2004). Usability issues such as navigation and help functions are also critical for the use of e-government services, particularly online transactions (Barnes & Vigden, 2007). These can be seen as barriers to using e-government information and services. In sum, citizens would be less willing to engage government online if they perceive problems.

Hypothesis 6: *Perceptions of problems with e-government information and services are negatively associated with engaging government online.*

Availability and Competition Effects

Availability of government information and services is likely to shape the extent to which citizens engage government online. At the local level, e-government Web sites are still mostly focused on information (Norris & Moon, 2005). Online transactions are rather rare. There are limited interactive services on government Web sites (Hart-Teeter, 2003; Thomas & Streib, 2003). Even the creators of government Web portals do not perceive the portals as a vehicle for interaction and transactions with government but simply as a channel for information delivery (Norris, 2005a). As for specific interactive features, about 15% of Web sites offer areas for posting comments or complaints (West, 2004). About 7% of Web sites offer broadcasting of government events, and about 1% of Web sites offer personalized information gathering targeted directly to the attention of the citizen (West, 2004). Thus, it is important to qualify the limited use of interactive functions according to actual availability.

Availability is the first barrier to actual utilization of government information and interactive services. However, availability is also a matter of awareness. If the user is not aware of the services, the user cannot utilize them. Some government officials have admitted that making the public aware of available services is sometimes a challenging task. We can expect that perceived availability is positively associated with the actual online engagement with governments.

Hypothesis 7: *Awareness of information and service availability is positively related to engagement with government online.*

Engaging government online should be put in its proper context. Online engagement is only one of several ways for citizens to interact with government. Citizens can visit government offices in person. They also have the option of writing letters or making phone calls. A 2003 national survey has shown that citizens still interact with government via traditional channels (Horrigan, 2004). When survey respondents were asked to rank methods of interaction, communication by telephone ranked the highest (42%) among other options such as Web site visit, in-person visit, e-mail correspondence, and letter writing. The use of government Web sites ranked second (29%). Nevertheless, in-person visits and e-mail correspondence remained viable options (20% and 18%, respectively). We will use willingness to engage government via traditional channels as a control.

Methods and Data

Models and Measures

This study analyzes three dimensions of citizen engagement with government online: accessing information, conducting transactions, or providing public policy input. Each of the hypotheses proposed in the conceptual framework will be tested against these three dimensions. Further, each dimension will then be tested in two models, using willingness and actual utilization to differentiate between intentions and use of e-government information and services. As a result, we have six models: the first three models capture willingness to engage with e-government and the next three models capture actual engagement with government online (See Table 1).

Willingness is measured by a scale-based query. Respondents are asked to rate the extent to which they agree with a statement, using a scale of "strongly disagree" (value=1) to "strongly agree" (value=5).[2] For the context of accessing information, the survey statement reads, "I would like to search for information on government Web site." For the context of conducting transactions and providing public policy input, the survey statement will begin similarly with the phrase of "I would like to," but each statement uses a different inserted phrase, such as "conduct transactions with government agencies online," or "participate in government policy making by providing my opinions and comments online."

Table 1. Operationalization of citizen online engagement with government

Dimensions of Online Engagement	Matched Survey Items
Getting government information online	A summation of scores for the following five survey items on the question "how often you look for the following information on government web sites" (Scale of 1-5; 1=never, 5=very often): (a) Look up contact information (e-mail, phone number) for government offices or officials; (b) Seek information about public policies or issues (environment, safety, etc.); (c) Get information about elections or voting; (d) Get information about public hearings or other policy forums; and (e) Get information about the impact of government decisions on your community.
Conducting transactions with government online	A summation of scores for the following three survey items on the question "how often you conduct the following activities on government web sites" (Scale of 1-5; 1=never, 5=very often): (a) File taxes (state or federal income taxes); (b) Purchase or renew licenses (driver's, business, hunting, fishing, and other licenses); and (c) Pay bills or tickets (i.e., utility bills, parking tickets).
Providing public policy input to government online	A summation of scores for the following four survey items on the question "how often you conduct the following activities on government web sites" (Scale of 1-5; 1=never, 5=very often): (a) Give comments to government officials; (b) Express a position on a government policy or initiative online; (c) Submit information to assist in ensuring public safety, protecting the environment, and so forth; and (d) File complaints.

The degree of engagement is measured by a score which evaluates both the number of activities and their intensity. For example, for the public policy input variable, this question is posed, "How often do you conduct the following activities on government Web sites: (a) give comments to government officials, (b) express a position on a government policy or initiative online, (c) submit information to assist in ensuring public safety, protecting the environment, and so forth, and (d) file complaints." Each activity is measured on a scale of 1-5 (1=never, 5=very often), and the total sum is the measurement of degree of engagement. Table 1 provides more details about the other two dependent variables.

The key independent variables identified in the conceptual framework and their measures are presented in Table 2. The measure of "political involvement" focuses on both willingness and actual action. "Community involvement" is a measure of the extent to which a citizen is involved in the community, including number of memberships in various organizations such as fraternities, labor unions, and youth groups. The questions are modeled after the U.S. General Social Survey to ensure comprehensiveness in naming community groups and to take into account intensity of involvement. The "utilization of information channels" construct is specific to learning about information and services accessible on government Web sites. This degree of specificity will let us pinpoint the government Web site activities as the foci of the framework.

The "perceived difficulties" construct measures the degree of perceived obstruction preventing online interaction with the government, as identified by the respondents. Similarly, the "perceived benefits" construct is specific to each dimension of civic engagement. This level of specificity matches the three dimensions of civic engage-ment. Likewise, the "availability" construct is specific to each dimension of civic engagement and each is measured according to the rating of availability of specific online activities on a scale of 1-5. The "competition" construct captures the com-petition effect of alternative channels of communication (such as personal visits to government offices or writing letters). This is a composite index, which takes into account use and level of satisfaction; both are critical factors in choosing one channel of communication over another. Standard demographic variables are used for control. Operationalization of each variable is in Table 2.

Research Design and Data Collection

The target population of this study was Internet users in the United States. The unit of analysis was the individual Internet user. We designed and implemented a two-stage data collection to achieve a sample of these Internet users and to collect relevant data on the conceptual constructs operationalized in Tables 1 and 2. Since our target population was Internet users, we felt that it is reasonable to reach respondents via the Internet. Moreover, despite their shortcomings, Internet surveys have become

Table 2. Conceptual constructs of determinants for engaging government online and their measures

Conceptual Constructs	Survey Items and Operationalization
Political Involvement	A summation of scores for the following two survey items on the question "how much you agree or disagree with the statement" (Scale of 1-5, 1 "strongly disagree" and 5 is "strongly agree"): (a) I am interested in politics and (b) I am active in lobbying, elections, and other political activities.
Community Involvement	The product of the total number of membership in the community and the level of activity. Total number of membership include those in the following 15 types of organizations: fraternal group, service group, veterans group, political club, labor union, sports club, youth group, school organization (PTA), hobby club, school fraternity/sorority, nationality group, farm organization, literary or arts group, professional society, and church organization. The level of activities is measured at the scale of 1-5 where 5 means "Very active" and 1 means "Very inactive."
Utilization of Information Channels	A count of the number of information channels being utilized to learn about the information and services provided on government Web sites. The list of channels include: newspaper advertisement, TV advertisement, radio advertisement, billboard, printed materials from government (newsletter, payment notice, postcard, etc.), e-mail, ad on a search engine (e.g., Google or Yahoo), online advertisement on a general Web site, online advertisement on a government Web site, and mobile advertisement (e.g., putting the government URL on a license plate).
Perceived Benefits	This is a rating of the following statements (scale of 1-5, 5 means "strongly agree" and 1 means "strongly disagree"). For information related models (Models 1 and 4), the rating for Question (a) is used. For online transaction models (Model 2 and 5), the rating for Question (b) is used. For public policy input, Question (c) is used. Question (a): I could benefit significantly from obtaining online information from government Web sites. Question (b): I could benefit significantly from conducting online transactions with government Web sites. Question (c): I could benefit significantly from submitting my opinions or comments on public policy issues online at government Web sites.
Perceived difficulties	A count of the number of the following barriers identified by the respondent: quality of information, accessibility of information, privacy, security (e.g., identity theft), too hard to obtain information, no person-to-person contact, and difficult to follow online instructions.
Availability and Competition	
Availability	This is a rating of the availability of the information and services relevant to a particular dimension of online engagement (scale of 0-4, 4 means "always available" and 0 means "not available"). For information related models (Models 1 and 4), the score is the rating of availability of public information such as recreation, businesses, health, and business opportunities. For online transaction models (Models 2 and 5), the score is the rating of availability of transactions with government agencies, such as paying taxes, getting driver or professional licenses, and getting permits. For public policy input models (Models 3 and 6), the score is the rating of the availability of online features to voice your opinion on public policy.

continued on following page

Table 2. continued

Competition Ranking	This is the ranking of various channels that citizens can use to interact with government. These channels include: (a) in person, (b) letter, (c) telephone, (d) e-mail, and (e) government Web site. The ranking is based on a composite index of frequency of use and satisfaction. A ranking score of 5 means the best option and a score of 1 means the least preferred option.
Demographics	
Income Level	This is done through ranking. 1. Below $20,000; 2. $20,000 - $29,999; 3. $30,000 - $39,999; 4. $40,000 - $49,999; 5. $50,000 - $59,999; 6. $60,000 - $74,999; 7. $75,000 - $99,999; 8. $100,000 - $149,999; and 9. over $150,000
Race	1= Caucasian and 0= other
Gender	1= male and 0= female
Age	Actual age at the time of the survey
Level of Education	This is done through ranking. 1. Completed some high school; 2. High school graduate; 3. Completed some college; 4. College degree; 5. Completed some postgraduate; 6. Master's degree; and 7. Doctorate, law or professional degree

an established data collection method and are considered a viable alternative to traditional survey methods (Dillman, 2000; Schonlau, Fricker, & Elliott, 2001).

We took several precautions in order to avoid the common pitfalls of Internet surveys, such as lack of control over the number of times an individual can take the survey, whether the survey respondent is a legitimate individual, and the overall quality of responses. First, we worked with a professional survey company, Survey Sampling International (SSI), Inc., to generate a panel of legitimate U.S. Internet users for the survey. Each person in the panel had to be registered with the survey company. We further employed commercial online survey software called *Opinio* to restrict the same individual from taking the survey twice based on their IP address. Further, the quality of responses was carefully assessed based on the time used to fill out the survey, the required fields, and demographic data from the survey company to validate with the same information collection through our online survey. Despite these efforts, it is important to recognize that online surveys, similarly to traditional surveys, are subject to nonresponse error (i.e., potential bias in the data if the non-respondents are significantly different from those who completed the survey).

A total of 5,000 survey invitations were sent out via e-mail by SSI on July 11, 2004, and the first stage of data collection ended within 10 days. This yielded 447 valid responses leading to a response rate of 9%, which is comparable with similar Web surveys (e.g., Comley, 1996; Smith, 1997). We achieved two objectives at the first stage. First, we collected additional demographic information such as race, age, income, and education to include in the data analysis. Second, we were able to identify those individuals who had previous experience with using online government information and services. At the second stage, we contacted those individuals to ask more detailed questions about their online civic engagement. The survey invitations were sent out on February 1, 2005. Two e-mail reminders were sent out on February 7 and 10, 2005. A total of 143 valid responses were generated at this stage, which translates into a response rate of approximately 3%. These responses form the basis of our analysis.

Data Analysis

The first analysis we conducted was to assess the extent to which the resulting sample after the two-stage of data collection is representative of the U.S. Internet user population. We benchmarked our sample against a national random sample of U.S. population obtained via the Pew Internet and American Life Project (2004), which included 2,925 Americans age 18 and over. For the comparison of demographic characteristics between our sample and the Pew sample, we included only those Pew respondents who had access to the Internet. This yielded a sample of Internet users (n=1,899). Given the random sampling used, the Internet user sample from the Pew study should be representative of the national Internet user population and can serve as a benchmark.

As Table 3 shows, we achieved representative sample of Internet user population by matching our sample to that of the Pew study. In particular, we match gender and age breakdowns of the Pew sample. Table 3 includes the percent distribution of the sample respondents that belong to various combinations of gender and age groups before and after weighting. For example, 9% of the sample respondents

Table 3. Age group breakdown by gender for creating a weighted sample to match pew data on Internet users

Female	Sample Distribution		Pew Data	Male	Sample Distribution		Pew Data
	Before Weighting	*After Weighting*			*Before Weighting*	*After Weighting*	
18-24	3%	6%	6%	18-24	1%	8%	8%
25-34	17%	10%	10%	25-34	2%	10%	10%
35-44	9%	13%	13%	35-44	7%	11%	11%
45-54	20%	11%	11%	45-54	9%	10%	10%
55-64	10%	7%	7%	55-64	15%	7%	7%
65+	3%	3%	3%	65+	6%	4%	4%
		50%	50%			50%	50%

Table 4. Models of various dimensions of engaging citizens online with government

Model #	Model 1	Model 2	Model 3	Model 4	Model 5	Model 6
Dependent Variable	*Willingness*			*Actual Utilization*		
	Public Info. Search	Online transactions	Public Policy Input	Public Info. Search	Online Transactions	Public Policy Input
Independent Variables						
Constant	1.717 (.427)	0.205 (.457)	0.578 (.427)	4.321* (1.944)	1.882 (1.607)	0.521 (1.496)
Political Involvement	0.080** (.032)	0.043 (.038)	0.131* (.038)	0.612*** (.147)	-0.173 (.133)	0.247 (.135)
Community Involvement	-0.015 (.010)	-0.019 (.011)	-0.015 (.011)	-0.037 (.044)	0.030 (.039)	0.099* (.039)
Utilization of Information Channels	0.007 (.039)	0.047 (.044)	0.009 (.044)	0.536** (.178)	0.127 (.156)	0.177 (.155)
Perceived Benefits	0.574*** (.082)	0.762*** (.075)	0.518*** (.080)	0.805* (.371)	1.242*** (.264)	0.568* (.279)
Perceived Difficulties	-0.029 (.041)	-0.034 (.044)	0.157*** (.045)	0.004 (.185)	-0.154 (.156)	0.049 (.157)
Availability and Competition						
Availability	-0.053 (.084)	-0.039 (.071)	0.156* (.079)	0.372 (.385)	1.120*** (.250)	0.559* (.276)
Competition	0.059*** (.016)	0.024 (.018)	0.027 (.017)	0.273*** (.074)	0.116 (.063)	0.154* (.061)
Demographics						
Income level	-0.016 (.029)	0.081* (.033)	0.045 (.032)	0.040 (.133)	0.130 (.115)	0.116 (.112)
Race (White vs. non-white)	0.372 (.223)	0.333 (.252)	-0.107 (.248)	0.136 (1.014)	-0.023 (.888)	-1.387 (.870)
Gender	0.288* (.141)	0.102 (.156)	-0.002 (.161)	-0.586 (.641)	1.057 (.549)	0.632 (.563)
Age	-0.013** (.005)	-0.003 (.005)	0.002 (.005)	-0.048* (.022)	-0.025 (.019)	0.032 (.019)
Education Level	-0.059 (.049)	0.006 (.056)	-0.099 (.054)	-0.089 (.222)	-0.447* (.196)	-0.288 (.191)
Model Fit						
R-Square	0.587	0.585	0.591	0.470	0.423	0.437
Adjusted R-Square	0.549	0.547	0.553	0.421	0.370	0.385

*, ** and *** denotes a coefficient significant at the .05, .01, and .001 level, respectively.

belong to the female, 35-44 age group before weighting, as opposed to 13% after weighting. After weighting (see "after weighting" and "Pew" columns), the sample distribution becomes representative of Pew data on Internet users for each gender and age combination.

Nonetheless, we recognize that our small sample size as well as sampling process may introduce some biases. Even after weighting according to age groups and gender, the sample data may not be able to achieve full representation on all demographic characteristics. As a result, this study should be viewed as exploratory in nature and generalization of the findings to all Internet users should be treated with caution.

We then employed OLS regression analysis to test the hypotheses generated in the analytical framework for three dimensions of online civic engagement both in terms of willingness and actual utilization. To address potential multicollinearity problems, we have run collinearity diagnosis for all models. Since all tolerance collinearity statistics are above 0.5, we concluded that multicollinearity is not an issue.[3] Multivariable regression analysis allows us to assess the significance as well as the direction of each hypothesized relationship. Thus, we are able to identify the independent effect of factors such as political involvement while controlling for age, education, and other demographics.

Results and Discussions

The study results are summarized in six regression models presented in Table 4. The first three focus on willingness and the remaining three capture actual engagement with e-government. Model 1 examines the influence of political involvement, community involvement, information channels, perceived benefits, perceived difficulties, and demographic characteristics on the willingness to conduct information searches on government Web portals (See Table 4). Models 2 and 3 measure the influence of the same variables on willingness to conduct online transactions and willingness to provide public policy input, respectively.

Model 4 measures the effects of political involvement, community involvement, information channels, perceived benefits, perceived difficulties, demographic characteristics, availability, and competition from off-line government services on actual utilization of government Web portals for information searches. Models 5 and 6 measure the effects of the same set of variables on actual utilization of online transactions and providing public policy input, respectively. The adjusted R-squares show substantial explanatory power for each of the six models. The following discussions present the general patterns observed in all six models and their theoretical and policy implications.

Engaging Government Online is a Multi-faceted Phenomenon

The first important finding suggests that engaging citizens with government online is a multifaceted phenomenon. Each dimension of engagement has its own dynamics. In particular, engaging citizens in online transactions with government (such as paying taxes) differs from citizens accessing online information and providing input on public policy. Political involvement as measured by interest and level of activities in politics is not significantly associated with transactions (see Models 2 and 5). On the other hand, political involvement is strongly associated with both the willingness and actual online engagement with government to access public policy information and provide input (see Models 1, 3, and 4).

This finding has both theoretical and policy implications. First, it seems important to differentiate between these two activities. Public administrators should examine how political involvement may create two different kinds of groups who interact with government online. Different strategies may need to be employed for promoting engagement when the target groups of online transactions and participatory governance differ.

Availability is Critical in Determining Utilization

The results also confirm the importance of availability, particularly for online transactions and interactive public policy input. For online transactions (see Model 5), perceived availability is significantly and positively associated with actual transactions (e.g., e-filing, purchasing or renewing licenses, paying bills or penalties, etc.). Similarly, perceived availability is significantly and positively associated with providing public policy input to government online in terms of both willingness and actual utilization (e.g., expressing a position on a government policy or initiative, submitting information to assist in ensuring public safety and protection of the environment, etc.) (see Models 4 and 6).

The significance of availability as an independent determining factor is particularly notable when all other factors are taken into account. Perceived availability, although positively related to accessing government information online, is not significant. Perhaps, governments are already doing a fair job in providing some important information online. Thus, in this specific case, availability seems to no longer be an issue.

The question of availability is critical in understanding both the supply and demand for e-government Web sites. Future researchers should consider treating supply and demand simultaneously rather than looking at supply or demand individually.

If public administrators want to improve their e-government efforts, perhaps they may need to better communicate the availability of such services.

Availability is an important prerequisite for citizens to utilize e-government services. Another key consideration is perception. Governments are sometimes being criticized for not being particularly effective in marketing their services. At times, transactions and options are available online but citizens are not aware of them. Governments need to consider using information channels more effectively to address the gap between the perception and reality of availability.

Perceived Benefits Are Conducive to Online Engagement

Perceived benefits are a critical factor in determining the willingness and utilization of e-government. This is the only factor that shows consistent significance in all six models. In almost all models, this factor has the highest level of significance compared to other variables. The results show that the more benefits citizens perceive, the more likely they will interact with government online.

The importance of perceived benefits lends support to the technology acceptance model (TAM). This seems to be a major factor in the adoption of new e-government information access and services. When the transaction involves obtaining permits or filing taxes, the perceived benefits may be convenience or a monetary advantage. For engaging citizens in public policy discussions, government must show how such discussions have a bearing on the content and direction of final policy decisions. Otherwise, citizens will not see any benefit in providing policy input and they would simply stop participating.

Political Activism Drives Online Public-Policy Engagement

Political activism emerges as a significant predictor for seeking policy information and engaging in public governance online (Models 1, 3, and 4). The relationship is positive. In contrast, for conducting online business transactions, political activism has no significant bearing (Models 2 and 5). An interpretation of these findings may be offered: political activism gives citizens the basic motivation for seeking public policy information and engaging government in public policy issues. Government Web sites provide new ways for doing so. In comparison, community involvement does not establish itself as a significant motivation for engaging government online. Having more and active membership in community organizations such as PTAs, hobby clubs, service groups, and so forth, does not show any significant relationship with engaging government online, with the only exception of utilizing online mechanisms to give comments to government. This suggests that membership in community groups, while controlling for other factors, only plays a role in giving government comments online.

The finding puts political activism at center stage, suggesting that interest in politics as well as actual participation in election and lobbying activities play a much more important role than general community involvement. Social capital as defined by community involvement in general does not translate directly into online civic engagement. Government Web sites seem to serve more as extensions of traditional methods of political participation rather than extensions of community building. If government aims to foster online public policy discussions, one important way is to augment political activities with electronic options.

Demographic Characteristics of Internet Users Have Limited Relevance

Our findings show that demographic characteristics play a limited role in determining willingness or actual utilization of online civic engagement options. When other factors are taken into account, income level does not impact searching for online government information or providing online input into policy. Age plays a role only in information searches but not in transactions or public policy input. Level of education plays a role only in conducting online transactions, but not in any other online activities. These findings suggest that, for our sample of Internet users, demographic characteristics have rather limited influence on user willingness and actual engagement with e-government.

Treating age, gender, race, and income level as controls, the findings demonstrated that those citizens who are politically involved off-line and perceive e-government as personally beneficial are more likely to use online government. This finding should be interpreted with caution, however, since it cannot be generalized to the general population. Our sample was limited to computer users who have access to the Internet already; in other words, higher income people who are not representative of the population at large. One possible explanation is that once a citizen has become part of the online community, factors such as perceived benefits and political activism seem to play important roles. At the same time, demographic characteristics become less significant.

Conclusion

Titah and Barki (2005) contend that despite the large amount of research on e-government, the field lacks a unified theoretical framework. One of the contributions of our study is the identification of specific variables that may facilitate or impede the adoption of e-government information and services. Our findings also provide an important step in understanding the supply and demand sides of online civic engagement. The proposed framework incorporates both the availability and competition effects of various communication channels, aiming to provide a more comprehensive view of online civic engagement. The framework combines several dimensions of online engagement, such as, e-government information searches, online business transactions, and contributing public policy input. The study is limited by the small sample size and its focus only on Internet users.

This study nevertheless highlights the importance of several key factors in explaining both the willingness and actual utilization of various online civic engagement options. Perceived benefits seem to be a key factor in explaining the intensity of online civic engagement. This validates the relevance of the technology acceptance model. In terms of policy recommendations, public managers need to have a better understanding of the specific kinds of benefits that citizens want.

Political involvement off-line emerged as a critical factor in explaining why citizens seek public policy information and provide public policy input online. In comparison, general community involvement does not play as significant a role as originally expected. E-government efforts need to take this into consideration to effectively engage citizens online.

Finally, perceived availability of e-government services seems to encourage citizens to interact with government online. Government can bridge the availability gap by providing more online business transactions and more opportunities for online public policy input. In addition, it is important to note that availability becomes less of a factor for engagement when sufficient amounts of information and types of services are made available.

Future research can build on the conceptual framework proposed in this study, which integrates insights from various fields. One fruitful area of research will be to explore the various elements that constitute perceived benefits. When governments learn from citizens, realizing that the connection between policy input and final policy decision is the most important element, governments will need to make that link a priority and communicate this to its citizens. Another avenue for future research is to differentiate between the three levels of government and test the models with longitudinal data to see how perceived availability shapes actual utilization over time. This approach will provide insights into the evolution and dynamics of supply and demand as they impact online civic engagement.

References

Ajzen, I., & Fishbein, M. (1980). *Understanding attitudes and predicting social behavior.* Englewood Cliffs, NJ: Prentice-Hall, Inc.

Andreasen, A. R. (1995). *Marketing social change.* San Francisco: Jossey-Bass.

Bandura, A. (1997). *Self-efficacy: The exercise of control.* New York: W. H. Freeman.

Barnes, S., & Vigden, R. (2007). Interactive e-government: Evaluating the web site of the UK Inland Revenue. *International Journal of Electronic Government Research, 3*(1), 19-37.

Brainard, L. (2003). Citizen organizing in cyberspace: Illustrations from health care and implications for public administration. *American Review of Public Administration, 33*(4), 384-406.

Carroll, J. M., & Rosson, M. B. (1996). Developing the Blacksburg electronic village. *Communication of the ACM, 39*(12), 69-74.

Comley, P. (1996). *The use of internet as a data collection method.* Paper presented at ESO-MAR, Edinburg, UK. Retrieved August 20, 2004, from http://www.virtualsurveys.com/news/papers/paper_9.asp

Davis, F. D. (1986). *A technology acceptance model for empirically testing new end-user information systems: Theory and results.* Unpublished doctoral dissertation, Sloan School of Management, MIT, Cambridge, MA.

Davis, F. D. (1989). Perceived usefulness, perceived ease of use, and user acceptance of information technology. *MIS Quarterly, 13*(3), 319-339.

Dillman, D. (2000). *Mail and Internet surveys* (2nd ed). New York: John Wiley and Son.

Dimitrova, D.V., & Chen, Y.C. (2006). Profiling the adopters of e-government information and services: The influence of psychological characteristics, civic mindedness, and information channels. *Social Science Computer Review, 24*(2), 172-188.

General Accounting Office (GAO) of the United States. (2001). *Characteristics and choices of Internet users.* Retrieved September 24, 2005, from http://www.gao.gov/new.items/d01345.pdf

Gibson, R. (2002). Elections online: Assessing internet voting in light of the Arizona democratic primary. *Political Science Quarterly, 116*(4), 561-583.

Graafland-Essers, I., & Ettedgui, E. (2003). *Benchmarking e-government in Europe and the US* (Statistical Indicators Benchmarking the Information Society [SIBIS]). Santa Monica: RAND.

Hart-Teeter. (2003). *The new e-government equation: Ease, engagement, privacy and protection.* Retrieved August 15, 2004, from http://www.cio.gov/documents/egov-poll2003.pdf

Ho, A. T. (2002). Reinventing local governments and the e-government initiative. *Public Administration Review, 62*(4), 434-444.

Horrigan, J. (2004). *How Americans get in touch with government: Internet users benefits from the efficiency of e-government, but multiple channels are still needed for citizens to reach agencies and solve problems.* Pew Internet & American Life Project.

Indiana Tobacco Prevention and Cessation (ITPC) Board. (2002). *Seeing is believing: How exposure to ITPC's media campaign affects tobacco knowledge, attitude, and beliefs among Hoosier adults.* Retrieved February 25, 2004, from http://www.in.gov/itpc/files/research_80.pdf

Larsen, E., & Rainie, L. (2002). *The rise of the e-citizen: How people use government agencies' Web site.* Washington, D.C.: Pew Charitable Trust. Retrieved September 2, 2007, from http://www.pweinternet.org

Lin, N. (2001). *Social capital: A theory of social structure and action.* Cambridge, UK: Cambridge University Press.

Lin, C. A. (2003). An interactive communication technology adoption model. *Communication Theory, 13*(4), 345-365.

Lynch, P. D., Kent, R. J., & Srinivasan, S. S. (2001). The global internet shopper: Evidence from shopping tasks in twelve countries. *Journal of Advertising Research, 41,* 15-23.

McNeal, R. S., Tolbert, C. J., Mossberger, K., & Dotterweich, L. J. (2003). Innovating in digital government in the American states. *Social Science Quarterly, 84*(1), 54-70.

Menard, S. (1995). *Applied logistic regression analysis.* Thousand Oaks: Sage.

Moon, M. J. (2002). The evolution of e-government among municipalities: Rhetoric or reality. *Public Administration Review, 62*(4), 424-433.

Mossberger, K., Tolbert, C., & Stansbury, M. (2003). *Virtual inequality: Beyond the digital divide.* Washington, D.C.: Georgetown University Press.

Nedovic-Budic, Z., & Godschalk, D. R. (1996). Human factors in adoption of geographic information systems: A local government case study. *Public Administration Review, 56*(6), 554-567.

Norris, P. (2001). *Digital divide: Civic engagement, information poverty, and the Internet worldwide.* New York: Cambridge University Press.

Norris, D. F. (2005a). Electronic democracy at the American grassroots. *International Journal of Electronic Government Research, 1*(3), 1-14.

Norris, P. (2005b). The impact of the Internet on political activism: Evidence from Europe. *International Journal of Electronic Government Research, 1*(1), 20-39.

Norris, D. F., & Lloyd, B. (2004, December 12). *The scholarly literature on e-government: Characterizing a nascent field.* Paper presented at the Special Interest Group, E-Gov, Pre-ICIS (International Conference on Information) Systems Workshop.

Norris, D. & Moon, J. (2005). Advancing e-government at the grassroots: Tortoise or hare? *Public Administration Review, 65*(1), 64-74.

Northrop, A., Dunkle, D., Kraemer, K., & King, J. (1994). Computer, police and the fight against crime: An ecology of technology, training, and use. *Information and the Public Sector, 3*(1), 21-45.

Pandey, S., & Bretschneider, S. (1997). The impact of red tape's administrative delay on public organizations' interest in new information technologies. *Journal of Public Administration Research and Theory, 7*(1), 113-30.

Pew Internet & American Life Project. (2004, May 24). *How Americans get in touch with government.* Retrieved July 22, 2004, from http://www.pewinternet.org/pdfs/PIP_E-Gov_Report_0504.pdf

Pratchett, L., & Krimmer, R. (2005). The coming of e-democracy. *International Journal of Electronic Government Research, 1*(3), i-iii.

Rice, R. E., & Atkin, C. K. (Eds.). (2001). *Public communication campaigns* (3rd ed.). London: Sage.

Rogers, E. (2003). *Diffusion of innovations* (5th ed.). New York: Free Press.

Rogers, E., Collins-Jarvis, L., & Schmitz, J. (1994). The PEN project in Santa Monica: Interactive communication, equality, and political action. *Journal of the American Society for Information Science, 45*(6), 401-410.

Schonlau, M., Fricker, R. D., & Elliott, M. N. (2001). *Conducting research surveys via e-mail and the Web.* Rand. Retrieved August 18, 2004, from http://www.rand.org/publications/MR/MR1480/

Scott, J. (2006). "E" the people: Do U.S. municipal government Web sites support public involvement? *Public Administration Review, 66*(3), 341-353.

Shelley, M., Trane, L., Shulman, S., Lang, E., Beiser, S., Larson, T., et al. (2004). Digital citizenship. *Social Science Computer Review, 22*(2), 256-269.

Skocpol, T., & Fiorina, M. (1999). *Civic engagement in American democracy.* Washington, D.C./ New York: Brookings Institution Press & Russell Sage Foundation.

Smith, C. B. (1997). Casting the net: Surveying an internet population. *Journal of Computer-Mediated Communication, 3*(1). Retrieved August 20, 2004, from http://www.ascusc.org/jcmc/vol3/issue1/smith.html

Thomas, J. C., & Streib, G. (2003). The new face of government: Citizen-initiated contacts in the era of e-government. *Journal of Public Administration Research and Theory, 13*(1), 83-102.

Titah, R., & Barki, H. (2005). e-Government adoption and acceptance: A literature review. *White paper.* Retrieved February 25, 2007, from http://whitepapers.techrepublic.com.com/whitepaper.aspx?&docid=162384&promo=100511

Tolbert, C., & Mossberger, K. (2006). The effects of e-Government on trust and confidence in government. *Public Administration Review, 66*(3), 354-369.

Venkatesh, V., & Davis, F. D. (2000). A theoretical extension of the technology acceptance model: Four longitudinal field studies. *Management Science, 46*(2), 186-204.

Weber, L., Loumakis, A., & Bergman, J. (2003). Who participate and why? An analysis of citizens on the Internet and the mass public. *Social Science Computer Review, 21*(1), 26-42.

West, D. (2004). E-Government and transformation of service delivery and citizen attitudes. *Public Administration Review, 64*(1), 15-27.

Whitehead, D. (2000). Using mass media within health-promoting practice: A nursing perspective. *Journal of Advanced Nursing, 32*(4), 807-816.

Witte, J., Amoroso, L., & Howard, P. (2000). Method and representation in Internet-based survey tools: Mobility, community, and cultural identity in Survey2000. *Social Science Computer Review, 18*(2), 179-195.

Endnotes

[1]   For an illustrative example, see Brainard et al., 2003.

[2]   The online survey did not differentiate between the three levels of government.

[3]   The tolerance statistics are in the range of .5 and 1.0. They are well above .2, a number below which would indicate a potential problem (Menard, 1995).

Chapter X

Citizen's Deliberation
on the Internet:
A French Case[1]

Laurence Monnoyer-Smith, University of Technology of Compiègne, France

Abstract

Within the frame of the deliberative democratic theory, development of information and communication technologies (ICT) has been proposed as a solution to enhance discussion in large groups and foster political participation among citizens. Critics have however underlined the limits of such technological innovations which do not generate the expected diversity of viewpoints. This chapter highlights the limits of a Habermassian conception of deliberation which restrains it to a specific type of rational discourse and harnesses citizen's expression within strict procedural constraints. Our case study, the DUCSAI debate, that is, the French public debate about the location of the 3rd international Parisian airport, shows that the added value of Internet-based deliberation rests in that it offers, under specific conditions, another arena of public debate. The chapter shows that hybrid forms of debate can widen a participant's profile, the nature of the participant's argumentation, and the participant's means of expression if it provides the opportunity to voice concerns the way the participant chooses to do so.

Introduction

In recent years, the theory of deliberative democracy has become the main, if not the dominant, approach in democratic theory. As John Dryzek (2000) puts it, "the final decade of the second millennium saw the theory of democracy take a strong deliberative turn" (p.1). Contrary to a century-long tradition of suspicion towards the ability of citizens to exercise wise scrutiny of government's activity and its will to dedicate the necessary time to complex political matters (Lippmann 1922), many theorists, inspired by John Dewey's work (1927), called in the early 1980s for a new approach to democracy (Barber, 1984; Cohen, 1986; Macpherson, 1977). The traditional "liberal rationalist" model has been challenged by a communitarian call for a grass-roots participation to politics as a pedagogic tool as well as a way to enrich the democratic debate in modern societies (Pateman, 1970). More recently, the work of U. Beck and A. Giddens has elucidated a new aspect of deliberation and participation in democracies as a consequence of reflexive modernization in risk societies (Beck, 1992; Beck & al., 1994; Giddens, 1990, 1991). Citizens are more eager to be involved in the decision-making process because they are directly concerned by potentially dramatic consequences of public policies (such as technological infrastructures, ethical-linked scientific programs, and so on). Therefore, with the growth of technological risk, technology assessment procedures limited to experts and scientists have been slowly replaced by public debates including lay people. Genetically modified organisms (GMOs), nuclear wastes, nanotechnology, embryonic manipulation, and so forth have formed the core themes of the first public debates.

The on-going crisis of representation which affects modern democracies since the mid-80s has also been interpreted as a symptom of a contested gap between elected officials and citizens (Norris, 1999). Therefore calls for a new type of communication and relationship between the public and its representatives have emerged, insisting on the normative value of public discussion (Guttman & Thomson, 1996; Habermas, 1984; Cohen, 1997a, 1997b).

The deliberative turn acknowledges an important switch in the conception of legitimacy: the legitimacy of a political decision emerges out of its deliberative process and not out of the institution which produces it (Manin, 1985, 1994). Therefore, an important feature of this theory rests in its procedural dimension: the legitimacy of a decision can only be recognized if a real deliberation occurs, that is, if conditions of "equal, reciprocal, reasonable and open-minded participation" (Mendelberg, 2002, p. 153) are fulfilled. Even if different perspectives persists among political theorists about the main features of an ideal deliberative democracy, they all agree on the fact that deliberation can be distinguished from other types of communication in that it supposes "an unconstrained exchange of arguments that involves practical reasoning and always potentially leads to a transformation of preferences" (Cooke,

2000, p. 948). Myriads of propositions have been made in order to actively engage citizens in political participation (from consensus conferences to deliberative pools); nevertheless, the core idea remains largely communitarian in spirit: "It is thought to promote tolerance and trust, lead to a heightened sense of one's role within a political community and stimulate further civic engagement" (Price, in press, p. 4).

The discursive dimension of deliberative democracy appears central in the academic literature as it focuses on the idea that political decisions should be the result of a rational process where only the "forceless force of the better argument" (Habermas, 1975) prevails over manipulation, aggregation of viewpoints, or force (Bohman & Regh, 1997; Cohen, 1989; Dryzek, 2000; Elster, 1998). A fundamental facet of deliberation then rests on the heavy constraints it imposes to participants, that is, in order to preserve the fairness of the debate, arguments have to be exchanged in the most civilized, detached, and articulated way.

The deliberative procedures then reach their own limits when it comes to putting them into practice; as many scholars have pointed out, public debates usually favor certain types of citizens, such as those who are outspoken and well educated men, and who feel comfortable within the procedure's format (Loader, 1998; Sanders, 1997; Wilhelm, 2000b; Young, 1996, 2000). As R. Blaug (1996) puts it, "the degree of abstraction required to posit a universal norm of communicative fairness moves his [Habermas] theory so far from the contexts in which specific discourses occur that he tends to gloss over the importance of rhetoric, persuasion and other aesthetic components of collective judgement" (p. 52). This leads to questioning of the heuristic value of discursive deliberation theory which can only be envisioned as a normative goal, yet not applicable in real life. Moreover, it might prevent one from recognizing, out of empirical experiments, attempts to deliberately use other forms of communication than discursive arguments and yet leading to normative agreements.

In this context, the Internet has been envisioned as an innovative tool to promote large discussion and deliberation among citizens and it revitalized an apathetic political involvement on the citizen's part. It "makes manageable large-scale, many to many discussion and deliberation" (Coleman & Gøtze, 2001, p. 17) and offers easy solutions to four traditional problems which have prevented people from fully participating in public debates because of the constraints they impose. Those problems are time, size, knowledge, and access (Street, 1997). Nevertheless, the extent to which the use of Internet has really enhanced the public sphere and introduced new actors in the democratic process through discussion and deliberation remains somewhat uncertain.

Many scholars acknowledge the inclusive potential of the new medium and demonstrate that online discussions reduce the potential influence of social status and diminish symbolic pressure on participants (Coleman, 2004; Klein, 1999; Pruijt,

2002). Group experiments suggest that, compared with face-to-face discussions, online deliberation tends to generate more open and direct exchange of ideas. Physical absence and the reduced visibility of social cues are generally interpreted as a positive factor on participants' interactions (Rains, 2005; Stromer-Galley, 2002).

On the other hand, critics have expressed three main reservations about the ability of the Internet to overcome the traditional flaws of face-to-face discussion, and posited that it might not be a suitable medium for deliberation. First, one of the main concerns is the question of access Even if Internet usage is now widespread in the population, a significant portion either has no material access or no competence to interact via a computer (Hill & Hugues, 1998; Luke, 1998). Price (in press) recently recognized in a summary of two large experiments that "people who showed up for the electronic discussions were, again in both projects, significantly less likely to be non-white than those who did not (about 3-4 percent difference), significantly older (by about 3 years in average) and better educated" (p. 12). Second, studies have shown controversial results of online discussion experiments, showing that they could encourage the fragmentation of the public sphere which leads to a "balkanisation of politics" (Bellamy & Raab, 1999). In this perspective, making available online a more heterogeneous scope of viewpoints could polarize the attention of people on Web sites they feel in harmony with (Dalhberg, 2001; Manin, 2005; Sustein, 2001). Third, effects on political behavior and participation are contested by authors like Putnam (2000) who emphasize that social capital cannot be reinforced through computer mediated communication. Political engagement necessitates physical and emotional contacts which are not provided by online discussion. Still, the academic debate remains quite open as these statements have been contradicted by recent experiments and observations (Coleman, 2004; Monnoyer-Smith, 2006a; Price, in press; Price & Capella, 2002; Stromer-Galley, 2003).

This chapter, based on a French case study of a public debate organized in 2001 by the National Commission of Public Debate (Commission Nationale du Débat Public, CNDP), aims to show how the online features of the debate Web site and its appropriation by citizens have overcome the constraints of its off-line version. I stress in this chapter that normative standards of deliberation, as they have been described by J. Habermas and J. Cohen, do not fully appreciate the inherent limitation of the deliberative process that *any* type of procedure implies by imposing a format of participation which might prevent some citizens from giving an opinion. Therefore, instead of evaluating online procedures under the normative banner of the ideal speech situation, one should analyze how complementary online and off-line procedures are, what type of participation they can enhance, and which citizen they could mobilize. In this perspective, the recent evolution of CNDP suggests that if multichannel contribution has developed a participative culture among civil associations, it has reached its limits for lay citizens whose writing aptitudes are limited.

Online participative systems still have to overcome a literacy gap which could be reduced by recognizing the argumentative potential of multimedia productions.

I suggest that a key dimension of a deliberative discussion rests on its ability to provide citizens with different types of procedural constraints. Hybrid systems offer them a wider scope of expression (from storytelling to photos or short videos for example) and welcome in the debate a larger portion of the population.

I will first present the French debate that our case study is based on and the methodology used by our multidisciplinary team. I will then show how actors' involvement is linked with the procedure and the Web site design. An analysis of the online argumentation will link technical aspects of the Web site with participants' argumentative strategies. I stress the fact that a real argumentation took place online which differs from the off-line one in some aspects. I will conclude that hybrid deliberative processes highlight the determinant role played by diverse arrangement structures. Therefore, the theory of deliberation has to reconsider its discursive anchorage if one is to open public debates to a large number of citizens.

The CNDP, an Original French Agency

The National Commission of Public Debate was created by a 1995 law as a concession from the government to civil associations following decades of conflicts and lack of citizen's consultation around important infrastructure projects (e.g., Mediterranean speed-train line, French-Spanish tunnel, high voltage power lines, etc.). Two years were necessary to set the Commission up and appoint its 21 members; a delicate balance between elected representatives, judges from various national courts, and user associations' representatives had to be found. Between 1997 and 2002, its scope of action was limited to finalized projects on public infrastructure about which the Commission had to organize public debates evaluating both their opportunity and characteristics. With the 2002 Act on Local Democracy, the Commission became an independent agency and could also decide to organize public debates on wider topics in order to help the government to shape a future policy. So far, only two debates of this kind have been planned: the first one on nuclear wastes (October- January 2006) and the second one on the public transport policy in the Rhone Valley (April-July 2006). Since its creation, the CNDP has directly organized 28 debates (mainly concerning new railways and motorways, and more recently nuclear infrastructures and wastes) and has assigned 19 to project managers (for less important infrastructures, under the Commission scrutiny). Its activity has increased significantly since the enlargement of its intervention perimeter in 2002, from 4 debates in the first period (1997-2002) to 24 up until today. Project managers have now included in their calendar the four necessary months of public consultation and discussion before finalizing any infrastructure project. Statistics show an important growth of information consultation on the CNDP's Web site. Pages viewed per day has increased from 297 in 2003 to over 3,300 in 2006; single visits per day has also boomed up from 56 in 2003 to nearly 900 in 2006.[2]

Our case study, the Ducsai Debate, was held between April and October 2001 and can be considered as a milestone for the CNDP. Specifically, appointed aside from its traditional boundaries, it was to test the future Commission's mission, enacted some months later by the 2002 Act on Local Democracy. For the first time, the Commission experimented new procedures by introducing an online version of the debate including a discussion forum.

"Ducsai" stands for "Débat d'Utilité Concertée pour un Site Aéroportuaire International" which literally means concerted usefulness debate about the location of an international airport, which, even in French, has never been heard of. This is the result of an awkward arbitrage by the Prime Minister between the Minister of Transport (Communist Party) and the Minister of Environment (Green Party), both members of the left wing coalition. The debate was supposed to involve all stakeholders in a public debate focused on the geographic location of the airport but not on the legitimacy of its existence.

The organization was improvised by the National Commission President who considered it to be an extraordinary democratic progress; for the first time in French administration history, citizens would be able to fully participate in a procedure which would have a direct impact on a highly strategic and political decision, before it was actually taken. Pierre Zemor selected 22 people (health specialists, sociologists, transport specialists, etc.) to form a board (called the Ducsai Mission) to help him animate, coordinate, and enlighten the debate. He also created a dedicated Web site on which information could be shared and arguments exchanged in order to "improve traditional public debates." Thirty-three public meetings were organized, first in Paris, then in potential location sites, and their transcription on the Internet fed the public forum, which was open to comments and questions for 6 months (including the summer months of July and August). Public meetings held in Paris were not as popular as those organized on potential sites; citizens were not yet informed and therefore not really involved. During the first phase (April through June) the public was mostly made up of experts from government agencies, national association members, and elected officials. Things changed during the summer as citizens mobilized themselves both through their networks and online. Between September and October, public meetings attracted a huge and very concerned crowd in small northern towns where the airport might have been potentially built. Citizens and associations formed the main public, elected officials and government agencies were outnumbered. One can estimate at around 1,500 as the number of people who had at least come to one public meeting.

The Web site was both dedicated to the debate and very informative. It included downloadable documents (aside from the extensive transcriptions) including maps and charts for an easier apprehension of the challenges at stakes, a simplistic discussion forum with no internal organization, and a very limited *a priori* moderation, but no search engine. Three hundred thirty-four messages were posted over a 6 month period by approximately 156 participants (some may have changed their names without us noticing). They sent from 1 to 11 messages, and 13 participants can be considered as "active" with 6 messages or more sent. Any actors in the debate could feed the Web site with documents, analysis, and comments, all of which has been widely used. The amount of information available online grew significantly once citizens got involved and *ad hoc* associations created a network of associations, during June 2001.

Of course, 156 (participants) might appear a narrow figure for a national debate which has involved more than 1,500 participants in public meetings. One has to recall that in 2001, only 5 million French households were connected to the Internet (95% without broadband). Today, these figures have increased to 10 million with 90% with broadband. The fact that the Ducsai debate mobilized only 156 people in 2001 has then to be put in perspective with the average Internet equipment and use at that time. As the Ducsai was the first of its kind in France, it had to deal with the novelty factor and poor equipment; nowadays National Commissions debates generate an average of 20,000 single visits and a few hundred questions through their discussion forums. In comparison, another 2001 debate, (EPA in the U.S.) counted over 300 participants for over 1,200 posts. Considering that the U.S. is 30 times bigger than France, it suggests that that our 156 participants was not such an insignificant figure at the time. The point here is that we witnessed with the Ducsai the beginning of a new participative trend which is considered by the National Commission as an essential asset to public meetings. I therefore do not pretend here that those 156 citizens are a representative sample of the population, but that we can learn from this emergent use, even with a limited sample.

During the debate, eight potential sites were considered according to various geographical, sociological, and economical characteristics and each of them has been extensively discussed in public. But more importantly the core idea of the necessity of a new airport has been the subject of passionate discussions both online and offline, even though it was not supposed to be a topic of the debate, and limited to the location of the airport.

By October, the CNDP gave its conclusion to the government with a list of criteria according to which the final decision should be taken (e.g., concerned population and protection against noise, distance to Paris, air traffic saturation) without expressing a preference for any of the eight locations selected. In November, after the debate's closure, while the government was analyzing the results and taking its decision on the debate, both *ad hoc* associations and more perennial ones mobilized their members through the Internet and by demonstrating in the concerned villages and towns. They were stressing that the DUCSAI debate had shown no need for a new airport, their argument being recently reinforced with the 9/11 tragedy. By mid-November, the final governmental decision fell: a little village named Chaulnes, in the Somme Valley, had been chosen. Quite unfortunately, in the selected area were buried hundreds of Second World War British and New Zealand soldiers. Outraged citizens and associations expressed their emotions and discontent with such a decision and started lobbying in order to slightly move the location and leave the cemeteries in their original position.

As the 2002 presidential campaigns started, these new networks created by the debate activated a strong lobbying strategy on candidates who publish online their comments about the actual left wing government decision. Jacques Chirac won the May 2002 presidential elections and his party (UMP) won a very large majority in Parliament. One of the first decisions taken by the new Transport Minister, also Mayor of Amiens, a northern city quite involved in the DUCSAI debate, was to cancel the former decision. The parliamentary commission mandated to assess the necessity of the airport a few months later, expressed no emergency in building such an infrastructure. Five years later, with increased concern for climate change and sustainable development central in the 2007 presidential campaign, the idea of a new airport seems to have been abandoned.

Research Questions

The purpose of this research was to evaluate the deliberative dimension of the DUCSAI debate and to compare its online and off-line versions. The specific features of this arrangement allowed us to question the impact of technical constraints on citizen's discussions. Academic literature on ICT-enabled debates and online forums has come to an ambiguous conclusion: there seems to be as many negative effects on deliberation as positive experiments of online discussions. On one side, the Internet has been offered as a solution to modern democracies' crisis of representation as it reaches apathetic citizens and gives them the opportunity to discuss, avoiding traditional time, space, and symbolic constraints of public expression (Blumler & Coleman, 2001; Coleman & Gøtz, 2001; Klein, 1999; Pruijt 2002; Rheingold, 1994). Empirical studies have shown that dissenters feel more liberated to express their views online than off-line as they do not have to cope with discontentment and manifestations of disapproval (Davies, 1999; Wallace, 1999). Jennifer Stromer-Galley (2002) considers for example that online conversations free people from the psychological barriers that otherwise would prevent them from getting involved in a deliberative process. Coleman (2004), evaluating the deliberative dimension of two parliamentary UK consultations, also clearly notes an inclusive phenomenon. He states that:

Most participants in both of the consultations were not the 'usual suspects': party members, lobbyist or people who lived in or around the Westminster village. The voices heard in these consultation forums would probably not otherwise be heard by parlementarians. (p. 16)

It seems though that this could be explained by the intense advertising and recruiting effort deployed by organizers to assure an heterogeneity of population participating in the consultation.

On the other hand, this heterogeneity has been questioned. If the Internet provides a space for different and alternative views, people also tend to participate and visit discussion forums and Web sites they share common values with and do not really look for controversies (Davies, 1999; Sustein, 2001; Wilhelm, 2000a, 2000b). The heterogeneity of people deliberating online is also narrowed by the social capital factor. Vincent Price and Joseph N. Capella (2002) state that their "examination of who participated to the Electronic Dialogue Events strongly supports the theoretical connections of social capital—voluntary associations, interpersonal trust and shared norms of civic values—to political engagement" (p. 322). A crucial element of deliberation, that is, its openness, the equality of parole, and its access, therefore seems to be jeopardized in the light of empirical data.

Behind these contradictory results, one can stress that less attention has been given to the technical frame of the deliberative artefacts used. Qualified as "mundane" aspects of the debate which should be taken care of (Ranerup, 2000), these technical and physical constraints play a great role in the participant's involvement. The software and the type of interaction it allows, the nature of the moderation, the appropriation of the interface by users, and their ability to manipulate it, all intervene in the success or failure of a deliberative experiment. Scott Wright (2006) notes that "the way in which the debates are framed may, through the design of the interface, generate the polarization discovered by Wilhelm and Davies." The impact of moderation on the deliberation is supported by his empirical analysis of BBC and government-run forums (Wright, 2005). Morison and Newman (2001) observe that "it seems that the interface affects the way people write and deliberate online, from the immediacy of chat systems to the stilted but carefully considered essays submitted to structured website bulletin boards" (p. 185).

With its hybrid format for public debates, the CNDP offers researchers interesting objects for observation and comparison between two types of deliberation, both dependant on technical and material constraints which affect citizen's mode of expression and involvement. Our research program has compared the impact of both online and off-line structures of the debate on its argumentative content. This has led to more theoretical considerations about the discursive anchorage of the deliberation theory.

Methodology

Case studies have a few shortcomings. One of them has been well summarized by Anthony Wilhelm (2000a): it is "the propensity of researchers, the media, and policy makers to want to generalize to all cyber democracy projects based on the findings from a single-shot study" (p. 25). He therefore takes the exemplary case of the Santa Monica Public Electronic Network (PEN) which with positive evaluation has been interpreted by many authors as a scientific element of proof that computer mediated communication discussion leads to an effective improvement of the local democratic process, dismissing that contextual elements were limiting the scope of the case study's conclusion. Then Wilhem (2000) pursues "we must be careful that we do not generalize beyond what the data tell us about various aspects of online public life within the community of study" (p. 25-26).

This drawback can be partially contained if the case study is completed with an important ethnographic research. Enlightening the context, the history of the debate and the evolution of its actors allow us to follow the case to witness its consequences in the concerned community and provide us with elements to better appreciate the qualities of discussion during the debate. As Stephen Coleman (2004) points out in his own case study on two online UK parliamentary consultations,

The environment and the structure of communication has a significant effect upon its content; synchronous chat rooms and peer-generated Usenet groups are no more indicative of the scope for online public deliberation than loud, prejudiced and banal political arguments in crowded pubs are indicative of the breadth of off-line political discussion. (p. 6)

On this basis, we have combined different approaches to our case study. The first one is both historical and, to a certain extent, ethnographical. We have conducted exploratory interviews with 25 actors (2 to 4 hours each) who have been involved in the Ducsai debate and also, for some of them, in long term discussions and negotiations with both Parisian airports (Orly and Roissy-Charles-de-Gaulle) about air traffic noise and pollution, in which the Ducsai debate takes place. These interviews gave us the opportunity to draw a broad picture of relations established between local associations, Aéroport de Paris (ADP, a private company managing both Parisian airports, Orly and Charles de Gaulle), and the government from 1974 (opening of Roissy) until December 2003(the date of our last interview, 2 years after the end of the Ducsai debate). Our objective was to relate the trajectory followed by the actors, their strategies, their birth, alliances, and disappearance from the "airport discussion" scene. Like Hiram Sachs (1995a,1995b) in his work on the nonprofit computer network Peace Net, I think that studying how public opinion has been formed is often overlooked, although it is of utmost importance to understand this single moment we were analysing in this long history. A content analysis of this material with Nudist© software allowed us to highlight the evolution of the debate's themes, even well after its end.

Another salient element of our methodology is its strong linguistic dimension; the discourse analysis conducted by our team had several levels. I will only describe in this chapter two of them. The first one is a comparison of arguments used by Internet participants on the forum and ordinary citizens during public debates. The purpose of this analysis was to focus first on the link between technical constraints and the nature of arguments and second on the variety and quality of them. Two "tree-type" maps of the argumentative structure (one for each modality of the debate) have been produced and the results are discussed below. The second discourse analysis has focused on the "quoted discourse" on the forum, that is, citations of others in someone's mail. The way participants have quoted each other has been compared with the characteristics of other online forums, and has been interpreted here to define the type of interaction developed between respondents on the forum. We acknowledge here that our two samples are of different sizes, therefore our conclusions constitute only trends of emergent uses qualitatively analysed which should be further explored in the future, in a more quantitative fashion.

Discussion

Two Arenas, Multiple Actors

I use the concept of arena (Dobry, 1992; Dodier, 1999; Renn, 1992) to describe the characteristics of these two spaces of discussion. It derives from an analysis of modern society as segmented in various spaces in which communication codes, legitimacy processes, regulation rules, and conflict nodes diverge. Therefore, the concept of arena is a heuristic tool to understand how different symbolic spaces manage their own discussion and how they can influence the political decision process.

An arena has two major characteristics (Joly & Assouline, 2001), and I would like to add a third one out of our observation of public debates:

- Specific access rules, the use of specific types of arguments, and resources they can mobilize in their interactions (power, money, fame, etc.). Some actors can belong to multiple arenas and develop different identities in each of them (e.g., company director in the economic arena, elected representative in the political arena, etc.)

- Each arena produces its own symbolic references which determine its relationship with the public, the nature of its internal conflicts, and their resolution patterns.

- Every arena is technically and materially configured. This encourages or prevents certain types of behavior from its participants and contributes structuring of its symbolic dimension.

The arena concept is of utmost pertinence here to describe how both the Web site and public meetings actually function as segmented symbolic spaces. Each of them has developed specific types of arguments, rituals, ways to envision a specific subject, tones used by participants to express themselves, access codes, and types of beliefs they can mobilize.

Therefore, the presence of different actors in different arenas is not surprising *per se*, it is not easy to master and be legitimate according to different arenas codes.

In our case study, despite our limited online sample, we can witness that the two arenas are quite distinct and overlap very little. Participants in public meetings rarely go online to pursue the debate, even if they keep an eye on the forum and publish site their official position paper on the Web. They are mainly official representatives of well-known associations when local militants or basic citizens constitute a majority of online participants (even if they did come to some local meetings). This confirms the flexible nature of the Internet which widens the variety of actors involved (Beierle, 2002; Coleman, 2001, 2004). Even if the use of nicknames sometimes makes it difficult to identify certain online participants, contents of mail suggests a limited involvement in the other arena. Only two individuals were identified as contributors on both sides. This characteristic explains the variety of arguments expressed online and the tone used by Internet users. Not only does one not write on a forum the same way as one speaks in public, but also, one does not have to follow the same speech ritual as that imposed on every public debate participant.

More importantly, due to the openness of the debate, its length, and its online archives, many actors have identified themselves as being concerned by the debate instead of being identified by the legitimate authority (Coleman & Gøtze, 2001). Here, the use of Internet as an archive keeper for deliberative processes has played a great role in public ability for future mobilization. Several months after the beginning of the procedure, two independent associations unaware of its existence were able to retrieve every element of the debate and then accurately make their contribution. The medium has therefore played an important role for those actors with no specific network contacts through which they could have access to precise data (such as up to date air traffic information, or landing trajectories of an Airbus 340).

The Internet has also created the conditions which have allowed people to prepare quickly and contribute serious input to the discussions. Contacts were made via e-mail between remote local associations and active individuals who then went off-line to meet. With information and the discussion forum being available online, the whole process of identifying the various actors' viewpoints and their weaknesses, making contact with alike-minded people, and getting organized as a powerful association has been extremely fast. Actors then organized themselves in associations, even federations, to improve the defence of their position and gain collective expertise in a very limited time (3 months). Once informed, they have participated actively and brought considerable expertise to the debate. All people interviewed mentioned that this first national debate experiment had set a precedent for future debates organized by the National Commission and therefore could be seen as a positive experience for them and their organization.

Another effect of multiple arenas is the enormous amount of knowledge gained by all actors. People have invested a great deal of time and passion in the debate. Starting from scratch, some of them have sought information from the administration and the Internet, asking questions in order to be able to discuss with the administration's experts. The former minister for the environment (Corinne Lepage) who, as a lawyer, was involved in trials over aircraft noise levels, the former minister of transport (J.-C. Gayssot who was in charge of this case), and several members of the National Commission expressed their amazement about how quickly ordinary people where able to find their way around complex administrative and technical dossiers concerning aircraft traffic, airport building constraint, and so forth. Some of them emphasized the role played by early retired and well educated people belonging to associations and their new attitude towards authority. The public aptitude for self-learning and rational discussion on complex matters clearly contradicts an important political science tradition of disregard (and even distrust) towards the average citizen (Almond, 1960; Converse, 1964; Lippman, 1922). We here follow Page and Shapiro's (1992) analysis that an informed and educated citizen properly involved in an appropriate deliberative process is perfectly able to give an articulate and stable opinion on any complex topic.

Actors have adapted to the procedure and chosen their arena of expression in such a way that it had led to a common building of new expectations and values that will determine future decisions about the airport (e.g., its location, its local implementation, and the respect of the environment). This constitutes a new analytical framework in which the concerned stakeholders already position themselves. The "urgency" argument used by the pro-airport group, stating that a decision to build the airport must be taken urgently because of the increased air traffic in the five past years that will soon bring Roissy to its limits, diminished during the debate under the pressure of the in-depth prospective analysis of air traffic evolution in a post 9/11 world presented by opponents to the project.

The DUCSAI debate has paved the way for the evolution of the Commission as an independent agency, after 2002. Their Web site has been formally redesigned in order to keep all debate archives and to offer an open area of expression to lay citizens and institutions willing to do so in a more or less official fashion. Every debate has its own Web site according to a predesign model with six sections within which the content varies (i.e., the debate organization, information, participation, news, press section, and links to related Web sites). If the information section has significantly grown in pages as multimedia documents are progressively integrated, the participation one has is reduced, in most debates, to a one-way communication. Stake holders and citizens can either ask questions or post comments and position papers; horizontal exchanges and discussion have been suppressed in most cases. In a recent interview, the Commission Vice-President justifies this by the nonappropriation of forums by Internet users; in two recent debates, only 15 persons went online for discussion. Two hypotheses, to be tested, can explain this disaffection for forums. The first is technical: the forums were so segmented in multiple themes and under-themes that a post had a limited chance to be seen by anyone, especially as the forum has been largely polluted by spam messages. This did not favor interaction between people. The second one seems to be a side-effect of a voluntary communication choice made by the Commission. All questions and comments written by mail (25%), during public meetings (50%), or online (25% in 2006) are now available online, with their answers from the appropriate authority and, most important, showing no traces of their media origins. In doing so, the perimeter for an online discussion has been jeopardized as there is no way to know who is online and who is not. The system seems to have reached its limits. If a new public is attracted to the debate via the Internet, it does not interact directly, as it used to do in the DUCSAI case, even if questions sometimes refer to one another.

Deliberation on the Forum:
Argumentation, Appropriation, and Design

I have concluded from the Ducsai case that it has been easier for 156 people online to discuss the legitimacy of the creation of a new airport than it has been for the other 1,500 participating in public reunions. First, because the design of procedure is more open to participants online than off-line, and second because the interactivity of the Internet allows users to manipulate this design to their own benefit. One has to notice that new Web site conceptions do not favor online deliberation as creativity is restrained by a controlled design and rational argumentation shows its limits for a larger inclusion of population.

Online Argumentation: ICT as a Source of Creativity

Despite the many claims that there was no real debate, a close analysis of the Ducsai online argumentation shows that participants have used various strategies to pass on their messages by avoiding thematic and technical limits installed by the Web site designer. Here I refer to the sociology of uses to interpret those strategies. I do not mean here that technical constraints were intentional, but rather they were more or less a result of a cumbersome public debate organization, by ill-experienced organizers, and lots of "bricolage," to quote Michel de Certeau. One has to notice that online debates are more easily appropriated by citizens than an off-line public debate which is shorter, often ritualized, and organized in such a way that interruptions and demonstrations cannot find a way to express themselves. Therefore, deliberation on the Internet offers new ways of expressing citizen's feelings and arguments because ICT can be adopted in a nonanticipated fashion. Here, creativity can become a fruitful resource for the deliberative process. Two examples illustrate this learning process.

The Ducsai debate was originally organized by the head of the National Commission who decided which would be the main issues discussed both on the Web site and during public meetings. As such, the Web site questions which are pertinent in the debate are formulated on the first page (e.g., the nature of the new airport and what type of traffic [it could have been passengers or freight or both]). The question of the airport's existence was not supposed to be part of the debate. But in fact, most interventions were focused on the "existence issue" and the Commission had to deal with that. It then included it in public meetings. Online, however, this issue was not mentioned as one that should be discussed, but in fact it was one of the hottest topics and nobody could prevent it (in public meetings people were sometimes reprimanded for going over old ground!). Users of the Internet here have played a great role in redefining the "legitimate" issue, sometimes with anger. Most of them have then argued against a specific location by showing how the idea of building a new airport was illegitimate. The thematic frame proposed on the Web site has been overcome by an argumentation strategy which cannot be easily stopped as in public meetings where the chairman interrupts for being off the subject. Online, the forum's moderator has never really interfered into discussions. He recalls having asked civil servants to answer some of the questions asked by citizens on the forum, but this is how far his intervention has really gone.

This absence of real moderation on the forum, partly due to an overload of work for a small team, and partly corresponding to a policy of free expression online, has emphasized the difference between the online and off-line debate. I here agree with J. Street and S. Wright (in press) on their analysis of the role played by moderation in an online deliberation: "The choice of moderation style can be significant (and positive) in shaping the quality and usefulness of the debates, particularly for government-run discussions." Nevertheless, because online debates are not subject to specific schedules, and because the "moderator" does not play the same role than the chairman—who is often showing authority towards participants in a public meeting—it has been easier for Internet users to extend the scope of the debate to nonexpected topics.

A second example reveals how smart Internet users can be. When they logged onto the Web site forum page, participants were invited to "ask a question," which is quite different to, for example, to "send your message," which is a common phrase used in public debate. It suggests that the participant is not in a position to exchange ideas with experts and the administration but instead that participant needs to be informed in order to appreciate the quality of the proposed program. This tiny detail reflects the difficulty the administration and public debate organizers have to conceive a real and balanced exchange of opinions, despite their claims. Internet users have overcome this strong suggestion by using the question mark to deliver their opinion. They used the "object" line on e-mails to sum up their positions ("useful debate?" "For Vatry," and so on) and very often their nickname has also been an indicator of their position (e.g., "no to the airport," "Juvincourt yes," "a countrywomen," etc.). Thanks to this little trick, a wide variety of opinions have been expressed and few discussions between users have occurred, although one has to notice the absence of civil engineers on the net. Most discussion and exchange with them happened off-line, during public meetings, or aside, thanks to personal contacts.

Lessons have been learned from the DUCSAI case. The Commission for instance keeps open every topic on a debate on his Web site as a counterpart of public meetings which are all focused on a specific topic except introductory ones. Participants are not compelled to "ask questions" and can now give their opinion in various forms (e.g., simple online statement, formal letter available in pdf format, or elaborated position paper), all of which are archived. Nevertheless, the formalization of each debate Web site does not leave much space for any local specificity or new form of creativity; online participation seems to have reached a new level. The domination of writing and rational argumentation still values a traditional way of expression which limits the inclusive potential of an interactive media to state or local institutions and an educated portion of the population. According to the Commission's Vice President, their main concern remains as: How do we include more people into the debate and how can we adapt our deliberation process to their mode of communication?

A Real Argumentation on the Forum

The comparison between online and off-line argumentation and their structure has shown that the extension of an actor's ways of participating to the debate is not detrimental to the debate's quality.

Three rhetorical questions have been covered on the Ducsai forum: For or against a new airport?; Its location?; and, Is the public debate a real and fruitful one? Almost all arguments expressed online have their counterparts off-line: the environmental one (noise pollution, worse quality of air…), the economical one (it is a very expensive public infrastructure, but, on another hand, it could enhance local economy), and the "alternative" one (there are other solutions to explore).

Nevertheless they slightly differ from each other. Public meetings have seen more elaborate and technical arguments developed. This has lead to an important analysis on the air traffic evolution in the last decade and in the near future. One can notice that each arena brings to the debate its own point of view on a specific topic; "private" and "public" interests have been defined and legitimized differently in each arena. Online, "private" concerns rightfully expressed themselves as enlightening some local consequences (Doury, 2005a), whereas off-line, the same set of arguments is inaudible; national authorities "represents" the national public interest and will not let it be challenged by local actors.

The reengineering of the Commission's Web sites has blurred frontiers between online contributions and traditional writing ones. With both of them indistinct from the user's point of view, it tends to legitimate a rational and extended argumentation. The proliferation of position papers and written contributions and the absence of forums have eliminated on-the-spot comments and quick exchanges we had seen in the Ducsai debate. Therefore, more research is now needed in order to evaluate the argumentative structure and content of online contributions.

Conclusion—Hybrid Debates:
A New Form of Deliberative Space?

Since the DUCSAI, the National Commission has developed its Web site and given voice to hundreds of people not able to attend public meetings and has spread information to associations and citizens. The Internet is now widely used and quite intertwined with off-line debates; questions, contribution, and their answers constitute the center of the participative process. Between February and May 2006, in a similar generic debate about the extension of the Parisian tramway, the CNDP counted more than 1,500 participants to meetings asking 300 questions, and 25,000 single visitors on the Web site asking more than 400 questions. It appears that since the DUCSAI, hybrid procedures have become a common way of participating to public decisions, even if it is not yet widely recognized and accepted by all political elites. We have here an unidentified deliberative object which presents certain characteristics of traditional deliberation (online and off-line meetings with arguments exchanged, a transparency of the procedure, and opened to all stakeholders), but which does not correspond to the canon of deliberation (Cohen, 1994; Habermas, 1997). It is a moving space, with actors entering and exiting, a wide use of rhetoric, emotions, and personal relationships.

This has brought us to question the heuristic value of a concept of deliberation which rests on a rather normative and discursive ground. Instead of incriminating the procedure for not being deliberative enough (not inclusive enough, transparent enough, sincere enough, and so on), one should reconsider what deliberation really is. If the concept of deliberation does not allow us to comprehend the existing situation, should we not reconsider it or rephrase it? This could be the theme of another chapter for instance, but I would like to stress here two dimensions of deliberation which have not been deeply considered by the theory.

First, material and technical factors shape deliberation and therefore contribute to excluding potential participants from debates. In our case study, the evolution from the first DUCSAI debate to more recent ones suggests that the inclusive potential of the Internet has now reached its own limits. Based on writing skills, contributions are as selective as oral ones which necessitate mastering emotions and commending symbolic authority. If Internet favors alternative ways of expressing arguments which enhance the heterogeneity of the public as it has been shown in the DUCSAI debate, it has not yet been configured to open itself to other forms of expression, such as images, mini-films, and other forms of multimedia productions.

By limiting debate to "public reason," one, by definition, limits the variety/plurality of people participating and tends to restrain it to articulated forms of oral/written argumentation. These criticisms have been formulated by Marion Young (1996) towards the habermassian conception of deliberation:

Restricting practices of democratic discussion to moves in a contest where some win and others lose, privileges those who like contest and know the rules of the game. Speech is assertive and confrontational is here more valued than speech that is tentative, exploratory or conciliatory. (p. 123)

Therefore, a procedural and discursive approach to deliberation not only excludes many potential participants from the debate, but also structures all discussion by imposing a unique type of constraint that might not fit with the creative potential of many citizens. We advocate here that production of norms rests within the creative capacity of every member of the deliberative process to express his or herself with one's own perspective as long as everybody listens to each other *in the format one chooses to do so*. In this perspective, new Web services and technology offer interactive and multimedia solutions which could help citizens to voice their concerns in an alternative fashion to writing. The wide use of cell-phone filming devices could be envisioned as a way of participating in online blogs, for instance.

Second, we have concluded from our case study that the use of ICT as another arena of expression has helped citizens to overcome traditional and symbolic face-to-face constraints (Davies, 1999; Stromey-Galley, 2002), such as its rituals, its forms of power, and its argumentative frame, by giving them a chance to build another deliberative space. It has become a somewhat creative space for individuals uncomfortable with the public meetings scheme. Nevertheless, actual Web site design and control by the National Commission has jeopardized citizen's appropriation of this deliberative space as there is less room for improvisation and creativity. Formatting and modelling discussion spaces within the debate tends to prevent us from welcoming other types of population in the discussion, especially those who have not framed their communication skills within those restricted boundaries. Therefore, the Internet should be considered as an alternative space for deliberation but not the "ultimate" one, as participants shape their expression according to the medium they use, which depends on various socioeconomic factors (Young, 1999).

I have tried in this chapter to show that there could not be such a thing as an "ideal procedure" as a true deliberative process should be as inclusive as possible and therefore could not be reduced to only one format. The potential of these new online and hybrid debates rests in their ability to mobilize citizen's creativity and use it within a larger deliberative frame than a traditional exchange of rational argument.

A next step in the theory of deliberation is now needed. It should rephrase the production of normative structures out of its discursive anchorage in order to show how argumentation can take various semiotic forms. I have tried elsewhere to start such a research program using Hans Joas' theory of creative action (Monnoyer-Smith, 2006b). In this perspective, hybrid deliberative processes are not measured out of a normative concept of deliberation but can be analyzed in their aptitude to include as many forms of expression as the local context justifies it. This could certainly lead to interesting field experiments and research analysis.

References

Almond, G. A. (1960). *The American people and foreign policy*. New York: Praeger.

Barber, B. (1984). *Strong democracy. Participatory politics for a new age*. Berkeley: University of California Press.

Beck, U. (1992). *Risk society: Toward a new modernity*. London: Sage.

Beck, U., Giddens, A., & Lash, S. (1999). *Reflexive modernization*. Stanford, CA: Stanford University Press.

Beierle, T. B. (2002). *Democracy on line. An evaluation of the national dialogue on public involvement in EPA decisions* (RFF Report). Washington, D.C. Retrieved March 24, 2006, from http://www.rff.org/rff/Documents/RFF-RPT-demonline.pdf

Bellamy, C., & Raab, C. D. (1999). Wiring up the deck-chairs? In S. Coleman, J. Taylor, & W. Van de Donk (Eds.), *Parliaments in the age of the Internet* (pp. 156-172). Oxford University Press.

Bohman, J., & Rehg, W. (Eds.). (1997). *Deliberative democracy*. Cambridge: MIT Press.

Cohen, J. (1989). Deliberation and democratic legitimacy. In A. Hamlin & P. Pettit (Eds.), *The good polity* (pp. 17-34). Oxford: Basil Blackwell.

Cohen, J. (1994). Critical viewing and participatory democracy. *Journal of Communication, 44*(4), 98-113.

Cohen, J. (1997a). Deliberation and democratic legitimacy. In J. Bohman & W. Rehg (Eds.), *Deliberative democracy* (pp. 67-92). Cambridge, MA: MIT Press.

Cohen, J. (1997b). Procedure and substance in deliberative democracy. In J. Bohman & W. Rehg (Eds.), *Deliberative democracy* (pp. 407-437). Cambridge, MA: MIT Press.

Cohen, J. R. (1989). Deliberation and democratic legitimacy. In A. Hamlin & P. Pettit (Dir.), *The good polity* (pp. 17-34). Oxford: Basil Blackwell.

Coleman, S. (2001). The transformation of citizenship? In B. Axford & R. Huggins (Eds.), *New media and politics*. London: Sage, 109-126.

Coleman, S. (2004). Connecting Parliament to the public via the Internet: Two case studies of online consultations. *Information, Communication & Society, 7*(1), 3-22.

Coleman, S., & Gøtze, J. (2001). *Bowling together: Online public engagement in policy deliberation*. London: Hansard Society Publishing.

Coleman, S., Hall, N., & Howell, M. (2002). *Hearing voices. The experience of online public consultations and discussions in the UK*. London: Hansard Society Publishing.

Converse, P. E. (1964). The nature of belief systems in mass publics. In D. E. Apter (Ed.), *Ideology and discontent* (pp. 206-261). New York: Free Press.

Cooke, M. (2000). Five arguments for deliberative democracy. *Political Studies, 48*(5), 947-969.

Dahlberg, L. (2001). Computer-mediated communication and the public sphere: A critical analysis. *Journal of Computer Mediated Communication, 7*(1), 1-28.

Davies, R. (1999). *The web of politics: The Internet's impact on the American political system.* Oxford University Press.

Dewey, J. (1927). *The public and its problems.* London: Allen & Unwin.

Dobry, M. (1992). *Sociologie des crises politiques.* Paris: Presses de la FNSP.

Dodier, N. (1999). L'espace public de la recherche médicale. Autour de l'affaire des ciclosporines. *Réseaux, 95,* 109-154.

Doury, M. (2005a, May 26-29). *Thesis and ethos: How to defend private interests without ruining one's image.* Paper presented at the IADA Congress, Bucharest, Romania.

Dryzek, J. S. (2000). *Deliberative democracy and beyond. Liberals, critics, contestations.* Oxford University Press.

Elster, J. (1998). *Deliberative democracy.* Cambridge University Press.

Giddens, A. (1990). *The consequence of modernity.* Cambridge: Polity.

Giddens, A. (1991). *The modernityand self-identity.* Cambridge: Polity.

Guttmann, A., & Thompson, D. (1996). *Democracy and disagreement.* Cambridge, MA: Harvard University Press.

Habermas, J. (1975). *Legitimation crisis.* Boston: Beacon Press.

Habermas, J. (1984). *The theory of communicative action.* Boston: Beacon Press.

Habermas, J. (1997). *Droit et démocratie. Entre faits et normes.* Paris: Gallimard.

Hill, K., & Hugues, J. (1998). *Cyberpolitics: Citizen activism in the age of the Internet.* Oxford: Rowman and Littlefield.

Joly, P.-B. & Assouline, G. (2001). Assessing debate and participative technology assessment in Europe, Final report. Grenoble: INRA Economie et Sociologie rurales, Teys: QAP Decision. Retrieved from http://www.inra.fr/internet/Directions/SED/sciencegouvernance/pub/ADAPTA/index.html

Klein, H. (1999). Tocqueville in cyberspace: Using the Internet for citizen associations. *The Information Society, 15,* 213-220.

Lippmann, W. (1922). *Public opinion.* New York: Mac Millan.

Loader, B.D. (Ed.). (1998). *Cyberspace divide: Equality, agency and policy in the information society.* London: Sage.

Luke, T. (1998). The politics of digital inequality: Access, capability and distribution in cyberspace. In C. Toulouse & T. W. Luke (Eds.), *The politics of cyberspace.* London: Routledge.

Macpherson, C. B. (1977). *The life and times of liberal democracy.* Oxford: Oxford University Press.

Manin, B. (1985). Volonté Générale ou Délibération ? Esquisse d'une Théorie de la Délibération Politique. *Le débat, 33,* 72-93.

Manin, B. (1994). On legitimacy and political deliberation. *Political Theory, 15*(3), 338-368.

Manin, B. (2005). Délibération et Discussion. *Swiss Political Science Review, 10*(4), 34-46.

Mendelberg, T. (2002). The deliberative citizen: Theory and evidence. *Research in Micropolitics, 6,*151-193.

Monnoyer-Smith, L. (2006a). Citizen deliberation on the Internet: An exploratory study. *International Journal of E-government Research, 2*(3), 58-74.

Monnoyer-Smith, L. (2006b). La délibération comme invention du politique. *Sciences de la Société, 69,* 51-70.

Morison, J., & Newman, D. (2001). Online citizenship: Consultation and participation in lew labour's Britain and beyond. *International Review of Law, Computers and Technology, 15*(2), 171-194.

Norris, P. (1999). *Critical citizens: Global support for democratic goernment.* Oxford: Oxford University Press.

Page, B., & Shapiro, R. (1992). *The rational public: Fifty years of trends in American policy preferences.* Chicago University Press.

Pateman, C. (1970). *Participation and democratic theory.* Cambridge University Press.

Price, V. (in press). Citizens deliberating online: Theory and some evidence. In T. Davies & B. S. Noveck (Eds.), *Online deliberation: Design, research and practice.* CSLI Publications/University of Chicago Press. Retrieved September 3, 2007, from http://www.ksg.harvard.edu/netgov/files/talks/docs/11_13_06_seminar_Price_citizens-delib_online.pdf

Price, V., & Cappella, J. N. (2002). Online deliberation and its influence: The electronic dialogue project in campaign 2000. *IT and Society, 1,* 303-328.

Pruijt, H. (2002). Social capital and the equalising potential of the Internet. *Social Science Computer Review, 20*(2), 109-115.

Putnam, R. D. (2000). *Bowling alone: The collapse and revival of American community.* New York: Simon and Schuster.

Rains, S. A. (2005). Leveling the organizational playing field-virtually. *Communication Research, 32*(2), 193-234.

Ranerup, A. (2000). Online forums as arena for political discussions. In T. Ishida & K. Ibister (Eds.), *Digital cities: Technologies, experiences and future perspectives* (pp. 209-223). Berlin: Springer Verlag.

Renn, O. (1992). The social arena concept of risk debates. In G. S. Krimski & D. Westport (Eds.), *Social theories of risk* (pp.179-196). Westport, CT: Praeger.

Rheingold, H. (1994). *The virtual community: Homesteading on the electronic frontier.* New York: Harper Perennial.

Sachs, H. (1995a). An ethnographic study about the computer networks. *Media, Culture and Society, 17*(1), 81-99.

Sachs, H. (1995b). Computer networks and the formation of public opinion: An ethnographic study. *Media, Culture & Society, 17*(1), 81-99.

Sanders, L. (1997). Against deliberation. *Political Theory, 25,* 347-375.

Street, J. (1997). Remote control? Politics, technology and 'electronic democracy.' *Journal of Communication, 12*(1), 27-42.

Stromer-Galley, J. (2002). New voices in the political sphere: A comparative analysis of interpersonal and online political talk. *Javnost/The Public, 9*(2), 23-42.

Sustein, C. (2001). *Republic.com*. Princetown University Press.

Wallace, P. (1999). *The psychology of the Internet*. Cambridge University Press.

Wilhelm, A. G. (2000a). *Democracy in the digital age: Challenges to political life in cyberspace*. London: Routledge.

Wilhelm, A. G. (2000b). Virtual sounding boards: How deliberative is online political discussion? In B.N. Hague & B. Loader (Eds.), *Digital democracy: Discourse and decision making in the information age* (pp. 154-178). London: Routledge.

Wright, S. (2005). Design matters: The political efficacy of government-run discussion forums. In R. Gibson, S. Oates, & D. Owen (Eds.), *Civil society, democracy and the Internet: A comparative perspective* (pp. 80-99). London: Routledge

Wright, S. (2006). Government-run online discussion fora: Moderation, censorship, and the shadow of control. *The British Journal of Politics and International Relations, 8*(4), 550-569.

Wright, S., & Street, J. (in press). Democracy, deliberation and design: The case of online discussion forum. *New Media and Society*.

Young, I. M. (1990). *Justice and the politics of difference*. Princeton University Press.

Young, I. M. (1996). Communication and the other: Beyond deliberative democracy. In S. Benhabib (Ed.), *Democracy and difference: Contesting the boundaries of the* political. Princeton University Press.

Young, I. M. (1999). Difference as a resource for democratic communication. In J. Bohman & William Rehg (Eds.), *Deliberative democracy* (pp. 387-398). Cambridge, MA: MIT Press.

Young, I. M. (2002). *Inclusion and democracy*. Oxford University Press.

Endnotes

[1] This paper is an updated version of an article published in the *International Journal of E-government research, 2*(3), pp. 58-74.

[2] These figures are available in the Commission's 2007 annual report.

Chapter XI

E-Government for an Inclusive Society:
How Different Citizen Groups Use E-Government Services in Europe

Jeremy Millard, Danish Technological Institute, Denmark

Abstract

This chapter examines the role of e-government in supporting an inclusive society by focusing on how government and e-government services are used, and who uses them. In this context, the socioeconomic and other characteristics of users and nonusers of e-government services are examined, as is the importance of the different user access channels, including the digital channel, and the consequences this has. The focus is also on user experiences of e-government and the role of human intermediaries in delivering services. In each case, the benefits and challenges of e-government for an inclusive society are documented and analyzed. Finally, conclusions are drawn concerning appropriate inclusion policy.

Introduction

There has been a relative dearth of studies and data on the user demand and usage side of e-government services compared with the supply side. This is both because it is much easier to collect supply side data from mainly public organizations than it is to collect usage data from citizens, and because chronologically roll-out takes place before take-up and use. This chapter presents new data and analysis (Millard, 2006) which, to some extent, redress this imbalance.[1] These findings are related to other sources and specifically to the issue of an inclusive society by examining the consequences of e-government for inclusion and how the benefits could be optimized.

The overall focus of the chapter is thus on the role e-government plays in an inclusive society by examining who the users of government and e-government are, the channels they use, and the role of social intermediaries in delivering e-government services.

Who Uses Government and E-Government Services

According to the eUSER survey, almost 70% of all adults had direct contact with the public administration in the previous 12 months, although the average number of contacts was only 1.6 per person during that period. Figure 1 shows the four main types of such service users and their main distinguishing characteristics, each of which is examined in the following.

Government Service User

Based on multivariate statistical analysis techniques, Figure 2 shows that a citizen's educational level is the most important factor determining whether or not they use government services. For example, citizens with a tertiary education are 2.5 times more likely to be government users than those with the lowest educational level, while Figure 3 shows that citizens in the over 65 age group are 1.9 times more likely to be government users than the 18-24 age group.

Other important factors include income, where citizens with over median income are 1.3 times more likely to be government users than citizens below the poverty level, and employment status which shows that unemployed citizens, followed closely by those who are early retired and invalids, are marginally more likely to be government users than other groups.

Figure 1. Characteristics of typical user groups

Government users are similar to general adult population, except are more likely to:	E-government users are similar to government users, except more likely to:	Social intermediaries for e-government are similar to e-government users, except more likely to:	Receivers of partial or full assistance from social intermediaries for e-government are similar to e-government users, except more likely to:
• have higher educational level • have higher income • be unemployed, early retired, or retired and invalided • be over 65 years old	• live in a country with high e-government roll-out • live in a country with high Internet roll-out • have well developed e-skills and e-attitudes • be in employment • be 25-34 years old • be male • use government services more often • use a wider range of government service types • use a wider range a different channels, not only digital	• be early retired, or permanently invalided • be unemployed • be 35-64 years old • live in a country with not very advanced e-government roll-out	• have low digital engagement or skills • be in manual or unskilled occupations • be not working or retired • be rare Internet users • live in a country with not very advanced e-government roll-out • be 50 plus years old • have low functional and low leisure online orientation • be female • have below secondary level education • have Internet access outside the home

Figure 2. Use of government services by education

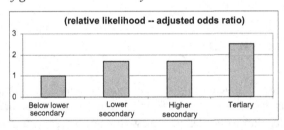

Figure 3. Use of government services by age

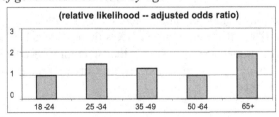

The data overall paint a picture of the typical government service user as an able, well educated, and higher income citizen who is in an older age group, and who is not working because of unemployment, invalidity, or retirement. Therefore, such citizens are those who couple the abilities and background to know about and access government with a strong need for such services. The issue remains that those citizens without such abilities and backgrounds, but who similarly need government services, are more likely to be socially excluded from using them.

E-Government Service User

Figure 4 shows that the media channel used when contacting government is still overwhelmingly face-to-face. However, other data show that there are very large differences between countries, so that Denmark is the leading country in the sample with over 40% of government users using e-channels, while in the Czech Republic, the figure is less than 9%. Also, in the UK and Ireland, the use of the postal services and the telephone has overtaken face-to-face. Overall, new digital media provide access for about 20% of all contacts with government, 17% of this via the Internet or e-mail, and about 3% via short message service (SMS).

Other data from this survey show that e-government users are more likely, when compared to government users, to use services supporting everyday life (such as related to work, housing, education, culture, transport, etc.), closely followed by taxes. Much of this is accessing information, but there is also increasing communication with civil servants. More formal and binding transactions, on the other hand, involved in calculating and submitting tax returns, making declarations or applying for permits (such as to the police or for building permission), and for receiving financial benefits and grants, are less popular as online services, but still increasing. Clearly the latter services can be more intimidating as they require the provision of personal data, and often the perceived need for more face-to-face and real time interaction, which can be more difficult to mediate electronically.

Figure 4. Media channel used when contacting government

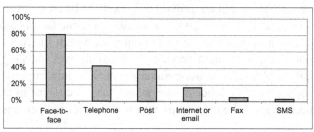

Figure 5. Media channel used for government services by type of user

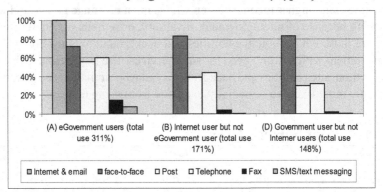

There is a strong tendency for the e-government user to use a wider range of government services, whether or not accessed online, than non e-government users. In addition, as shown in Figure 5, e-government users use government services on average 3.1 times a year compared with non e-government users who only tend to use government services 1.5 times a year. Further, when examining the range of **media channels** used, e-government users are "**flexi-channelers**" and "channel balancers," in that 60% to 70% of them also use other channels and freely make channel choices suited to their preference, to the specific service, and to the specific task in hand.

This is in some contrast to non e-government users who tend much more to be "single channellers," relying mainly on the face-to-face channel to access government services. The strong overall conclusion is, therefore, that the individual e-government user tends to use government services more than non e-government users for a wider range of such services, and to do so through a more flexible channel mix, which includes both electronic and traditional channels. The behavior of e-government users is thus typically somewhat different from government users.

The profile of e-government users is also quite different from government users, as illustrated in Figure 1. According to the eUSER multivariate data analysis, the factors determining whether or not an individual is likely to be an e-government user are country, Internet, or skill related, while sociodemographic factors are much less significant. Thus, an individual living in a country with high Internet availability and high roll-out of e-government services, and having well developed e-skills and e-attitudes, is highly likely to use e-government. The only important sociodemographic factor seems to be labor market status, that is, citizens in employment are 2.4 times more likely to be e-government users than retired persons. This is in some contrast to users of government services generally (rather than e-government services specifically) where, education, income, labor market status, and age are the most important factors. Encouraging e-government use is thus more a question of providing access and skills, rather than tackling income, education, or age issues, although the latter are important for wider **inclusion** issues, and this clearly has important policy implications.

However, it is still the case that those e-government users who use the Internet from PC platforms tend to be in higher income groups, of lower age, and with a tertiary education. In contrast to this, the eUSER data show that access to e-government services through **handheld** devices, like mobile phones or PDAs (personal digital assistants or organizers, that is, "m" or mobile government), is both becoming more important generally, and is particularly important for people who are otherwise likely to be digitally excluded. These include groups with below secondary level education, those not working (but not unemployed), or those invalided, as well as those living in countries where access is a greater problem.

E-Government Social Intermediary

Figure 6 shows that using e-government services on behalf of others (i.e., as a "social intermediary" in a context of what can be termed the "social use" of e-government) is undertaken by about 11% of all users of government services. The data also show that 53% of users of e-government do so for their own purpose, 51% as part of their job, and 42% on behalf of family or friends, the latter thus being termed "social intermediaries" for e-government.

In terms of national differences, countries with the highest e-government use are also those with the highest use on behalf of family or friends; those countries include Ireland, Denmark, the UK, and France. In addition, Ireland and France stand out as having greater use on behalf of family and friends than they do for their employer, and are also conspicuous as having by far the highest ratios of use for family or friends in relation to total e-government use, perhaps because of their strong family and community centered culture.

Further, it can be seen that the **new member states** (NMS) have the lowest e-government use for family or friends in terms of total government use, as well as an average or a lower than average percentage in terms of total e-government use. The former relates to their lower overall use of e-government, and the latter, perhaps, to the higher ratio of total e-government use on behalf of their employer. The latter appears to be an important route in the NMS for people to become familiar with e-government.

This picture changes, however, when it comes to the number of people assisted by social intermediaries, as shown in Figure 7, where the NMS are all above the mean

Figure 6. E-government users: On whose behalf (own purpose, for family/friends, or for employer)

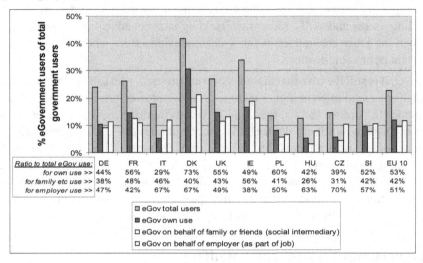

Figure 7. Average number of other persons assisted by social intermediaries for e-government

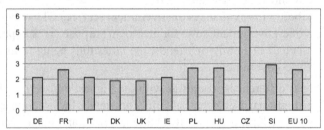

of 2.6, with the Czech Republic soaring to 5.3. This may be due to the fact that the NMS, particularly those in this sample, generally have greater access problems and lower **digital skills**, so that more of the population may need to use e-government via the more skilled social intermediaries. Part of the explanation for this could also be that it reflects different levels of development (particularly sophistication and user friendliness) of e-government services in these countries.

The mean of 2.6 other persons assisted by social intermediaries for e-government, coupled with the generally high numbers of such intermediaries (10% of total government users and 42% of e-government users), indicates that the phenomenon is probably a lot more widespread and important than has previously been appreciated.

Figure 1 also shows that there is a quite striking profile of a social intermediary for e-government as one who tends to be a user of a large number of different e-government services, with both a functional and leisure orientation to the Internet, and who belongs to the group of early retired, permanently invalided, not employed, or otherwise not working before the formal retirement age.

Moreover, social intermediaries tend to have well developed application and technical **digital skills**, to be interested in new technology, to have a mixed educational background (either very little or very high), and to live in countries which are only "emerging" in terms of e-government readiness, as opposed to those which are "intermediate" or "advanced." They also tend to be male, between the ages of 35 and 64, and with quite low income, although these latter factors are not statistically significant. Thus, overall, social intermediaries are far from being typical e-government users or Internet "nerds," but are instead likely to be individuals with plenty of free time and with good **digital skills** and orientation in not very advanced e-government countries. Such people, of which could be a large number, represent an important resource to help deliver the benefits of e-government.

There is also some evidence of **civil servants** acting as intermediaries as part of their job.[2] User inclusion and personalization strategies could include a "one-to-one" relationship between the citizen and the public sector, where an individual civil servant, a small team of civil servants, or an electronic agent, have the responsibility to fully support individual (or groups of) users, whether these be citizens or businesses. This concept could be crystallized around the term "citizen account manager" (in order to draw an analogy with "key account managers" in business) or citizen service activist, while the term "street-level bureaucrat" has been used. Intermediated and personalized support and services can best be provided in this way to users if deep knowledge is available about each individual, obtained through highly intelligent digital systems, including electronic agents, but also, critically, through human and personal experiences based on tacit knowledge which digital systems cannot always capture and which is only built up through trust established by close contact over time. Thus, this role moves on from the earlier one-stop-shop concept, in which a user approached a single desk (or portal) for further access to different services, but where the desk officer did not necessarily have any prior relationship with the user, to a concept based on longer-term and more stable relationships.

User Receiving Assistance from an E-Government Social Intermediary

Figure 8 shows that on average 18% of all e-government users receive some help from an intermediary, while 7% receive complete help. Support from an intermediary is highest in the new member states, which may be due to greater access problems and lower **digital skills,** so that more of the population may need to use e-government via

Figure 8. Users receiving support from an e-government social intermediary

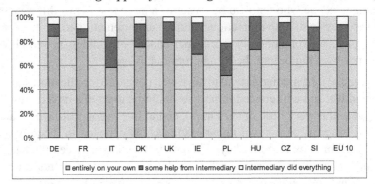

the more skilled social intermediaries. This probably also reflects different national levels of e-government service development, particularly in terms of sophistication and user friendliness. Italy and Ireland are the only older member states with greater than average numbers of users receiving help from a social intermediary.

As with social intermediaries themselves, Figure 1 shows that the profile of the typical citizen receiving assistance in using e-government is also highly specific. Such assisted users are very likely to have low digital engagement and skills, to be in manual and unskilled occupations, to be a rare Internet user, and to live in countries with low Internet penetration. They also tend to be 50 years old and over, demonstrate a markedly low functional and low leisure online orientation, be female rather than male, have a below secondary level education, be unemployed or not working, have an income below the poverty level or no higher than median income, have Internet access outside the home, and have started to "use" the Internet only very recently. These latter factors are, however, not statistically significant.

Overall, it is clear that users assisted by e-government social intermediaries tend to be in otherwise socially- and digitally-excluded groups, who would normally not receive any benefits from e-government services.

Flexi-Channeling for an Inclusive Society

Both the eUSER data and other sources show that a multichannel, rather than single channel, strategy can successfully reach out to existing users in new ways, as well as to previously excluded users, both by providing new channels and through better tailored and more appropriate services. Although the face-to-face and increasing telephone channels remain most important, particularly to **disadvantaged** groups, the use of electronic channels is rapidly increasing and channel balance is dynamic and evolving. Digital systems in the back-office can also help the civil servant provide better services to users in traditional ways, and this may be for the time being more important. (OECD, 2005).

There is evidence that appropriate channel strategies, built on good user research, increase service uptake and channel migration, as well as generate cost efficiencies within individual public sector departments (EDS, 2005). There can also be increasing user fulfillment given that, in the absence of well thought out channel strategies, many citizens regularly demonstrate that they are prepared to trade off inconvenience, poor environments, and service for the reliability of traditional channels only. Overall experience of the **flexi-channel** approach shows that success means (Millard & Shahin et al., 2006):

- Providing better services for the user, which are flexible, accessible, direct, rapid, complete, of high quality, easy to use, more secure, and ensure fulfillment.

- That channel strategies should be designed to match channel features with actor requirements (e.g., user needs, cost efficiency, etc.), and that a business case needs to be developed to provide the basis for rational decision making.

- That appropriate organizational changes in terms of organizational integration, administrative, or legal rules should be made.

- That appropriate human resource characteristics, in terms of staff culture, ways of working, jobs and roles, numbers, qualifications, skills, and competencies, are necessary.

- That technological architectures must be in place which enable channels to interoperate instead of merely coexist, that is, they must ensure integration of channels and applications, take account of phases in user sessions, and switch points between channels, as well as the reuse of data and of generic service components, and this will often require the integration of backend business processes.

Examples of successful **flexi-channel** strategies from the private sector include Amazon (the most successful e-retailer) which now is also moving into multichannels and exploring ways to acquire physical outlets (e.g., by entering into cooperation with the book store retailer Waterstones in the UK). This is both good for Amazon and for Waterstones by developing physical coffee shops, environments for reading, discussion groups, and so forth. Also, Tescos (the UK's largest retailer) is both increasing its physical and e-outlets. There seems to be a strong move in some sectors to multichannels and switching between channels, so that more "e" leads to more "p" (physical), and vice versa. The public sector should learn from this, especially in policies to support an inclusive society. Wider evidence from other areas of digital application shows that creating more online participation does not mean creating less human or physical participation, but typically quite the opposite, as Figure 5 amply illustrates.

Despite the benefits of a **flexi-channel strategy** for **inclusion**, there is much evidence of strong moves away from multichannels towards single digital channels. The efficiency program in the UK targets services where most of the users are already online, such as students applying for higher education. Government-to-business online services like corporation tax are already mandatory for large businesses in many countries (e.g., Spain, Denmark, and UK) and are fast also becoming so for SMEs (Denmark). Even where multichannel options are maintained, all are rapidly becoming supported by digital and shared databases. The move to the single "e" channel means the full automation of services which can sometimes lead to less information being accessible, for example, when citizens cannot change or even check their medical records. However, it should also be borne in mind that the traditional system may not have been any better than this and that provision costs also need to be considered.

Problems and tensions could arise if the movement to a single e-channel quickens and extends to nonspecialists target groups, perhaps triggering a "reverse-engineering" of **e-inclusion** in the medium to longer term. When everything is "e" and "e" is virtually without cost, and if efficiency is prioritized higher than inclusion, human contact will become expensive, given that labor costs compared to other costs will rise dramatically. Thus, the already included and better-off citizens will use their resources and skills to access human contact with government in situations where this gives them a better service (e.g., in terms of personal advice, care, social support, etc.). The excluded and worse-off citizens will, however, only have recourse to the ubiquitous and inexpensive e-services, and will not be able to supplement these with human contact. The e-exclusion of today will thus be replaced by the h-exclusion of the future, where "h" refers to human service contact. The European Union (EU) may need to run h-inclusion programs. (Millard et al., 2006). Indeed, the financial sector, which often leads in terms of using digital systems for service provision, is already moving strongly to the standard e-channel solution. In Finland, for example, e-banking is now the norm and provides a high quality service with no access costs. However, if personal face-to-face financial advice is desired, a relatively large charge is made for this. If government goes down the same route, there could be serious **inclusion policy** issues.

Conclusion and Recommendations

Users often report that they do not care how a service is delivered, or who delivers it, as long as it is easy, cheap, quick, and provides service fulfillment. The evidence and analysis presented in this chapter show that there are two often overlooked strategies for including **disadvantaged** users in the benefits provided by government services, that is, flexi-channeling and social intermediaries. From the strictly digital policy perspective this could provide a challenge as both involve the blending of electronic and nonelectronic channels. As in other policy areas, it is necessary to avoid the trap of assuming that the e-channel provides all the answers, particularly when seen from the perspective of the (**disadvantaged**) citizen.

On the one hand, using nonelectronic channels, including social intermediaries, could be a barrier to users' own use of e-services, but on the other hand, interme- diaries are clearly already able to include many citizens who would otherwise be excluded. One way of envisaging flexi-channeling and the use of intermediaries is as a powerful transition phase for many, prior to their own use of e-services. This is certainly the historical pattern of diffusion of new technology in which leaders (temporarily) assist laggards, such as radio in the 1920s, TV in the 1950s, and PCs and tele-cottages in the 1980s and 1990s.

This chapter has also shown, however, that flexi-channeling is extremely important in its own right and may not be a temporary phase at all. It involves informed and skilled users switching between channels according to their personal preferences, to the service being accessed, and to the task involved, and is strongly associated with both greater and more successful use of government services generally. Such flexi-channeling strategies are used much more by e-government users than others, and this appears to be a deliberate choice based on each channel's own strengths and weaknesses, which taken together are highly complementary and beneficial to users.

Extrapolation into the future leads to the prediction that most if not all activities which become "routine," which manipulate, match, and mine data, and which require access to information and systematized intelligence, will become codified and automated by digital systems, resulting in the squeezing out of direct human presence. In the future, on the other hand, human presence will focus even more than at present on activities which humans are innately better equipped to do than machines. Fortunately, this still appears to encompass a large potential area of growth in the numbers and quality of tasks, revolving around the use and creation of implicit and tacit knowledge. These areas include care, teaching, consulting, counseling, advising, controlling and coordinating, decision and policymaking, creating, brainstorming, empathizing, socializing, and so forth. In each case, of course, such human presence will increasingly be strongly supported by powerful digital systems. (Millard et al., 2006).

In contrast to these flexi-channeling strategies used by e-government users, many non e-government users access government services through **social intermediaries**. This is already providing immense benefits by ensuring that potentially **disadvantaged** users, who may otherwise not receive the services they need, successfully receive them. The types of individuals receiving assistance from social intermediaries for e-government tend to be those who are otherwise beyond the digital divide and excluded from e-government, as well as from other information society benefits, and who are living in countries which are not leading in e-government.

The social intermediaries themselves represent a potentially rich resource, given that up to half of all e-government users are already acting in this way and assist many other individuals. It is clear that assistance networks bringing online benefits to a large number of people, who would not otherwise enjoy them, already exist. It is also likely, of course, that this is nothing new, and that such networks have existed at family and community levels—helping to disseminate the benefits of public and private services—long before the Internet provided another channel. **Policy** design should recognize and promote these networks in a flexi-channel future.

It was noted above that there is a serious e-government **digital divide**, and that online services seem, even more than traditional government services, to be used by a social elite rather than by a representative cross section of adults. However, traditional channels, including the increasingly important telephone-based services, are likely to continue to be offered and used by all types of users, including those beyond the digital divide, as described above. Moreover, these human and physical channels are more and more supported and enhanced by digital systems as part of the user interface of a transformed and digitized back-office. In addition, there are burgeoning examples of e-channels which are increasingly being used by those beyond the digital divide, such as mobile devices. This chapter has not looked at digital TV, as it is not yet widely rolled out for government services, but also here the potential seems significant.

Despite these conclusions, however, this chapter has shown that people who themselves use e-channels for government seem thereby to increase their overall interaction with government and to obtain important benefits which non e-government users do not readily enjoy. So, although the weaker members of society will continue to be served particularly by traditional channels, and increasingly by mobile devices or social intermediaries, the overall benefits they receive from government are still likely to remain considerably less than mainstream e-government users.

Thus, in addition to recognizing and promoting flexi-channeling and the role of social intermediaries for e-government, **inclusion policy** should also promote wider own-use e-government take up. This chapter has shown that the important factors involved are not sociodemographic but rather related directly to e-government supply and Internet penetration, as well as to individual skills and online engagement. These are factors which can be tackled within the present policy time frame as concrete strategies with relatively easily recognized and measurable results and impacts.

References

Electronic Data Systems Corporation (EDS). (2005). *Delivering modern services strategy: EDS input to first stages of e-government Unit consultation in the UK*. London, England: Electronic Data Systems Corporation.

Millard, J. (2006). E-government services. Deliverable D5.2, current demand/supply match. *eUSER project: Evidence-based support for the design and delivery of user-centered online public services* (European Commission IST 6th Framework IST Program). Retrieved September 6, 2007, from http://www.euser-eu.org

Millard, J., Shahin, J., Warren, R., & Leitner, C. (2006). Towards the e-government vision for EU in 2010: Research policy challenges. *2020 visions*. Seville, Spain: Institute of Prospective Technological Studies/ European Commission DG JRC.

OECD. (2005). Multi-channel service delivery. *E-government for better government*. Paris: Organization for Economic Co-operation and Development.

Endnotes

[1]   eUSER provided a statistically valid telephone interview sample of over 10,000 adults across ten EU member states (the Czech Republic, Denmark, France, Germany, Hungary, Ireland, Italy, Poland, Slovenia, and the United Kingdom,), as well as studies on the supply side, on good practice, and on user-orientation issues related to e-health, e-government and e-learning services (http://www.euser-eu.org).

[2]   Such as civil servant "intermediaries" operating out of small citizen offices located in the more deprived areas of Berlin, and using a digital suitcase to visit old people's homes, hospitals, and the like, as information empowered front-line staff. Also, in Seattle in the USA a system of mobile civil servants visiting citizens, rather than citizens traveling to the town hall, is being established based on the capabilities of the city digital backbone. (Millard et al., 2006)

Chapter XII

The Utilization of Online Policy Forums on Government Web Sites and the Practice of Digital Democracy

Chan-Gon Kim, Rutgers University – Newark, USA

Marc Holzer, Rutgers University – Newark, USA

Abstract

The Internet provides a new digital opportunity for realizing democracy in public administration, and this study raises a central question: What factors determine public officials' acceptance of the practice of digital democracy on government Web sites? We focused on online policy forums among many practices of digital democracy. To gauge public officials' behavioral intentions to use online policy forums on government Web sites, we examined individual and organizational factors, as well as system characteristics. We administered a survey questionnaire to Korean public officials and analyzed a total of 895 responses. Path analysis indicates that three causal variables are important in predicting public officials' intentions to use online policy forums: perceived usefulness, attitudes toward citizen participation, and information quality. We discuss implications of this study for practices and theories of digital democracy.

Introduction

Today the Internet is changing the operation of governments. A large number of citizens can access a large volume of information simultaneously and conduct online transactions with government agencies 24 hours a day and 7 days a week. In addition, citizens can register their opinions on government Web sites through online discussions and online polls anywhere and anytime. Thus the concept of digital democracy is emerging. New electronic means have the potential to increase citizen participation in government and to ensure that citizens' preferences are reflected in the policy-making process.

Despite the fact that digital democracy is possible in public agencies, there are wide variations in adopting and implementing practices of digital democracy among government agencies at the federal, state, and local levels. Decisions at the organizational level do not necessarily bring changes in the attitudes and behaviors of individual public administrators. In other words, policy adoption is different from program implementation, and factors affecting these two are also different (de Lancer Julnes & Holzer, 2001). Successful innovation implementation is determined by human factors, or end-users' acceptance of the innovation (Nedovic-Budic & Godschalk, 1996). Organizational members can reject or not fully utilize an innovation (Leonard-Barton & Deschamps, 1988). The literature on implementation has indicated that street-level bureaucrats have considerable resources with which to influence policy outcomes (Hill, 2003; Lipsky, 1980). While some research has examined the adoption of e-government at the organizational level (Ho, 2002; Ho & Ni, 2003; Moon, 2002; Weare, Musso, & Hale, 1999), little research has been done at the micro level with regard to attitudes and behaviors of public administrators toward digital democracy.

This study examines why and how public administrators accept the practice of digital democracy on government Web sites when they make and implement public policies. Since public administrators offer and maintain government Web sites, supplying the space for digital democracy on a government Web site and utilizing it is a prerequisite for such democracy in public administration. The major research question of this study is: What factors determine public administrators' acceptance of the practice of digital democracy on government Web sites? More specifically, this study focuses on a single practice of digital democracy and aims to examine the impact of individual, organizational, and system characteristics on administrators' intentions to use online policy forums on government Web sites.

Digital Democracy in Public Administration

Citizens' involvement in public affairs through the Internet has brought about the use of several essentially similar terms such as "digital democracy," "electronic democracy," "e-democracy," "virtual democracy," "teledemocracy," and "cyber-democracy." This study uses the term "digital democracy" to describe the use of government Web sites for citizens' participation in public affairs. The main characteristic of the new information and communication technology (ICT) is digital data transfer (Hague & Loader, 1999), and "digital democracy" is defined as "a collection of attempts to practice democracy without the limits of time, space, and other physical conditions, using ICT or computer-mediated communication instead, as an addition, not a replacement for, traditional analogue political practices" (Hacker & van Dijk, 2000, p. 1).

Online citizen participation can enrich democratic processes and build public trust by enabling public agencies to receive broader and more diverse opinions from citizens than those available through traditional means of off-line participation (Holzer, Melitski, Rho, & Schwester, 2004). Through online discussions, members of the public can learn from each other, and public administrators can become better informed, sometimes through the experience and hidden expertise of the public (Coleman & Gotze, 2001). Several scholars have suggested typologies of digital democracy (Kakabadse, Kakabadse, & Kouzmin, 2003; Norris, 2005; Tsagarousianou, 1999). With regard to the current state of digital democracy, information disclosure on government Web sites is full-fledged, and many agencies are receiving feedback on policy issues from citizens through the Internet. However, online discussion is just emerging, and decision making through government Web sites, such as electronic referenda, is still relatively infrequent in government (Kim, 2004; Norris & Moon, 2005).

Online Policy Forums

An "online policy forum," or an online discussion forum, is a place on the government Web site where public officials or citizens can post discussion topics on policy issues and exchange their views on those topics over a period of time. Online policy forums can take several formats. Public officials can participate in forums as discussants or citizens can discuss issues among themselves without officials' participation. Discussion topics can be offered by the government or registered online by citizens. There are also two types: issue-based forums and policy-based forums. At an early stage of policy-making, issue-based forums are organized to collect ideas and opinions. At a later stage of policy-making, policy-based forums are offered to solicit responses about a draft policy (OECD, 2003).

Although online policy forums are still emerging and not universally utilized yet in public agencies, there are several exemplary cases of online discussion forums around the world (Coleman & Gotze, 2001; Holzer et al., 2004; OECD, 2003). At the central government level, the National Dialogue of Public Involvement was implemented by the Environmental Protection Agency (EPA) in 2001 to offer online discussions between public administrators and citizens (www.network-democracy. org/epa-pip) with 1,261 message postings in 10 days (Beierle, 2002; Holzer et al., 2004). The Hansard Society e-democracy program has been piloting a series of online discussion forums (www.tellparliament.net) for the UK Parliament since 1998 (Coleman, 2004). At the state level, Minnesota offered an online policy forum, *Issue Talk* (http://issuetalk.state.mn.us), from January 7th to 18th in 2002, inviting more than 600 comments and ideas about the state budget shortfall (Minnesota Planning, 2002). Cases at the local government level include online forums for the city of Kalix (www.kalix.se), Sweden, for the North Jutland County in Denmark (www.nordpol.dk), and for Bologna, Italy (www.comune.bologna.it) (Coleman & Gotze, 2001; OECD, 2003). Recently, several governments have introduced online policy forums which have been recognized as good practices such as ConsultQld in Queensland, Australia (Hogan, Cook, & Henderson, 2004), DanmarksDebatten in Demark, Wolverhampton e-panel in UK (European Commission, n.d.), and Cyber Policy Forum at the Seoul Metropolitan Government, South Korea (United Nations, 2007).

Conceptual Framework

Since a government Web site can be viewed as an information system (IS) for public administrators, the theories of information system use can be applied to explain and predict public administrators' use of such sites. Kling and Jewett (1994) classify theories of information systems use into two broad types: rational systems models and natural systems models. The rational systems model views organizations as instruments designed to pursue specific goals and considers the efficiency of achieving those goals the most important value. By contrast, the natural systems model assumes that organizational members share a common interest in the survival of the organization, and that organizational behavior is oriented toward the pursuit of this end. In this model, organizations resemble natural systems that are like living organisms (Kling & Jewett, 1994; Scott, 1992). We conducted a comprehensive literature review, and an updated classification is presented in Table 1. The prevailing theory of information systems use is based on the rational systems model, and the technology acceptance model (TAM) (Davis, 1989) has been the dominant model for an individual's technology acceptance (Adams, Nelson, & Todd, 1992; Mathieson, Peacock, & Chin, 2001).

Based on previous research on an individual's technology acceptance and utilization of information systems, this study proposes a model to explain public administrators' acceptance of online policy forums on government Web sites when public agencies introduce such forums in their organizations. Since the characteristics of the Internet are different from other information technologies, these factors have been considered in formulating the conceptual framework of this study. Previous information technology innovations were mainly used by organizational members

Table 1. Theories of information systems use

Theories	Research	Variables Affecting IS Use
1. RATIONAL SYSTEMS EXPLANATIONS		
A. IS Implementation Research	• Kwon and Zmud (1987) • Lucas, Ginzberg, and Schultz (1990)	• individual, structural, technological, task-related, and environmental factors • user acceptance, system characteristics, management support, user knowledge of system purpose and use, organizational support, and so forth.
B. IS Success Model	• DeLone and McLean (1992, 2003)	• information quality, system quality, and service quality
C. Application of the Theory of Planned Behavior	• Ajzen (1985, 1991)	• attitude, subjective norms, and perceived behavioral control
D. Technology Acceptance Model	• Davis (1989)	• attitude, perceived usefulness, and perceived ease of use
E. Application of Innovation Diffusion Theory	• Rogers (1995)	• relative advantage, compatibility, complexity, trialability, and observability
2. NATURAL SYSTEMS EXPLANATIONS		
A. Cultural/political perspectives	• Kling (1980), Kling and Jewett (1994) • Walsham (1993)	• power politics, coalition building, and forwarding agendas • interpretive approach, and organizations as cultures and political systems
B. Sociotechnical Systems Theory	• Kraemer, Dutton, and Northrop (1981), Danziger, Dutton, Kling, and Kraemer (1982) • Danziger and Kraemer (1986)	• political, socioeconomic technological environment, political/administrative system attributes, computer package (hardware, software, procedures, management policies), and orientation of computing • organizational environment, computer package, and user characteristics
C. Theory of Technology Enactment	• Fountain (2001)	• objective information technology, organizational forms, institutional arrangements, and enacted technology

without interaction with citizens; but using a government Web site for purposes of digital democracy requires interaction between public administrators and citizens. Thus, when studying online dialogue, factors affecting users' attitudes and behaviors should be considered in contexts different from those utilized in studying other information technologies.

The basic constructs of this study are "perceived usefulness" and "behavioral intention," which are derived from the technology acceptance model (Davis, 1989) and the Theory of Planned Behavior (Ajzen, 1985, 1991). The dependent variable in this study is a public administrator's behavioral intention to use online policy forums on a government Web site. A public administrator's behavioral intention to use such forums is considered a predictor for actual use of online policy forums. The public administrator's perceived usefulness of online policy forums is an intervening variable that mediates the relationship between independent variables and the behavioral intention. We assume that independent variables have impacts on the dependent variable directly or indirectly through perceived usefulness. A survey of the literature on variables that affect individuals' attitudes toward, and use of, information technology generated a substantial number of factors (Anandarajan, Simmers, & Igbaria, 2000; Davis, 1989; DeLone & McLean, 1992, 2003; Finlay & Finlay, 1996; Igbaria, Guimaraes, & Davis, 1995; Lucas, 1978; Ranerup, 1999; Thong & Yap, 1995). Among them, nine factors are considered important in predicting a public official's perceived usefulness and behavioral intention to use online policy forums. These independent variables can be divided into three broad categories: (1) individual factors, (2) organizational factors, and (3) system characteristics. Individual factors include Internet attitudes, attitudes toward citizen participation, and knowledge about digital democracy. Organizational factors refer to supervisor support, IS department support, and innovation-supportive organizational culture. System characteristics include the ease of use of online policy forums, information quality, and perceived risk in online discussion. Taking account of all relationships between these factors, the conceptual framework of this study is presented in Figure 1. According to empirical research, there is a close relationship between intention and behavior (Davis, 1989; Davis, Bagozzi, & Warsaw, 1989; Sheppard, Hartwick, & Warsaw, 1988). This study focuses on intentions and relevant factors but does not measure actual use of online policy forums. However, behavioral intention can be used as a surrogate for predicting actual use of online policy forums.

Individual Factors

Previous research found that favorable Internet attitudes are associated with the frequent use of the Internet (Anandarajan et al., 2000; Spacey, Goulding, & Murray, 2004). Thus we expect that administrators' Internet attitudes will influence

Figure 1. A model of public administrators' acceptance of online policy forums on government Web sites

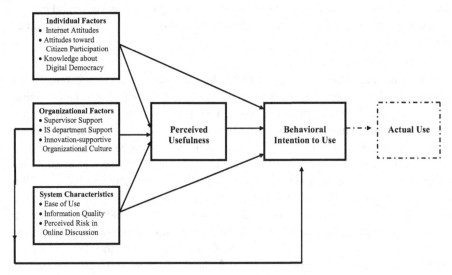

the perceived usefulness of online policy forums and behavioral intentions to use online policy forums.

Hypothesis 1-1. *A public administrator's favorable Internet attitudes will positively affect his/her perceived usefulness of online policy forums.*

Hypothesis 1-2. *A public administrator's favorable Internet attitudes will positively affect his/her behavioral intention to use online policy forums.*

To implement digital democracy, public administrators must interact with citizens and allow citizen participation in policy making and implementation through the government Web site. Wang (2001) found that both managers' and public administrators' willingness to be accountable was related to increased citizen participation. Thus public administrators' favorable attitudes toward citizen participation are prerequisite to the use of practices of digital democracy.

Hypothesis 2-1. *A public administrator's favorable attitudes toward citizen participation will positively affect his/her perceived usefulness of online policy forums.*

Hypothesis 2-2. *A public administrator's favorable attitudes toward citizen participation will positively affect his/her behavioral intention to use online policy forums.*

Research on the use of management information systems (MIS) has shown that education, training, experience, and skills of individuals using the technology are associated with perceived usefulness and actual use of information systems (Agarwal & Prasad, 1999; Igbaria, 1990, 1993; Igbaria et al., 1995; Igbaria, Parasuraman, & Baroudi, 1996; Nelson & Cheney, 1987). Thong and Yap (1995) found that businesses with CEOs who are more knowledgeable about information technology (IT) are more likely to adopt IT. Research found that knowledge about the Internet affects the use of the Internet (Finlay & Finlay, 1996). If public administrators are knowledgeable about digital democracy, they will understand the importance of digital democracy and perceive the usefulness of practices of digital democracy as high and use online policy forums frequently.

Hypothesis 3-1. *A public administrator's high level of knowledge about digital democracy will positively affect his/her perceived usefulness of online policy forums.*

Hypothesis 3-2. *A public administrator's high level of knowledge about digital democracy will positively affect his/her behavioral intention to use online policy forums.*

Organizational Factors

In MIS research, organizational support—such as manager support and information center (IS department) support—was found to affect system usage (Anandarajan et al., 2000; DeLone & McLean, 2003; Igbaria, 1990, 1993; Igbaria et al., 1995, 1996; Lucas, 1978; Thompson, Higgins, & Howell, 1991). Supervisors may encourage or discourage subordinates to use online policy forums in their work. In addition, an IS department that is in charge of managing the government Web site may facilitate implementing practices of digital democracy in agencies.

Hypothesis 4-1. *Supervisor support for using online policy forums will positively affect a public administrator's perceived usefulness of online policy forums.*

Hypothesis 4-2. *Supervisor support for using online policy forums will positively affect a public administrator's behavioral intention to use online policy forums.*

Hypothesis 5-1. *IS department support for using online policy forums will positively affect a public administrator's perceived usefulness of online policy forums.*

Hypothesis 5-2. *IS department support for using online policy forums will positively affect a public administrator's behavioral intention to use online policy forums.*

As long as a certain culture exists within an organizational unit, the activities of organizational members can be influenced by the culture. According to Subramaniam and Ashkanasy (2001), innovation takes place when organizational members are opportunistic, not constrained by many rules, and willing to take risks and experiment with new ideas. According to previous research, businesses with more innovative CEOs are more likely to adopt IT (Thong & Yap, 1995), and top managers' risk-taking propensity is positively associated with IT innovativeness (Moon & Brestchneider, 2002). Since online policy forums are new innovations, public administrators who work in an innovative organizational culture may try new inventions.

Hypothesis 6-1. *Innovation-supportive organizational culture will positively affect a public administrator's perceived usefulness of online policy forums.*

Hypothesis 6-2. *Innovation-supportive organizational culture will positively affect a public administrator's behavioral intention to use online policy forums.*

System Characteristics

The influence of perceived ease of use on perceived usefulness and behavioral intention is derived from the technology acceptance model (Davis, 1989). Public administrators have several means of gathering information from citizens in the decision-making process, such as face-to-face meetings, telephone conversations, or government Web sites. Thus perceived ease of use of online policy forums is directly related to the use of online policy forums.

Hypothesis 7-1. *A public administrator's positive perception of the ease of use of online policy forums will positively affect his/her perceived usefulness of online policy forums.*

Hypothesis 7-2. *A public administrator's positive perception of the ease of use of online policy forums will positively affect his/her behavioral intention to use online policy forums.*

Previous research found that the quality of information had significant influence on the perceived usefulness of an information system (Klobas, 1995; Kraemer, Danziger, Dunkle, & King, 1993; Lin & Lu, 2000). We can view the government Web site as an information system that produces information for public administrators when citizens register their opinions on online policy forums. Public administrators judge whether the information provided by online citizens is reliable and valid, or whether the online information is of uncertain quality. If the quality of online information is high, then public administrators may perceive the usefulness of online policy forums positively and continuously use those forums. Therefore, the following hypotheses are formulated:

Hypothesis 8-1. *A public administrator's perception of high information quality of online policy forums will positively affect his/her perceived usefulness of online policy forums.*

Hypothesis 8-2. *A public administrator's perception of high information quality of online policy forums will positively affect his/her behavioral intention to use online policy forums.*

Online relationships are established between users of the Internet when they are engaged in electronic conversation through a chat room or a discussion forum. The lack of face-to-face contact leads to greater anonymity in online interactions, and online citizens might behave with less good will (Friedman, Kahn, & Howe, 2000). If public administrators perceive a high risk in using online discussion forums, they might not write on online forums.

Hypothesis 9-1. *A public administrator's perception of high risk in online discussions will negatively affect his/her perceived usefulness of online policy forums.*

Hypothesis 9-2. *A public administrator's perception of high risk in online discussions will negatively affect his/her behavioral intention to use online policy forums.*

The Impact of Perceived Usefulness on Behavioral Intention

The importance of perceived usefulness as one of the determinants of the intention to use an information system has been stressed by the technology acceptance model (Davis, 1989). Perceived usefulness influences user acceptance of the information system because of the value of outcomes from using the system. Public administrators can utilize online information submitted by citizens through online discussion on the government Web site. If public administrators perceive the usefulness of online policy forums as positive, they will use online policy forums more frequently.

Hypothesis 10. *A public administrator's positive perception of the usefulness of online policy forums will positively affect his/her behavioral intention to use online policy forums.*

Research Methodology

Sample and Data Collection

The unit of analysis in this study is individual public administrators, and the population of this study is defined as public administrators who work in public agencies that have adopted online policy forums, and make and implement public policies in their agencies in South Korea. Our focus is on individual public administrators' use of online policy forums in South Korea, which is the leader in broadband penetration in the world (Organization for Economic Cooperation and Development, 2001) and places second in terms of Internet usage rate among its population (International Telecommunication Union, 2004). South Korea obtained a fifth-place ranking in terms of the e-government readiness index and was sixth in terms of the e-participation index constructed by the United Nations[1] (2004). South Korea has been vigorously promoting e-government and digital democracy, with many public agencies adopting online policy forums. All Ministries except one among 18 Ministries offer online policy forums, and 12 upper-level local governments among 16 offered online policy forums as of January, 2005. Thus South Korea is a particularly good case for the study of digital democracy.

This study mixed purposive sampling and cluster sampling. To select appropriate public agencies, we used several criteria, such as the frequency of online policy forums, the number of message postings per forum, and the highest and average number of message postings per forum. Then, a total of 13 public agencies were selected, including four central government ministries, two upper-level local governments, and seven lower-level local governments. Among 18 ministries at the central government of South Korea, four ministries were relatively active as shown in Table 2 in terms of the frequency of online forums and the number of message postings. The ministries selected for the survey were the Ministry of Information and Communication, the Ministry of Government Administration and Home Affairs, the Ministry of Unification, and the Ministry of Health and Welfare. Among them, the Ministry of Unification's "Online Public Hearing" (www.unikorea.go.kr) was the most active, offering six online forums in 2004, with 731 participants on average per forum. Discussion topics were offered by government or registered by citizens on government Web sites. Most online forums lasted for 15 to 30 days, and any citizens or officials could post messages. We applied the same methodology to selecting several local governments. Among 16 upper-level local governments, the Seoul Metropolitan Government and Gyeonggi Province were actively promoting online policy forums and were selected for the survey. Seoul Metropolitan Government's "Cyber Policy Forum" (http://forum.seoul.go.kr) provided discussion topics every month in 2004, with the average number of 120 participants per forum. Gyeonggi Province offered five online policy forums in 2004, with 82 participants on average per forum (http://www.gg.go.kr/0502new/news/join/dojung/dojung01/index.html). Among 232 lower-level local governments, seven district offices were deemed appropriate for this study: Gangnam, Gangdong, Guro, Jungnang, Seongbuk, Yangchon, and Gangseo.

Table 2. Statistics of online policy forums for 18 ministries in South Korea (2004)

Ministry	Selection of discussion topics	Online forums with message postings 21 - 50	Online forums with message postings above 50	The highest number of message postings per forum
Unification	Offered by government	0	6	1,257 (average 731)
Information and Communication	Offered by government	0	2	99 (average 96)
Government Administration and Home Affairs	Offered by government	0	2	1,281 threads (average more than 817)
Health and Welfare	Offered by government	0	2	167 (average 120)
Gender Equality and Family	Offered by government	3	2	110 (average 60)
Education and Human Resources Development	Offered by government	2	1	106
Construction and Transportation	Offered by government	0	1	258
Agriculture and Forestry	Offered by government	0	1	252
Finance and Economy	Offered by government	0	1	85
Science and Technology	Offered by citizens	1	0	11
Labor	Offered by government	1	0	29

continued on following page

Table 2. continued

Culture and Tourism	Offered by government	1	0	18
Commerce, Industry, and Energy	Offered by both government and citizens	1	0	39
Foreign Affairs and Trade	Offered by government	1	0	36
Maritime Affairs and Fisheries	Offered by government	1	0	27
Environment	Offered by government	0	0	10
Justice		0	0	0
National Defense		0	0	0

Then we selected several divisions at each public agency. Selected divisions were those that posted discussion topics on their agency's Web site or those related to discussion topics registered by citizens. A total of 34 divisions were selected in the central government, 29 divisions in upper-level local governments, and 31 divisions in lower-level local governments. We mailed questionnaires to a manager at each agency in central and local governments between February 11th and 15th of 2005. Then these managers distributed the questionnaires to all public administrators who make and implement public policies in their divisions, which had posted discussion topics or had topics registered by citizens on government Web sites for the past two years. Questionnaires were distributed to 300 officials at the central government, 320 at upper-level local governments, and 390 at lower-level local governments. Thus the total sample selected for this study was 1,010 as presented in Table 3.

Questionnaires were accompanied by a cover letter that stated that participation was voluntary and that responses were anonymous, encouraging honest responses for this study. We did not ask a respondent's name, phone number, resident registration number, address, or date of birth. After respondents completed the questionnaires, they voluntarily returned them by mail. After excluding incomplete questionnaires, we collected 895 questionnaires, and the response rate was 88.6% across governments.

Table 3. Distribution and collection of the questionnaire

Level of government	Agency	Number of divisions for survey	Distribution	Collection	Response rate
Central Government Ministries	Ministry of Information & Communication	8 divisions	70	62	88.6%
	Ministry of Government Administration & Home Affairs	8 divisions	90	86	95.6%
	Ministry of Unification	9 divisions	70	64	91.4%
	Ministry of Health & Welfare	9 divisions	70	65	92.9%
	Subtotal	*34*	*300*	*277*	*92.3%*
Upper-level Local Governments	Seoul Metropolitan Government	22 divisions	240	230	95.8%
	Gyeonggi Province	7 divisions	80	69	86.3%
	Subtotal	*29*	*320*	*299*	*93.4%*
Lower-level Local Governments	Gangnam District Office	12 divisions	120	80	66.7%
	Gangdong District Office	3 divisions	40	23	57.5%
	Jungnang District Office	3 divisions	55	50	90.9%
	Guro District Office	3 divisions	40	39	97.5%
	Seongbuk District Office	5 divisions	60	59	98.3%
	Yangchon District Office	4 divisions	60	54	90.0%
	Gangseo District Office	1 division	15	14	93.5%
	Subtotal	*31*	*390*	*319*	*81.8%*
Total		**94**	**1,010**	**895**	**88.6%**

Measurement and the Survey Instrument

This study used a five-point Likert-type questionnaire to measure the attitudes and beliefs of public administrators. We combined several questions to measure a variable and created a composite measurement by summing individual items for each variable. Questionnaire items are summarized in the Appendix. Factor analysis and Cronbach alpha coefficients showed the unidimensionality and reliability of the instrument. Variables of this study are as follows:

- **Negative Internet attitudes:** A public administrator' negative attitudes toward the Internet.

- **Attitudes toward citizen participation:** A public administrator' willingness to allow citizen participation in the policy-making process.

- **Knowledge about digital democracy:** A public administrator's knowledge about digital democracy.

- **Supervisor support:** The degree to which a public administrator's supervisor emphasizes citizen input through online policy forums in policy processes and encourages employees to use online policy forums in their work.

- **IS department support:** The degree to which IS department supports a public administrator's using online policy forums in public agencies.

- **Innovation-supportive organizational culture:** The degree to which a public administrator works in an innovative organizational culture in public agencies.

- **Perceived ease of use:** The degree to which a public administrator expects the use of online policy forums to be free of effort.

- **Information quality:** The degree to which online information submitted by citizens is valuable and of high quality.

- **Perceived risk in online discussion:** The degree to which a public administrator perceives risks when communicating with citizens online.

- **Perceived usefulness:** A public administrator's subjective perception that using online policy forums will increase the job performance.

- **Behavioral intention:** The degree to which a public administrator has the intention to use online policy forums in work.

Results

Descriptive Statistics

Following factor analysis and reliability tests, appropriate constructs were established, and the descriptive statistics for 11 research variables are presented in Table 4. On average, public officials in South Korea seemed to believe that organizational culture is moderately innovative ($M = 3.68$), and they tended to have moderately high behavioral intentions to use online policy forums in the near future ($M = 3.55$). However, they think that they have only a little knowledge about digital democracy ($M = 2.58$), perceived low risk in online discussion ($M = 2.83$), and low supervisor support for using online policy forums ($M = 2.89$). When we examined a correlation

Table 4. Descriptive statistics for research variables

Variable	N	Mean	Std. Deviation
Negative Internet Attitudes	891	3.52	.95
Information quality	515	3.07	.63
Perceived usefulness	512	3.24	.64
Perceived risk in online discussion	883	2.83	.80
Supervisor support	861	2.89	.75
IS department Support	867	2.99	.81
Attitudes toward citizen participation	891	3.36	.73
Organizational culture	892	3.68	.68
Knowledge about digital democracy	892	2.58	.83
Ease of use	508	3.42	.64
Behavioral intention	889	3.55	.67

matrix, perceived usefulness and behavioral intention have positive relationships with several variables. None of the independent variables show correlations above 0.8 among themselves, which implies that multicollinearity would not be a problem in regression analysis.

Path Analysis

To test hypotheses, we analyzed data using SPSS and employed path analysis. Path analysis was developed by Sewall Wright as a method for examining relationships among all variables and testing causal models when multiple variables are involved in a theoretical model (de Vaus, 1986; Loehlin, 1998; Pedhazur, 1997). In path analysis, a path diagram graphically displays the pattern of causal relationships among a set of variables. An arrow from one variable to another indicates a direct effect, and a two-headed curved arrow indicates the correlation between two variables. We assume that the relations among the variables in the path model are linear and additive, the residual of each endogenous variable is not correlated with one another or with other endogenous variables, there is a one-way causal flow in the model, and the variables are measured on an interval scale without error. Then path analysis can be reduced to the solution of several multiple linear regression analyses (Pedhazur, 1997, p. 771). When we examined the assumptions of multiple regression, they were also met, including normality of residuals, linear relationships between variables, homoscedasticity, and no perfect collinearity.

In path analysis, each path is given a path coefficient, a beta weight (standardized regression coefficient) in regression analysis that shows how much impact the variable has on another variable. Since these path coefficients are standardized numbers, they can be compared with each other in terms of the degree of importance of each variable.

To control for the effects of other known influences on regression models, we examined two variables: age and gender. When we removed these two control variables in regression analysis, R^2 for the model without control variables was similar to R^2 for the original regression model with control variables, and the magnitude of the regression coefficients changed little. Among research variables, Internet attitudes, innovation-supportive organizational culture, and perceived risk in online discussion had no significant impacts on either perceived usefulness or behavioral intention. Thus these independent variables were removed in path analysis.

The initial path analysis produced all path coefficients regardless of statistical significance or meaningfulness of coefficients. To trim the path model and make it more parsimonious, insignificant or unimportant path coefficients can be removed from the model. Accordingly, two criteria were used in deleting a few path coefficients: the significance and importance of the coefficient. Path coefficients not significant at the 0.1 level were deleted, and path coefficients less than 0.05 were deleted from the model. Thus three paths were removed from the original path model: the path from knowledge about digital democracy to perceived usefulness, the path from supervisor support to behavioral intention, and the path from information quality to behavioral intention. All path coefficients in the final model are statistically significant at the 0.05 level, R^2 for the model predicting perceived usefulness is 0.572, and R^2 for the model predicting behavioral intention is 0.417. This means that 57% of the variation of perceived usefulness is explained by five independent variables, and 42% of the variation of behavioral intention is explained by four independent variables and perceived usefulness. The final path model is presented in Figure 2.

The total causal effect of each predictor on behavioral intention was calculated by adding the direct and indirect effects in the final path model. To obtain indirect effects, we multiply the path coefficients of all of the indirect routs. The results of effect analysis are presented in Table 5. Total causal effects for all predictor variables are significant at or below the 0.05 level. With regard to the magnitude of the total causal effect of each predictor on behavioral intention, the order of importance is as follows: (1) perceived usefulness (0.359); (2) attitudes toward citizen participation (0.220); (3) information quality (0.199); (4) ease of use (0.17); (5) IS department support (0.16); (6) knowledge about digital democracy (0.168); and (7) supervisor support (0. 042).

In path analysis, model-implied or model-predicted correlations between two variables using path coefficients should reproduce the original correlations or observed correlations (Heise, 1969; Klem, 1995; Kline, 1998; Pedhazur, 1982; Schumacker

Figure 2. Final path model

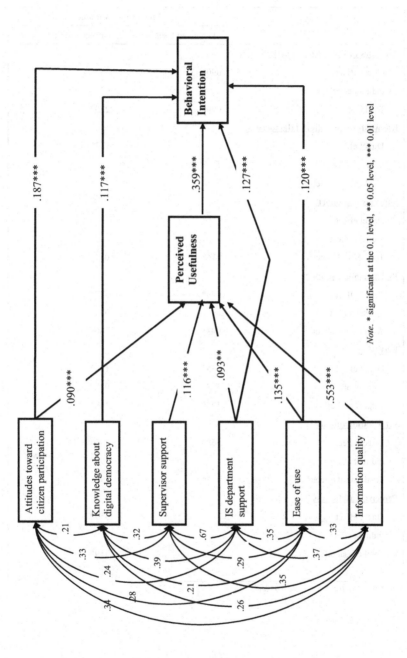

Table 5. Decomposition of effects for the final path model

Causal variable	Endogenous Variable	
	Perceived Usefulness	Behavioral Intention
Attitudes toward citizen participation		
Direct effect	.090*	.187*
Indirect effect		.032*
Total causal effect	.090*	.220*
Knowledge about digital democracy		
Direct effect		.117*
Indirect effect		
Total causal effect		.117*
Supervisor support		
Direct effect	.116*	
Indirect effect		.042*
Total causal effect	.116*	.042*
IS department support		
Direct effect	.093*	.127*
Indirect effect		.034*
Total causal effect	.093*	.160*
Ease of use		
Direct effect	.135*	.120*
Indirect effect		.048*
Total causal effect	.135*	.168*
Information quality		
Direct effect	.553*	
Indirect effect		.199*
Total causal effect	.553*	.199*
Perceived usefulness		
Direct effect		.359*
Indirect effect		
Total causal effect		.359*
R^2	.572	.417

*Note. * significant at or below the 0.05 level.*

Table 6. Correlation residuals from the final path model

Variable	1. ACP	2. Know	3. SPV	4. IS	5. EOU	6. Info	7. PU
1. ACP	–						
2. Know	0	–					
3. SPV	0	0	–				
4. IS	0	0	0	–			
5. EOU	0	0	0	0	–		
6. Info	0	0	0	0	0	–	
7. PU	.0001	.0129	.0001	0	0	.0001	–
8. BI	.0065	.0046	.0386	.0084	.0001	.0095	.0183

Note. Abbreviated variable names refer to the following variables:

ACP = attitudes toward citizen participation   Know = knowledge about digital democracy
SPV = supervisor support   IS = IS department support
EOU = ease of use   Info = information quality
PU = Perceived usefulness   BI = behavioral intention

& Lomax, 1996), and it is desirable to have correlation residuals with absolute values less than 0.1 (Kline, 1998). We calculated a predicted correlation in the path model by adding causal effects—direct and indirect effects—and noncausal effects—spurious and unanalyzed effects. Spurious effects occur when a third variable has causal paths to both an independent variable and a dependent variable, while unanalyzed effects occur due to effects from correlations between pairs of source variables (Davis, 1985; Klem, 1995; Kline, 1998; Pedhazur, 1982). In our model, correlations range from 0.21 to 0.39 between pairs of source variables, and these effects were considered in analyzing the impact of independent variables on dependent variables.

The final path model appears to fit the data fairly well. Applying the criterion that the difference between the original and reproduced correlations should not exceed 0.1, we find that correlation residuals in the absolute values for all correlations are well below the 0.1 criterion (Table 6). Thus, the final path model reproduced all of the observed correlations, and the model is relevant in predicting public administrators' behavioral intention to use online policy forums in South Korea. The final path model confirms that "perceived usefulness" mediates between some predictors and "behavioral intention." Information quality does not directly affect behavioral intention, but affects it indirectly through perceived usefulness. Perceived usefulness provides only a partial mediation for attitudes toward citizen participation, supervisor support, IS department support, and ease of use.

Conclusion

This study examined what factors determine public administrators' acceptance of online policy forums on government Web sites for digital democracy and how individual, organizational, and system characteristics affect public officials' intentions to use online policy forums in South Korea. Hypotheses 2-1, 2-2, 3-2, 4-1, 5-1, 5-2, 7-1, 7-2, 8-1, and 10 were supported, but hypotheses 1-1, 1-2, 3-1, 4-2, 6-1, 6-2, 8-2, 9-1, and 9-2 were not supported at the 0.05 significance level.

First, perceived usefulness of online policy forums is the strongest factor affecting public administrators' behavioral intentions to use online policy forums. Path analysis reveals causal relationships between behavioral intention, perceived usefulness, and other predictors. Perceived usefulness has been found to play a mediating role between some predictors and behavioral intentions.

Second, public administrators' favorable attitudes toward citizen participation are positively associated with the perceived usefulness of online policy forums and their intentions to use online policy forums. If public administrators have negative attitudes toward citizen participation, online policy forums cannot be utilized in the policy-making

Third, the information quality of online policy forums is the major factor affecting public administrators' perceived usefulness of online policy forums. It has the largest impact on perceived usefulness among the nine factors.

Fourth, perceived ease of use of online policy forums is a predictor for perceived usefulness of online policy forums and behavioral intentions to use online policy forums. If public administrators feel that online policy forums are easy to access and use compared to other methods of gathering citizens' opinions, they will utilize online policy forums more frequently.

Fifth, IS department support for using online policy forums is related to the perceived usefulness of online policy forums and behavioral intentions to use online policy forums. Public officials may perceive online policy forums as useful when IS departments encourage officials to consider citizens' opinions in the policy-making process.

Sixth, public administrators' knowledge about digital democracy is positively associated with their behavioral intention to use online policy forums. In other words, the more knowledgeable public officials are about digital democracy, the more likely they are to use online policy forums for digital democracy in public administration.

Seventh, Internet attitudes, innovation-supportive organizational culture, and perceived risk in online discussion are not predictors for either perceived usefulness of online policy forums or behavioral intention to use online policy forums. Considering the fact that South Korean public administrators are heavy users of the Internet, Internet attitudes may have no impact on our model. Unlike other discussion

Table 7. Summary of hypotheses testing process

Hypotheses	Results	Hypotheses	Results
H. 1-1. Internet attitude → Usefulness	Not supported	H. 6-1. Organizational culture → Usefulness	Not supported
H. 1-2. Internet Attitudes → Behavioral intention	Not supported	H. 6-2. Organizational culture → Behavioral intention	Not supported
H. 2-1. Attitudes toward citizen participation → Usefulness	Supported	H. 7-1. Ease of use → Usefulness	Supported
H. 2-2. Attitudes toward citizen participation → Behavioral intention	Supported	H. 7-2. Ease of use → Behavioral intention	Supported
H. 3-1. Knowledge about digital democracy → Usefulness	Not supported	H. 8-1. Information quality → Usefulness	Supported
H. 3-2. Knowledge about digital democracy → Behavioral intention	Supported	H. 8-2. Information quality → Behavioral intention	Not supported
H. 4-1. Supervisor support → Usefulness	Supported	H. 9-1. Risk in online discussion → Usefulness	Not supported
H. 4-2. Supervisor support → Behavioral intention	Not supported	H. 9-2. Risk in online discussion → Behavioral intention	Not supported
H. 5-1. IS department support → Usefulness	Supported	H. 10. Usefulness → Behavioral intention	Supported
H. 5-2. IS department support → Behavioral intention	Supported		

forums operating in the private sector, the government's online policy forums may strongly regulate messages posted on their Web sites, so public administrators may not perceive much risk when they write in online policy forums. As South Korea has been promoting administrative reforms at all public agencies, innovation-supportive organizational culture may not be an important factor.

Since digital democracy is still emerging for many public agencies, the results of this research can be helpful for successful implementation of the concept. Path analysis reveals that perceived usefulness, attitudes toward citizen participation, and information quality are the major determinants of behavioral intention among individual, organizational, and information system factors. Policy makers, elected officials, and managers should focus on increasing the level of those three factors in order to facilitate digital democracy. Leaders within public administration organizations should pay attention to online policy forums and utilize information provided by citizens in the policy-making process so that public administrators may perceive the usefulness of those policy forums. Since public administrators' use of online policy forums involves citizen participation in the policy-making process through government Web sites, officials' favorable attitudes toward citizen participation are indispensable to digital democracy. On the part of citizens, they should understand policy issues and provide good discussions on policy issues through government Web sites so that public administrators can perceive the usefulness of online policy forums and utilize them. This was consistent with the analysis of comments from respondents who emphasized that the quality of information, mature citizenship, and citizen's competence in policy issues are prerequisite to the success of digital democracy. Many officials commented that opinions on online policy forums were often posted by narrow, self-interested parties, and some officials complained that abusive or malicious opinions were posted on government Web sites.

Theories of digital democracy have hypothesized that the Internet has a potential to broaden and deepen citizens' participation in decision making in government and improve the quality of decisions by ensuring deliberative public debate. Although several studies have been conducted at the organizational level to find characteristics of agencies that have adopted practices of e-government, research on individual public administrators is rare. This research underscores several implications for developing theories of digital democracy. First, this study suggests that the acceptance of practices of digital democracy at the individual level should be distinguished from the adoption of such practices at the organizational level. This study also finds that the level of individual public administrators' acceptance of practices of digital democracy varies within an agency that has adopted those practices. Second, this study indicates that the causal path model is valid in explaining public administrators' behavioral intentions to use online policy forums. This model can be extended to public administrators' acceptance of other practices of e-government or digital democracy, such as online opinion polls/surveys, online public hearings, and electronic town meetings. As these practices take place online, there are no essential differences between online forums and other practices.

The generalizability of this study across countries is limited because the samples were selected from public officials in South Korea. We expect that individual, organizational, and IS system characteristics will differ between public officials in South Korea and other countries, and one previous study did show that the pattern of relationships between variables in IS research was different between countries (Igbaria & Zviran, 1991). Thus comparative, cross-national research is necessary to more fully understand the implementation process for digital democracy. In addition, future research might compare public administrators' willingness to use the practice of digital democracy between public administrators who work at agencies that adopted such practices and those who work at agencies that did not introduce such practices in their organizations.

References

Adams, D. A., Nelson, R. R., & Todd, P. A. (1992). Perceived usefulness, ease of use, and usage of information technology: A replication. *MIS Quarterly, 16*(2), 227-247.

Agarwal, R., & Prasad, J. (1999). Are individual differences germane to the acceptance of new information technology? *Decision Sciences, 30*(2), 361-391.

Ajzen, I. (1985). From intention to actions: A theory of planned behavior. In J. Kuhl & J. Beckmann (Eds.), *Action control: From cognition to behavior* (pp. 11-39). New York: Springer- Verlag.

Ajzen, I. (1991). The theory of planned behavior. *Organizational Behavior and Human Decision Processes, 50*, 179-211.

Anandarajan, M., Simmers, C., & Igbaria, M. (2000). An exploratory investigation of the antecedents and impact of interne usage: An individual perspective. *Behaviour & Information Technology, 19*(1), 69-85.

Beierle, T. C. (2002). *Democracy on-line: An evaluation of the national dialogue on public involvement in EPA decisions.* Retrieved February 17, 2005, from

http://www.rff.org/Documents/RFF-RPT-demonline.pdf

Coleman, S. (2004). Connecting parliament to the public via the Internet. *Information, Communication & Society, 7*(1), 1-22.

Coleman, S., & Gotze, J. (2001). Bowling together: Online public engagement in policy deliberation. *Hansard Society.* Retrieved October 14, 2004, from http://bowlingtogether.net/bowlingtogether.pdf

Danziger, J. N., Dutton, W. H., Kling, R., & Kraemer, K. L. (1982). *Computers and politics: High technology in American local governments.* New York: Columbia University Press.

Danziger, J. N., & Kraemer, K. L. (1986). *People and computers: The impacts of computing on end users in organizations.* New York: Columbia University Press.

Davis, J. A. (1985). *The logic of causal order.* Beverly Hills: Sage.

Davis, F. D. (1989). Perceived usefulness, perceived ease of use, and user acceptance of information technology. *MIS Quarterly, 13*(3), 319-340.

Davis, F. D., Bagozzi, R. P., & Warsaw, P. R. (1989). User acceptance of computer technology: A comparison of two theoretical models. *Management Science, 35*(8), 982-1003.

de Lancer Julnes, P., & Holzer, M. (2001). Promoting the utilization of performance measures in public organizations: An empirical study of factors affecting adoption and implementation. *Public Administration Review, 61*(6), 693-708.

DeLone, W. H., & McLean, E. R. (1992). Information systems success: The quest for the dependent variable. *Information Systems Research, 3*(1), 60-95.

DeLone, W. H., & McLean, E. R. (2003). The DeLone and McLean model of information systems success: A ten-year update. *Journal of Management Information Systems, 19*(4), 9-30.

De Vaus, D. A. (1986). *Surveys in social research.* London: George Allen & Unwin.

European Commission. (n.d.). *EParticipation good practices from the eGovernment good practice framework.* Retrieved March 30, 2007, from http://ec.europa.eu/information_society/activities/egovernment_research/doc/eparticipation/eparticipation_good-practices.pdf.

Finlay, K., & Finlay, T. (1996). The relative roles of knowledge and innovativeness in determining librarians' attitudes toward and use of the Internet: A structural equation modeling approach. *Library Quarterly, 66*(1), 59-83.

Fountain, J. E. (2001). *Building the virtual state: Information technology and institutional change.* Washington, D.C.: Brookings Institution Press.

Friedman, B., Kahn, P. H., & Howe, D. C. (2000). Trust online. *Communications of the ACM, 43*(12), 34-40.

Hacker, K. L., & van Dijk, J. (2000). What is digital democracy? In K. L. Hacker & J. van Dijk (Eds.), *Digital democracy: Issues of theory and practice* (pp. 1-9). Thousand Oaks, CA: Sage Publications.

Hague, B. N., & Loader, B. D. (Eds.). (1999). *Digital democracy: Discourse and decision making in the information age.* London: Routledge.

Heise, D. R. (1969). Problems in path analysis and causal inference. *Sociological Methodology, 1*, 38-73.

Hill, H. C. (2003). Understanding implementation: Street-level bureaucrats' resources for reform. *Journal of Public Administration Research and Theory, 13*(3), 265-282.

Ho, A. T. (2002). Reinventing local governments and the e-government initiative. *Public Administration Review, 62*(4), 434-444.

Ho, A. T., & Ni, A. Y. (2003). Explaining the adoption of e-government features: A case study of Iowa County Treasures' office. *American Review of Public Administration, 34*(2), 164-180.

Hogan, M., & Cook, N., & Henderson, M. (2004, April 14-15). *The Queensland government's e-democracy agenda.* Paper presented at the Australian Electronic Governance Conference, University of Melbourne, Australia. Retrieved March 30, 2007, from http://www.public-policy.unimelb.edu.au/egovernance/papers/16_Hogan.pdf

Holzer, M., Melitski, J., Rho, S., & Schwester, R. (2004). Restoring trust in government: The potential of digital citizen participation. *Report of IBM Center for the Business of Government.* Retrieved October 25, 2004, from

http://www.businessofgovernment.org/pdfs/HolzerReport.pdf

Igbaria, M. (1990). End-user computing effectiveness: A structural equation model. *Omega, 18*(6), 637-652.

Igbaria, M. (1993). User acceptance of microcomputer technology: An empirical test. *Omega, 21*(1), 73-90.

Igbaria, M., Guimaraes, T., & Davis, G. B. (1995). Testing the determinants of microcomputer usage via a structural equation model. *Journal of Management Information Systems, 11*(4), 87-114.

Igbaria, M., Parasuraman, S., & Baroudi, J. J. (1996). A motivational model of microcomputer usage. *Journal of Management Information systems, 13*(1), 127-143.

Igbaria, M., & Zviran, M. (1991). End-user effectiveness: A cross-cultural examination. *Omega, 19*(5), 369-379.

International Telecommunication Union. (2004). *Internet indicators: Hosts, users, and number of PCs*. Retrieved February 11, 2005, from http://www.itu.int/ITU-D/ict/statistics/at_glance/Internet03.pdf

Kakabadse, A., Kakabadse, N. K., & Kouzmin, A. (2003). Reinventing the democratic governance project through information technology? A growing agenda for debate. *Public Administration Review, 63*(1), 44-60.

Kim, S.-T. (2004). *E-government: Theories and strategies*. Seoul, Korea: Bummunsa.

Klem, L. (1995). Path analysis. In L. G. Grimm & P. R. Yarnold (Eds.), *Reading and understanding multivariate statistics* (pp. 65-97). Washington, D.C.: American Psychological Association.

Kling, R. (1980). Social analyses of computing: Theoretical perspectives in recent empirical research. *Computing surveys, 12*(1), 61-108.

Kline, R. B. (1998). *Principles and practices of structural equation modeling*. New York: Guilford Press.

Kling, R., & Jewett, T. (1994). The social design of work life with computers and networks: A natural systems perspective. In M. C. Yovits (Ed.), *Advances in computers* (Vol. 39, pp. 239-293). San Diego: Academic Press.

Klobas, J. E. (1995). Beyond information quality: Fitness for purpose and electronic information resource use. *Journal of Information Science, 21*(2), 95-14.

Kraemer, K. L., Danziger, J. N., Dunkle, D. E., & King, J. L. (1993). The usefulness of computer-based information to public managers. *MIS Quarterly, 17*(2), 129-148.

Kraemer, K. L., Dutton, W. H., & Northrop, A. (1981). *The management of information systems*. New York: Columbia University Press.

Kwon, T. H., & Zmud, R. W. (1987). Unifying the fragmented models of information systems implementation. In R. J. Boland & R. A. Hirschheim (Eds.), *Critical issues in information systems research* (pp. 227-251). New York: John Wiley & Sons.

Leonard-Barton, D., & Deschamps, I. (1988). Managerial influence in the implementation of new technology. *Management Science, 34*(10), 1252-1265.

Lin, J. C., Lu, H. (2000). Towards an understanding of the behavioural intention to use a Web site. *International Journal of Information Management, 20*, 197-208.

Lipsky, M. (1980). *Street-level bureaucracy: Dilemmas of the individual in public services*. New York: Russell Sage Foundation.

Loehlin, J. C. (1998). *Latent variable models: An introduction to factor, path, and structural analysis* (3rd ed.). Mahwah, NJ: Lawrence Erlbaum Associates.

Lucas, H. C. (1978). Empirical evidence for a descriptive model of implementation. *MIS Quarterly, 2*(2), 27-41.

Lucas, H. C., Ginzberg, M. J., & Schultz, R. L. (1990). *Information systems implementation: Testing a structural model*. Norwood, NJ: Ablex Publishing.

Mathieson, K., Peacock, E., & Chin, W. W. (2001). Extending the technology acceptance model: The influence of perceived user resources. *The Data Base for Advance in Information Systems, 32*(3), 86-112.

Minnesota Planning. (2002). *Issue talk: State budget shortfall.* Retrieved January 12, 2005, from http://www.mnplan.state.mn.us/pdf/2002/IssueTalkSummary.pdf

Moon, M. J. (2002). The Evolution of e-government among municipalities: Rhetoric or reality? *Public Administration Review, 62*(4), 424-433.

Moon, M. J., & Brestchneider, S. (2002). Does the perception of red tape constrain IT innovativeness in organizations? Unexpected results from simultaneous equation model and implications. *Journal of Public Administration Research and Theory, 12*(2), 273-291.

Nedovic-Budic, Z., & Godschalk, D. R. (1996). Human factors in adoption of geographic information systems: A local government case study. *Public Administration Review, 56*(6), 554-567.

Nelson, R. R., & Cheney, P. H. (1987). Training end users: An exploratory study. *MIS Quarterly, 11*(4), 547-559.

Norris, D. F. (2005). Electronic democracy at the American grassroots. *International Journal of Electronic Government Research, 1*(3), 1-14.

Norris, D. F., & Moon, M. J. (2005). Advancing e-government at the grassroots: Tortoise or hare? *Public Administration Review, 65*(1), 64-75.

Organization for Economic Cooperation and Development. (2001). *The development of broadband access in OECD countries.* Retrieved February 14, 2005, from http://www.oecdwash.org/DATA/DOCS/broadband_access.pdf

Organization for Economic Cooperation and Development. (2003). *Promise and problem of e-democracy: challenges of online citizen engagement.* Retrieved October 18, 2004, from http://www1.oecd.org/publications/e-book/4204011E.PDF

Pedhazur, E. J. (1982). *Multiple regression in behavioral research* (2nd ed.). New York: Holt, Rinehart and Winston.

Pedhazur, E. J. (1997). *Multiple regression in behavioral research* (3rd ed.). Forth Worth: Harcourt Brace College Publishers.

Ranerup, A. (1999). Internet-enabled applications for local government democratisation. In R. Heeks (Ed.), *Reinventing government in the information age* (pp. 177-193). London: Routledge.

Rogers, E. M. (1995). *Diffusion of innovations* (4th ed.). New York: The Free Press.

Schumacker, R. E., & Lomax, R. G. (1996). *A beginner's guide to structural equation modeling.* Mahwah, NJ: Lawrence Erlbaum Associates.

Scott, W. R. (1992). *Organizations: Rational, natural, and open systems* (3rd ed.). Englewood Cliffs, NJ: Prentice Hall.

Sheppard, B. H., Hartwick, J., & Warsaw, P. R. (1988). The theory of reasoned action: A meta-analysis of past research with recommendations for modification and future research. *Journal of Consumer Research, 15*(3), 325-343.

Spacey, R., Goulding, A., & Murray, I. (2004). Exploring the attitudes of public library staff to the Internet using the TAM. *Journal of Documentation, 60*(5), 550-564.

Subramaniam, N., & Ashkanasy, N. (2001). The effects of organizational culture perceptions on the relationship between budgetary participation and managerial job-related outcomes. *Australian Journal of Management, 26*(1), 35-54.

Thompson, R. L., Higgins, C. A., & Howell, J. M. (1991). Personal computing: Toward a conceptual model of utilization. *MIS Quarterly, 15*(1), 125-143.

Thong, J., & Yap, C. (1995). CEO characteristics, organizational characteristics and information technology adoption in small businesses. *Omega, 23*(4), 429-442.

Tsagarousianou, R. (1999). Electronic democracy: Rhetoric and reality. *Communications, The European Journal of Communication Research, 24*(2), 189-208.

United Nations. (2004). *UN global e-government readiness report 2004*. Retrieved December 10, 2004, from http://www.unpan.org/egovernment4.asp

United Nations. (2007). *Compendium of innovative e-government practices*. Retrieved March 30, 2007, from http://unpan1.un.org/intradoc/groups/public/documents/UN/UNPAN023997.pdf

Walsham, G. (1993). *Interpreting information systems in organizations*. Chichester, UK: John Wiley & Sons.

Wang, X. (2001). Assessing public participation in U.S. cities. *Public Performance & Management Review, 24*(4), 322-336.

Weare, C., Musso, J. A., & Hale, M. L. (1999). Electronic democracy and the diffusion of municipal Web pages in California. *Administration & Society, 31*(1), 3-27.

Endnote

[1]   E-government readiness index is calculated by averaging the Web measure index, the telecommunication infrastructure index and the human capital index. The e-participation index evaluates the extent of information provision on government Web sites and citizens' online participation in policy-making.

Appendix

Perceived Usefulness of Online Policy Forums

Respondents were asked for the extent of their agreement/disagreement with: A. Online policy forums have been useful for making better decisions in my organization; B. Using online policy forums has improved decision-making in my organization; C. Online policy forums have been helpful in doing my organization's task at hand; D. I find online policy forums to be effective in inviting citizens' opinions in the policy-making process; E. Using online policy forums has improved citizen-government relationships in my organization; F. Online policy forums have strengthened public trust in my organization.

Behavioral Intention to Use Online Policy Forums

Respondents were asked for the extent of their agreement/disagreement with: A. I intend to access online policy forums during the time when an online discussion is held on topics related to my work in the near future; B. I predict that I would access online policy forums frequently when an online discussion is held on topics related to my work in the future; C. I intend to use online policy forums in the future to invite citizens' opinions in the policy-making process; D. I am likely to use online policy forums in the near future when citizens' opinions are needed in decision-making in my job; E. I am wiling to discuss policy issues with citizens on online policy forums in the near future.

Negative Internet Attitudes

Respondents were asked for the extent of their agreement/disagreement with: A. Soon, our lives will be controlled by the Internet; B. People are becoming slaves to the Internet.

Attitudes Toward Citizen Participation

Respondents were asked for the extent of their agreement/disagreement with: A. Citizens' participation in government affairs should be increased beyond the current extent of participation; B. Involving citizens in the policy-making process would improve the quality of decisions and public service; C. Ordinary citizens should have the same chance of influencing government policy.

Knowledge About Digital Democracy

The following questions were asked to measure public administrators' knowledge about digital democracy. A. In the past two years, how many times have you attended education, training, workshops, seminars, or lectures which include topics related to e-government, digital democracy, or informationalization? (never = 1, more than three times = 5); B. How often have you read articles on e-government, digital democracy, or informationalization in newspapers, magazines, or books? (never = 1, more than once per two weeks =5); C. I am familiar with the term "digital democracy" and its meanings (strongly disagree = 1, strongly agree = 5); D. Please rate your knowledge about best practices of e-government or digital democracy at home and around the world. (no knowledge = 1, a lot of knowledge = 5).

Supervisor Support for Using Online Policy Forums

Respondents were asked for the extent of their agreement/disagreement with: A. My supervisor has given me support to use online policy forums; B. My supervisor has shown an interest in citizens' opinions posted on online policy forums; C. My supervisor has encouraged me to consider citizens' opinions posted on online policy forums in my work; D. My supervisor has urged me to find discussion topics to be posted on online policy forums.

IS Department Support for Using Online Policy Forums

Respondents were asked for the extent of their agreement/disagreement with: A. The IS department in my agency has provided support for my using online policy forums; B. The IS department in my agency has encouraged me to use online policy forums; C. The IS department in my agency has provided most of the necessary help, consulting, and guidance to get us to use online policy forums; D. The IS department in my agency has emphasized the advantages of using online policy forums.

Innovation-Supportive Organizational Culture

The following questions were asked to measure innovation-supportive organizational culture. (1) Please tell us to what extent you agree or disagree with the following statements. A. Being innovative is very important in my organization, B. Having a willingness to experiment is very important in my organization; (2) In regard to organizational culture, please indicate the importance of doing the following: A.

Coming up with a new idea to provide public service, B. Trying new ways of doing things, C. Questioning old ways of doing things.

Perceived Ease of Use of Online Policy Forums

Respondents were asked for the extent of their agreement/disagreement with: A. I find online policy forums to be easy to access; B. Using online policy forums does not require a lot of my mental effort; C. It is easy to search and read messages posted on online policy forums; D. Online policy forums are easy to use compared to face-to-face meetings with citizens when I need opinions from citizens.

Information Quality

Respondents were asked for the extent of their agreement/disagreement with: A. Online policy forums provided the precise information that I needed in decision-making in my organization; B. Citizens' diverse perspectives were reflected in opinions registered on online policy forums; C. Online policy forums provided sufficient information that I needed in decision-making in my organization; D. Opinions registered by citizens on online policy forums were new information that was not previously available; E. Citizens' opinions on online policy forums were relevant to the work of my organization.

Perceived Risk in Online Discussion

Respondents were asked for the extent of their agreement/disagreement with these statements: A. I am concerned that online citizens will criticize my writing if I write on online policy forums; B. It is risky to write on online policy forums because online citizens may post offensive messages by taking advantage of anonymity; C. I am concerned that unknown online citizens will behave with less good will in an online discussion than in a face-to-face meeting.

Chapter XIII

The Evolution of Web Governance in the Federal Government

Julianne Mahler, George Mason University, USA

Priscilla M. Regan, George Mason University, USA

Abstract

Over the last 10 years, federal agencies have undergone a major transformation in the way they manage programs and internal administration, in their relations with Congress, and in their dealings with clients and citizens. Agencies now work in electronic environments of e-mail, electronic documents and filings, intranets, and the Internet. This article seeks to describe and to account for the emergence of what is now being termed Web governance. *Briefly, Web governance is concerned with the control of content and design for agency Web sites. We explore the evolution of the process by which Web governance decisions are being made government-wide and at individual federal agencies. We look to changing patterns of administrative process in order to help account for the emergence of controls, and we find evidence of the importance of networking and of disbursed, self-designing processes.*

Introduction

Over the last 10 years, federal agencies have undergone a major transformation in the way they manage their programs and internal administration, in their relations with Congress, and in their dealings with clients and citizens. Rather than operating in a slow, cumbersome paper and briefing-book environment, agencies now work in electronic environments of e-mail, electronic documents and filings, intranets, and the Internet. This transformation has occurred as a result of e-government laws, agency initiatives, citizen demands, and technology-industry support. But the transformation recently has generated calls for exerting tighter control over the content and management of federal agency Web sites, creating uniform standards for presentation and accessibility, and establishing more centralized procedures for tracking and approving material on the Web sites. These new policy efforts include the creation of more elaborate procedures for approving Web site content in many federal agencies. Since 2002, OMB also has been charged with overseeing the creation and implementation of government-wide standards to guide the look and performance of federal Web sites, and more elaborate procedures for tracking and approving the content of sites are being created at the agency level.

Here, we are concerned with the development of these new governance efforts. How are decisions about the control of Web content decisions being made government-wide and within agencies? What kinds of processes and influences shaped the emerging guidelines and approval procedures at the agency and government-wide levels? How has this governance process been governed? We seek to describe the emergence of what is now being termed *Web governance*, the authoritative control of content and design for agency Web sites. At stake may be a significant change in how decisions about Web site content are being made and who makes them.

What should we expect the development of Web site governance tools to look like? Decentralized, self-organizing management long has been thought to be the hallmark of high technology enterprises. Since the 1960s, a shift from mechanistic to organic organizational processes has been associated with high technology. Burns (1963) saw in the emerging high technology industrial sector the development of new organizational forms based on continuous task redefinition, flexible network structures, lateral communication, and cooperative problem solving. Current research on the kinds of collaborative work settings and problem solving capacities of intranets and the Internet shows how intranets and the Internet fulfill some of these early ideas about lateral communication and knowledge management (Allcorn, 1997; Scott, 1998). Self-organizing, learning organizations are thought to be fostered by the open, wide dissemination of information made possible with intranets and the Internet. Harvey, Palmer, and Speier (1998) find that intranets are the "supporting information technology infrastructure that is most effective in creating and maintaining ... a learning environment" (p. 341). Research on the evolution of creative, interactive intranets sees them as emerging from the bottom up, in several places simultaneously, rather than in an orderly, centralized process (Scheepers & Rose, 2001). Our own earlier research shows the promise, still often unfulfilled, of intranets to foster collaborative management and problem solving (2002).

Decisions about intranets and the Internet may reflect new ideas about how work is managed in the information-intensive setting of the public sector. Peristeras, Tsekos, and Konstantinos (2002) note that with the advent of widespread information and communication technologies that made e-government possible, public administration is approaching a paradigm shift. Increasingly, public work is allocated to ad hoc groups with specific goals, but these groups are given considerable autonomy and allowed to be self-regulating in achieving those goals. The tight control over information and knowledge needed to make decisions in large government bureaucracies may be giving way in many cases to disbursed information housed in many parts of many organizations and accessible to a widening range of interested individuals inside and outside the organization. Knowledge management, based on stimulating and capturing innovative solutions to public problems, replaces more restricted problem-solving approaches (Brown & Duguid, 1991). Tacit knowledge rather than routine procedures may be recognized increasingly as a legitimate means to address issues.

Thus, rather than relying on rule-governed hierarchical control to coordinate effort, work and workers become increasingly self-organizing, using the networks of relations made possible by Internet and intranet connections (Martin et al., 2002). Networks replace hierarchies, as workers find ways to partner with agencies and other private and non-profit partners in order to achieve the public purpose (Goldsmith & Eggers, 2004). Large-scale routine technologies are replaced by communities of practice in which knowledge of how to achieve the desired ends is located in tacit practice, shared by those connected by interests and perhaps only secondarily by organizational settings (Brown & Duguid, 1991). These communities are based not on the relationships mapped out on organization charts but rather on the shared understanding of how to do work based on expectations built up over past interactions (Weick, 1979).

If this disbursed and self-designing process characterizes the emerging efforts to create a set of principles to guide the agency Web site content decisions, we should expect to see a Web site governance process and result that represent wide participation, collaboration rather than control, and self-organizing procedures rather than tightly held, top-down control over participation.

However, the stakes for content management decisions and policies are high. The Web sites are seen as an increasingly critical agency resource for managing relations with the public and other branches of government (Mahler & Regan, 2004, 2005). There may be struggles over control of this resource rather than collaboration and openness. In a small way, this research question begins to test the depth to which the new collaborative management paradigm can survive serious competition over a valued agency resource.

Methodology

The research conducted to examine the development of Web governance procedures consists of a set of three interlocking case studies. First, we examine the history of the decisions that OMB and Congress made about how to proceed to create government-wide Web content rules. Second, we track the evolution of the interagency groups that actually drafted the OMB rules. Finally, we look at what agencies have done on their own to create Web content governance procedures.

These three case studies are based on interviews with staff responsible for content management at various offices in seven agencies as well as agency staff who participated in several formal and informal interagency councils concerned with content management issues and Web governance. In this endeavor, we spoke with agency personnel during the summer and fall of 2004. We also spoke with current and former OMB staff members tasked with overseeing the development of government-wide requirements. These interviews were conducted in the fall of 2004. In addition, we perused publications and online documents, setting out the developing procedures within agencies such as rules for posting decisions and memorandums of understanding about authorization to post content. It is important to note, however, that written rules have not been developed in all cases. We also gained access to interagency recommendations and government-wide guidelines.

In order to investigate the development of content management procedures within agencies, we selected seven agencies with varying levels of Web site development and sophistication, as judged in West's (2003) fourth annual rankings of federal Web sites. These rankings are based on the quality of online publications, online databases, audio and video clips, advertisements, fees, privacy and security policies, comment forms, readability levels, and presence and number of online services. Although these features are not directly relevant to our interest in content management for agency Web sites, they do provide an overall measure of the sophistication and professionalism of a Web site. Using the West rankings we selected two agencies rated most highly (FCC and HUD); three in the middle (FDA, DOT, and EPA); and two at the bottom of the rankings (EEOC and NLRB). On a 100-point scale, the agencies we studied ranked as shown in Table 1.

The West rankings allow us to compare agencies with well-developed Web presence to those just beginning to offer more kinds of information online. Variations in stages of development may be important to decisions about content management and governance.

Table 1.

Agency	West Rating
FCC	73
HUD	62
FDA	53
DOT-FAA	51
EPA	50
EEOC	41
NLRB	38

Interviews were conducted with selected agency staff responsible for information technology, information management, program content, and public relations in each of our agencies. Our interviews were semi-structured with a template of questions about the approval process for Web content and changes in the approval process from paper release of information. We interviewed a total of 18 agency officials in 10 offices and seven former and current staff members at OMB. In some large, multidivisional departments, we interviewed Web content staff members in program divisions as well as in upper-level public relations, sometimes located in the top administrators' offices. Interviews lasted at least a half hour and often extended an hour and a half. Subsequent phone calls and e-mails allowed us to clarify and elaborate on the information gleaned during the interview.

Government-Wide Efforts to Control Web Sites by Congress and OMB

The current role of OMB's oversight of the development of federal Web sites has evolved over the past 25 years from a series of legislative measures and executive orders. The Paperwork Reduction Act (PRA) of 1980 and its 1986 amendments encouraged agencies to coordinate information collection in order to relieve citizens of excessive duplication of reporting requirements and to give OMB the authority to oversee this coordination. OMB's authority for agency information management expanded with the 1995 amendments to the PRA, giving them greater responsibilities for developing federal information technology (IT) performance standards, and procurement through use of its budget oversight capacities. The Clinger-Cohen Act, also known as the Information Technology Management Reform Act (ITMRA), almost immediately amended the 1995 PRA and created a Chief Information Officer (CIO) for each agency. As implemented under OMB Circular A-130, CIOs were charged with creating and enforcing a program in order to integrate IT into agency operations and to set up cost-effective IT acquisitions programs. President Clinton's Executive Order 13011 established the CIO Council, chaired by OMB, to provide an interagency forum in order for CIOs to exchange information and to make recommendations about the development of effective IT management strategies. The composition and the contributions of this interagency council are the subject of the next section.

There have been some questions raised, however, about the adequacy of OMB's budget oversight role as a tool for encouraging the adoption of these policies and the appropriateness of the CIO Council as a forum for accomplishing Web policy goals (Relyea, 2002). Indeed, in our interviews with agency personnel, there was general agreement that OMB has not done very much that is helpful and that its role primarily has been a reactive one concerned with putting out fires rather than creating a vision. However, one respondent was less critical, seeing OMB as providing gentle direction. Even those who were critical noted that OMB has so much under its jurisdiction that Web content issues were of relatively minor importance compared to preparation of the budget and regulatory review.

The use of the CIO Council to develop policies and strategies in order to develop the information content capacities of federal agencies also has been called into question. Interviews with agency staff and stakeholder groups outside the government revealed a common view that the CIO Council was focused too narrowly on technology and, therefore, was not the appropriate group to develop or to oversee Web content policies. One respondent noted that OMB sees the CIO Council and CIOs as key because agency Web sites began as IT projects. OMB and the CIOs were seen as viewing issues of Web governance too narrowly and overemphasizing the role of information technology in making Web site visits possible and de-emphasizing the role of Web managers and content providers in making it worth the visit. Another respondent noted that the *I* in CIO Council is often forgotten and that CIOs start with the tool and ask what can they do with it rather than asking what needs to be done.

Concerns about content issues as distinct from the primarily technological focus of the CIO Council soon gained more attention as Congress passed the E-Government Act of 2002. This act made use of an evolving, informal interagency forum in order to develop guidelines for content management. This interagency forum, its success, its antecedents in voluntary action among content managers in federal agencies, and its inclusive self-organizing process stands as an interesting model of collaborative planning

Interagency Initiatives

As Congress deliberated about the E-Government Act of 2002, the question of the role and expertise of CIOs was raised as a policy issue. Interest groups, especially the library community, and some federal officials advocated that the CIO Council not be given responsibility for developing Web content policy. Instead, they promoted the establishment of a new group that could be derived from and draw upon the expertise of an existing, informally-constituted group of Web managers. Consistent with this perspective, Section 207 of the E-Government Act established the Interagency Committee on Government Information (ICGI) (information and documents on the ICGI are available online at http://www.cio.gov/documents/ICGI.html). The purpose of Section 207 was "to improve the methods by which Government information, including information on the Internet, is organized, preserved, and made accessible to the public." Specifically, the ICGI is charged with the following:

- Consulting with interested communities.
- Conducting studies and submitting recommendations to the Director of OMB and the Archivist of the National Archives and Records Administration (NARA).
- Sharing effective practices for access to, dissemination of, and retention of federal information.

The ICGI conducts its work through an executive committee under the direction of the CIO Council and a number of working groups (see Table 2), which have the responsibility for drafting policy recommendations for final approval by the executive committee.

Most relevant to the issue of governance structures for Web content is the Web Content Standards Working Group, which, on June 9, 2004, issued its recommended policies and guidelines for federal public Web sites. The group developed its recommendations through a three-step process:

- First, it compiled all existing Web content requirements from laws, regulations, presidential directives, and other official documents.
- Second, it reviewed federal Web sites and identified common practices that promote usability and good customer service.
- Third, it solicited suggestions through a comment form on the FirstGov.gov Web site. (Web Standards, Work Plan, http://www.cio.gov/documents/ICGI. html)

Table 2. Working groups of the ICGI

Working Group	Membership	Jurisdiction
"Categorization of Government Information" Working Group	Nine members who represent all three branches of the federal government; chair appointed by OMB	Responsible for recommendations on standards for the organization and categorization of government information so that it is searchable electronically in ways that are interoperable across agencies
E-Gov Access Work Group	20 members from several federal agencies including most prominently GPO, OMB, HUD and GSA	
Electronic Records Policy Working Group	Eighteen members for the Cabinet level departments and from NARA; chair appointed by NARA	Responsible for developing recommendations on public access to government information on the Internet and in electronic form
Web Content Standards Group of the Web Content Management Working Group	Twenty-two members, almost all from cabinet level departments; chair designated by OMB	Developing guidance on standards for agency websites to assist public users in their use of websites
Public Domain Directory Group of Web Content Management Working Group	Fifteen members, with the majority from NARA and GSA; chair designated by OMB	Developing a public domain directory of public Federal Government websites and a repository of federally funded research and development

In addition to input from the interagency group, it also identified 14 advisers from government agencies who worked directly on agency Web sites and had expertise in specific areas, including information architecture, library science, usability, records management, and FOIA. In April 2004, the Working Group completed its draft recommendations, posted them for public comment on the ICGI Web site, and sent them to stakeholders and Web content experts. It received more than 100 sets of comments from the public during a three-week vetting period. This Working Group recognized that the development of Web content policies was an ongoing process, requiring structure and, to that end, recommended that OMB establish a Web Content Advisory Council.

The larger Web Content Management Working Group also has developed and posted on FirstGov.gov the Federal Web Content Managers Toolkit. This contains a compilation of laws and regulations, a list of common practices, and tools including a listserv, discussion forum, and library. This Web site is easy to use and complete. For example, common practices simply are listed, and each one is linked to a more detailed explanation with further links to examples from current federal Web sites and other resources. The Web site also solicits additional examples from other agencies that would then be linked from the Toolkit.

Both the results and the process leading to the recently released draft guidelines for content are noteworthy. In general, the process that the ICGI and its various working groups have followed is one that is bottom-up, collaborative, and rewarding for participating agency staff and for the agency as a whole. Congressional statutes and OMB guidelines set out fairly specific goals, but they neither dictated implementation details nor dictated a process. Although Congress required the establishment of the ICGI, OMB might have elected to actively oversee this process through its own Office of Information and Regulatory Affairs or through the CIO Council, but instead, OMB allowed the ICGI the autonomy that Congress seemed to have intended for it. The ICGI subsequently allowed the working groups considerable autonomy and allowed agencies to select representatives to the working groups. The result has been a process that largely is owned by the agency staff who had developed expertise and interest in e-government through direct experience in their own agencies. The working groups have given agency heads a means by which to recognize staff personnel. In this process, no one agency was designated as the best or the model. Instead, the concept of best practices was used in an ecumenical fashion, and almost all agencies have been able to contribute some practice to the mix. The working groups adopted a clearly collaborative, open process rather than a competitive, closed process.

The key to understanding how this open distributive process emerged lies in a development from the HUD Web site, one of the earliest sites and one whose development was directed by program managers rather than agency Web technology staff. The trajectory of the Web site of the Department of Housing and Urban Development, which was an early department-wide and award-winning Web site, is summarized on HUD's state of the Web yearly reports (http://www.hud.gov/library/bookshelf15/). The aspect of the HUD case that is particularly relevant in order to understand the emergence of the interagency policy guidelines for content was the evolution of the Federal Content Managers Forum from HUD's own internal Departmental Web Team. This team, created in 1999, was composed of a network of program office and field office Web managers. By 2000, a Deputy Secretary's Task Force on Web Management investigated Web management at other federal agencies as a basis for developing its own recommendations on the duties of content managers, which put HUD actors in touch with those with similar responsibilities in other agencies. In 2001, the HUD Web team organized a new working group of federal agency Web content managers, Federal Web Content Managers Forum, to share experiences, discuss problems, and identify best practices in content management. In its second year, the Forum sponsored a Web Content Managers Seminar with attendance from more than 100 Web content managers from 40 agencies. This Forum now has a listserv of 400, and its membership provided the basis for identifying the content managers to serve on the ICGI.

The vision of the Web site as a tool for program administration and agency management grew from early experiences of a small number of actors in a few agencies. This vision of the potential uses of the Internet in program administration was alluded to in legislation since the mid-1990s, but the means to do this, the techniques for incorporating the communication and information exchange potential of the Web for public management, had yet to be developed. It was this task as much as the creation of content guidelines that the Interagency Web Content Managers Forum initiated. Using the Internet to accomplish the mission and to serve constituencies of the agency was not an obvious extension of what the agency had been doing with letters, paper publications, notices, and so forth. It involved the imagining of new program tasks and novel kinds of program products that depended on innovative practices. These practices did not grow up in a vacuum. The cross-agency collaboration provided the sounding board that made these discoveries possible.

This unusual source for the ICGI, composed of agency personnel who were informally and voluntarily drawn to the problems of content management, reflects not just a new source of ideas for OMB committees and guidelines but also the emergence of new self-organizing processes in public management. Do we see the decentralized, self-organizing process at the agency level, as well? Is a similar process occurring as agencies move to develop Web content governance processes? Our agency case studies give us an opportunity to look for evidence of this process at the agency level as well.

Agency Governance Initiatives

We began by asking who controls the content and design of agency Web sites. Now, after considering the external actors who may be influencing the course of information management decisions, we consider forces inside the agency. At the agency level, we investigated where the decisions about Web content are being made and what procedures are emerging about who can create and post content. We questioned actors about the approval processes emerging for Web content and what kinds of standards for content were developing. Together, these issues constitute what we mean by governance, the authoritative control of content and design for agency Web sites. We found that the approval processes and the principles that actors thought were served by the approval process varied widely among the agencies in the study. Two issues that capture much of what we found are the degree of centralization and the location of Web content authorization.

In an earlier project (2004), we found that practices surrounding the control of content on federal Web sites were highly variable. While most respondents said that the degree of centralization in the Web content approval process essentially was unchanged from the approval process for print releases, some said that it was becoming more centralized over time, and some said less. There also were distinct differences in perceptions about where Web content approval decisions were made. In almost all cases, top-level agency Web content managers reported that the program offices had almost complete autonomy over the initiation and control of the content of the sites. However, virtually without exception, the Web posters or Webmasters in subordinate program offices identified an elaborate and careful hierarchical procedure for review and approval of content. What this suggests is that agencies are struggling to find ways to control the creation of new content on Web sites. Some upper-level managers are trying to prevent Web site postings from becoming (or remaining) a "free for all", as one respondent put it, and some program officers are trying to exercise their accustomed autonomy in these decisions.

Behind these struggles are differences in perspective about how to make the sites useful and accessible for different audiences. These are the stakes that respondents see as important to the mission and integrity of their organizations. Thus, a major trend was that the challenges that agencies face in arriving at content decisions are tied closely to the character of their mission and to emerging ideas about who their stakeholders are, how they can be served, and how the agency's mission is advanced through the use of the public Web site.-

A number of respondents described tension or conflict in their agency over the control of the Web site content. Most often, the conflicts were between program officials in the subdivisions of the agency and public affairs offices at the agency director's level. In one regulatory agency, there was a struggle over where responsibility for authorizing new content would reside: in the information technology division or in public affairs in the director's office. A memo of understanding was created to divide responsibility between them, assigning one the authority for content and the other the authority for the look and feel of the site. In another agency, tension between the public affairs in the top-level administrator's office and the subunits was resolved with the creation of a central advisory committee to oversee content decisions. In two cases, the main conflict appears to be between program offices and legal counsel. In two other cases, we heard how the IT division gave up or did not seek to control Web content decisions, only to realize later what a significant organizational resource such control was. In each case, efforts by IT staff to wrest control from content managers were unsuccessful. But in another agency, IT dominates. The CIO is the agency's representative to the federal Web Content Managers Forum and does not communicate new developments from that group to the content managers in agency's subdivision. Finally, we found one case in which the shift away from IT control has been gradual, so that now, half of the content managers are in public affairs. In most agencies, IT handles the server technology and, in some cases, the intranet, but not the Internet content.

A point of contention we did not anticipate concerns the location of the Web content manager within the agency. In some ways, this issue is related to the friction over the public relations uses of the sites. Earlier in the evolution of the agency Web site, the control of the sites typically resided with the information technology staff. In a few cases, the program managers (e.g., HUD) were able to gain control of content decisions. In other cases, content decisions migrated to the IRM function of the library staff. Increasingly, the content functions previously described are now located in Public Affairs or the Director's office. This reflects a shift away from viewing the Web site as a technical feature of the agency but does not resolve other issues about the uses of the sites for public relations and programs.

We also saw friction in agencies over who was to be the principal audience for the Web site and how they were to be served. In some cases, we saw disagreement over the relative weight to give to serving the needs of the technical users vs. the average users and who those average users were. In most cases, the proliferation of pages has meant that many user groups are served.

Interviews also revealed a debate between those who thought that the Web site should be used for public relations and those who saw it as a tool for communicating program information to the public. The latter often took the form of emphasizing the public education mission of the site. Almost all our respondents who defined themselves as Web managers emphasized the public education perspective. The friction was played out over such issues as whether the secretary's picture should appear on the department's home page. These debates indicate how ideas for using the Web site to serve the mission are unfolding. Similar debates are occurring at the state level, where Eschenfelder found that agencies with weaker public education missions have smaller Web sites (2004).

These conflicts and the typical uncertainties about who should authorize important postings led some of the agencies in our study to create formal procedures or institutions for making posting decisions. In others, as noted, the program actors seem to have greater independence, leading to a "wild west" approach, in the words of one respondent. This freedom is said to create inconsistent policy and legal positions. Some agencies have confronted these problems directly by creating governance structures. Three have developed procedures or institutions to govern content decisions, while three more are at varying stages of trying to create such structures.

Agency Reactions so Far to the OMB Guidelines

Actors we spoke with in agencies with larger and more fully developed Web sites (2004) were not concerned about the guidelines on Web content developed by ICGI and released by OMB. There appear to be several reasons for this. The larger sites already are meeting and exceeding the guidelines, which, in any case, their Web content representatives likely had a hand in producing. Of the agencies we examined, HUD, FDA, and EPA, in particular, were well represented on the ICGI. Several noted that they only needed to tweak current practices in order to meet the guidelines.

Many respondents also noted that the legislative and administrative backing for the guidelines gave legitimacy to practices that already are reasonably widespread. They expected that the guidelines would serve as useful justifications within their agencies for changes that they wanted to pursue. One respondent noted that the guidelines would be a useful spur for the upgrades that they wanted to make. Further, the guidelines are limited in scope, focusing on format and accessibility features of sites and not broaching the more controversial issues of how the sites will serve the agency mission. The provisions that were identified most often as real constraints were those related to privacy, but these requirements already exist under other legislative and OMB auspices. Not being able to contact users in order to follow up on usability surveys to users was seen as a drawback, but not one tied to the guidelines particularly.

Discussion

In characterizing the process and actors of the emerging Web content governance procedures, we expected that the process generally would reflect the common characterization of the Internet environment as decentralized and collaborative. We were only partly correct. We did see elements of this kind of process at the interagency level, with guidelines that may be only marginally intrusive on agency Web content decisions. There seem to be few real objections raised to the proposed guidelines, since they make only modest demands about format and virtually none about content. We typically did not see this kind of process at the agency level, however. Within the agencies, the process appears to reflect business as usual within large bureaucratic organizations with subdivisions and levels jockeying for control. In the interagency setting, we saw a different process, however. The interagency process we observed in the development of the content guidelines and the agency participation in that development illustrates a trend identified by many observers as a shift in the way work is organized as a result of the information and communication technologies of the Internet.

The reality of networks and communities of practice is clearly evident in this case. Several respondents from the Forum and the ICGI note that much of what they are establishing in the guidelines is the already-agreed-upon community practices. In this effort, those who early on recognized the different roles for Web content management, Internet technology support, and management were important in setting the stage for the later collaborative processes. These early adopters were the discoverers of these practices. The desire of small groups within agencies to find others with whom to discuss the difficulties of creating useful content and wishing for a group with which to share emerging ideas on how to do this led to the creation of a community of Web content managers.

Later, as OMB implemented the provisions of the PRA and the E-Government Act, it did not impose top-down control in part, several of our respondents noted, because they were sympathetic to the concerns of the Web content managers. The resulting ICGI rested on the network forged by the Forum, in effect allowing those who would be using the guidelines to have a role in creating them. This informally created network exchanged information about new practices and later best practices. They were a community of practitioners sharing knowledge based not on policy mandates or on professional standards but on their trial-and-error experiences, extending the opportunities for vicarious learning. The early members of the Forum bring experiences to the group in order to find support and inspiration. Without accepted norms or procedures to follow, they created their own community and their own guides to practice. This non-formal, non-canonical process is a clear manifestation of the kind of paradigm shift in public organizations noted previously.

References

Allcorn, S. (1997). Parallel virtual organizations: Managing and working in the virtual workplace. *Administration and Society, 29*(4), 412-439.

Brown, J. S., & Duguid, P. (1991). Organizational learning and communities-of-practice. *Organization Science, 2*(1), 40-57.

Burns, T. (1963, January). Industry in a new age. *New Society, 31.*

Electronic Records Policy Working Group. (2004). *Recommendations for the effective management of government information on the Internet and other electronic records* (A Report to the Interagency Committee on Government Information). Retrieved October 20, 2004, from http://www.cio.gov/documents/ICGI

Eschenfelder, K. R. (2004). Behind the Web site: An inside look at the production of Web-based textual government information. *Government Information Quarterly, 21*(3), 337-358.

Goldsmith, S., & Eggers, W. (2004). *Governing by network.* Washington, DC: Brooking Institution Press.

Harvey, M., Palmer, J., & Speier, C. (1998). Implementing intraorganizational learning: A phased-model approach supported by intranet technology. *European Management Journal, 16*(3), 341-354.

Mahler, J., & Regan, P. M. (2004, September 3). *Crafting the message: Agency Websites and political control.* Paper presented at the American Political Science Association Meetings, Chicago, Illinois.

Mahler, J., & Regan, P. M. (2005). Agency Internets and changing dynamics of congressional oversight. *International Journal of Public Administration, 28*(7/8), 553-565.

Martin, D., Rouncefield, M., & Sommerville, I. (2002). Applying patterns of cooperative interaction to work (re)design: E-government and planning. In *Proceedings of the*

SIGHI Conference on Human Factors. Retrieved October 10, 2005, from http://www. dirc.org.uk/publications/inproceedings/papers/65.pdf

Office of Management and Budget. (2002, February 27). *E-government strategy: Implementing the president's management agenda for e-government*. Retrieved October 10, 2005, from http://www.whitehouse.gov/omb/inforeg/infopoltech.html

Office of Management and Budget. (2004, March 8). *FY-2003 report to Congress on implementation of the e-government act*. Retrieved October 10, 2005, from http://www. whitehouse.gov/omb/inforeg/infopoltech.html

Office of Management and Budget. (n.d.). *Circular No. A-130, revised, memorandum for heads of executive departments and agencies*. Retrieved October 10, 2005, from http://www.whitehouse.gov/omb/circulars/a130/print/a130trans4.html

Peristeras, V., Tsekos, T., & Tarabanis, K. (2002). *Analyzing e-government as a paradigm shift* (UNTC Occasional Paper Series No. 1). Paper presented at the Annual Conference of the International Association of Schools and Institutes of Administration, The United Nations Thessaloniki Centre for Public Service Professionalism. Retrieved October 10, 2005, from unpan1.un.org/intradoc/groups/public/documents/UNTC/ UNPAN007008.pdf

Relyea, H. C. (2002). E-gov: Introduction and overview. *Government Information Quarterly, 19*(1), 9-35.

Scheepers, R., & Rose, J. (2001). Organizational intranets: Cultivating information technology for the people by the people. In S. Dasgupta (Ed.), *Managing Internet and intranet technologies in organizations: Challenges and opportunities* (pp. 1-20). Hershey, PA: Idea Group Publishing.

Scott, J. (1998). Organizational knowledge and the intranet. *Decision Support Systems, 23*(1), 3-17.

Strejcek, G., & Theil, M. (2002). Technology push, legislation pull? E-government in the European Union. *Decision Support Systems, 34*(3), 305-313.

Weick, K. (1979). *The social psychology of organizing* (2nd ed.). Reading, MA: Addison-Wesley.

West, D. M. (2003, September). *State and federal e-government in the United States, 2000*. Retrieved October 10, 2005, from http://www.InsidePolitics.org

This work was previously published in International Journal of Electronic Government Research, Vol. 2, Issue 1, edited by D. F. Norris & P. Fletcher, pp. 21-35, copyright 2006 by IGI Publishing, formerly known as Idea Group Publishing (an imprint of IGI Global).

Chapter XIV

Service, Security, Transparency, and Trust:
Government Online or
Governance Renewal in Canada?

Jeffrey Roy, University of Ottawa, Canada

Abstract

The objectives of this article are twofold: first, to examine the main conceptual dimensions of electronic government (e-government); and secondly, to critically assess both the current responses and future prospects of Canada's public sector. The first sections of the paper are primarily conceptual as they delve into e-government's meaning and scope by presenting a set of major thematic challenges driving public sector reform. The paper then provides a critical assessment of recent reforms and new initiatives undertaken by the Government of Canada. Building on this analysis, the article aims to sketch out the major issues and challenges likely to confront Canadian governance. Of particular interest is whether or not a sufficient balance exists in focusing on dimensions of e-government and e-governance in order to adapt effectively to a more informational, digital, and interdependent world.

Introduction

The objectives of this article are twofold: first, to examine the main conceptual dimensions of electronic government (e-government); and secondly, to critically assess both the current responses and future prospects of Canada's public sector. In order to be more precise on the scope of this paper, the following definition of e-government is useful as a starting point:

The continuous innovation in the delivery of services, citizen participation, and governance through the transformation of external and internal relationships by the use of information technology, especially the Internet[1].

This definition helps to underscore the links between government and governance in such a context, and the fluid nature of roles and relationships both within the public sector and across various stakeholders externally. The latter term—governance—may be defined in a general way as the manner and mechanisms by which resources are coordinated in a world where power and knowledge are increasingly distributed (Paquet, 1997). The rise of electronic governance (e-governance) denotes processes of coordination made possible or even necessary by the advent of technology and, in particular, the spreading of online activities (Allen et al., 2001).

This starting point has been extended as of late by many groups suggesting that e-government is more simply and holistically about achieving good government. This perspective underscores the widening canvass of e-government as digital technologies and online activities permeate most all aspects of the public sector. For some, e-governance is distinguishable from e-government in that the former comprises a more fundamental sharing and reorganizing of power across all stakeholders and the citizenry, whereas the latter is more focused on modernizing existing state processes to improve performance with respect to existing services and policies (Peristeras et al., 2002; Riley, 2003). For others, and more in line with the definitions adopted above, e-government must be viewed as encompassing both administration and democracy (Bertelsmann, 2002).

Despite rather fluid terminology, such viewpoints offer a useful guide for the conceptual review provided by the first half of this article. Section two explores e-government from a primarily internal perspective, examining the governance of online service delivery and homeland security as two distinct but quite related facets of e-government. Section three examines more outwardly rooted governance themes related to transparency and trust and their connection to broader debates concerning democratic reform. The interdependence of such inward and outward considerations also matters due to the holistic context of a public sector encompassing both internal and external dimensions.

Section four then undertakes a critical assessment of e-government in Canada. Building on this analysis, section five looks forward to sketch out the major issues and challenges likely to confront Canadian government. The purpose of this discussion is less a definitive blueprint of what the future will yield and more some informed guidance as to how the public sector in Canada is likely to evolve. Of particular interest is whether or not a sufficient balance exists in focusing on administrative and democratic adaptation, internally and externally, in line with the emerging contours of a more informational, digital, and interdependent world.

Service and Security

Remarkably new by any historical measure, the rapid emergence of e-government around the world and the specific nature of its current evolution can be viewed as stemming from two separate yet interrelated episodes over the past decade—on the one hand, the rise of the Internet and electronic commerce (e-commerce) during the 1990s; and on the other hand, the terrorist attacks of September 11, 2001. While their origins are quite distinct, they share many contemporary governance challenges.

With respect to e-commerce, growth and expansion are linked to an online population that has now surpassed half a billion people worldwide. Yet, despite progress in most regions of the world, this group remains relatively concentrated in the developed world within the most advanced economies of Asia, Europe, and North America (Geiselhart, 2004). This concentration stems in part from the catalytic role played by the private sector. Indeed, within industry the Internet has served three main purposes in shaping market behavior and organizational dynamics: a source of product and process innovation, an efficiency tool, and an alternative channel of client service. The widening scope of digital technologies means that few, if any, industries are exempt from some degree of transformation (Andal-Ancion et al., 2003).

For governments, all of these Internet-induced changes are relevant. Much of e-government reflects private sector activity that has both encouraged and pressured public sector organizations to act in a similar manner. Fiscal constraints imposed by a quasi-competitive system of global investors and domestic politics, as well as a strategic desire to generate cost savings and reallocate spending to new and politically attractive priorities, make the nexus between technology management and efficiency a central concern in government today (McIver & Elmagarmid, 2002; Pavlichev & Garson, 2004). Thus, multinational corporations and national governments (and large subnational ones) may be viewed similarly in terms of seeking to deploy new governance capacities (Cairncross, 2002).

A more careful examination of government, however, reveals important differences across the private and public sectors. Efficiency, for example, is a much more politically contested principle in government. Stakeholders such as unions and political parties may oppose worker mobility and job cuts, moves generally applauded in the market sector. Although private corporations may aggressively cater to select clients, governments remain wedded to broader public interest responsibilities involving all citizens.

These public interest considerations are tied to political accountabilities that, in turn, shape both the feasibility and the perceived appropriateness of e-government as a service-delivery strategy. The modest and uneven results of online service delivery by governments, even in those countries leading in Internet use, is indicative of both the complexities and diverse preferences characterizing a citizenry and its relations with its government (Hart-Teeter, 2003). Indeed, it is not clear whether citizens are demanding online services or governments are pushing them, and the requisite mix of incentives and results to move citizens online remains elusive (Roy, 2003). This elusiveness, in turn, is reflected in dispersed and uneven political leadership, both in terms of the relative importance of online service delivery as a strategic objective and the level of resources and authority allocated to undertake necessary change.

These necessary changes are primarily about fostering more horizontal governance to cut across traditionally separate vertical entities, perhaps the single most crucial organizational challenge to realizing citizen-centric portals and service delivery mechanisms (Allen et al., 2005; Fountain, 2001). Achieving this horizontal collaboration, therefore, requires political will and a set of organizational mechanisms to facilitate information sharing and joint action (Batini et al., 2002). There are both structural and cultural impediments to such mechanisms, reflecting traditional resource allocation processes and separate accountability systems based on vertical hierarchy and, in the case of Parliamentary models, ministerial accountability (Allen et al., 2005).

The danger is that in the absence of strong action to overcome these limitations—the rhetoric of portals as a basis for integrative services—one stop encounters and more seamless governance remains just rhetoric. Moreover, strengthened government-wide coordination, implying some degree of central authority, runs counter to the thrust of new public management reform in the 1980s and early 1990s that emphasized organizational autonomy and flexibility. Striking a new balance is proving to be a formidable challenge (as the Canadian experience, examined below, demonstrates).

The terrorist acts of September 11, 2001 have brought out similar governance dilemmas, albeit with an added sense of urgency. Governments have been quick to establish new anti-terrorism and homeland security measures that often create new pressures for horizontal coordination and government-wide action. Information management and interoperability over a safe and secure digital architecture become precursors to improved security for citizens.

In many ways, security efforts are in keeping with the definition of e-government offered at this article's outset. Online service delivery has relied upon a secure infrastructure in order to underpin the technological feasibility of interacting and transacting via the Internet (Holden, 2004). Nonetheless, today cyber-security may also be viewed as one element in a broader public safety or homeland security agenda that denotes an important reshaping of e-government in terms of purpose and focus. A commonality of service delivery and homeland security is an emphasis on coordination across government and capacities to transcend organizational boundaries in order to focus on the needs of the citizen. A similar necessity for both agendas is a sophisticated and reliable digital architecture to underpin government-wide capacities for action.

There are differences, as well, that are important in shaping how e-government is viewed both within and outside the public sector. On the service delivery side, most governments have pursued a more collaborative model, facilitating horizontal coordination across separate units in an effort to achieve better results for the citizen as a consumer of public services (Allen et al., 2005). In comparison, the dramatic imposition of homeland or domestic security as a response to recent terrorist activities has accentuated a more centralized form of organizational response. The United States Department of Homeland Security is a case in point, internalizing coordination within a broader, more central command and control structure accountable directly to a senior Cabinet appointee of the President. Yet, challenges of balancing hierarchies and networks, structure and flexibility, control and collaboration remain stark (Kamark, 2004).

It may well be that a heightened political profile of security and terrorism corresponds to a public demand for action and clarity and, as a result, stronger and more centralized forms of leadership. This point underscores how an evolution or dramatic shift in the mood of the public can shape the organization of government. The heightened security-minded focus on centralization and clarity is accelerating attention and investments made in cyberspace, technology, and internal governance reform, changes that may well bolster the level of seriousness and internal competencies within government devoted to deploying and managing digital technologies (Clifford, 2004; Dutta & McCrohan, 2002).

How and to what ends such deployments occur are dependent on many variables, particularly the views of the citizenry and their elected representatives. Internet use is expected to rise and grow more prevalent, suggesting that more individuals will look to conduct their affairs with their governments online when feasible (Hart-Teeter, 2003). Uncertainty remains, however, as public attitudes are intertwined with service comparisons across online and offline channels and broader socio-economic and political shifts. Privacy of information is a case in point. In North America, prior to 2001, there was often trepidation in the minds of citizens with respect to the government's collecting, sharing, and using personal information, even if better service resulted (Joshi et al., 2002). More recently, governments have been comforted, and perhaps even driven, by a public now rebalancing security and privacy concerns. Yet, despite this rebalancing, and even with broad support for stronger homeland security measures, the American public remains suspicious of government handling of personal information (Hart-Teeter, 2004).

This contrast (openness versus secrecy), a major point of departure between deploying digital technologies as a means of serving citizens and one centered on public safety, brings to light the central and related aspects of transparency and trust as two inter-related and important dimensions of e-government and e-governance.

Transparency and Trust

According to some commentators, we live in the age of transparency (Tapscott & Ticoll, 2003). Although this particular invocation targets private corporations facing heightening investor and public scrutiny, ultimately rendering secrecy and information containment counterproductive, the message and underlying forces driving it also hold much relevance for government. Transparency drives this need for greater openness and responsiveness, as secrecy invites suspicion, resulting in questions, exposure, and increased costs and complexities down the line (Mitchinson & Ratner, 2004).

Governments are not immune to such pressures. From one perspective, e-government has accelerated this emphasis on openness, as governments themselves have moved to provide much more information online, but the Internet has underpinned expanded capacities for neutral observers and vested interests to find and share information, expose secrets and shortcomings, and mobilize public opinion accordingly.

The relationship between trust and transparency is complex and consequential, and it is bound to become more so as online access widens and usage expands. The notion of trust in government and political processes is multifaceted and complex. Parent et al. distinguish between specific and diffuse forms of political trust.

Specific support refers to satisfaction with government outputs and the overall performance of political authorities. Diffuse support refers to the public's attitude toward regime-level political objectives. (Parent et al., 2004, p. 1)

This differentiation underscores the potentially different ways in which citizens may judge precise forms of government action and democratic institutions more generally. Therefore, there may be related differences in how e-government is viewed as a set of customer relationship mechanisms (defined primarily by service delivery and responsiveness) versus how e-governance might come to be viewed (encompassing broader elements of legitimacy and accountability).

In their own discussion of how e-government might contribute to rising trust in the public sector, Tolbert and Mossberger (2003) offer a more encompassing approach bridging, to some degree, these two dimensions. The authors point to potential improvements in both administrative and democratic systems by making government more responsive, transparent, accountable, accessible, responsible, efficient, effective, and participatory. Their findings provide cautious testament to the notion that e-government's degree of online transparency is positively correlated to the level of trust accorded by citizens along some of these dimensions (Parent et al., 2004; Tolbert & Mossberger, 2003). Similarly, some experts see online information reporting as a key (although underutilized) component of performance management and heightening political and managerial accountability to the citizenry (Lee, 2004).

The relationship between homeland security, transparency, and e-government is illustrative. In the United States, despite an expanded realm of powers and secrecy, public opinion would seem to accord dramatically higher levels of confidence in those public organizations pursuing security-related matters (particularly frontline emergency services but also intelligence agencies) than in the federal government generally (Hart-Teeter, 2004). At the same time, widening demands for transparency and openness remain central to such matters, arguably an important factor in shaping the sorts of responses put forth by government[2].

Other areas of public sector operations—procurement and contracting—underscore such trends. With the Internet and increasingly ubiquitous digital technologies, e-government relies on closer forms of collaboration and partnering between private sector specialists and government organizations (Langford & Harrison, 2001). This relational complexity is heightened by a wider focus on openness and a loss of the traditional common ground joining industry and government. This loss may not necessarily be negative as both sectors seek new arrangements to foster more collaborative governance in a much more open manner, with transparency extended to the widest possible range of stakeholders (Allen et al., 2002; Paquet, 1997). In navigating such volatility, an essential element (and often an elusive one) is trust (Lane & Roy, 2000; Lawther, 2002).

Yet this point applies more generally to the broad spectrum of relational governance challenges driving e-government. Trust is centrally positioned at the nexus between the primarily internally driven administrative reforms of e-government's architecture and the related and more externally rooted pressures for e-governance reflected in widening debates on openness and engagement. Thus, the nature of trust is likely to be increasingly tied not only to online performance measures such as information and transactions provided by governments, but also to online process considerations more in line with a broader participatory and multi-stakeholder environment that challenges conventional notions of authority (Northrup & Thorson, 2003).

In such an environment, democratic legitimacy—the importance of maintaining and/or strengthening trust between public sector institutions and citizens—is a central and fluid concern. The notion of citizen engagement, for instance, implies a more meaningful and ongoing democratic role for the public beyond merely electing representatives, and the Internet is a powerful venue for a more widely informed and highly educated citizenry disgruntled with largely representational systems of democratic governance (Palfrey, 2004; Geiselhart, 2004).

Accordingly, a reconsideration of the relative balance between representational and more participative forms of democracy is growing as the Internet's potential to facilitate a broader conversation across all stakeholders and the public at large is also an argument for inclusiveness, as proponents of e-democracy espouse. Conversely, the difficulties in structuring such a conversation and, indeed, questions surrounding whether online exchanges can facilitate meaningful venues for democratic decision-making are real, and they represent critical design issues in terms of making use, or partial use, of cyberspace (Fountain, 2002; Lenihan, 2002a; Norris, 2000; Oliver & Sanders, 2004). A general observation is that the systemic introduction of more digital forms of democracy would constitute a major revolution in the structure and functioning of the public sector apparatus (Fountain, 2002). There is, nonetheless, widening experimentation with democratic reform, much of which involves online capacities (MacIntosh et al., 2002), and while a wholesale redesign of democratic governance seems unlikely in the short term, ongoing mixes of acceptance, resistance, and incremental change have resulted (Allen et al., 2001).

In all aspects of online activity, questions surrounding the level of trust and confidence of citizens in the digital technologies themselves are important (Bryant & Colledge, 2002). Much like online service delivery channels have been slow to evolve in many jurisdictions, it will not be tomorrow when online mechanisms replace current democratic practises. Moreover, as with homeland security, approaches and demands may vary with circumstance, as a strong public appetite for action and clear accountability may, at times, co-exist uneasily with demands for greater participation and power sharing. This latter tension reflects a source of contention at the heart of how democratic government and governance will co-evolve and adapt to the new circumstances of an online and interconnected world.

E-Government and E-Governance in Canada

Canada provides a useful basis for examining e-government. As one of the world's most advanced countries by measures of economic wealth, quality of life, and Internet access and affordability, Canada has been aggressively bolstering its usage of digital technologies in order to realize the promise of e-government.

The impetus for a key component of e-government federally evolved from a broader effort—Connecting Canadians—that was crafted in the mid-1990s and led by the federal Department of Industry. In the Speech from the Throne on October 12, 1999, outlining its objectives and priorities, the Government of Canada stated:

By 2004, our goal is to be known around the world as the government most connected to its citizens:

The Government On-Line Initiative (GOL) was launched to meet this commitment. The goal of GOL is to provide Canadians with electronic access to key federal programs and services. The initiative focuses on grouping or "clustering" online services around citizen's needs and priorities, rather than by government structures. (Coe, 2004, p. 6)

The Government showcases citizen satisfaction surveys, and Canada's reputation internationally has also been bolstered by international observers such as Accenture Consulting that ranked Canada as a global leader—a recognition largely predicated on the Government's main portal (www.gc.ca) that, in the spirit of integrated service delivery, is grouped according to clusters of services and specific client groups[3].

Despite such acclaim, evidence suggests that the changes and investments made to date have been insufficient to overcome the inertia of more traditional and vertical processes of ministerial accountability and silo operations that comprise primarily separate and autonomous political fiefdoms. "Silos continue to reign" (Coe, 2004, p. 18).

Coe's (2004) examination of GOL pilot projects—interdepartmental experiments to integrative services—reveal a widespread lack of shared accountability to facilitate collaboration. Managers are frustrated by tensions between horizontal intent strategically and vertical constraints operationally. In her review of GOL, the Auditor General underscores a similar absence of a coordinated architecture required to balance vision and planning: "With only high-level expected outcomes, there is no clearly defined end state for GOL. The government will have difficulty measuring progress and performance toward 2005 objectives" (Auditor General of Canada, 2003, p. 10). Such findings are indicative of the growing need for more rigorous collaborative mechanisms and performance frameworks to both facilitate shared action and gauge progress, particularly in service delivery agendas that transcend traditional reporting relationships (Public Policy Forum, 2003; Stowers, 2004).

Similar challenges also characterize security efforts. Over the past three years, security has become a high priority with financial investments and organizational reorganizations to improve domestic capacity[4]. In findings remarkably similar to the GOL experience, the Auditor General again concludes that horizontal coordination has been inadequate.

Overall, these gaps and deficiencies point to a requirement to strengthen the management framework of issues that cross agency boundaries, such as information systems, watch lists, and personnel screening. (Auditor General of Canada, 2004, p. 39)

In another example, the Auditor General reports on an effort to create an Integrated National Security Assessment Centre (INSAC) in 2003 to "use intelligence from many sources to produce timely analyses and assessment of threats to Canada" and distribute this information accordingly (Auditor General of Canada, 2004, p. 24). The findings illustrate the difficulties of joint action:

The latter four organizations (Foreign Affairs, Citizenship and Immigration, Solicitor General and Privy Council Office) have not yet provided a representative. Foreign Affairs said that its resources should more properly address the threat to its personnel and assets abroad and that increasingly scarce resources from a "foreign ministry" should not be devoted to matters that are better left to domestic agencies. Immigration told us it supports the concept and attributes its absence to the lack of permanent funding available for that purpose. Solicitor General Canada said that although it has not assigned a specific representative, its officials are fully engaged in all functions and work initiated by the Centre. The Privy Council Office told us that it has no intelligence collection mandate but is actively involved on a daily basis in the processing of information produced by INSAC. (Auditor General of Canada, 2004, ibid.)

The centrality of information sharing and interoperability lies at the heart of GOL and security. Notably, despite the added and significant possibility of invoking national security in the latter case, unlike the former, privacy concerns remain a significant barrier to cross-agency action, although the Auditor General herself remains suspicious that its relevance is not properly understood or defined.

We noted that privacy concerns were often cited as the reasons why agencies could not exchange information. However, officials were not able to show us any legal opinions, specific references to legislation, or judgements as a basis for that position. (Auditor General of Canada, 2004, p. 17)

In a separate, closely related study, the Senate Standing Committee of National Security and Defence conducted a three-year review of security readiness and emergency preparedness, once again noting similar concerns. The Senate report quotes a senior official's assessment of what is required for the newly formed Office of Critical Infrastructure Protection and Emergency Preparedness (OCIPEP) to fulfill its coordination role in responding to a major emergency. "The challenge," he said, "is that this would require an unprecedented level of cooperation inside and outside of government" (Standing Senate Committee, 2004, p. 14).

An important lesson of governance would seem applicable to both GOL and security. In both cases, despite a similar need for horizontal action, capacities for doing are lacking. Moreover, there are important connections between GOL and security. A major component of the former is the secure channel, initially conceived as a core mechanism to conduct transactions with citizens, but now also a central focus of cyber-security. For example, OCIPEP is the government's primary agent in improving cyber-security. Thus, their separate fortunes may also shape their collective and integrative prospects for success.

The responses of the recently reconstituted federal government (under a new Prime Minister) in December 2003, address such dilemmas in a familiar manner—centralized authority within an enlarged political entity and, it is hoped, a clear and decisive mandate to ordain the coordination necessary to improve homeland security. Thus, the earlier attempts to pursue a more collaborative and horizontal approach to security management have been significantly abandoned in favor of a more centralizing approach. Given the disappointing results of GOL to take hold and strengthen government-wide capacities, it is not unreasonable to expect that similar centralizing tendencies may result here as well, particularly as security becomes a common plank of service delivery and homeland safety.

The danger with such an evolution is the disconnect between centralizing the internal architecture for e-government in terms of government-wide capacities for service delivery and homeland security, and the more participative nature of e-governance externally, fueling calls for openness, engagement, and more decentralized and collaborative decision-making models. This cleavage is underscored by widening dissatisfaction with the Canadian Parliamentary model as a whole, driven in large part by the political and managerial dominance of central agencies, and the Prime Minister's Office in particular (Savoie, 1999). Such characterizations are indicative of an operating culture much more axed on top-down communication than consultation.

In response to such a critique, democratic reform proposals offered by the new government have focused predominantly on the role of the legislature—Parliament—in an effort to re-engage elected officials through a variety of measures to lessen the dominance of the Prime Minister's Office. In short, the emphasis is on refurbishing the current representational model in very precise manners in the hopes of reversing its steady decline in the eyes of the citizenry[5].

Yet the widening canvas of e-governance and more participative democratic forms create contradictions in terms of the messages conveyed to citizens. This contradiction stems from the emphasis on citizen engagement as a principle embraced by the government, particularly within the public service. Supported and reinforced by Ministers who routinely convey similar sentiments in public, citizen engagement promises a more direct voice to the public and to key stakeholders in shaping policy decisions and service delivery processes through new and innovative forms of consultation and participation. The Government has staked out cyberspace as one means of pursuing expanded public engagement, stating online that it is committed to finding new and innovative ways to consult with and engage Canadians.[6]

The digital gap between reforming Parliament and engaging Canadians is considerable, as digital technologies (and the Internet specifically) are utterly absent in terms of both usage and debate from Parliamentary chambers, the traditional focal point of open and public deliberation (Lenihan, 2002b). Politicians appear increasingly out of step in this regard, particularly when, unlike their elected masters, public servants have fewer qualms envisioning a very different future (hypothetically, 2013).

Representative democracy in Canada has not been replaced, but it has become more participative. Democracy is no longer just voting every four or five years, but a continuous, engaged, informed and collaborative dialogue involving all players. (E-Government Policy Network, 2004, p. 9)

Presently within the Parliamentary model, the scope of such participation remains a source of tension, one likely to intensify as a key determinant in public trust[7]. Moreover, as Canadians seek more voice, in the absence of clarity on how to do so, the impacts of transparency are nonetheless widely displayed via a relentless series of scandals involving mismanagement or alleged corruption[8]. This more reactive form of transparency provides testament to the view that, while it is arguably unlikely that governments are erring more often at present than in historical terms, their failures are now more likely to be exposed, and to a greater affect. As a result, trust and cynicism are impacted, inversely related in a negative spiral.

Such difficulties suggest that e-government, if unaccompanied by significant efforts at political and institutional reform, may do little more than reinforce the existing tendencies of a particular state system (Karakaya, 2003; Wilson & Welch, 2004). In the case of the Canadian Parliamentary model, the problem is compounded by the tension between these inward, reactionary tendencies of government, on the one hand, and the intensifying outward pressures for greater openness and participation on the other.

Contested Path Ahead

In attempting to summarize the key lessons and expectations that may be derived from the preceding discussion, there are a number of lessons that stand out—lessons that will be influential in shaping the future of e-government and e-governance in Canada and elsewhere. They are as follows:

The rise of online connectedness as a driver of e-government heightens the need for horizontal coordination to transcend internal organizational boundaries, and this point applies to both service delivery and security-related processes.

Such horizontal governance requires both technological and political reforms in order to align performance objectives, decision-making processes, and accountability mechanisms in a suitable manner.

Governance is increasingly becoming more transparent and participative with resulting pressures for democratic reform certain to intensify.

Such pressures may nonetheless encounter resistance within existing political structures and culture.

Public confidence and trust in government are central to shaping e-government and e-governance reforms, representing critical determinants in the ongoing capacity of the public sector to adapt.

As one goes down the list, these points become increasingly more strategic and complex managerially, and with greater consequences democratically. If an incremental path is insufficient, where does one begin to orchestrate more systemic changes required to achieve some of the transformational potential that most all governments have acknowledged as worthy of pursuit?

First, a more holistic reform process requires a broader and more encompassing view of e-government and e-governance in keeping with the definition offered at the outset of this article. The Government of Canada's current difficulties stem largely from subsuming governance as a primarily internal facet of public sector modernization without adequately embracing the interface between internal and external reforms, both administratively and democratically.

Even with respect to present internal governance reforms associated with service delivery improvements, a key inhibitor of performance is misinformation and a lack of public understanding surrounding what the government is attempting to do and how objectives are being pursued. For example, in response to the Auditor General's criticism of GOL's horizontal capacities, the federal government's response is to defensively point to a considerable array of horizontal mechanisms now in place.

The GOL governance structure, which was strengthened in 2002, includes a 15-member deputy minister-level committee and a 16-member assistant deputy minister-level committee that meet at least every six weeks and oversee the work of three subject-matter expert committees on service transformation, information and other policies, and architecture. In addition, three inter-departmental committees focus on the information technology, information management, and service delivery "communities of practise." (Auditor General of Canada, 2003, p. 13)

Such responses may not only be insufficient internally, but also counterproductive externally with respect to the views of the citizenry. This is so since the formal templates of how government functions, as presented to the public, correspond less and less to the more complex and interdependent realities of governing, and of organizing to govern. The public senses this drift, becoming frustrated and cynical at not being genuinely invited and trusted as a stakeholder. The missed opportunity (and the potential source of a further decline in trust) is that a public more knowing and understanding of the challenges faced by governments would likely be more supportive in embracing experimentation, innovation, and systemic change.

This point may well be particularly consequential for citizens—government relations within the context of homeland security, with its added layers of secretive operations often contentiously co-existing with mechanisms of oversight and pressures for greater transparency more generally. In Canada, there has been little effort to engage citizens in discussions about security priorities and means, with the only mechanism for public openness being an inquiry established reactively to address alleged potential mismanagement and shed some light on an otherwise secretive governmental apparatus[9].

Therefore, while e-government may carry some positive potential for greater trust and better accountability, the evidence in Canada suggests that any such benefits are mitigated by a public's rightful sense that it really does not understand how government works until after the fact when judgements are formed within a confrontational culture of political blame and media sound bites. Perhaps more than elsewhere, the centralized and inward Parliamentary system is prone to this danger, reinforcing a "culture of secrecy" that is "indicative of a government leadership which is unsympathetic to the right of access" (Reid, 2004, p. 82).

The other major challenge faced by the Government of Canada extends to all levels of government, as the vision of more seamless forms of governance need not apply exclusively to any one government, but rather to the public sector as a whole. Horizontality, interoperability and online integrative portal capacities are issues that will increasingly drive a wider need for new intergovernmental capacities collectively, encompassing all levels government (Fletcher, 2004; Paquet & Roy, 2004).

In Canada, GOL is envisioned to become intergovernmental, providing citizen-centric service delivery across all levels of government. Yet the structures for doing so are completely absent. Similarly, in terms of domestic security and emergency preparedness, where the stakes are arguably higher, the situation is similar, as a recent Senate report provides an important examination of the extended implications and dangers of stymied federal coordination for the country as a whole. The Committee found major intergovernmental blockages that are particularly harmful to local governments and frontline delivery agents most in need of informational and tangible resources in order to respond to crises of various sorts (Fletcher, 2004; Paquet & Roy, 2004, p. 10).

Whether the public endorses a primarily competitive view of federalism and inter-governmental relations or a more collaborative view, is a critical variable in shaping e-government's future. Some observers suggest that the federal government may well be the beneficiary of a more digital future as citizens maintain their national attachment, facilitated in part by online connectivity, while lessening their tradition-ally strongest ties to provincial governments since these latter identities may erode in visibility and relevance over time (Gibbons, 2004). Some early research in the United States supports this notion, pointing to a relatively higher level of confidence and trust online accorded by citizens to federal and local governments than at the state level (Tolbert & Mossberger, 2003).

Sensing this danger, the provinces may be less willing to seek more integrative governance solutions that erode their presence. Moreover, in comparison to other countries, both federal and unitary, the absence of an intergovernmental dimension to e-government's architecture should be underscored as a key concern and notable handicap for the future of Canada's public sector. Although the current CIO Council (comprised of voluntary participants by senior public managers from federal and provincial governments) could evolve into a collective entity, it is currently not empowered in such a fashion.

At some point, the parameters of Canadian federalism and the processes interlinking all levels of government will need to be significantly rethought from their 19th-century traditions toward the more digital and interdependent era of the present century. Yet that point remains some time in the future, as e-government's current evolution is first and foremost shaped by structures rooted in history.

Conclusion

Federally, and in response to the title of this article, e-government would appear to be mainly about getting "government online," despite an accelerating dissatisfaction with the broader system of democratic governance surrounding it, an untenable situation unlikely to generate any greater trust in government (Paquet, 2004).

Much of what is required to reframe governance has been recognized. Lenihan, for example, points to two over-arching meta-principles that must take hold: collaborative and inclusive governance (Lenihan, 2002a). Hunold (2001) invokes a more deliberative democracy via wider openness and participation across the citizenry, public service, and elected officials. While such fundamentals are a sound beginning, there often remains a gulf separating techno-enthusiasts on the one hand and governance architects on the other. Perhaps in the best performing organizations from any sector today, this disconnect may be less pervasive (Van Grembergen, 2004); however, such a divide certainly characterizes many governments at present, including the Government of Canada.

For e-government and e-governance to co-evolve in a positive manner, the technical design work of deploying technology must become more fully integrated with those overseeing governance design (or in some instances, redesign). An important starting point is fostering stronger and wider deliberative mechanisms from within government in order to acknowledge, be more inclusive of, and benefit from the expanding set of discursive networks outside of government. In this manner, more deliberative and more virtual forms of democracy must become mutually reinforcing. Demographics will make this tie more essential, as the first generations of those not knowing a time without online commercial, familial, and civic engagements will see no valid reason to exempt the political sphere from this reality (Cherny, 2000).

More concretely, within Canada's Parliamentary model, the absence of a publicly recognizable mechanism with organizational and political authority (e.g., a Minister or Central agency) to address the nexus between the internal and technical architecture of online government and the broader political, civic, and participatory contexts of democratic governance, is a major deficiency. An appropriate response may not necessarily be yet another layer of centralization such as the one now in fashion for security, but rather a collaborative mechanism with the means, legitimacy, and flexibility to act innovatively. Major priority areas, such as modernizing service delivery and improving public safety, have exposed the flaws of an inherently vertical and hierarchical system that often implies individual responsibility and accountability with a single Minister in a fashion no longer feasible. Thus, collaborative behaviour, in order to be effective, will rely upon elected officials embracing new mechanisms with shared accountabilities and integrative results (Coe, 2004). Such mechanisms will need to be both conceived and gauged more proactively and transparently than in the past, making use of wider circles of engagement encompassing all relevant stakeholders.

In sum, within the confines of service, security, transparency, and trust, the current struggles of the federal government are likely to be accentuated by the significant investments now being made into the structural and policy directions of the first two components without a corresponding effort to widen the governance canvas in a corresponding and meaningful fashion. The provincial level, as a network of 10 potential laboratories of governance reform that share common Parliamentary traditions may offer more promise in the short term. Many of these governments appear more intent on pursuing wider experimentation democratically and more participative forms of governance that could, in turn, shape e-government's path more positively within their jurisdictions, federally, and for the country as a whole.

References

Allen, B., Juillet, L., Paquet, G., & Roy, J. (2001). E-government in Canada: People, partnerships and prospects. *Gov. Info. Quarterly, 30*(1), 36-47.

Allen et al. (2002). E-governance and the partnership imperative. *Optimum Online, 32*(4), 36-47.

Allen, B., Juillet, L., Paquet, G., & Roy, J. (2005). *E-government and Collaboration: Structural, Accountability and Cultural Reform* (forthcoming, Ideas Group Publishing).

Andal-Ancion, A., Cartwright, P., & Yip, G.S. (2003, Summer). The digital transformation of traditional business. *MIT Sloan Management Review*, 62-74.

Auditor General of Canada (2003). *Information Technology: Government Line*. Ottawa: Office of the Auditor General of Canada.

Auditor General of Canada (2004). *National Security in Canada—The 2001 Anti-terrorism Initiative*. Ottawa: Office of the Auditor General of Canada.

Bertelsmann Foundation (2002). E-government—Connecting efficient administration and responsive democracy. *Postfach*. Retrieved from: www.begix.de

Batini, C., Cappadozzi, E., Mecella, M., & Talamo, M. (2002). Cooperative architectures. In W.J. McIver & A.K. Elmagarmid (Eds.), *Advances in Digital Government—Technology, Human Factors and Policy*. Boston: Kluwer Academic Publishers.

Bryant, A., & Colledge, B. (2002). Trust in electronic commerce business relationships. *Journal of Electronic Commerce Research, 3*(2), 32-39.

Cairncross, F. (2002). *The Company of the Future*. Cambridge: Harvard Business School Press.

Cherny, A. (2000). *The Next Deal—The Future of Public Life in the Information Age*. New York: Basic Books.

Clifford, M. (2004). *Identifying and Exploring Security Essentials*. Upper Saddle River, NJ: Pearson Prentice Hall.

Coe, A. (2004). *Innovation and accountability in 21st century government: Government on-line and network accountability*. [Working paper]. Kennedy School of Government, Harvard University.

Dutta, A., & McCrohan, K. (2002). Management's role in information security in a cyber economy. *California Management Review, 45*(1), 67-87.

E-Government Policy Network, Government of Canada (2004). Transforming government and governance for the 21st century: A conceptual framework. In L. Oliver & L. Sanders (Eds.), *E-Government Reconsidered: Renewal of Governance for the Knowledge Age*. Regina: Canadian Plains Research Center.

Fife, R. (2004). Ottawa plans $500M security fix. *National Post, 22*(04), 1.

Fletcher, P. (2004). Portals and policy: Implications of electronic access to U.S. federal government information and services. In A. Pavlichev & G.D. Garson (Eds.), *Digital Government: Principles and Best Practises*. Hershey, PA: IGP.

Fountain, J.E. (2001). *Building the Virtual State: Information Technology and Institutional Change*. Washington, DC: Brookings Institution Press.

Fountain, J.E. (2002). Electronic government and electronic civics. [forthcoming]. In B. Wellman (Ed.), *The Encyclopaedia of Community*. Sage Publications.

Geiselhart, K. (2004). Digital government and citizen participation internationally. In A. Pavlichev & G.D. Garson (Eds.), *Digital Government: Principles and Best Practises*. Hershey, PA: IGP.

Gibbons, R. (2004). Federalism and the challenge of electronic portals. In L. Oliver & L. Sanders (Eds.), *E-Government Reconsidered: Renewal of Governance for the Knowledge Age*. Regina: Canadian Plains Research Center.

Gronlund, A. (ed.). (2002). *E-Government—Design, Applications and Management*. Hershey, PA: IGP.

Hart-Teeter (2003). *The New e-Government Equation: Ease, Engagement, Privacy and Protection*. Washington, DC: Council for Excellence in Government.

Hart-Teeter (2004). *From the Home Front to the Front Lines: America Speaks Out About Homeland Security*. Washington, DC: Council for Excellence in Government.

Holden, S.H. (2004). *Understanding Electronic Signatures: The Key to e-Government*. Washington, DC: IBM Center for The Business of Government.

Hunold, C. (2001). Corporatism, pluralism, and democracy: Toward a deliberative theory of bureaucratic accountability. *Governance: An International Journal of Policy and Administration, 14*(2), 151-167.

Joshi, J.B.D., Ghafoor, A., & Aref, W.G. (2002). Security and privacy challenges of a digital government. In W.J. McIver & A.K. Elmagarmid (Eds.), *Advances in Digital Government—Technology, Human Factors and Policy*. Boston: Kluwer Academic Publishers.

Kamarck, E.C. (2004). Applying 21st-century government to the challenge of homeland security. In J.M. Kamensky & T. Burlin (Eds.), *Collaboration—Using Networks and*

Partnerships. IBM Center for The Business of Government: Rowman and Littlefield Publishers Inc.

Karakaya, R. (2003). *The use of the Internet for citizen participation: Enhancing democratic local governance?* [Paper] Political Studies Association Annual Conference, University of Leicester.

Lane, G., & Roy, J. (2000). Building partnerships for the digital world. *Lac Carling Government Review, 2*(1), 23-29.

Langford, J., & Harrison, Y. (2001). *Partnering for e-government: Challenges for public administrators.* [Paper]. Institute of Public Administration of Canada Conference, Edmonton. Retrieved from: http://www.ipaciapc.ca/english/menu.htm

Lawther, W. (2002). *Contracting for the 21st Century: A Partnership Model.* Washington: PricewaterhouseCoopers Endowment for The Business of Government.

Lee, M. (2004). *E-reporting: Strengthening Democratic Accountability.* Washington, DC: IBM Center for The Business of Government.

Lenihan, D. (2002a). *E-government, Federalism and Democracy: The New Governance.* Ottawa: Centre for Collaborative Government.

Lenihan, D. (2002b). *E-government: The Message to Politicians.* Ottawa: Centre for Collaborative Government.

MacIntosh, A., Malina, A., & Farrell, S. (2002). Digital democracy through electronic petitioning. In W.J. McIver & A.K. Elmagarmid (Eds.), *Advances in Digital Government—Technology, Human Factors and Policy.* Boston: Kluwer Academic Publishers.

Marche, S., & McNiven, J.D. (2003). E-government and e-governance: The future isn't what it used to be. *Canadian Journal of Administrative Sciences, 20*(1), 74-86.

McIver, W.J. & Elmagarmid, A.K. (eds.). (2002). *Advances in Digital Government—Technology, Human Factors and Policy.* Boston: Kluwer Academic Publishers.

Mitchinson, T., & Ratner, M. (2004). Promoting transparency through the electronic dissemination of information. In L. Oliver & L. Sanders (Eds.), *E-government Reconsidered: Renewal of Governance for the Knowledge Age.* Regina: Canadian Plains Research Center.

Norris, P. (2000). Global governance and cosmopolitan citizens. In J.S. Nye & J.D. Donahue (Eds.), *Governance in a Globalizing World.* Cambridge: Brookings Institution Press.

Northrup, T.A., & Thorson, S.J. (2003). The web of governance and democratic accountability. *Proceedings of the 36th Hawaii International Conference on System Sciences.*

Nugent, J.H., & Raisinghani, M.S. (2002). The information technology and telecommunications security imperative: Important issues and drivers. *Journal of Electronic Commerce Research, 3*(1), 1-14.

Oliver, L., & Sanders, L. (eds.). (2004). *E-government Reconsidered: Renewal of Governance for the Knowledge Age.* Regina: Canadian Plains Research Center.

Palfrey, J.G. (2004). *Submission to the workshop on Internet governance.* International Telecommunications Union. Harvard Law School: Berkman Center for Internet and Society.

Paquet, G. (1997). States, communities and markets: The distributed governance scenario. In T.J. Courchene (Ed.), *The Nation-state in a Global Information Era: Policy Challenges the Bell Canada Papers in Economics and Public Policy, 5,* 25-46. Kingston: John Deutsch Institute for the Study of Economic Policy.

Paquet, G., & Roy, J. (2004). Smarter cities in Canada. *Optimum Online, 33*(1).

Paquet, G. (2004). There is more to governance than public candelabras: E-governance and Canada's public service. In L. Oliver & L. Sanders (Eds.), *E-government Reconsidered: Renewal of Governance for the Knowledge Age.* Regina: Canadian Plains Research Center.

Parent, M., Vandebeek, C.A., & Gemino, A.C. (2004). Building citizen trust through e-government. *Proceedings of 37th Hawaii International Conference on System Sciences.*

Pavlichev, A., & Garson, G.D. (eds.). (2004). *Digital Government: Principles and Best Practises.* Hershey, PA: IGP.

Peristeras, V., Tsekos, T., & Tarabanis, K. (2002). *E-government or e-Governance: Building a Domain Model for the Governance system.* University of Macedonia: United Nations Thessalokiki.

Public Policy Forum (2003). *Clusters and Gateways Survey: Preliminary Results.* Ottawa.

Reid, J. (2004). Holding governments accountable by strengthening access to information laws and information management practises. In L. Oliver & L. Sanders (Eds.), *E-government Reconsidered: Renewal of Governance for the Knowledge Age.* Regina: Canadian Plains Research Center.

Riley, T.B. (2003). *E-government vs. E-governance: Examining the Differences in a Changing Public Sector Climate.* Ottawa: Commonwealth Centre for E-Governance.

Roy, J. (2003, Summer). The relational dynamics of e-governance: A case study of the city of Ottawa. *Public Performance and Management Review, 26,* 1-13.

Savoie, D. (1999). *Governing from the Centre: The Concentration of Power in Canadian Politics.* Toronto: University of Toronto Press.

Standing Senate Committee on National Security and Defence. (2004). *National Emergencies: Canada's Fragile Front Lines.* Ottawa: Parliament of Canada.

Stowers, G.N.L. (2004). *Measuring the performance of e-government.* Washington, D.C.: IBM Center for The Business of Government.

Tapscott, D., & Ticoll, D. (2003). *The Naked Corporation—How the Age of Transparency will Revolutionize Business.* Toronto: Viking Canada.

Tolbert, C., & Mossberger, K. (2003). *The effects of e-government on trust and confidence in government.* [Working Paper]. OH: Kent State University.

Van Grembergen, W. (ed.) (2004). *Strategies for Information Technology Governance.* Hershey, PA: IGP.

Wilson, W. & Welch, E. (2004). Does e-government promote accountability? A comparative analysis of Website openness and government accountability. *Governance: An International Journal of Policy, Administration and Institutions, 17*(2), 275-297.

Endnotes

[1] Among other jurisdictions, the Government of Mexico has recently adopted this definition, although its precise origins are unknown.

[2] Decisions made by governments today that likely would not have been monitored and questioned publicly in the past are now regularly deliberated more openly and politically. For instance, a recent study on the attitudes of Americans on this topic shows majority support for the Patriot Act, but a strong desire to see its performance and suitability publicly debated (Hart-Teeter, 2004).

[3] There are three main sub-selections from the main portal: Canadians, non-Canadians, and businesses, the logic being that the sorts of information and services required by online visitors generally falls into one of these three camps. Accordingly, with just a few clicks, users are more likely able to find the information they seek.

[4] Specifically, in the 2001 Federal Budget, the government allocated $7.7 billion in new funds over five years on a range of initiatives and reforms centred on public security, safety, and anti-terrorism. Following the Auditor General's report, one public opinion poll conducted in April 2004 showed rising support among Canadians for higher spending on anti-terrorism (55% of those surveyed) and military defence (54%) (Fife, 2004).

[5] The thrust to date of the announced reforms mainly envision reduced partisan control within Parliament by empowering members to vote more freely and by extending more power to committees to review legislation proposed by government (introduced in February 2004, there is insufficient experience to gauge any impact on such measures, but the hope is a more discursive and bolstered legislative branch to lessen executive branch dominance, notably that of the office of the Prime Minister).

[6] As one example, a new consultation portal has been established (www. consulting-canadians.gc.ca), suggestive of online citizen engagement, but more a communications tool and clearinghouse to provide information and links to consultations across departments (which vary in online usage).

[7] This point reflects a tension in the current Canadian system as public servants are consulting citizens more regularly (more than 30 such initiatives are listed on the consultation portal in April 2004), mechanisms that are examples of public servants reaching out to the public and inviting input. Many Parliamentarians (i.e., those outside of Cabinet, within the legislative branch) are uneasy about this trend since a strict reading of the machinery of government would indicate only that they have such authority, and public servants are limited to serving Ministers in the executive branch.

[8]   Over the past several years, numerous examples have emerged federally, featuring alleged political and operational mismanagement, including gun control registration, human resource assistance programs, and, most recently, the so-called sponsorship scandal based on government communication spending, primarily in Quebec during the 1990s following the provincial referendum on sovereignty in 1995. The scathing Auditor General's report (completed in November 2003 but released in February 2004) embroiled the new government in controversy ever since, resulting in a formal public inquiry.

[9]   The inquiry is to examine the case of a Canadian citizen deported on suspicions of terrorism from the United States to Syria, where he was interrogated and tortured. The issues of information management (gathering and sharing, both within and between governments) and internal governance may also facilitate a broader consideration of government's expanded roles and responses in homeland security. However, as with most such highly legalistic inquiries, the forum is primarily viewed as a vehicle for exposing error and assigning fault.

[10]   Reporting a wide range of federal (provincial) local barriers to coordinated action, the Senate report states, "It is imperative that federal, provincial and territorial governments act in common cause, and with common urgency in devising strategies and tactics, and allocating resources and training, to ensure optimal responses to major emergences" (Standing Senate Committee, 2004, p. 41).

This work was previously published in International Journal of Electronic Government Research, Vol. 1, Issue 1, edited by P.D. Fletcher & D. Norris, pp. 40-58, copyright 2005 by IGI Publishing, formerly known as Idea Group Publishing (an imprint of IGI Global).

Chapter XV

Generational Differences in IT Use and Political Involvement:
New Directions

Mack C. Shelley, II, Iowa State University, USA

Lisa E. Thrane, Wichita State University, USA

Stuart W. Shulman, University of Pittsburgh, USA

Abstract

A structural equation model analysis of data from a 2003 national random sample survey (n = 478) on information technology (IT) reveals important direct and indirect effects of generational demographic and attitudinal differences on electronic forms of political participation. Younger respondents reported more support for IT and fewer technological disadvantages, compared to older respondents. Younger respondents showed more desire for public IT availability and e-political participation, whereas older respondents preferred traditional electoral involvement. The more educated held more favorable views of IT generally and of public IT access more specifically. Better-educated respondents were more active civically, in both traditional and electronic forms of participation. Supportive technological views led to greater e-political participation and stronger interest in e-elections. Respondents with less concern and fear about IT were more likely to act as digital citizens and were more involved in e-politics and e-elections. Proponents of public IT access were more supportive of e-elections. Our model suggests that e-citizenry will compound existing social divisions as nonelectronic voices are marginalized and electronic voices are amplified.

Generational Differences in Information Technology Use and Political Involvement

Past research has demonstrated that generational differences play an important role in linking information technology (IT) literacy and usage with political outcomes such as partisanship, elections, or public policy decisions (Fox, 2004). Other sociodemographic differences, together with generational effects, define what has become known as the "digital divide" (Castells, 1999; Warschauer, 2003). Attitudes toward the availability and use of IT play an important role in contemporary political theory and outcomes regarding political participation.

Complex contemporary issues regarding full participation by older members of the political community revolve around the rapidly expanding reliance on electronic sources of access that all too frequently are unfamiliar to older adults, for the purpose of commenting on pending government rules and the corresponding increased use of exclusively online "e-rulemaking" by public agencies (e.g., Garson, 2005; Shulman, Thrane, & Shelley, 2005). A related IT research front has emerged regarding the global need to adapt technologies that often have been developed of, by, and for the young to the needs of the elderly (e.g., Jaeger, 2005; Thrane, Shelley, Shulman, Beisser, & Larson, 2005). Making "young technologies" available and functional to older users requires careful attention to cognitive, social, and education differences, as well as to the vastly divergent life histories that separate younger "with it" technology users from their elders. An area of particularly critical current application of research on the generational dimension of the digital divide lies in the need to provide and evaluate functional online information and referral systems for services supporting the elderly—and especially the disabled elderly—that can cut successfully across generationally different modes of seeking and following up on sources of assistance for service delivery (e.g., Auh & Shelley, 2006; Shelley & Auh, 2006). The importance of combined online, telephone, and in-person contacts cutting across generations is driven home by the ongoing multiyear Aging and Disability Resource Center initiative of the U.S. Center for Medicare and Medicaid Services and the Administration on Aging to establish information and referral capability for the elderly and disabled in nearly every state.

In this chapter, we define IT literacy operationally as a self-reported ability to use computer hardware and software for self-expression, to communicate with other individuals and organizations, to locate and process information electronically, and to engage in problem-solving activities. Past research demonstrates that IT literacy is greater among younger members of society, those with higher incomes and more education, those of more advantaged ethnic groups (white non-Hispanic and Asian), and those with IT resources more readily available at home, work, or in readily-accessible public locations such as libraries or other public buildings (Mossberger, Tolbert, & Stansbury, 2003; Norris, 2001; Servon, 2002). A number of studies have identified unequal levels of IT literacy as a significant barrier to equity in citizenship (NRC, 1999; Wilhelm, 2000). Survey data have been useful for fleshing out the characteristics of the population of nonusers of the Internet, as well as particular obstacles and concerns that explain IT nonuse.

This study assesses the impact of generational and socioeconomic status differences on IT literacy and political participation. It argues that cohort differences have a direct influence on traditional and electronic forms of political engagement, but also suggests that interest in and support for technology are key factors in shaping notions of digital citizenry. In addition, this research evaluates whether e-political participation occurs at the expense of more traditional forms of electoral involvement.

Literature Review

Studies consistently show that age, race, language, and disabilities are significant predictors shaping IT literacy, even when controlling for socioeconomic status (Cooper, 2000; Goslee, 1998; Novak & Hoffman, 1998). Income and education increase the likelihood of access to and use of computers and the Internet (NTIA, 2000, 2002; UCLA, 2000; Wilhelm, 2000) as well as access to broadband (NTIA, 2004). The purchase of a home computer, or general access to and availability of computers, is widely considered to be dependent on income. Some scholars (e.g., Compaine, 2001), however, in situating the rollout of computers and the Internet historically, have concluded that access to computers and connectivity to the Internet in fact is diffusing at an unprecedented rate compared to other technologies such as television, radio, and electricity.

In a study of residents of Los Angeles, California, age had no effect on the centrality of the Internet to everyday life; however, older respondents had fewer IT skills than their younger counterparts (Loges & Jung, 2001). Age seems to become a barrier to Internet use among those over 65 years in age (Lenhart, Rainie, Fox, Horrigan, & Spooner, 2000). Concerns about privacy may be an important consideration for elders' use of IT (Dennis, 2001; Lenhart et al., 2000). To this end, Loges and Jung (2001) recommend that Internet training should put seniors at ease by addressing these privacy concerns.

Compared to their older counterparts, citizens 30 years of age and younger are more likely to use the Internet as a news source on a weekly basis. Age, sex, education, size of locality, and e-information collection have been shown to be significant predictors of political involvement (Pew Research Center for the People and the Press, 2000). Shah and colleagues (Shah, McLeod, & Yoon, 2001) found that reliance on the Internet for information had a positive effect on "Generation X"ers' civic participation. The Internet may encourage civic and political participation while bolstering both off-line and online communication (Katz et al., 2001) and strengthening community-level participation (Alexander, 1999; Brants, Huizenga, & Van Meerten, 1996). Research findings suggest that traditional political participation is reinforced by e-activities (Weber, Loumakis, & Bergman, 2003). In turn, the Internet may lead users to expand their political knowledge (Horrigan, Garrett, & Resnick, 2004).

Compared to nonusers, Internet users are more likely to use other kinds of technology, including cell phones, as well as print and broadcast media (Lenhart, Horrigan, Rainie, Allen, Boyce, Madden, et al., 2003); others suggest that use of the Internet and other technologies is mutually reinforcing (Katz, Rice, & Aspden, 2001). Among Midwesterners, the desire for computing skill promoted positive attitudes toward e-government (Shelley, Thrane, Shulman, Lang, Beisser, Larson, et al., 2004). Attitudes toward IT and desire to enhance computer skills may compound the impact of sociodemographic constructs, intervening between personal or group characteristics and e-political participation.

Theory

Technological literacy, almost by its very definition, evokes images of generational differences in orientations to politics and of age-related variation in levels of political interest and political involvement, ranging from simply gathering information passively to voting actively in elections at all levels. The theoretical structure undergirding our study is based on well-established past research linking generation gaps to political outcomes. Our theoretical approach is predicated on the notion of a younger, "with it" cyber-literate generation living a vastly different political reality than an older generation for which the use of Internet technology is somewhat episodic and for whom the very thought of making serious use of IT is filtered through and sometimes blocked by feelings of technophobia or IT inadequacy. College, high school, and even grade school students who can program and Websurf circles around their parents provide a stereotype that all too often reflects reality.

Our theoretical base informing this analysis is the extensive literature of political science, political psychology, and political sociology addressing the relationships between generations and politics (e.g., Abramson, 1989; Greenstein, 1969; Jennings & Niemi, 1974, 1981). More specifically, our models are informed by, and reflect, generational differences in voting behavior elucidated by Miller and Shanks' (1996) multistage generational persistence model of societal change (Kiesler, Morgan, & Oppenheimer, 1981; Sears, 1981). Miller and Shanks (1996) postulate that:

The voter sentiments involved in a series of taxpayer revolts, the drive for term limits, or the 1994 Republican conception of a revolutionary reduction in the role of the federal government may be only the most recent manifestation of a general rejection of partisan politics by young, newly eligible voters that began in the 1970s. (p. 23)

Generational explanations, broadly speaking, capitalize on the inevitability of actuarial tables, which guarantee replacement of older political generations by younger ones and the ultimate dominance of the ideas that gain greatest credence among the survivors within the electorate. More specifically, Miller and Shanks argue, reduced participation in U.S. electoral politics was a consequence of post-1964 generations "that were dramatically less engaged by, and less likely to participate in, national politics than were their predecessors at the same stages of their adult lives" (p. 41). Although life-cycle effects lead the electoral participation rates of a given generational cohort to increase, as the cohort ages over time, from the Miller and Shanks perspective, trends from the 1970s through the early 1990s toward lower voting turnout combined with plunging interest and trust in government and politics are traceable to the replacement of habitual older voters by more heavily nonvoting and politically disinterested younger cohorts, particularly since 1972. Period effects also played a leading role in these generational vicissitudes, particularly the rising cynicism regarding government and politics highlighted by war, political assassinations, civil rights, the making of a counterculture, and Watergate-era political crime, cover-up, and presidential resignation.

The three fundamental tenets of the Miller and Shanks (1996) approach are equally relevant to the present investigation:

(1) Younger cohorts are particularly vulnerable to influence by historical events in their political environment; (2) older cohorts may entertain a 'lifelong openness to change,' but, in fact, reveal great stability in the persistence of earlier orientations; and (3) even in the face of large historical events, long-term societal change may occur largely as a consequence of generational replacement. (pp. 43-44)

In addition, social connectedness, otherwise expressed as social cooperation, community integration, or social involvement (e.g., Knack, 1992; Teixeira, 1987), plays an important role both in Miller and Shanks' study and in our investigation of generational differences associated with the virtual societal linkages that characterize contemporary IT literacy. However, unlike Miller and Shanks' reliance on bloc recursive models, in which a single equation is enhanced by successive addition of new sets of predictor variables (Agresti & Finlay, 1997), we employ structural equation modeling (SEM), which is appropriate when causal interpretations are desired measuring both the direct and indirect effects of exogenous (independent) variables (typically, demographic variables) on endogenous (dependent, often behavioral outcomes) variables and the effects of some endogenous variables on other endogenous variables (Bollen, 1989; Bollen & Long, 1993; Jöreskog & Sörbom, 1996a, 1996b). We also conceptualize the role of education differently from Miller and Shanks (p. 56), who focus on the profound increases in voting participation that are associated with greater educational attainment offsetting overall declines in voter turnout in more recent electoral cohorts.

Methods

Sample

The national sampling frame consisted of phone numbers appearing in telephone directory listings, which represented three regions of the country. Adults (age 18 and above) living in Colorado, Iowa, and Pennsylvania were eligible for participation. These states were chosen to provide data from a state (Colorado) with a substantial minority population and Rocky Mountain political culture that generally is resistant to liberal positive governmental "intrusion," a state (Pennsylvania) with an older and more established political culture generally supportive of a "big government" role and of political action by labor unions and other organized popular interests, and a state (Iowa) with a characteristically Midwestern streak of independence and an economy in transition from agriculture to postindustrial service sector dominance. All three states are politically competitive and, among survey researchers, have reputations for relative openness to telephone interviews. Respondents ($n = 478$ completed interviews, of which 150 were from Pennsylvania, 157 from Colorado, and 171 from Iowa) were interviewed in 2003 using computer-assisted telephone interviewing methodology. Reported sample percentages are statistically valid within ±4.5% at the 95% confidence level over all three states. For individual states, the 95% confidence intervals are ±7.8% for Colorado, ±7.5% for Iowa, and ±8.0% for Pennsylvania. Standard random digit dialing protocols were employed and screening calls were used to locate a random sample of adults in each of the three states. Businesses, group quarters, teen-lines, vacation homes, numbers with an undetermined eligibility status, and nonworking numbers were eliminated from the sample. In addition, the sample was weighted prior to data analysis by age, sex, and geography, to ensure representativeness both within and across states (Larson, Anderson, & Anderson, 2003).

Respondent demographics generally reflect the characteristics of the sampling frame. Women and men were nearly equally represented (52% and 48%, respectively). Nearly nine in every ten were White (89%), with other racial/ethnic origins including Black (5%), Hispanic (4%), American Indian/Alaskan Native (1%), and Asian or Pacific Islander (1%). The age breakdown was 18-30 years (23%), 31-50 years (42%), 51-70 years (22%), and 70+ years (13%). On average, respondents were 46 years old. Five percent of respondents reported not completing high school, 24% had achieved a high school degree, 8% had a technical or vocational certificate, 24% had some college but without degree completion, 24% had a 4-year degree, and 15% had a graduate degree. Nearly two-thirds were married or living as married (59%), and 23% had never been married. Eight percent were divorced, 9% widowed, and 1% separated. Nearly a quarter of respondents lived in a rural area (23%); another 18% residing in a town of less than 10,000; 22% in a town of 10,000-50,000; 11% in a city of 50,000-100,000; and 26% in a city of 100,000 or more. The overall response rate was 31.4%, ranging from 37.4% in Iowa to 26.7% in Pennsylvania.

Measures

The following variables were employed in statistical analysis. Response categories for **age** were 1 = "18-37 years," 2 = "38-50 years," 3 = "51-64 years," and 4 = "65+years." **Education** was treated as a continuous variable, with response categories of 1 = "non-completion of high school," 2 = "high school diploma," 3 = "trade school," 4 = "some college," 5 = "undergraduate degree," and 6 = "graduate or professional degree." Higher values reflect increased levels of education; the mean is 3.81.

Using Statistical Package fo the Social Sciences software, we performed principal components factor extraction, with varimax rotation using Kaiser normalization, on the values of responses to the seven items measuring attitudes toward technology. This resulted in two factor-derived scales: the advantages of IT, and the disadvantages of IT (Table 1). **IT Advantages** is a scale comprised of three items (with factor loadings given in parentheses, denoting the correlation between each item and the factor with which it is associated): "The Internet is a good source of information about state, national and world news." (.76); "Using email would be a good way for people to contact their public officials." (.72); and "I enjoy learning how to use new technological devices." (.65). Individual item response categories range from 1 = "strongly disagree" to 4 = "strongly agree." Higher values of the scale indicate more support for IT. **IT Disadvantages** is a four-item scale: "I am concerned that personal information stored in computer systems might not be kept confidential." (.73); "Our society is becoming too dependent on computers." (.71);

Table 1. Factor solution for attitudes toward technology (Varimax rotation) (n=478)

	Factor Solution	
Item	IT Advantages	IT Disadvantages
Enjoy using new technology	.65	
Internet is a good source of information	.76	
E-mail is a good way to contact public officials	.72	
Difficult to keep up with technology		.59
Society is too dependent on computers		.71
Personal information stored in computers might not be kept confidential		.73
Information on the Internet is not true		.48

Note. Absolute values less than .40 are omitted to ease interpretability

"It is difficult for me to keep up with the changes in technology." (.59); and "A lot of the information that appears on the Internet is not true." (.48). Individual item response categories ranged from 1 = "strongly agree" to 4 = "strongly disagree." Lower values of this scale reflect a distrust of IT.

Two factor scales were extracted from the eight political participation items (Table 2). The **traditional electoral participation** scale was constructed from three items. The largest factor loadings (correlations with the relevant factor) were for "How often do you vote in elections that involve only local issues, and candidates for local offices, such as mayor, city council, or school board?" (.91) and "How often do you vote in elections that involve candidates for state and national offices, such as president, governor, senators or representatives?" (.90). Individual item response categories ranged from 1 = "never" to 5 = "always." The third item, "People can be involved in the political process in many ways, such as keeping informed about issues, writing letters, and attending meetings, as well as campaigning or voting," had a less robust factor loading (.64). Individual item response categories ranged from 1 = "not at all" to 5 = "a great deal." Higher scale values reflect more involvement in traditional political participation. The **e-political participation** scale was constructed of five items, with "Have you ever used the Internet to get information about political issues, current affairs, or elected officials?" (.85), "Have you ever used the Internet to get news?" (.75), and "Have you ever used the Internet to get information about the views or background of a candidate for political office?" (.67) having the largest factor loadings. Measures of more intense participatory commitment had lower factor loadings: "Have you ever responded to an email or Internet petition or given your opinion in an on-line political discussion?" (.58) and "Have you ever used the Internet or email to contact elected or appointed public officials?"

Table 2. Factor solution for political participation (Varimax rotation) (n = 478)

Item	Factor Solution	
	Traditional Electoral Participation	E-political Participation
How often vote in local elections	.91	
How often vote in state/national elections	.90	
Involvement in political process	.64	
E-contact with appointed public officials		.56
Used Internet for political information		.85
E-information about political candidate		.67
Used Internet to get news		.75
Responded to Internet petition		.58

Note. Absolute values less than .40 are omitted to ease interpretability.

(.56). Individual response categories were 0 = "no" and 1 = "yes." Higher scale values indicate more involvement in e-politics. Missing values were not replaced for these items. For the e-political participation measure, we used the square root transformation to induce normality. Unless otherwise indicated, all factor scores were obtained by principal components extraction and varimax rotation, with the Anderson-Rubin (1956) procedure used to save the resulting factors as uncorrelated standard normal composite variables with mean 0 and standard deviation 1. Unless otherwise indicated, missing values were replaced through mean substitution.

Public IT access was formed as the mean of two items: (1) "Computers should be available to the general public in places like public libraries, so that people who cannot afford to buy a computer can use one if they want to," and (2) "Instruction and workshops on how to use the Internet should be available to the general public in places like public libraries at no charge." Individual response categories ranged from 1 = "strongly disagree" to 4 = "strongly agree." Higher values of this construct indicate respondents' greater support for public IT access and instruction. The **e-elections** construct measures interest in having elections held on the Internet: "I think someday elections should be held on the Internet." Individual item response categories ranged from 1 = "strongly disagree" to 4 = "strongly agree." Higher values indicate more desire for e-electoral participation. To induce normality, a square root transformation was applied to both measures.

Research Questions

We used these variables to answer the following research questions:

1. How are demographic traits (e.g., age and education) and attitudes regarding traditional political participation, e-political participation, IT advantages, IT disadvantages, public IT access, and e-elections interrelated?
2. To what extent can the outcomes of support for traditional political participation, e-political participation, and e-elections be causally related to age, education, and attitudes regarding IT advantages, IT disadvantages, and public IT access?
3. What is the relative magnitude of direct and indirect components of the causal links among these variables?
4. How well do these results conform to the generational interpretation of differences in levels of use and support for IT?

Results

Correlations

Pearson product-moment correlations among the variables examined in this study, together with descriptive statistics, are presented in Table 3. In regard to the exogenous (independent) variables, as age increased, education declined ($r = -.27$). The pattern of correlations suggests that the exogenous variables were meaningful predictors of the measured outcomes. Younger respondents reported more IT advantages ($r = -.34$) and fewer technological disadvantages ($r = -.34$). Younger people also were more likely to suggest that IT should be made available to the public ($r = -.31$). On the other hand, older people engaged in traditional electoral participation more often than did their younger counterparts ($r = .36$), but were less inclined to engage in e-politics ($r = -.42$) or to support e-elections ($r = -.15$). Education had a positive relationship with IT advantages ($r = .28$) and IT disadvantages ($r = .17$). Education also increased support for public IT access ($r = .24$) and for both traditional political engagement ($r = .15$) and e-political participation ($r = .41$).

Those who saw more advantages to technology had more positive attitudes toward public access to IT ($r = .26$). Support for IT had a positive association with e-political participation ($r = .40$) and e-elections ($r = .23$). The desire for public IT access declined as the disadvantages became more pronounced ($r = .12$). Those who saw

Table 3. Correlation matrix (n = 468)

	1	2	3	4	5	6	7	8
1 Age	--							
2 Education	-.27**	--						
3 IT advantages (factor score)	-.34**	.28**	--					
4 IT disadvantages (factor score)	-.34**	.17**	-.00	--				
5 Public IT access	-.31**	.24**	.26**	.12**	--			
6 Traditional electoral participation (factor score)	.36**	.15**	-.01	-.14**	-.01	--		
7 E-political participation (factor score)	-.42**	.41**	.40**	.28**	.20**	-.04	--	
8 E-elections	-.15**	.06	.23**	.21**	.19**	-.12*	.18**	--
Mean	2.13	3.81	.00	.00	3.29	.00	1.37	1.75
Standard Deviation	1.11	1.53	1.00	1.00	.53	1.00	.36	.22

* $p < .05$; ** $p < .01$.

more IT disadvantages were more likely to favor traditional forms of politics (r = -.14). Perceiving fewer IT disadvantages was associated with higher levels of support for e-political participation (r = .28) and e-elections (r = .21). Favoring pubic IT access increased support for e-politics (r = .20) and e-elections (r = .19). As traditional electoral involvement increased, support for e-elections declined (r = -.12). E-politics and e-elections were positively correlated (r = .18).

Structural Equation Model

Our path analysis structural equation model, estimated with LISREL 8.50 statistical software using the maximum likelihood procedure, fit the data well (Figure 1). The chi-square lack-of-fit test was nonsignificant (χ^2 = 11.86; df = 10; p = .31). The goodness of fit index (GFI) was .99, and the adjusted goodness of fit index (AGFI) was .98, while the normed fit index (NFI) was .98 (Bentler & Bonett, 1980); values of each of these measures closer to 1.00 indicate a better fit of the model to the data. The values of the root mean square error of approximation (RMSEA = .02) and Akaike information criterion (AIC = 63.7) (Akaike, 1987) also confirm that the reduced model accurately reproduces the relationships among the variables contained in the model. With 18 cases per parameter, the estimates meet the usual criteria for being stable and reliable (Bollen, 1989). Direct effects are displayed in Figure 1 by arrows that go directly from a predictor variable on the left to a dependent variable to its right, without passing through any other variable in between. In contrast, indirect effects are relationships between a left-hand-side predictor variable and a right-hand-side dependent variable that are mediated by passing through one or more other variables in between. Cross-multiplying the regression coefficients for any combination of paths that connects a predictor variable on the left with a dependent variable on the right, and then summing these results, determines the magnitude of indirect effects. The total effect of a predictor variable on a dependent variable is the sum of its direct and indirect effects.

There are statistically significant direct effects from age and education to dimensions of attitudes toward technology and political interest. As age declined, respondents reported more support for IT (β = -.33) and fewer technological disadvantages (β = -.34). Younger persons showed more desire for public IT availability (β = -.26) and e-political participation (β = -.20). However, older-aged respondents had a pronounced preference for traditional electoral involvement (β = .43). Those with higher levels of education held more favorable views toward IT (β = .22) and positive attitudes toward public IT access (β = .17). In addition, better-educated respondents were more active civically in both traditional (β = .26) and electronic forms of participation (β = .25).

Those who had a positive attitude toward IT were aware of its less valuable dimensions (β = -.15). Direct effects also were found between the attitudes toward

Figure 1. Reduced model

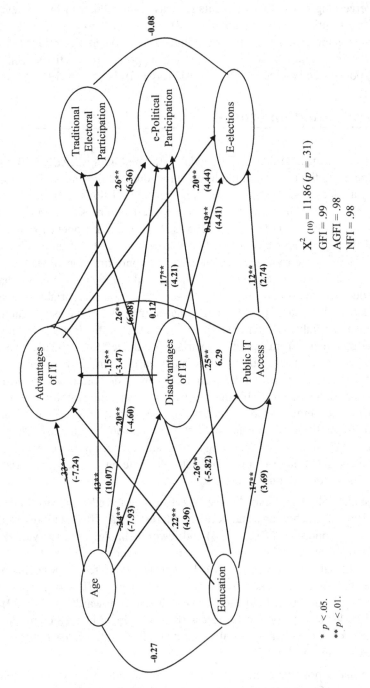

technology factors and citizenship activities. A positive attitude toward technology led to greater involvement in e-political participation (ß = .26) and an interest in e-elections (ß = .20). Individuals with less concern and fear about IT were more supportive of digital citizenship. They were more involved in e-politics (ß = .17) and more likely to be proponents of e-elections (ß = .19). Advocates of public IT access were more interested in e-electoral participation (ß = .12).

The path model displayed in Figure 1 demonstrates how some predictors may have an intervening effect on the outcome measure; in general, however, these indirect effects had minimal influence. Total effects are decomposed into direct and indirect effects in Table 4. Age has an indirect positive effect on IT advantages. Younger persons saw fewer IT disadvantages, while those who held positive views of IT were also capable of seeing its detrimental influences. This indirect effect (.05) accounted for 13% of the total effect. A statistically significant indirect effect was found between age and e-political participation; the direct effect accounted for 61% of the total effect (-.20). For the most part, the effect of age on e-politics was mediated through IT advantages. As age increased, IT advantages declined, while IT advantages had a positive impact on e-political participation. The indirect effect that passed through both the negative and positive aspects of IT played a less prominent role. In addition, education also indirectly increased support for e-politics; this indirect effect (.06) accounted for 19% of the total effect. Higher levels of education led to stronger support for IT, which in turn led to a more positive attitude toward e-politics. Age decreased support for e-elections through several channels (-.16) (i.e., IT advantages, IT disadvantages, and public IT access); the effects were strongest through IT advantages and disadvantages. Education also had an indirect impact (.06) on e-elections through public IT access and IT advantages, but more so through the latter construct.

Conclusion

Generational differences are mirrored in orientations to technology and voting patterns, with younger cohorts favoring cyber involvement while older citizens prefer more traditional forms of citizenship. Successively older cohorts are increasingly likely to hold pessimistic attitudes about IT, which short-circuits their participation and interest in e-politics. In addition, older respondents held less favorable attitudes toward IT access than did their younger counterparts. It may be that older respondents see fewer IT benefits in their own lives, and they may speculate therefore that other citizens are better off without technology as well. Opting for digital citizenship decreases respondents' engagement in voting and the political process. There may be a trade-off, as younger people exchange community involvement for e-citizenry and invest less in their communities as a result.

Table 4. Decomposition of total effects for reduced model

Predictor Variable		Dependent Variable	Total Effect	Direct Effect	Indirect Effect	Standard Error	t-statistic	Direct Effect as % of Total Effect
Age	⇒	IT advantages	-.38	-.33	.05	.04	-7.24**	87%
Education	⇒	IT advantages	.22	.22		.03	4.96**	100%
Age	⇒	IT disadvantages	-.34	-.34		.04	-7.93**	100%
Age	⇒	Public IT access	-.26	-.26		.02	-5.82**	100%
Education	⇒	Public IT access	.17	.17		.02	3.69**	100%
IT disadvantages	⇒	IT advantages	-.15	-.15		.04	-3.47**	100%
Age	⇒	Electoral participation	.43	.43		.04	10.07**	100%
Education	⇒	Electoral participation	.26	.26		.03	6.08**	100%
Age	⇒	E-politics	-.33	-.20	-.13	.01	-4.60**	61%
Education	⇒	E-politics	.31	.25	.06	.01	6.29**	81%
IT advantages	⇒	E-politics	.26	.26		.01	6.36**	100%
IT advantages	⇒	E-elections	.20	.20		.01	4.44**	100%
IT disadvantages	⇒	E-politics	.21	.17	-.04	.01	4.21**	81%
IT disadvantages	⇒	E-elections	.22	.19	-.03	.01	4.41**	86%
Public IT access	⇒	E-elections	.12	.12		.02	2.74**	100%
Age	⇒	E-elections	-.16		-.16	.00	-6.34**	0%
Education	⇒	E-elections	.06		.06	.00	4.17**	0%

Total Effect = Direct Effect + Indirect Effect.

* p ≤ .05 (i.e., |t-value| ≥ 1.96); ** p ≤ .01 (i.e., |t-value| ≥ 2.56).

Not surprisingly, education promotes IT literacy and extrinsic efficacy. Greater educational attainment has the net effect of stimulating support for technology and viewing public computer availability and Internet instruction favorably. Citizens' acquisition of technological skills is consequential for the educated, which in turn leads respondents to endorse Internet-based elections. Education has a direct impact on citizens' empowerment and voice in technological and traditional electoral participation and an indirect influence through IT benefits.

Older citizens and the less educated may face unique challenges that influence their desire to become fluent with IT. The process of becoming a digital citizen is influenced by technological attitudes that may widen the digital gap. By permitting some citizens to conduct their routine business with the government more easily, IT appears to be widening the gap between the IT literate and those without basic navigational skills. As society becomes increasingly dependent on e-government, social barriers will be compounded if nonelectronic voices are marginalized from political participation.

These findings provide evidence supporting the tenets of the Miller and Shanks (1996) thesis regarding age and political activity. The positive direct effect of age on electoral participation denotes that older respondents were more likely to say they engage in traditional forms of politics and government. This relationship is enhanced by the negative direct effect between age and electronic forms of political participation; younger respondents clearly prefer this more contemporary and innovative mode of engagement vs. the preference among their elders for more traditional patterns of political involvement. Although the effect is entirely indirect, the negative relationship between age and e-elections similarly demonstrates the positive valence for newer electoral cohorts of "with it" modes of casting votes that older cohorts may find to be inappropriate, insecure, or simply too new and untested.

It is unknown at this time if Miller and Shanks' previous findings are replicable. We believe that our extension of the Miller and Shanks model works better as an explanatory mechanism than as a tool for prediction. The explanatory nature of our findings is inherent both in limitations of the data and in the bounded rationality that is imposed by the lack of specific research-based knowledge about which variables determine outcomes in the rapidly-evolving "digital divide" arena. It is simply too early to have a clear idea about what determines individual or group cyberpolitical outcomes.

This study is limited in that it is cross-sectional, although it does provide evidence of longer-term trends. Care must be taken in drawing conclusions about the processes at work because the data do not allow clear evaluation of these mechanisms over time. The study's results are based on data collected in three states, and may not be generalizable to all regions in the U.S. Although the model may fit well and be defensible theoretically, it does not imply causality. Nonetheless, this study suggests that e-government magnifies social divisions, as age dictates IT involvement and empowers younger IT-savvy citizens to shape contemporary and future policy. Future research may do well to investigate whether the evident effect of age on preferences for e-government will continue as cohorts age in place within the electorate. Life cycle patterns and the impacts of dramatic events, such as political bombshells or key technological innovations, certainly are expected to be important, and efforts to tease out the differential effects of age, period, and cohort should continue to provide a fertile source of future research as well as exciting opportunities to enhance knowledge in this rapidly-evolving aspect of modern governance. Of particular relevance for the future research agenda is whether the digital divide will persist at about its current level, become more severe, or be reduced. In any event, it is evident that among the major driving forces influencing the consequences of the digital divide are generational and other societal differences that separate the electorate into technological haves and have-nots.

To the extent that IT literacy affects political participation, it is important to ascertain how meaningful that difference might be. Neither our findings nor other comparable research provides a direct answer yet to whether a higher level of IT literacy increases overall political participation or shifts the forms or quality of participation. In particular, it is crucial to understand to what extent, if at all, IT literacy affects the important dimensions of voting. It is unclear whether IT literacy benefits Republicans, Democrats, third parties, or independent candidates. It also is unclear whether IT literacy raises voting participation overall or in more specific ways; for example, in national rather than state or local elections, or in elections with high-salience, hot-button issues rather than when only more mundane concerns are at issue.

Ultimately, a number of policy considerations are connected to what we know now, and what we will learn, about the societal and political impacts of IT literacy. Whether IT literacy will—or should—be encouraged will depend in very large part on which political interests are perceived to benefit from expanded technological literacy and who is in power, as well as the limited budgets and bounded rationality available to policymakers. Even if a clear consensus emerges among political elites to pursue policies that encourage substantially expanded IT literacy, there is no certainty that society will respond quickly, positively, or strongly to such initiatives. Engineering societal change is risky business, all the more so when generational differences in preexisting levels of IT literacy mean that the targeted audience will be operating from multiple perspectives and with vastly different receptiveness. It will require a richly textured implementation to make such a policy innovation effective and lasting. The challenges of achieving a democracy of the Internet are all the more evident in emerging areas including service delivery for the aging and disabled and the processes of electronic commenting and e-rulemaking.

Acknowledgment

This research was made possible with a grant (EIA-0113718) from the National Science Foundation. Any opinions, findings, conclusions, or recommendations expressed in this material are those of the authors and do not necessarily reflect those of the National Science Foundation. This manuscript is based on papers prepared for presentation at the dg.o 2004 conference (May 24-26, 2004) and the 2004 Annual Meeting of the American Political Science Association (September 2-5, 2004). Additional support was provided by the Center for Medicare and Medicaid Services Grant #11-C-91931/7-01 and Administration on Aging Grant #90AM2821 for the Aging and Disability Resource Center, the evaluation of which was made possible thanks to the expert efforts of Dr. Seongyeon Auh, Postdoctoral Research Associate in the Research Institute for Studies in Education (RISE) at Iowa State University, Minsun Lee, RISE Graduate Research Assistant, and Mary Anderson and Mary Ann Young, Iowa Department of Elder Affairs.

References

Abramson, P.R. (1989). Generations and political change in the United States. *Research in Political Sociology, 4,* 235-280.

Agresti, A., & Finlay, B. (1997). *Statistical methods for the social sciences* (3rd ed.). Upper Saddle River, NJ: Prentice-Hall.

Akaike, H. (1987). Factor analysis and AIC. *Psychometrika, 52,* 317-332.

Alexander, J. (1999). Networked communities: Citizen governance in the information age. In G. Moore, J. Whitt, N. Kleniewski, & G. Rabrenovic (Eds.), *Research in politics and society* (pp. 271-289). Stamford, CT: JAI.

Auh, S., & Shelley, M.C., II. (2006, April). *Iowans' needs assessment for the Iowa Aging and Disability Resource Center: The Iowa family survey report* (Report to the Iowa Department of Elder Affairs and the Centers for Medicare and Medicaid Services). Ames, IA: Research Institute for Studies in Education.

Bentler, P.M., & Bonett, D.G. (1980). Significance tests and goodness of fit in the analysis of covariance structures. *Psychological Bulletin, 88,* 588-606.

Bollen, K.A. 1989. *Structural equations with latent variables.* New York: Wiley.

Bollen, K.A., & Long, J.S. (Eds.). (1993). *Testing structural equation models.* Newbury Park, CA: Sage.

Brants, K., Huizenga, M., & Van Meerten, R. (1996). The new canals of Amsterdam: An exercise in local electronic democracy. *Media, Culture, & Society, 18,* 233-247.

Castells, M. (1999). The informational city is a dual city: Can it be reversed? In D.A. Schön, B. Sanyal, & W.J. Mitchell (Eds.), *High technology and low-income communities* (pp. 24-42). Cambridge, MA: MIT Press.

Compaine, B. (2001). Declare the war won. In B.M. Compaine (Ed.), *The digital divide: Facing a crisis or creating a myth* (pp. 315-335). Cambridge, MA: MIT Press.

Cooper, M.N. (2000). *Disconnected, disadvantaged, and disenfranchised: Explorations in the digital divide*. Retrieved on December 15, 2000, from http://www.consumersunion. org/pdf/disconnect.pdf

Dennis, E.E. (2001). Older Americans and the digital revolution. In L.K. Grossman & N.N. Minow (Eds.), *A digital gift to the nation: Fulfilling the promise of the digital and Internet age* (pp. 175-182). New York: Century Foundation Press.

Fox, S. (2004). *Older Americans and the Internet*. Retrieved on June 8, 2005, from http:// www.pewinternet.org/pdfs/PIP_Seniors_Online_2004.pdf

Garson, G.D. (Ed.). (2005). *Handbook of public information systems* (2nd ed). New York: Marcel Dekker.

Goslee, S. (1998). *Losing ground bit by bit: Low-income communities in the information age*. Retrieved on December 15, 2000, from http://www.benton.org/Library/Low-Income/home.html

Greenstein, F.I. (1969). *Children and politics* (rev. ed.). New Haven, CT: Yale University Press.

Horrigan, J., Garrett, K., & Resnick, P. (2004, October 27). *The Internet and democratic debate*. Retrieved September 6, 2007, from http://www.pewinternet.org

Jaeger, B. (Ed.). (2005). *Young technologies in old hands: An international view on senior citizens' utilization of ict*. Copenhagen, Denmark: DJØF.

Jennings, M.K., & Niemi, R.G. (1974). *The political character of adolescence: The influence of families and schools*. Princeton, NJ: Princeton University Press.

Jennings, M.K., & Niemi, R.G. (1981). *Generations and politics*. Princeton, NJ: Princeton University Press.

Jöreskog, K.G., & Sörbom, D. (1996a). *LISREL 8: User's reference guide*. Chicago: Scientific Software International.

Jöreskog, K.G., & Sörbom, D. (1996b). *LISREL 8: Structural equation modeling with the SIMPLIS command language*. Chicago: Scientific Software International.

Katz, J., Rice, R., & Aspden, P. (2001). The Internet, 1995-2000: Access, civic involvement, and social interaction. *American Behavioral Scientist, 45*(3), 405-419.

Kiesler, S.B., Morgan, J.N., & Oppenheimer, V.K. (Eds.). (1981). *Aging: Social change*. New York: Academic Press.

Knack, S. (1992). Civic norms, social sanctions, and voter turnout. *Rationality and Society, 4,* 133-156.

Larson, J.M., Anderson, L.L., & Anderson D.G. (2003, September 9). *Methodology report for technology and citizenship survey*. Ames, IA: Center for Survey Statistics and Methodology, Iowa State University.

Lenhart, A., Horrigan, J., Rainie. L., Allen, K., Boyce, A., Madden, M., et al. (2003). The ever-shifting Internet population: A new look at Internet access and the digital divide. *Pew Internet & American Life Project*. Retrieved on April 20, 2003, from http://www. pewinternet.org/reports/toc.asp?Report=88.Pdf

Lenhart, A., Rainie, L., Fox, S., Horrigan, J., & Spooner, T. (2000, September 21). *Who's not online: 57% of those without Internet access say they do not plan to log on.* Retrieved September 6, 2007, from http://www.pewinternet.org

Loges, W., & Jung, J. (2001). Exploring the digital divide: Internet connectedness and age. *Communication Research, 28*(4), 536-562.

Miller, W.E., & Shanks, J.M. (1996). *The new American voter*. Cambridge, MA: Harvard University Press.

Mossberger, K., Tolbert, C.J., & Stansbury, M. (2003). *Virtual inequality: Beyond the digital divide*. Washington, D.C.: Georgetown University Press.

National Research Council. (1999). *Being fluent with information technology.* Washington, D.C.: National Academy Press.

National Telecommunications and Information Administration (NTIA). (2000). *Falling through the net: Toward digital inclusion.* Retrieved on July 7, 2002, from http://www. ntia.doc.gov/ntiahome/digitaldivide/

National Telecommunications and Information Administration (NTIA). (2002). *A nation online: How Americans are expanding their use of the Internet.* Retrieved on July 8, 2002, from http://www.ntia.doc.gov/ntiahome/ dn/index.html

National Telecommunications and Information Administration (NTIA). (2004). *A nation online: Entering the broadband age.* Retrieved on June 8, 2005, from http://www. ntia.doc.gov/reports/anol/

Norris, P. (2001). *Digital divide: Civic engagement, information poverty, and the Internet worldwide*. New York: Cambridge University Press.

Novak, T.P., & Hoffman, D.L. (1998). *Bridging the digital divide: The impact of race on computer access and Internet use.* Retrieved on October 24, 2000, from http://ecom-merce.vanderbilt.edu/papers/race/ science.html

Pew Research Center for the People and the Press. (2000). *Internet sapping broadcast news audience.* Retrieved September 6, 2007, from http://www.people-press.org/reports/ display.php3? ReportID=36

Sears, D.V. (1981). Life-stage effects in attitude change, especially among the elderly. In S.B. Kiesler, J.N. Morgan, & V.K. Oppenheimer (Eds.), *Aging: Social change* (pp. 183-204). New York: Academic Press.

Servon, L.J. (2002). *Bridging the digital divide: Technology, community, and public policy.* Malden, MA: Blackwell Press.

Shah, D., McLeod, J., & Yoon, S. (2001). Communication, context, and community: An exploration of print, broadcast, and Internet influences. *Communication Research, 4*(28), 464-506.

Shelley, M.C., II, & Auh, S. (2006, October). *The needs and satisfactions of aging and disabilities resources in a rural state in the U.S.: Lessons from the Iowa case.* Paper presented at the 3rd International Conference on Healthy Ageing & Longevity, Melbourne, Australia.

Shelley, M., Thrane, L., Shulman, S., Lang, E., Beisser, S., Larson, T., et al. (2004). Digital citizenship: Parameters of the digital divide. *Social Science Computer Review, 22*(2), 256-269.

Shulman, S., Thrane, L., & Shelley, M. (2005). Erulemaking. In G.D. Garson (Ed.), *Handbook of public information systems* (2nd ed.) (pp. 237-254). New York: Marcel Dekker.

Teixeira, R.A. (1987). *Why Americans don't vote: Turnout decline in the United States, 1960-1984.* New York: Greenwood Press.

Thrane, L.E., Shulman, S.W., Shelley, M.C., Beisser, S.R., & Larson, T.B. (2005). Does computer training translate to e-political empowerment among midwestern senior citizens? In B. Jaeger (Ed.), *Young technologies in old hands: An international view on senior citizens' utilization of ict* (pp. 159-173). Copenhagen, Denmark: DJØF.

UCLA Internet Report. (2000). Surveying the digital future. *UCLA Center for Communication Policy.* Retrieved on November 15, 2000 from http://www.ccc.ucla.edu

Warschauer, M. (2003). *Technology and social inclusion: Rethinking the digital divide.* Cambridge, MA: The MIT Press.

Weber, L., Loumakis, A., & Bergman, J. (2003). Who participates and why? An analysis of citizens on the Internet and the mass public. *Social Science Computer Review, 21*(1), 26-42.

Wilhelm, A.G. (2000). *Democracy in the digital age: Challenges to political life in cyberspace.* New York: Routledge.

About the Contributors

Donald F. Norris is a professor and chair of the Department of Public Policy, and Director of the Maryland Institute for Policy Analysis and Research at the University of Maryland, Baltimore County. He is a specialist in public management, urban affairs, and the application, uses, and impacts of information technology in public organizations. He holds a BS in history from the University of Memphis and both an MA and a PhD in government from the University of Virginia.

* * *

Henri Barki is Canada research chair in information technology implementation and management at HEC Montréal and a fellow of the Royal Society of Canada. His research has been published, or is forthcoming, in *Annals of Cases on Information Technology Applications and Management in Organizations, Canadian Journal of Administrative Sciences, IEEE Transactions on Professional Communication, Information Systems Research, Information & Management, INFOR, International Journal of Conflict Management, International Journal of e-Collaboration, International Journal of e-Government Research, Journal of AIS, Journal of Management Information Systems, Management Science, MIS Quarterly, Organization Science,* and *Small Group Research.*

Tony Carrizales is an assistant professor of public administration at Marist College, School of Management. Carrizales is an associate director for the E-Governance Institute at Rutgers University – Newark and managing editor for the *Journal of Public Management and Social Policy*. Carrizales received his master's degree in public administration from the Cornell Institute of Public Affairs and his PhD in public administration from Rutgers University – Newark.

Yu-Che Chen is an assistant professor of e-government and public management at the Northern Illinois University, USA. Chen's research interests include management of e-government projects and IT-enabled collaboration in management networks. He has published in *Public Performance and Management Review, Social Science Computer Review, Government Information Quarterly, Public Administration Quarterly*, and other journals. He also published IBM reports on IT outsourcing and the use of IT in combating global health-related crises. Chen teaches e-government and program evaluation courses. He serves on the IT committee of the National Association of Schools of Public Affairs and Administration and the editorial board for the *International Journal of Electronic Government Research*.

Daniela V. Dimitrova is an assistant professor in the Greenlee School of Journalism and Communication at Iowa State University. She received a PhD in mass communication from the University of Florida and an MA from the University of Oregon. Dimitrova teaches classes in multimedia production, international communications, and communication technology and social change. Her research interests focus on news framing of conflict events and international political communication. Dimitrova's record includes research articles in the following journals: *The Harvard International Journal of Press Politics, Gazette, Journalism Studies, Journal of Computer-Mediated Communication, Social Science Computer Review* and *Telecommunications Policy*.

Marc Holzer is the dean and board of governors professor in the School of Public Affairs and Administration at Rutgers University – Newark. Dr. Holzer is the executive director of the National Center for Public Productivity and the E-Governance Institute. He is the founder and editor-in-chief of the *Public Performance and Management Review*. Dr. Holzer is a past president of the American Society for Public Administration and a fellow of the National Academy of Public Administration. Dr. Holzer holds a PhD in political science and master's degree in public administration, both from the University of Michigan.

Chan-Gon Kim is the vice mayor of the Guro District in Seoul, South Korea. Kim has served as a career public official for 26 years, initiating and implementing a variety of programs. In particular, he is applying new information and communication technologies to provide public services to citizens in innovative ways. He previously served as an associate director of the E-Governance Institute at Rutgers University – Newark. Kim received his PhD in public administration from the School of Public Affairs and Administration at Rutgers University – Newark and a master's in pubic administration from the University of Georgia.

Benjamin A. Lloyd holds a BA from Towson University and a Master of Public Policy from the University of Maryland, Baltimore County. From 2003 to 2005,

Ben was a research assistant at UMBC's Maryland Institute for Policy Analysis and Research. He resides in Harford County, Maryland.

Jeremy Millard (senior consultant, Danish Technological Institute) has 30 years experience working with new technology, education, and training and in consultancy in the UK, Denmark, Europe, as well as globally. He has worked extensively with local and national governments and regional development agencies in all parts of the world. He is the coordinator of the European Best eEurope Practices Project, which presents and analyses the impact of good practice in e-government and other areas, and led a study for the European Commission on the reorganization of government back-offices for better electronic public services in 2004. He is currently working on user issues in e-government, and is surveying European e-government research and relating this to the major European economic and social policies.

Laurence Monnoyer-Smith, associate professor, is head of media studies at the University of Technology of Compiègne where she gives the introductory lecture on deliberative democracy and new technology. Her work is focused on the uses of ICT in politics in order to enhance political participation (electronic voting and deliberation plateforms). She has participated in several European/French contracts on e-voting and e-deliberation since 1999 and has published many articles on the subject.

Aroon Manoharan is currently pursuing his doctorate in public administration at the School of Public Affairs and Administration, Rutgers University – Newark. His research interests include public performance measurement and reporting, survey research, e-government, and public transit issues. He currently serves as the assistant editor of the *Journal of Public Management and Social Policy*. He received his Master of Public Administration from Kansas State University in 2005.

Mack C. Shelley, II (mshelley@iastate.edu) is university professor of statistics, educational leadership and policy studies, and political science, and director of the Research Institute for Studies in Education, Iowa State University. His research has addressed American government, public policy, and research methods and statistics.

Stuart W. Shulman (shulman@pitt.edu) is an assistant professor in the School of Information Sciences, with a joint appointment in the Graduate School of Public and International Affairs, and a senior research associate in the University Center for Social and Urban Research, at the University of Pittsburgh. His other research focuses on the impact of electronic rulemaking in citizen-government interaction.

Genie Stowers is professor of public administration at San Francisco State University. Her primary field of research is e-government and distance education. She teaches in the fields of public budgeting and finance, public policy and policy analysis, statistical applications, and information management.

Lisa Thrane (Lisa.Thrane@wichita.edu) is an assistant professor at Wichita State University. Her research interests include deviance, mental health, social inequality, digital citizenship, and research methods.

Ryad Titah is a PhD candidate at HEC Montréal. His research interests are in information technology adoption and impact in both public and private organizations. His doctoral dissertation focuses on conceptualizing and measuring the nonlinear relationships among individual and organizational factors explaining e-government capability development, adoption, and impact. He holds an MSc in information technology, a DESS in marketing, and a LSc in economics. His work has been published in journals such as *Information Systems Research, Information Technology and People, International Journal of e-Government Research*, and in academic conferences such as ACFAS and ICEG.

Index